METROPOLIS TO:
Albæ.
D1179749
MOSCVÆ VRBIS
LOCA INSIGNIORA
1 Magni Ducis arx, dicta Czargorod.
2 Magni Ducis conclauia noua
3 Ecclesia S. Michaelis.
4 Aula, siue atrium vel Palatium Patriarchæ.
5 Conclaue, seu cœnaculum e latere exstructum, e quo magnus Dux populo se conspiciendum præbet, aut unde Principis Edicta populo proclamantur.
6 Tabernæ siue pergula, in quibus diuersi generis animalium pelles, aliæque merces diuenduntur.
7 Curia ciuium et Cancellaria prope quas Vnguentorum officinæ seu Pharmacopolæ.
8 Legatorum externorum Aula siue Hospitium.
9 Carceres seu Custodiæ reorum
10 Tabernæ pictorum
11 Externorum Mercatorum Aula siue Hospitium.
12 Forum in quo fœnum et diuersi generis tentoria seu domunculæ venduntur
13 Aquæ calidæ seu Thermæ
14 Magni Ducis hortus.
15 Poganiski iesoro seu lacus
16 Equile M. Ducis
17 Armamentarium.
18 Forum equarium
19 Domus Fusoria.
20 Glinski aula.
pars urbis dicta Kitaigorod
urbis, suo circumdata muro, dicta Bielgorod
Tertia pars urbis versus Septentrionem vocata Skorodum.

THE FALL OF EAGLES

By the same author

THE PRIVILEGE WAS MINE

THE FALL OF EAGLES

PRECURSORS OF PETER THE GREAT

ZINAÏDA SCHAKOVSKOY

Translated from the French by J. Maxwell Brownjohn

Harcourt, Brace & World, Inc.

New York

first American edition

Printed in Great Britain under the title *Precursors of Peter the Great*

Library of Congress Catalog Card Number: 64-18294

Printed in the United States of America

To
Sviatoslav de Malewsky-Malevitch
with love

CONTENTS

ILLUSTRATIONS

(Between pages 160 and 161)

ACKNOWLEDGMENTS

I SHOULD like to express my gratitude to the many people who have encouraged me in my work, also to those who have helped me to carry it out, in particular: M. Michel Dunin-Barkovsky, who has been good enough to undertake a great deal of preliminary research for me from 1949 onwards; to M. Vladimir Boutchik, Librarian of the Institute of Advanced Slavonic Studies, Paris, whose devotion has never flagged; to the librarians of the Lenin Library, Moscow, who helped me to acquire a knowledge of ancient manuscripts which I should have had great difficulty in deciphering on my own; to Professor Dimitry von Mohrenschild, who holds the Chair of Russian Civilization at Dartmouth College, U.S.A.; to M. Robert Prudhon-Kienast, Professor of History at the Lycée Henri IV; to Prince Dimitry Golitzine; and, in particular, to Professor Pierre Pascal, who has kindly lent authoritative support to some of my interpretations of historical fact and cleared up points which might have aroused controversy. My thanks are also due to the French Ministry of Foreign Affairs, which generously gave me access to the archives of the Quai d'Orsay. Finally, it would be impossible for me to omit the name of Mademoiselle Hélène Charra, who has lavished such care and enlightened attention on my manuscripts for so many years.

Michael (first Romanov tsar
1613–45
= (ii) Eudoxia Streshn

(10 children, 6 of whom died young)

Irina

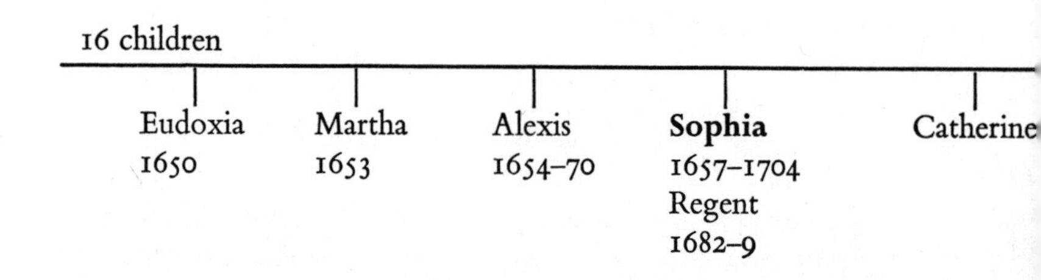

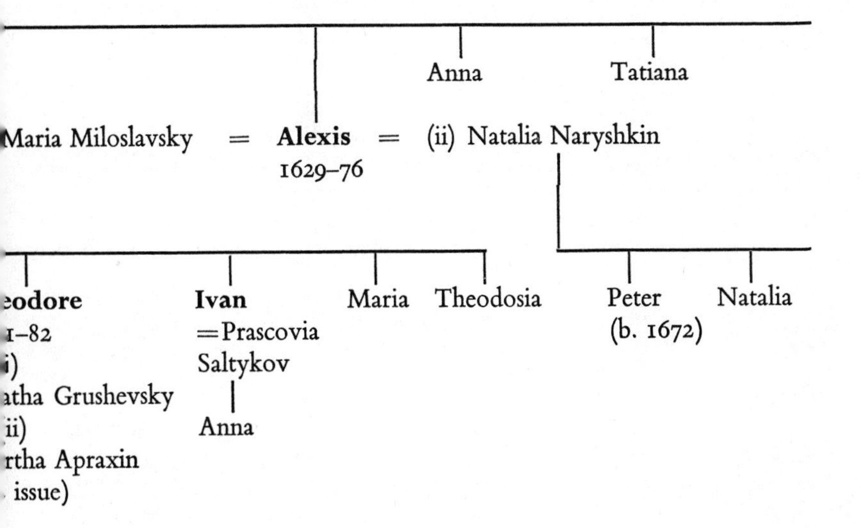
Princess Maria Dolgorukov
Anna
Tatiana
Maria Miloslavsky = Alexis = (ii) Natalia Naryshkin
1629–76
eodore
1–82
i)
atha Grushevsky
ii)
rtha Apraxin
issue)
Ivan
=Prascovia
Saltykov
Anna
Maria
Theodosia
Peter
(b. 1672)
Natalia

PREFACE

THERE is no more fascinating period in the history of Russia than the seventeenth century, with its maelstrom of conflicting trends. Ancient customs and new ideas, the quasi-Byzantine traditions of Kievan Russia, the still vivid memories of the Time of Troubles and Polish intervention, the oppressive legacy of Tatar occupation, the first moves towards repairing the broken links with Western Europe – all these factors combine to form a picture of a national way of life that was at once intense and kaleidoscopic.

It is always futile to cut history into segments, and it is just as difficult to select from a wealth of colourful personalities and events and be satisfied with that selection. In choosing to open this book with the birth of the child who was to become the Regent Sophia, I wished to underline a precise point in history, a period when Great Russia – or Muscovy, as it was still called – was proffering its unexploited resources and potentials to the West. The fascination exerted on Europe by Peter the Great has been such as to obscure his predecessors, but – at the risk of exploding a myth – Peter was not a spontaneous apparition. His father Alexis Michaelovitch, his brother Theodore and his sister Sophia were responsible for launching the country on a new European career. This salutary evolution began under Tsar Alexis, and only evolution could, in the long run, lead the country towards civilization 'in depth'. The revolutionary reforms introduced by Peter, who, in the words of Pushkin's poem, 'made the Russian people rear like a courser above a chasm' (that is to say, maintained a precarious balance), violated the laws of natural development. Any movement which presses on regardless and ruthlessly discards good and bad alike lacks roots, especially when it relies on force and coercion, expedients which tend to corrupt rather than civilize.

This book is intended both as a portrait of a period and as a biography of an exceptional woman. Far from attempting a clinical analysis of a century, I shall simply indicate landmarks, sketch in scenery and arrange hitherto lifeless figures on the stage of their destiny, which was to be that of Russia as well.

Russia was shaking off her immobility and seeking to adapt herself to the rhythm of Europe. With a prudent lack of haste, Tsar Alexis accompanied her on a step towards the West.

PART ONE

TSAR ALEXIS

(1657–76)

'I wish to disabuse sundry persons who believe that the boundaries of Christendom extend only to Hungary, even though Russia is one of the foremost bulwarks of Christendom, and though that Empire is larger and more powerful, populous and abundant than one might believe.'

The Condition of the Empire of Russia and the Grand Duchy of Muscovy, by Captain Margeret (in the service of Boris Godunov, 1598–1605)

CHAPTER ONE

TSAR ALEXIS MICHAELOVITCH, son of the first sovereign of the house of Romanov, was a man of imposing mien with a full, ruddy-complexioned face, white skin, large gentle eyes and a mouth ever ready to break into a smile. As master of the country and the men who inhabited it, the monarch did not take his responsibilities lightly. Russia was a large country.[1] In the east, her frontiers were bounded by the Donetz, the Desna and the Psel, beyond which stretched the steppes of the Crimean Tatars; in the west, it abutted on Lithuania, Poland, Livonia and Sweden; in the north, it extended beyond the Polar Circle and into the Arctic Ocean. The most diverse races inhabited it. Tsar Alexis Michaelovitch had only to survey the geographical chart drawn up by Theodore Godunov to see the full extent of his task. With the Baltic Sea in Swedish hands, the Black Sea closed by the Tatars and contact with the West barred by Poland, the only direction in which the country could expand and develop its relations with the West was northwards, and Alexis was patiently working to open up other routes.

On October 4th, 1657, however, cares of state were laid aside in favour of rejoicing. His Holiness Patriarch Nikon was about to solemnize a new royal baptism in the Cathedral of the Assumption. On September 17th of the same year, clerks had made the following entry in the Court annals: 'A daughter has been born to the Lord Tsar and Grand Prince of all the Great, Little and White Russias, Autocrat: the Lady Tsarevna and Grand Princess Sophia Alexeyevna.'

A daughter did not, of course, carry any weight from the dynastic point of view. The Terem or gynaeceum of the Kremlin already housed two little princesses, Eudoxia and Martha, and their brother Alexis, who had just turned four, was heir to the throne. However, the birth of any Christian soul was an occasion for rendering thanks to the Almighty. Clouds of incense rose once more to the vaulted ceilings surmounted by

[1] Seventeenth-century Russia occupied an area of 30 by 16 degrees, or some 450 by 240 German miles. A German mile being equivalent to about 7.5 kilometres, this area measured 3,375 by 1,800 kilometres, or approximately 6,000,000 square kilometres (2,347,800 square miles).

their five gilded cupolas, wreathing the columns decorated with brilliant frescoes. Candles glimmered, illumining the icons and gilding of the iconostasis and casting reflections on the mosaic-covered floors and brocaded vestments of the officiating priests.

The cathedral had been built in 1479 by Aristotele Fieravanti of Bologna (called Aristobal Fioravante by the Russians), who had wisely drawn his inspiration from the ancient Cathedral of Vladimir. Chroniclers of the fifteenth century sang its praises in the following terms: 'It is marvellously majestic and large, light and resonant and lofty.' But the Cathedral of the Assumption was more than an architectural success. It was still the city's spiritual and national centre, and the whole of the Kremlin was disposed round it like a worthy setting round some precious jewel. The Metropolitans of Moscow slept their last sleep there, the Tsars were anointed and crowned there, and their baptisms, marriages and obsequies were all celebrated there. The cathedral housed the finest icons of the twelfth to the sixteenth centuries, sent from all parts of Russia: Jesus of the Golden Hair, Jesus of the Piercing Eye, the Holy Virgin of Vladimir and the tragic and triumphant Vision of the Apocalypse. Other icons illustrated great moments in the country's history, on the principle that every victory was a divine miracle.

At the time of Sophia's birth, the Kremlin was at once the Tsar's palace, the seat of government and administration (since the *prikazy* or government departments were situated within its precincts), the meeting-place of national consultative assemblies, and an educational centre. The Monastery of the Miracle of the Kremlin was destined before long to become the birthplace of the first Russian Academy. The Kremlin was also the place to which the populace flocked on days of general wrath or rejoicing.

From the Cathedral Square or, still better, from the summit of the belfry-cum-watch-tower of Great St John, the beholder could inspect the surrounding country-side and glimpse, lost in its wooded undulations, the little Kremlins which guarded the approaches to the capital, especially to the south, which had always been the greatest source of danger.

As early as the beginning of the sixteenth century, Sigismund Herberstein, ambassador of the German Emperor, marvelled at the Kremlin's importance.

'In this city,' he wrote, 'there is a fortress so large that, apart from the Tsar's magnificent residences, it contains the living-quarters of the Metropolitan, the Sovereign's brothers, courtiers and very many other persons. Numerous churches are also to be found there, so that it almost resembles a town.'

* * *

In accordance with custom, Tsar Alexis had invited his boyars and friends to a banquet, which undoubtedly took place in the Granovitaya Palata or Palace of Facets whose amazing façade of carved stones can still be seen today. The annals inform us that:

> On October 16th, in honour of the birth of the Lady Tsarevna and Grand Princess Sophia Alexeyevna, a banquet [was held] at the residence of the Lord Tsar and Grand Prince Alexis Michaelovitch. There were present His Holiness Patriarch Nikon, the Tsarevitches of service, and the Tsarevitch Alexis Alexeyevitch.

We can reconstruct this state banquet from accounts given by those who attended it.

The Palace of Facets had two floors. On the upper floor, approached by a monumental exterior staircase, was the throne-room and the audience-chamber where foreign ambassadors were received. The latter was also used for family or national festivities and sometimes for Councils of State.

It was a square room of immense proportions, with a floor area of nearly 5,000 square feet and a ceiling comprising four vaults supported by a central column. The light fell in profusion on mural paintings of the sixteenth century, recently renovated on the orders of Tsar Alexis by Simon Ushakov, one of the leading icon-painters of the day. Biblical scenes, parables and episodes in Russian history were all represented. There was the great prince Yaroslav of Kiev sharing out towns among his twelve sons, for instance, and the Byzantine emperor Constantine offering the crown of Caesar to another Russian prince. Looking down on Alexis Michaelovitch's guests from their stations between the windows were portraits – known as 'persons' – of princes, tsars and monarchs ranging from Yaroslav the Wise to Boris Godunov.

The chamber was maintained at an agreeable temperature, even at the height of winter, by a modern and ingenious system of heating which introduced warm air into the room through ventilators leading from a furnace installed in the basement.

In the centre of the chamber was an enormous pyramid-shaped dresser with a square base, on which were ranged vessels of gold and silver. Four vases over three feet high took the place of flowers, and precious stones gleamed on the brocade and velvet robes of the guests.

The company seated itself in order of precedence: first the Tsar's son and the Patriarch, then the princes and boyars, then other dignitaries of inferior rank. Ambassadors sat facing the sovereign's table.

The tables were covered with small cloths, but eating utensils were few and far between. There was a salt-cellar, a pepper-pot and a vinegar cruet to every four guests. Also on the table was an hors-d'œuvre of pickled cucumber, sour cream and plums in vinegar, to be eaten with the vodka which opened the banquet. Other beverages followed, including various wines, Malmsey and mead.

We do not know whether this was a feast-day or a day of abstinence. In the former case, the meal would traditionally have begun with roast swan, followed by other roasts – perhaps fifty different dishes – all ruined for foreign palates by the garlic and onion of which the Russians made such lavish use.

Even if the dinner given by the Tsar to celebrate Sophia's birth took place on a day of abstinence such as Wednesday or Friday, the guests would have had no claim on our sympathy. Dishes permitted on fish-days included caviare served with greenstuff, clear fish soup, stuffed sturgeon, stewed pike, fish pies and smoked fish, so there was still a guarantee of fifty or sixty dishes.

Gentlemen stewards clad in belted Dalmatics and wearing *terliks* embellished with precious stones carried in the dishes at a trot – which may have accounted for the fact that they changed their clothes three times during a banquet.

The Tsar presided over the gathering with a benevolent smile on his florid and good-natured features. If he ate little or nothing himself, he did not omit to honour particularly favoured guests from time to time by sending them bread from his own table, or salt, which was an even greater token of esteem. Each time he did so, all the guests rose and saluted the person singled out for this honour.

At the entrance to the chamber, which gave on to a vast antechamber, a small and discreet window marked the location of a secret room occupied on such occasions by the recluses of the Terem, who were thus enabled to satisfy their curiosity without infringing the rules of propriety.

It was to the Terem that Tsarevna Sophia was taken immediately after her baptism, and it was there, in the logical course of events, that she would end her days, ignored for ever by history and the world.

It is quite probable that, while the birth of the Tsar's daughter was hailed with popular and official rejoicing, Sophia's mother and aunts leant over her cradle with feelings not untinged by melancholy. The lot of a tsar's daughters was an unenviable one. The people saw them only on the day of their baptism and never heard their names again, except when prayers were offered during divine service or alms were distributed on their behalf. Their nannies, nurses and governesses bore them off at birth and took permanent charge of them. The daughters of boyars, known as the 'upstairs *boyaryshni*' because the Terem was situated on the upper floors of the Palace, came and shared their childhood games. Acting as maids of honour and companions, they diverted the captive princesses with girlish chatter, and their gossip provided them with a reflection of a world which they would never know. Carefully selected mistresses were entrusted with the task of teaching them to read and even (times having changed) to write. *Igrizy* or entertainers came to organize their games and school them in traditional dances such as *Khorovod*, the round dance which was a relic of the pagan rituals of ancient Russia. In the evening, *bakharki* lulled them to sleep in their feather beds with stories handed down from times immemorial.

The tsarevnas occasionally left Moscow, their faces shielded from the gaze of onlookers by the curtains of massive Court carriages, to undertake pilgrimages to monasteries or, with equal secrecy, to visit one or other of the pleasure palaces which stood some versts from the capital – Kolomenskoye, for instance, or Izmailovo, where the Tsar liked to fly his hawks and hunt bear in the Russian fashion, with a knife.

The tsarevnas of Moscow had never taken on a distinct personality. Theirs was a collective anonymity which flowed like a dark and silent stream from one generation and one reign to the next. How did a Christian nation and a country which saw itself as heir to Byzantium come to adopt the Muslim practice of hiding women away and denying them a life of their own?

From the twelfth century onwards, Russia had regarded the monastic life as the ideal mode of existence. Daughters and widows of feudal princes were attracted in large numbers to the peace of the cloisters, and the custom of semi-monastic existence gradually became an established feature of the family life of well-born ladies. Between feudal Russia and Muscovite Russia lay a long period of Tatar occupation, during which rape and violation of womenfolk by the infidel provided an additional reason for their seclusion. What had once been merely a protective measure necessitated by circumstance soon became a custom which persisted after the Tatars' defeat. The *domostroy* or code of family life which evolved at the beginning of the sixteenth century saw women as nun-like creatures devoted to their duties and mindful of their purity, their hands always busy with embroidery, their lips never opened save in prayer, their destiny never to emerge from the family domain.

If girls of noble lineage were subject to the rules of the Terem, they were at least permitted to taste the joys of marriage and motherhood. They were married off without their consent, it is true, but if their husbands were distasteful to them they always had their children to console and occupy them. Again, if they were widowed and elderly enough to be immune to malicious gossip, some of the recluses even turned into Roman matrons, managing their estates, leading an active life and often playing a part in the social or religious life of the country.

The Tsar's daughters, by contrast, could never hope for a husband. It would be a stain upon the Tsar's honour to give his daughter to one of his subjects, even if she had been born of a mother who was not a princess of the blood. As for marrying a Muscovite tsarevna to a foreign prince, experience had long ago dashed all hopes of this. The Tsar's family was separated from the dynasties of Europe by a religious gulf. Gone were the days when foreign kings regarded it as an honour to solicit the hand of a Rurikid princess, as in the twelfth century, when the house of Rurik united all the reigning families of Christendom by marriage. Tsar Ivan the Terrible had encountered nothing but snubs when he contemplated marrying Queen Elizabeth, and the broken engagement of Irina, sister of Tsar Alexis, was too recent and too humiliating a tragi-comedy to be forgotten by the royal family.

The story is sufficiently instructive to merit re-telling here. Irina, elder sister of Tsar Alexis, was thirteen when her father, Tsar Michael, decided to marry her off. The candidate was Prince Valdemar of Denmark, a son of the King but also the product of a morganatic marriage and, as such, less likely to prove a problem than other foreign princes. Valdemar was twenty years old, handsome, fair-haired and grey-eyed. He spoke Latin, French, Italian and German. Negotiations soon got under way, and Valdemar, accompanied by an ambassador extraordinary, betook himself to Moscow under the name of Count Schweitz-Holstein. The success of the project was prejudiced at the very outset by an incident concerning royal titles. The Danish prince demanded that the King's title should take precedence over that of the Tsar. Obtaining no satisfaction on this point, he made his way home to Denmark. Before long the Russians resumed the offensive and set out for Denmark again, taking with them 2,000 roubles' worth of sables earmarked as payment for the good offices of intermediaries.

In January 1644, thirteen years before Sophia's birth, Valdemar reappeared in Moscow in the role of Irina's official fiancé. The Danish prince was somewhat apprehensive about his future bride's physical charms, since custom prescribed that she should remain out of sight. As for Irina, she managed, by a typically feminine ruse, to catch a glimpse of her betrothed, perhaps through the secret window mentioned above. All went well until the day when the Patriarch sent a priest to the prince in an attempt to convert him to Orthodoxy. Valdemar refused and demanded to be released from his engagement, but Tsar Michael would not hear of it.

Departure under such circumstances would have dishonoured his house and made him the laughing-stock of the whole country. The affair dragged on, punctuated by exchanges of letters, negotiations, conferences and discussions. In an understandable state of exhaustion, the prince finally accepted the fact that Irina would not change her religion, and consented to shoulder the burden of any sin which she might be committing by marrying a husband who was not Orthodox. To keep him on the hook, the boyars constantly harped on Irina's beauty, going out of their way to stress that the princess had never been drunk in her life. (Irina was hardly thirteen at the time.)

In 1645 the prince wrote to the Tsar complaining that he was being treated worse by the Russians than he would be by the Turks or the Tatars. Under pressure, Valdemar agreed that his children should be reared in the Orthodox faith. He even promised to keep Lent in so far as his health permitted, and affirmed that he would gladly accede to the Tsar's wishes by wearing Russian dress and observing all national customs which were not incompatible with his honour. That, however, was as far as he would go. 'I shall not renounce my faith, even though the Tsar crucify me,' he declared, adding: 'Let them do with me what they will, but speedily, for pity's sake.'

Fortunately for Valdemar, Michael died in 1645 and was succeeded by Alexis. The latter at once atoned for his father's unfair behaviour by allowing Irina's ill-starred suitor to return home. Free at last, Valdemar thanked him effusively.

Like the other tsarevnas, Irina remained an old maid. and she no doubt felt a pang of regret at the thought that her niece was destined to suffer a similar fate. Had she only known it, there was latent significance in the baby's name, Sophia, 'wisdom', a name which only one woman in the Kremlin had borne before her: Sophia Paleologa, niece of the last Emperor of Byzantium and wife of Ivan III, an intelligent and politically adroit princess.

But then, who could have foreseen that a little princess destined by birth to a life of obscurity would be the first woman since Olga the Wise of Kiev to take the reins of government into her own hands and rule the land of Russia?

In the meantime, Sophia was just a baby in a feminine universe ruled by the women who lived behind the ornate windows of the Terem. Tsarina Maria, the Tsar's wife, was a member of the Miloslavsky family. Beautiful, placid, reared in the old tradition and devoid of personality, her role was to ensure the continuity of the house of Romanov. Before marrying her, Tsar Alexis had set his heart on a young lady called Vsevolozhsky, and it was common knowledge in Moscow that his tutor Morozov, anxious not to forfeit his influence over his royal pupil, had scotched the affair rather crudely by persuading her hairdresser to pull her tresses so hard, on the day of her presentation at court, that the girl swooned and was at once suspected of epilepsy. Alexis settled for Maria Miloslavsky, the girl recommended by Morozov, who followed up this success by marrying the new Tsarina's sister soon after the royal wedding had taken place.

Maria counted for little in the Terem. Her frequent pregnancies produced a succession of children, some of whom died at an early age. By a strange quirk of fate, the surviving girls were as robust as the boys were sickly and delicate.

The woman who ruled the family and the Terem was the Tsar's sister, Irina, the unfortunate ex-fiancée of Valdemar of Denmark. Being some years older than the Tsar, she had taken the place of his mother. Matriarch and supreme arbiter in family matters, Irina performed her duties without any sense of personal ambition.

Her sister Anna resembled her, but her younger sister Tatiana was cast in a different mould, and was later to become Sophia's ally and adviser. Sophia was preceded by three surviving children: Eudoxia, Martha, and the heir apparent, Alexis Alexeyevitch, a handsome but delicate boy of lively intelligence. She was followed in 1659 by Catherine, in 1661 by Theodore, and then by Ivan, Maria and Theodosia in that order.

Life in the Terem was governed by strict protocol, and the Tsarina's court was modelled on that of the Tsar. The number of courtiers, officials and retainers employed by the Kremlin ran into thousands. Some of them lived in the Kremlin itself, while others were quartered in the city and served the Tsar in rotation.

'Upstairs' in the Terem, the Tsarina's court was composed almost entirely of women. Various duties were performed by the daughters, wives and widows of boyars and dignitaries, who acted as treasurers, judges, ladies-in-waiting, ladies of the bedchamber and stewardesses. About a hundred men had the right to enter the Tsarina's apartments. Chosen for their respectability and good character, they were for the most part men who had recently been ennobled by grants of land. Some of them acted as janitors and others superintended the heating of the apartments. A substantial number of young pages aged between ten and fifteen, sons of the Tsar's boyars and officials, ran errands for the ladies of the palace, accompanied the Tsarina on journeys and provided her with an escort. At the age of fifteen, these youths entered the service of the Tsar.

Each of the tsarevnas, as Alexis's sisters and daughters were called, had a court of her own consisting of three women of the household. These young girls fulfilled the duties normally performed by men and boys in the Tsarina's court.

Life in the Terem followed a well-worn path. Apart from the little dramas and pleasures typical of a closed community, there was nothing to break the monotony of the passing days except the frequent prayers which the *domostroy* required to be said in the morning, in the evening and before undertaking a task of any kind. Little by little, however, a breath of fresh air invaded the Terem in the wake of the tutors who instilled into the younger generation a taste for literature and, more than that, a taste for a livelier existence and a spirit of enterprise.

There is a singular dearth of references to Sophia's childhood in documents of the period. Although she was the Tsar's daughter, she was an insignificant being whose doings, sayings and character were evidently considered unworthy of notice. We know that, like the other royal children, she must have accompanied the Tsarina's court on its pilgrimages to the Monastery of the Holy Trinity and St Sergius, and that she spent the summer months at Kolomenskoye or Izmailovo, but she is never mentioned. Sophia only emerges from collective anonymity at the age of six, but even then we learn little enough about her personality. She is never more than a reflection of the people surrounding her and, above all, of Simeon Polotski, the erudite 'Latinist' monk who became her tutor and whose lessons she apparently followed with closer attention than her sisters.

Although our information is scanty, we can at least immerse ourselves in the environment in which Sophia grew up. We can familiarize ourselves with the people among whom she spent her childhood and adolescence, and whose influence left its mark on her. Isolated though it was, the Terem opened its doors to the Tsar's intimates, and these intimates included men who merit our attention because they were involved in dramatic events which affected the whole country.

'The tsarevnas,' Kotoshikhin wrote in his memoirs, 'live like hermits, seeing little of the world and little seen by it, continually devoting themselves to prayer and fasting, bathing their eyes in tears.' Fettered by tradition, crushed beneath its weight and impatient of its restraints, Sophia, the girl whom no one deigned to notice, was preparing what was destined to be a spectacular revenge.

CHAPTER TWO

RISING before day-break, boyars, noblemen and officials, musketeers and soldiers, merchants and artisans, peasants and priests, beggars and *yurodivy* ('devout simpletons'), counsellors of the Tsar and foreigners in his service all left their quarters and made their way toward the heart of the capital. On foot and on horseback, in carriages or sleighs, depending on the weather, rich and poor alike waited for one of the Kremlin's gates to open and allow them to enter its precincts.

The Tsar and his family had also risen at dawn. The Terem Palace was a blend of the magnificent and the bizarre. It was, in fact, composed of several *izbas* or abodes linked by corridors, passages, halls and interior and exterior staircases, some of them opening on to spacious terraces. On the ground floor were the ceremonial rooms, and above them private apartments belonging to members of the royal family.

The decoration of the Tsar's apartments and those of his family had been entrusted to Simon Ushakov and other celebrated national painters. The walls bore portrayals of Biblical scenes or – a daring innovation – historical figures. The ceilings were richly ornamented with designs picked out in mica, silver and pewter. The solid oak floor-boards were covered with Indian and Persian carpets. Each apartment contained a *seny* or large hall which served as a living-room. Like every other room in the Terem, it had the traditional 'red corner' or corner of honour, which was marked by icons before which lights burned night and day. There was very little furniture. The only table in the room stood in the 'red corner', together with 'the Tsar's seat', 'the Tsarina's seat' and (sometimes) 'the Patriarch's seat'. The 'seat' was normally a throne but occasionally took the form of an armchair. One of Alexis Michaelovitch's 'seats' was covered with safian, the most costly Persian leather, 'adorned with an enchased design of seven silver trumpets embossed in silver'. The seat's interior was upholstered in Turkish satin on a silver ground and embroidered with multicoloured silks and gold thread. In 1664 Tsarina Maria had a 'seat' in the form of an armchair of gilded wood upholstered with velvet.

Chairs and armchairs were not yet in general use. The only seats available to the other inmates of the Kremlin and their guests were benches, with or without backs, covered with cushions and arranged along the walls. Cupboards being a rarity, the space beneath these benches was filled with chests and trunks. Depending on the occupant of the suite, the table served as a repository for objects such as pieces of needlework, valuable chess-boards, books and – always and everywhere – the Bible and religious works.

The traditional table was a plain and solid article of furniture. The red or green cloth which normally covered it was replaced on festive occasions by one of *lamé* satin or silk interwoven with gold. However, modern styles were already gaining favour in the Kremlin, and other tables of German and Polish origin were appearing in the Terem at this period. These had 'lion's paw' feet and were decorated in the most delicate colours applied on gold and silver leaf.

In 1670 the Tsar acquired a logwood table encrusted with Venetian shell-work. At its centre was a crowned and bicephalous eagle with wings spread in a circle, while at each extremity was a Sirine, a bird of mythical rather than heraldic nature and drawn from national folklore, which seemed to indicate that the table had been executed by a Russian craftsman. In the same year, the Persian Armenian Saltanov made Tsarevitch Theodore a table on which were portrayed the proverbs of King Solomon.

Inset wall-cupboards took the place of wardrobes, and clothes were still folded away in coffers and handsomely ornamented chests. Articles such as pieces of jewellery and plate, goblets and hanaps, cups and valuable trinkets were kept in the dressers which each member of the family possessed. Alexis Michaelovitch had retained his childhood toys, presents from his grandfather, the Patriarch Philaret. These included 'a silver elephant on which sits an Arab with an axe' and 'a bear in vermeil'.

The Muscovites were extremely fond of watches and clocks, and the royal family owned a bizarre assortment of Russian and foreign time-pieces, each of which showed the time in the manner of its land of origin. Russian watches told the time by dividing the day into two parts: day from sunrise to sunset, and night from sunset to dawn. Despite their popularity, mirrors were not permitted to further the ends of coquetry at this austere court, but were used only when dressing, combing one's hair or adjusting a head-dress. For the rest of the time temptation was banished by covering them with silk or velvet curtains or shutting them away in small cupboards. Antique mirrors were of miniature proportions, but in 1665 the ambassador of the Netherlands, Jacobus Borel, presented the Tsar with a mirror more than six feet long and framed in tortoise-shell, and by 1667 Tsarina Natalia, who succeeded Maria Miloslavsky, owned an intricately ornamented mirror supported by 'two maidens and some birds'.

The palace was carefully cleaned each day by a whole army of retainers and servants, and each year during Holy Week the great spring-clean made it shine like a new pin in time for Russia's greatest religious festival.

As for beds, the use of which was confined to the nobility, those in the Kremlin were surmounted by testers draped with cloth of gold and covered with eiderdowns of the softest quality.

Halls and rooms were scented with incense, rose-water, essence of citronella and ambergris supplied by the Court apothecaries.

* * *

Leaving the crowds massed in front of the Frolov Gate to make their way into the Kremlin courtyard and await the Tsar's appearance, let us take a look at the latter's apartments at his hour of rising. The walls were hung with leather embossed with designs picked out in gold. Since it was still dark, footmen had lit candles in the hanging chandeliers, which assumed a variety of shapes such as stags' or horses' heads, geese and coiled serpents. Before the icons – needless to say – night-lights flickered and threw dancing shadows. Arranged on the Tsar's table were a copy of the Ulozhenye Code, a German watch in the form of a dog, a silver and crystal whistle adorned with three small bells, sundry documents, a sand-castor and a tube filled with water for moistening swan's quills, a black-lead pencil capped with an emerald, a slate and a slate pencil, a pair of gold-rimmed spectacles, four pen-knives and a golden pen.

The other rooms in his suite contained five hundred prints, wood and copperplate engravings, and geographical charts, notably the one drawn up by Theodore Godunov and the map of the world compiled by Lopotitsky in 1663. The varied selection of books in the library was testimony to Alexis Michaelovitch's love of religion, science and literature. A parrot stirred restlessly in its large gilded cage, for birds were popular in the Kremlin. Canaries sang in each apartment, and parrots had been much in favour ever since 1490, when the first one was presented to the Grand Prince of Moscow by Emperor Maximilian, husband of Marie de Bourgogne. They could be purchased in Moscow at the 'Court of Merchants'.

Like every Christian on Russian soil, Alexis Michaelovitch began his day with prayers. His first steps took him in the direction of his private chapel, where his confessor was already awaiting him, and the first sight that met his eyes was his collection of priceless icons and gorgeous frescoes.

Oriental patriarchs and Russian pilgrims sent or brought him souvenirs from distant lands: a candle from Constantinople, some sand from the Jordan, a palm leaf from Jerusalem.

While the Tsar was hearing Mass and receiving Communion, the *prikazy* or government departments were opening their doors; cooks and scullions were bustling about in front of their vast ovens, preparing pies of meat, cabbage, mushrooms and fish, soups of all kinds, enormous sturgeon and salmon, mutton, goose, swan and sides of beef; the noblemen responsible for serving the wines were ordering up casks of vodka, wine and mead from the cellars; the grooms and coachmen in the royal stables were grooming the Tsar's horses, checking the gleaming harness and polishing the ornate gold saddles; master-armourers and their apprentices were resuming their daily work, and every department and workshop in the Kremlin was a hive of activity.

Meanwhile, the motley and ill-assorted crowd waiting outside the Frolov Gate had been admitted to the Kremlin. In front of the 'Courtyard of Honour' where the Tsar's palace stood, boyars, noblemen and soldiers dismounted from their chargers and carriages, leaving them in the care of footmen. Since it was forbidden to enter on horseback or carrying arms, rich and poor alike approached the Terem Palace on foot and unarmed. The towers and turrets of the palace gleamed with pale and dreamlike splendour in the first rays of the sun. Its walls, pierced by small, elaborately ornamented windows, were decorated with multicoloured designs whose reds, blues and greens mingled in kaleidoscopic profusion.

After Mass, the Tsar distributed alms to the poor and gave orders for food to be sent from his table to foreign ambassadors and persons whom he wished to single out for special favour. Then, in all his majesty, effortlessly wearing his long robes of heavy brocade spangled with precious stones, Alexis Michaelovitch ceremoniously made his way to the Duma, or Council of State, where his boyars and senior officials were waiting. Luxuriant of beard and bright of eye, the Tsar prepared to hear reports and make decisions affecting the great country which represented his patrimony.

Next to the Palace of the Terem was another palace occupied by the Grand Sovereign Patriarch. It, too, was thronged with visitors. An unbroken stream of humanity converged on the head of the Russian Church, some to receive his blessing, others to request his intercession or obtain alms. Voivodes leaving for the country, boyars and officials assigned to new posts, bishops, priests and monks, some from Moscow and others from remote parts of the provinces, all came to consult him or submit their plans for comment. Individuals of every kind and condition sought his advice or asked him to share their joys and sorrows. No event in the life of a Russian family could take place without the blessing of the Church. If a house was to be built, its foundations had to be blessed. If two brothers quarrelled, the Patriarch was called upon to settle the dispute. If a father proposed to marry off his daughter, he sought the approval of his spiritual chief. If a merchant was preparing an expedition to the uncharted lands of Asia or a dispossessed widow was seeking justice, the Patriarch was the logical person to consult. All brought him a present according to their means, sometimes a large sum of money, sometimes a simple piece of cloth, sometimes a length of gold brocade or a small wax candle, sometimes a chalice made by one of the great goldsmiths or a fish caught that morning in the Moskva. A man named Ipatiev once presented the Patriarch with a whole nestful of cygnets. The gifts were redistributed so that the poor were not sent away empty-handed. Monasteries and churches received grants towards the cost of building or decoration, foreign monks were invited to work on theological texts. Part of the money was set aside for prisoners and invalids, another sum provided a girl with a dowry...

While the Tsar was deliberating with his councillors and the Patriarch was receiving petitioners, other crowds were swarming into the huge Ivanovsky Square, dominated by the belfry of Ivan the Great, where government notaries received their clients and explained new administrative measures to those already lost in a maze of legal formalities. Ivanovsky Square was the place where contracts were drawn up, loans were negotiated, real estate was bought and sold and people 'hired' themselves out, that is to say, sold themselves into virtual slavery for a fixed period in return for a sum of money. Public scriveners, brandishing their goose-quill pens, composed petitions for the illiterate. Striving hard to make themselves heard above the general hubbub, *dyaky* (government clerks) read, or rather bellowed out the Sovereign's latest decrees and ordinances to the good people of Moscow and elsewhere.

Down in the lower, worse-lit rooms within the precincts of the Kremlin, government clerks and officials laboured unceasingly to discharge day-to-day business. Bearded pen-pushers scratched away with goose-quills, dipping them in the heavy copper ink-wells before them. The tables were covered with red cloth and the seats were benches covered with wool-stuffed cushions. Hours of work were long – twelve hours at a stretch – and the atmosphere in the rooms, overheated in winter and swarming with flies in summer, was oppressive in the extreme. Archives and files were kept in the large chests studded and bound with iron which lined the walls. Each table was illuminated by tallow candles. The only people allowed to have wax candles, which smoked less, were heads of departments. Antechambers and doorways were thronged with couriers waiting to carry dispatches, documents and correspondence not only to Moscow but to the farthest corners of Russia.

Anyone who knew how to read and write had a chance of bettering himself. Many a young man languishing in the stifling discomfort of the Kremlin offices cherished secret hopes of becoming an ambassador. In the meantime he had to resign himself to years as a common clerk, ill-paid, constantly tempted by bribery and constantly under threat of the bastinado.

It was from one of these *prikazy* that Gregory Kotoshikhin escaped, to find freedom and an ignominious death in the West. An extremely interesting personality and the author of a remarkable work entitled *On Russia in the Time of Tsar Alexis Michaelovitch*, Kotoshikhin was a young official in the Prikaz of Foreign Affairs. He was intelligent and shrewd, though not over-scrupulous, judging from a report by Adolph Ebers, a Swedish diplomat resident in Moscow at the time: 'This man, Russian in origin but a good Swede by sentiment, has promised to inform me of what passes in his country.'

Gregory had some reason to complain of his lot. He was sentenced to the bastinado for making a minor error when transcribing the Tsar's titles, an experience scarcely calculated to intensify his patriotism. The bastinado being a very commonplace punishment, Kotoshikhin's career was not ruined by this misdemeanour. At the time of the second war with Poland he was attached to the army commanded by the voivode Prince Yury Dolgoruky. On being ordered by his commander-in-chief to carry out an irregular order, Kotoshikhin refused to obey (let us give him the benefit of the doubt and assume that he did so from a rare access of conscience rather than from fear of the consequences) and, to escape Dolgoruky's wrath, fled to Poland. From there he went to Germany and eventually to Sweden. As an intelligent man, Kotoshikhin could not fail to compare conditions in his native land with those prevailing in foreign countries and was struck by the advantages of life in the West. Accordingly, he set out to describe the manners and customs of his native Russia, a project in which he was encouraged by Count Magnus de la Gardie. In *On Russia in the Time of Tsar Alexis Michaelovitch*, Kotoshikhin, who adopted the Polish nom de plume Selitski, has bequeathed posterity a vivid picture of the Russia of his day.

Poor Kotoshikhin-Selitski was certainly a great deal less virtuous than he tried to appear in his memoirs. Having entered the service of Sweden, his native land's most implacable foe, he became a Lutheran because Lutheranism suited his new nationality better than Orthodoxy. He remained Russian in his fondness for the bottle, however, and it was during a drunken brawl that he killed Daniel Anastasius, his landlord and the husband of his mistress. Kotoshikhin met his end on a Swedish gibbet. His bones were strung on copper wire and preserved for many years as a curiosity by Upsala Museum – a macabre but peculiarly apt conclusion to the career of a shrewd adventurer. 'Thus ended the life of Selitski, a man of Russian origin and superior intelligence,' remarks the Swedish translator in a preface to his work.

* * *

Leaving Kotoshikhin's colleagues poring over their mountains of paper, let us emerge from the Kremlin and take a glance at Moscow in the time of Alexis Michaelovitch. The capital was developing rapidly and its population steadily increasing. Large seigniorial mansions, churches and monasteries were springing up everywhere. Foreigners visiting Moscow at this period estimated that its population already exceeded that of Prague, Paris or London, and the beauty of the site on which it was built reminded them of a 'White Jerusalem'.

Outside the walls of the Kremlin in Red Square ('red' meaning beautiful), where, surmounted by its multicoloured domes and looking for all the world like some strange and gargantuan flower, stood the Church of the Intercession of the Holy Virgin and St Basil, the hum of activity was even more intense than in the Kremlin squares. St Basil's had been built for Ivan the Terrible by two Russian architects named Barma and Poznik, to commemorate his conquest of Kazan. Alexis Michaelovitch ordered it to be repainted and redecorated. Like the Kremlin Palace, which was an agglomeration of small apartments, the church was a composite building made up of nine chapels. It was visible from a considerable distance on all sides.

In the square, the only static points in a sea of movement were the merchants' open-air booths, stalls and calashes. The din was infernal. Barkers touted for customers, brawls and disputes raged. Here, one of the *yurodivy* or 'devout simpletons' shouted his prophecies and imprecations amid a clatter of chains; there a puppeteer, surrounded by a group of loungers, used his voice and nimble hands to illustrate the adventures of Petrushka – none other than a long-Russianized equivalent of Italy's Petruochio. Lacking a stage, the showman simply supported the folds of his caftan on a brass ring, forming an improvised platform on which the hero played abominable tricks on the constable and was predictably thrashed.

Despite the stern disapproval of Patriarch Nikon, who compelled Tsar

Alexis to take measures against public entertainers, tradition died hard. The Church still regarded showmen, lutanists, cithern-players and street singers as perverters of Christian morality and henchmen of the Devil, and in 1667 the Tsar, who was personally fond of diversions and amusements, indulged the Patriarch by issuing a decree confirming the interdict proclaimed in 1648.

But the showmen still plied their trade. *Gussly* or lutes continued to twang an accompaniment to the voices of blind minstrels as they sang of ancient wars. Mead and spirits still gladdened the heart, and passers-by still stumbled over the recumbent forms of those who had imbibed too deeply. On the Lobnoye Miesto, which still exists today, a *dyak* proclaimed the latest government decrees, struggling to make himself heard above the tumult. A little farther on, a thief imprisoned in the stocks was receiving his ration of knout – not that the sight discouraged his colleagues, who worked their way dexterously through the dense crowds in defiance of the constables' attempts to instil a respect for law and order. The great clock on the Frolov Tower punctuated the passage of time each hour with its booming voice, and at regular intervals the bells pealed out from every belfry in Moscow and its suburbs, marking the hours of divine worship.

Near a bridge some distance away was the booksellers' quarter, where, amid the rattle of the brand-new pumps bringing water from the Moskva to the Kremlin Palace, one could buy primers at a kopek apiece, books, woodcuts and engravings of foreign origin.

The capital was built in concentric circles of which the Kremlin formed the focal point. The annexes and offices of the palace had overflowed its walls, and the old streets of the Arbat bore their names, e.g. Bread Street, Knife Street, Cloth Street and Cook Street.

The frequent and appalling conflagrations which regularly devastated the capital, most of whose houses were constructed of wood, had given rise to strict controls on building, though only the rich could afford to have houses of stone or brick. Noblemen and wealthy merchants owned veritable estates in the middle of the city, some of them maintaining as many as five hundred domestic servants, all of whom had to be lodged on the premises. Each man of substance possessed a chapel or private church of his own. A boyar's court was virtually an autonomous state whose lord and master could call on the services of any craftsman or tradesman without having to step outside his domain: tailors, cobblers, joiners, gardeners or embroiderers in gold thread. Screened from the gaze of the curious, an inner garden allowed the women and girls of the great houses to take the air without risking annoyance from passers-by.

Adjoining it was a kitchen garden which made good any deficiencies in the menu if bad weather interrupted the flow of supplies to the household from the boyar's country estates. It is sad to remember that all this opulence was founded on the sweated labour of peasants and serfs, who had to furnish their masters with foodstuffs, firewood, tallow, wax, woven cloth and a multitude of other necessities.

Moscow's traditionally austere and colourless exterior was assuming a gayer appearance under Alexis Michaelovitch. New buildings were enlivened by a blend of red brick and white stone, and one of the happier modes of ornamentation was the growing use of decorative slabs of faience as a facing for façades and interior walls. Roofs were covered with handsome tiles laid in tiers.

Streets and suburbs took their names from the trade or occupation pursued by their inhabitants, e.g. gunners, printers, bell-founders, stablemen, grooms, coiners and postilions.

As foreign trade increased in volume and the economic life of the country developed and became more centralized, so the common people gradually assumed more importance. Certain merchants became advisers to the Tsar. The bourgeoisie once more started to live on the same footing as the boyars, as they had done in the days of the free republics of Pskov and 'Great Lord' Novgorod. Their houses, palatial though some of them were, were all built in Moscow's commercial centre, the Gostinnyy Dvor or Court of Merchants. In the five years between 1660 and 1665, a new 'Court' was built in the Kitay Gorod. This was a large rectangle enclosed by stout walls and bounded at each corner by a watch-tower. The shops and warehouses, all built of stone, gave on to the inner courtyard. Trades were concentrated in groups, and it was fruitless, for instance, to attempt to buy a pair of boots in the corn-chandlers' section.

Everything was carefully controlled, and for once foreigners were compelled to admire the efficiency of Russian organization. There was a special section for jewellers, another for wholesalers of wood, and others for armourers, soap-merchants, bootmakers and drapers. Piety forbade the sale of icons, but there was no objection to bartering them. Foreign merchants had a section of their own near their Russian colleagues. A little farther on, Armenians, Hindus, Persians and Tatars displayed splendid wares from the Orient: carpets, precious stones, jewels set in gold filigree, spices, mirrors encrusted with mother-of-pearl and tortoise-shell, bolts of many-hued silk . . .

As one left the centre of the city behind, so the quarters and suburbs became poorer. The *possads*[1] were inhabited by workmen, small shop-

[1] Inner suburbs.

keepers and musketeers who pursued a manual occupation in their spare time and lived in hopelessly overcrowded conditions. It has been estimated that as many as three hundred trades were represented in the area, which was the centre for workshops and small businesses employing free labour and also the place from which the more adventurous spirits slipped away to join the Cossacks. But in every quarter, however wretched the neighbouring houses, Russian steam-baths were to be found, and, whatever foreigners said of them, Russian workmen and peasants of the period kept themselves cleaner than their Western counterparts.

The people of the possads were scarcely better off than the peasants in their villages. They had no beds, merely simple wooden alcoves just large enough for the whole family to curl up inside and heated in winter by large Russian stoves. Window-panes were made of mica, and a family often shared its room with chickens and domestic animals.

There were churches and monasteries everywhere. Many an otherwise wretched-looking hovel betrayed a preoccupation with things aesthetic. Householders who were skilful with axe and knife would often carve friezes and designs in the woodwork round their windows and above their doors.

The quarter where the weavers were established was 'Khamovniki', where Tolstoy was to live in years to come. The weavers had put their pennies together and built a handsome church dedicated to St Nicholas, most venerated of all saints. The farriers lived still farther out, and on the outskirts of the city lived the postilions, who travelled the ill-kept roads of their vast country in all weathers, carrying passengers, merchandise or supplies for armies in the field.

Also to be found in Moscow was the royal Apothecaries' Garden, where medicinal herbs were grown. In the reign of Alexis a foundlings' home had been established in the new Monastery of the Virgins, opposite the Field of the Virgins. There were also hospitals patronized by Theodore Rtistchev the Compassionate, a friend of the Tsar. Prisons tended to be places of transit rather than of long-term detention.

An appalling stench pervaded the 'Court of Cattle' or cattle-market, where beasts were brought by road and unceremoniously slaughtered behind the butchers' stalls. Offal was thrown into a near-by pond, which soon won the name 'pool of corruption'. Fifty years later, when cleansed and purified, it came to be known as the 'pool of purity'.

As for the city morgue, the Muscovites euphemistically called it the 'House of the Good Lord' and those who worked there 'Those of the House of the Good Lord'.

Crowds were as dense and traffic as heavy in the better-class neighbourhoods as in the wretched alleys of the suburbs. The narrow and ill-paved streets were clogged with merchants' calashes and the carriages of the rich, whose footmen could only force a passage by dint of much shouting and jostling. The masses who thronged the streets and squares of the capital were placid yet emotional, credulous yet anxious not to deviate from Orthodoxy, patient yet prone to sudden outbursts of fury quite as violent as the fires that so often engulfed their homes.

To watch these people as they paused to gape at the showman's trained bear or spent a kopek on the bread rolls or *kalatchi* which, so it was said, were only good when made with water from the Moskva, was to realize that they belonged to a fundamentally anarchic community overlaid with a veneer of order. Urchins moved among the crowds hawking meat or cabbage pies. One of them, Alexander Menshikov, was later to win fame as the lieutenant of Peter the Great. Enterprising nuns eager to swell their convent's resources sold hot *bliny* in the shadow of its venerable walls. Despite government decrees, vodka was always obtainable. The strangest rumours and most fantastic tales spread and circulated from mouth to mouth. Talkative, turbulent, eating and drinking when the opportunity arose and locked in a perpetual struggle for survival, some of the masses accepted their destiny and others rebelled against it. But amid all the trivial chatter, oaths and drunken singing, impassioned theological disputes raged just as they once did in old Byzantium, where public places were so often the scene of violent religious arguments.

* * *

Lapped by the stormy waves of Muscovite life was a strange little island known as the Nemetskaya Sloboda or German Quarter – though a brief excursion into etymology shows that the expression Nemetskaya was not exclusively German in connotation. *Nemets* (plural: *nemtsy*) came from the word *nemoy*, meaning a mute, i.e. someone who could not speak Russian. Thus, people of this period used to talk of a 'French *nemets*', an 'English *nemets*' or an 'Italian *nemets*'.

Large numbers of foreigners were already living on the banks of the Yauza in the reign of Ivan the Terrible. The Time of Troubles scattered them, but from the advent of the first Romanov onwards they returned in ever-increasing numbers. At first they settled haphazardly among the native population, some in the neighbourhoods occupied by the Khokhly or Little Russians and others in the 'Mestchanskaya' of the 'Mesto', the place where émigrés from the small towns in the south-west had concentrated. The foreign colony included men of all types: doctors and charlatans, jewellers and technicians, apothecaries, officers and soldiers in the Tsar's service, merchants, manufacturers, numerous adventurers and a substantial sprinkling of common or garden thieves. Their relationship with the Muscovites was not always one of peaceful coexistence. Apart from anything else, the Church regarded their customs and religions, which they practised freely, as likely to corrupt Russian morals, and viewed the potential consequences of foreign infiltration with some anxiety.

'One day,' wrote Olearius, 'the foreign officers' wives took umbrage at the presumption of the foreign merchants' wives, who claimed the right to sit next them in the pews of the Protestant church. (It is plain to see that the Russians were not the only people to be sensitive where precedence was concerned.) One thing led to another, words flew thick and fast, and the ladies resorted to violence on the very threshold of the church. A pitched battle took place, with much ferocious hair-pulling. As luck would have it, the Patriarch of Moscow drove by in his carriage. Calling to his coachmen to halt, he sent them to ask the reason for the squabble. On being told, the Patriarch decided that the authority of the church, even if Protestant, lay within his jurisdiction, and that it devolved on him to remedy such disorders. So he summarily ordered the profaned temple to be destroyed.' Klyuchevsky dates this incident *circa* 1643, in the reign of Michael.

In 1652 Alexis Michaelovitch ordered all foreigners to leave the interior of the city and settle on the banks of the Yauza. The Russian government allotted a plot of land to each man and each family, and before long the new German Quarter became a Western island in a Russian sea.

Meyerberg estimated that there were more than a thousand foreigners in Moscow in 1660, but this number was destined to grow. The streets of the 'Quarter of the Dumb' were broad, and its houses, which were built mainly of wood, stylish and well-appointed. It was a world apart, and a far freer world than that of Russia. Everyone lived as he pleased, without changing his ways or abandoning the customs of his distant homeland. There were two Lutheran churches, a Reformed church, a German school and maybe a Catholic church and chapel as well. Ideas, fashions, comforts, amusements, music, song and theatre all spread from this cultural oasis and became diffused throughout Moscow, where boyars and merchants eagerly surrendered themselves to the pleasurable influences of the West.

Near the German Quarter there later came into being a village known as Lefortovo, after Lefort, a Genevese officer in the service of Peter the Great. It was composed of houses owned by the leading lights of the foreign colony, interspersed with smaller establishments belonging to the soldiers of Lefort's regiment.

* * *

When darkness came, the whole city fell asleep to the barking of dogs and the tap of night-watchmen's staffs. Musketeers mounted guard round the Kremlin. 'Holy Virgin, pray for us!' a man's voice would cry. 'Saint Nicholas, pray for us!' came the response, and again: 'Holy Angels and Archangels, pray for us!' Distant voices took up the cry, re-echoing from tower to tower and hill to hill: 'Saints of Moscow, pray for us!' And then, from still farther away, came the cry of sentries belonging to the newly formed provincial regiments: 'Glory to Suzdal!', 'Glory to Tula!', 'Glory to Kiev!', 'Glory to Moscow!'

CHAPTER THREE

SOPHIA'S sparkling mind, her taste for politics and literature and her capacity for assessing people and situations could only have come from her father, who was later to beget Peter the Great. But there was one great difference between them: Sophia never lost her temper, and remained in command of herself even when assailed by anger or anxiety. Though she was not devoid of passion, her actions were always dictated by reason. She was a girl destined to immerse herself in a man's world, and guile – a defect or attribute entirely lacking in the Tsar's fundamentally straightforward nature – was to be a valuable weapon in her armoury.

The Terem was dominated by the figure of the husband and father. Klyuchevsky's portrait of the Tsar bears the stamp of nobility.

> He was an extremely endearing blend of loyalty to the old Russia and receptiveness to all novelties that were useful or pleasant ... The very embodiment of the well-ordered and assimilated piety in which the religious sentiment of ancient Russia had for so long been steeped, the Tsar prayed and fasted like a monk. During Lent and Assumption the Tsar ate only once a day on Sundays, Tuesdays, Thursdays and Saturdays, his meal consisting of cabbage or mushrooms without butter or oil, and fruit. On Mondays, Wednesdays and Fridays, no matter what the particular fast, he neither ate nor drank the whole day. He attended divine office for five or six hours at a time and prostrated himself between a thousand and fifteen hundred times daily. He was a veritable man of prayer, and one who simultaneously and harmoniously combined mortification of the flesh with spiritual intensity of the soul.

Extremes were repugnant to Alexis Michaelovitch, who sought harmony and balance in all things. He was conscious not only of his duty as sovereign but also of the sovereign's responsibility to God. He enjoyed considerably more personal power than his father had done, and his mastery over the country was as undisputed as that of Ivan the Terrible. But, even though the autocrat in Tsar Alexis could write: 'God has blessed Us and appointed Us, the Sovereign, to govern and judge Our people to

East and West, to North and South,' his Christian sentiments were so strong that they robbed him of overweening pride in the power conferred on him by Heaven. 'It were better to govern with tears, diligence and humility before God than by force and pride,' he wrote to one of his voivodes. He was never jealous of his power, and nothing pleased him more than to be able to share it with the men who enjoyed his confidence.

In 1652, Alexis Michaelovitch wrote to Prince Nikita Odoyevsky:

'And We, the Grand Sovereign, do pray each day to the Creator and His Immaculate Mother and all the Saints that the Lord God enable Us, the Grand Sovereign, and you, the boyars, to govern the men of His earth in accordance with justice and truth, in unity of spirit with you.'

Tsar Alexis was fond of writing. From his pen, so skilled at tracing the intricate flourishes and convolutions of the old Russian alphabet, there flowed a stream of letters to those whom he wished to commend or console – or chastise, for his warm and generous heart was matched by a lively and volatile temperament. Compassion was one of his major virtues. In 1652 the son of Prince Nikita Odoyevsky, voivode of Kazan, died of a pernicious fever. On hearing the news, the Tsar immediately wrote to the bereaved father:

'And you, Our voivode, do not grieve beyond measure. Assuredly, one cannot help but mourn and weep, but in moderation, so that the Lord be not vexed. Do not grieve, Prince Nikita,' the Tsar concluded. 'Trust in God and have confidence in Us.'

What made the Tsar's fits of rage all the more violent was that he detested being forced to be angry and flew into a fury when obliged to punish anyone. That was why he occasionally 'corrected' boyars guilty of negligence with his own august hand, only to regret his outbursts later. Presumptuousness, arrogance and irresponsibility were the main targets of his wrath.

In 1660, a voivode of his named Prince Ivan Khovansky suffered a bloody defeat in Lithuania and lost most of his army. The Tsar summoned a meeting of the Duma. For want of a better idea, Ivan Miloslavsky, brother of Tsarina Maria, started to run the unfortunate general down. 'If it please the Sovereign to entrust the command of his armies to me,' he declared, 'I shall bring back the King of Poland himself a prisoner.'

'How dare you boast of your prowess in war, you mischievous buffoon!' cried the Tsar. 'What have been your victories hitherto?' And, still hurling abuse, he wrenched at his brother-in-law's beard and kicked him bodily out of the council chamber.

The son of the first Romanov had a happy childhood, an almost unique experience for a Tsar of Muscovy. His father Michael, a physically delicate man with a melancholy disposition and little taste for power, had left his own father, Patriarch Philaret, to govern Russia on his behalf, and Alexis Michaelovitch's grandfather played an important part in his education.

When he looked back on his childhood the Tsar saw himself at the age of six, learning the alphabet and poring over his first reading matter: the Ten Commandments and the Shorter Catechism. At the age of seven he graduated to the Psalms, followed by the Acts of the Apostles. At ten, Alexis could read, write, chant vespers, matins, canons and litanies, and thread his way through the complex rituals of the Orthodox Church as well as any monk and sometimes better. On coming to the throne he was quick to seize upon any errors or omissions on the part of officiating clergy, and would not hesitate to leap from his chair in the middle of a church service in order to berate the offending deacon or cantor in the harshest terms. He enjoyed playing the verger's role, too, and happily snuffed or lit the candles before their icons, feeling quite as at home in a cathedral as in his own house.

There was nothing pompous about him, despite his firm conviction that he must rule the country in an autocratic way and thus expunge what he deemed to be the weaknesses of his father, who had frequently convened quasi-parliamentary national assemblies before taking urgent measures. The power was his, but he was determined to use it for the good of his subjects. Every man was a potential friend. He enjoyed throwing etiquette overboard and dining *en famille* with one or other of his boyars like any ordinary neighbour.

The son of his intimate associate, Ordyn-Nastchokin, an extremely promising young man, was so fired by the tales told by his Polish friends that he 'chose freedom' and fled to the West. Deeply affected, Ordyn-Nastchokin informed the Tsar of this disgrace in person and asked to be relieved of his high offices. The Tsar at once made for his writing-desk.

> You have requested me to release you. Why do you ask this of me? I suppose that it is through grief. But is it so astounding that your son has been foolish? He is a young man. He wished to see the world of the Lord and His works. Even as a little bird flies hither and thither and returns to its nest, so your son shall soon remember his nest and return to you.

Alexis was not afraid of oaths. His own were quite as ripe as those of his peasants, and he used them with unabashed fluency and considerable wit.

On one occasion a monastery treasurer who had drunk more deeply than was wise picked a quarrel with the musketeers of the monastery garrison, killed the non-commissioned officer commanding them and ordered their weapons and clothing to be thrown out of doors. The Tsar was enraged by this insult to his soldiers, but, even though it would have been only too easy for him to take draconian measures against the impetuous treasurer, he confined himself to sending him a letter. The superscription ran:

'From the Tsar and Great Prince Alexis Michaelovitch of all the Russias to the enemy of God, the betrayer of Christ, the disparager of the House of Miracles, the accursed foe, the evil and worthless malefactor Nikita ... '

While verbally chastising his rebellious subject, however, the Tsar took care to stress that it was not the personal affront which had excited his wrath. 'Take note, angel of Satan,' he continued, 'that wordly honour is important only to you and to your father, the Devil. To me, a sinner, all the honour of this world is no more than dust. Are we precious, you and I, in the eyes of the Lord? Are our proud thoughts worth aught to Him if His fear dwells not in us?'

And the monarch who could have imprisoned or even killed his wayward subject merely concluded by saying that he, the Tsar, would pray to the Lord for protection against the doings of the wicked treasurer. 'For how otherwise could I protect myself against you?' he added.

Passionately interested in all that was new, Alexis Michaelovitch was fascinated by anything of Western origin. Whether by chance or by his grandfather Patriarch Philaret's deliberate design, his tutor as a child had been the boyar Ivan Morozov, a man with numerous failings but one positive quality: a strong attachment to Western Europe. Alexis and his brother were dressed 'in the German fashion' from an early age, a little revolution which was to have far-reaching consequences. Their toys, which also came from abroad, included picture-books, cards and a miniature suit of armour made by the German Peter Schaldt. By the time he was twelve, the future occupant of the throne already owned a small but varied library comprising, among other things, a grammar, a cosmography printed in Lithuania and a lexicon. These were quite enough to whet his appetite for reading and stimulate his curiosity about the outside world. When he grew up, Alexis supplemented his education by delving deeply into the humanities and sciences and by conversing with foreigners. He spoke Polish, knew Greek, and had read almost all the Slavo-Russian literature available in his day.

Peace and virtue reigned in the Tsar's palace. Like those of his father Michael and his son Theodore after him, Alexis Michaelovitch's morals were above reproach. The Russian Court was completely innocent of the illicit love-affairs and clandestine vices so characteristic of foreign courts of the time.

Such was the atmosphere that prevailed in the Kremlin when Sophia attained the age of reason.

* * *

The Tsar's friends had access to the Terem, and there were occasions on which Alexis Michaelovitch welcomed them to his family circle and conversed with them in the 'upstairs' apartments. One constant visitor to the palace was Theodore Rtistchev 'the Compassionate', whose appointment as tutor to Tsarevitch Alexis, the heir apparent, indicated how much value the Tsar placed on human integrity.

Like the monarch's other intimate associates, Theodore Rtistchev was not a member of the senior nobility, but, as his biographer Kashkin said later, he embodied 'the world's supreme Christian ideal'. Rtistchev's reputation for compassion and piety was so great, in fact, that an anonymous contemporary wrote his biography during his lifetime. It read almost like a hagiography – a circumstance rendered all the more remarkable by the fact that laymen always have great difficulty in passing for saints.

Born four years before Tsar Alexis in 1625 and therefore an almost exact contemporary, Theodore Rtistchev very probably entered Court service at an early age, and his entire life was spent in the Tsar's immediate circle. On the occasion of the Tsar's marriage to Maria Miloslavsky, Rtistchev's sister Anna was appointed an 'upstairs boyarina' or lady-in-waiting to the new Tsarina, with the result that the Tsar's children came to look upon Rtistchev as a sort of respected uncle.

Rtistchev was reared in a pious and – despite its lack of means – charitable family. He devoted himself to religion from an early age, doing penance, meditating and helping the unfortunate. It is hard to picture a man so pure and so devoid of vanity and conceit living amid the pomp and intrigue of the Court. Even today, it seems almost improper to discuss a man whose virtues daunted even the most sceptical and malicious of his contemporaries. Theodore Rtistchev remained true to himself throughout his career in the Kremlin, displaying genuine humility and gentleness at all times. He steadfastly declined to participate in Court entertainments, and, although he was married and the father of a family, his life closely resembled that of a lay monk.

Rtistchev was, in a certain sense, the Tsar's conscience. His influence over him was very great, but he never took advantage of it except to further the spiritual, educational or charitable aims to which he devoted his energies.

The Tsar sometimes sent Rtistchev abroad on missions, and on one occasion appointed him envoy plenipotentiary charged with concluding a peace treaty with Poland. He also entrusted him with the education of his heir and nominated him a boyar, a high distinction which Rtistchev humbly declined. Whatever the task in hand, Theodore Rtistchev always strove to act with perfect charity, reconciling enemies, pouring oil on troubled waters and never under any circumstances seeking to enhance his personal prestige. Though less well-known to foreigners than Ordyn-Nastchokin, the Minister for Foreign Affairs, Rtistchev made a great impression on the few visitors who met him. Mayerberg, ambassador of Emperor Leopold I, declared that 'at the age of forty, Theodore Rtistchev possesses more wisdom than an old man', and Ordyn-Nastchokin, who normally judged his compatriots so harshly, held him in the highest esteem. 'He is the most resolute and upright of all those in the palace,' he used to say.

To be frank, Rtistchev's virtues were so great that it is hard to fit him into an historical work at all, but he played such an important role that he cannot be excluded from the century which, in Klyuchevsky's words, 'he illumined like a beacon'.

As one of the most influential members of the 'Zealots of Religion', the society founded at Court, Theodore Rtistchev was also one of the first to urge the amendment of liturgical and religious books, agitate for a system of national education and stress the need for establishing a proper welfare organization in the country.

Rtistchev was a man of action who quickly translated words into deeds. He engaged a group of thirty monks from the monastery at Kiev and other monasteries in Western Russia and established them in Moscow at his own expense. Using money given him by Tsar Alexis, he founded the capital's first free academy in 1649 and enrolled himself as its first pupil. At his instigation, monks were commissioned to translate works written in foreign languages and instruct Russians in philosophy, the sciences, and Greek, Slavonic and Latin rhetoric. He spent whole nights with learned professors, assimilating their knowledge. His example was infectious, and in 1667 the parishioners of the church of St John the Apostle decided to open a school in their parish – not an elementary school, it may be added, but a school which taught Slavonic, Greek and Latin and the liberal sciences. It is known that, in quest of someone to sponsor their application to the Tsar, they turned to a man 'of honour and virtue', who can only have been Rtistchev himself.

Surrounded by parochial squabbles great and small, appalling religious strife and intrigue for influence and power, Theodore Rtistchev went his lonely way untempted by wealth and glory. Rubbing shoulders with arrogant and uncouth boyars, with unscrupulous coxcombs like Ilya Miloslavsky, the Tsar's brother-in-law, with a 'man of fire' like Archpriest Avvakum or with a 'man of stone and will' like Nikon, it was always he who spread peace and reconciliation, speaking not only of principles and ideas but also of charity and Christian brotherhood. Like the Minister of Foreign Affairs, Ordyn-Nastchokin, he worked to destroy whatever corrupted national life, but he concentrated on quite another sphere. If Rtistchev strove to influence the laws he did so in the spirit of modern social reform, anxious to reinforce the charitable impulses of private individuals with a powerful and government-supported welfare organization. At his instance, Tsar Alexis ordered a census to be taken of the poor of Moscow. Those who were genuinely ill were placed in two charitable institutions specially created for the purpose, while the able-bodied were found work. A start had been made. Under Theodore and Sophia, a number of important charitable institutions were founded in Russia. Hospitals and asylums originally set up under the auspices of the Church were later taken over by the State.

A large number of facts reported by contemporaries of Theodore Rtistchev the Compassionate bear witness to his unwearying pursuit of the good.

In 1654, Rtistchev accompanied the Tsar on his Polish campaign. As a civilian, he travelled by coach, but he crammed so many sick, destitute and wounded men into the vehicle en route that before long there was no room for him and he had, despite his own infirmities, to proceed on horseback.

To ensure that the unfortunates whom he picked up during his travels were cared for, Rtistchev took advantage of any halt, however brief, to set up small hospitals in the towns and villages through which the Tsar's column passed. The money given him by the Tsar was not enough to finance his good works, but other donations flowed in and the Tsarina herself sent him large sums. Rtistchev was a self-appointed Minister of Goodness. He purchased Russian prisoners from the Tatars and took an interest in foreign prisoners who had fallen into Russian hands. His charitable nature made no distinction between Greek and Jew. He visited prisons, bringing help and sympathy wherever he went.

It is recorded that, when offered a good price for one of his properties near Arzamas, Rtistchev preferred to sell it to the local inhabitants for less because they needed it and could not raise the full sum. Rtistchev cared so little about his personal reputation that he often came to people's aid under a cloak of anonymity: for instance, he sent a consignment of wheat to the famine-stricken Vologda region at his own expense but pretended that he was only acting as an agent for some anonymous philanthropists.

No peasants and serfs lived better than those on estates belonging to Rtistchev, who advanced them the wherewithal to develop their farmsteads and took care not to overburden them with taxes. He reduced the price of one of his estates in return for an undertaking on the purchaser's part to continue to treat the peasants as he himself had treated them. Reports of his virtue became so widespread that the Cossacks of Little Russia wanted him as Prince of Malorussia, i.e. the Tsar's viceroy.

Rtistchev, while enthusiastically supporting religious reform, was so tolerant towards those who disagreed with him that he lost no time in coming to the aid of Avvakum and other Old Believers who were fighting against all that he held most dear.

Sophia's elder brother Alexis, a precocious and delicate boy like his younger brother Theodore, was brought up by Theodore Rtistchev the Compassionate and Wise to fear God and love his neighbour. As for Sophia herself, the virtuous example set by that saintly man probably made less impression on her than the worldly-wise cynicism of her uncle Ivan Miloslavsky and old Morozov, her relative by marriage, both of whom were frequent guests in her mother's apartments.

Morozov was an old fox whose contemporaries described as being 'as avid for gold as a drunkard is for wine'. An intelligent but unscrupulous man, Tsar Alexis's former tutor had steered clear of public affairs ever since his activities sparked off the Salt Rebellion, an insurrection which proved a sore trial to the young Tsar during the early years of his reign.

Ivan Miloslavsky, Sophia's uncle, was a man abundantly endowed with guile, cunning and the spirit of intrigue. Tsar Alexis prudently kept him out of high office, and everyone recalled how brutally he had punished him for his braggadocio by humiliating him in the presence of the Duma.

Blood, however, is thicker than water. Alexis Michaelovitch did not hesitate to shield Morozov from the retribution which he so richly deserved for his part in causing the Salt Rebellion, just as he tolerated his brother-in-law's presence without believing in his merits. Like many another worthy monarch before and since, he allowed his wife's relatives to make their nest in his palace and feather it to their heart's content.

* * *

Although Tsar Alexis had his favourites he chose them all with the greatest discernment – all, that is to say, except Morozov, whose defects he was too inexperienced to recognize when he first mounted the throne. The Tsar entered relationships with his eyes open. Being neither cruel nor debauched, he selected men who would not indulge his non-existent vices but would share the burdens of his position. No Russian tsar was ever surrounded by better-chosen friends.

The great Nikon was, of course, an exceptional man, and Theodore Rtistchev was the very epitome of virtue, but Athanasius Nastchokin was a statesman of unique ability.

His long face made even longer by a heavy beard, the Prime Minister and Minister of Foreign Affairs was not a member of the senior nobility and could never have assumed the responsibilities which he discharged with such brilliance had it not been for the Tsar's favour.

The origins of the Nastchokin family were obscure, but some traced it back to an Italian named Ordini who entered the service of Prince Alexander of Tver at the beginning of the fourteenth century. Ordini's son was said to have been wounded in the cheek while fighting the Tatars, which would explain the surname Nastchokin, derived from 'on the cheek'. In the seventeenth century the Ordyn-Nastchokins belonged to the provincial petty nobility of the Pskov region, which meant that they were established near the Baltic frontiers, so important at this period. The fact that the Ordyn-Nastchokin estates were not far from the West may well have had something to do with the elder Nastchokin's decision to give his son a first-class education despite his limited means. Athanasius not only studied mathematics and science but knew Latin and later learnt Polish.

Like all gentlemen's sons, Athanasius entered the Tsar's service at a very early age. Michael, who still occupied the throne at the time, dispatched him to the Swedish frontier to negotiate a settlement of the demarcation dispute with Queen Christina's government. Possessing neither money nor influential relatives, he rose to high office solely on his personal merits. As Minister of Foreign Affairs and Chancellor of State at a period when the traditional rights of precedence still held sway (they were not abolished until the reign of Theodore Alexeyevitch), he not unnaturally encountered fierce opposition on the part of many illustrious boyars.

From the days of his youth onwards, Athanasius Ordyn-Nastchokin always performed his appointed tasks to complete satisfaction. He acted firmly but diplomatically when the Pskov rebels tried to assassinate him at the beginning of Alexander Michaelovitch's reign, and his star remained in the ascendant from then on. In 1654 the Tsar sent him to guard the Russo-Lithuanian and Russo-Livonian frontiers, and he acquitted himself admirably. In 1658 he negotiated an armistice with the Swedes at Valiesarsk, and, thanks to his inexhaustible reserves of patience, obtained better terms for Russia than anyone had dared hope for. In 1665 Ordyn-Nastchokin was made voivode or military governor of the Pskov district. Two years later he became the chief architect of the Treaty of Andrussovo, which ended thirteen years of war between the Russians and the Poles and guaranteed Russian control of the right bank of the Dnieper.

Behind all these dates and treaties there looms the unique figure of Athanasius Ordyn-Nastchokin himself, great devotee of Western Europe and critic of the Russian way of life. His colleagues took exception to his wide knowledge of alien customs and derisively nicknamed him 'the foreigner'. No one but Tsar Alexis appeared to support or even to respect him, and neither his political flair nor his diplomatic finesse were ever appreciated by his compatriots. He was forced to fight a war on two fronts: on the one hand, against foreigners – for whom he felt an intellectual affinity – because he considered their ways superior to those of his fellow-countrymen, and, on the other, against the distrust of the Russians themselves. What made Ordyn-Nastchokin's position even more uncomfortable was that he possessed a stubborn conscience and a rigid moral sense. He never hesitated to reproach others for their shortcomings (his diplomatic Achilles' heel) and took a certain relish in denouncing the evils of the government and the stupidity of its members. His only mainstay and prop was the Tsar, and it was to the Tsar that he addressed his numerous and eloquent letters of complaint. Alexis Michaelovitch may have had no vices but he was not without the failings common to the best of men, and did not take kindly to being pestered with recriminations and complaints, some of which he found pedantic in the extreme.

'Of all men,' Ordyn-Nastchokin wrote to his sovereign, 'none is more vilified for his services to you than I.' And again: 'I am as unnecessary to the men of the Duma as great affairs of state are unnecessary to them.'[1]

By contrast, foreigners who met Ordyn-Nastchokin held him in the highest regard. Alexis Michaelovitch's English doctor, Collins, considered the Russian minister to be in no way inferior to the greatest statesmen of the West.

A search of his archives disclosed plans for far-reaching reforms and studies on problems of all kinds. As we have said, Ordyn-Nastchokin regarded Western Europe's organizing ability as a thing to be emulated, but despite his nickname he was a great patriot and a man of imperialist aspirations. Since Russia was in a state of permanent conflict with Poland (over Little Russia) and with Sweden (over the Baltic), he made it his first concern to secure a lasting peace with Poland, believing that Poland alone stood in the way of the unification of the Slavic world and that once this

[1] Quoted by Klyuchevsky.

union was achieved Sweden would no longer represent a threat. Ordyn-Nastchokin was the only man of his day, apart from the unfortunate Croat, Krizhanitch, to cherish pan-Slavist dreams.

The Tsar took his time before elevating Ordyn-Nastchokin to the supreme order of Russian nobility, that of boyar, despite his senior position. When granting him the lesser status of gentleman of the Duma he sweetened the pill by accompanying his appointment with the following letters patent:

> We honour you, Athanasius, for your great and numerous services to Our person. Mindful of God and His Holy Commandments, you give drink to them that thirst, clothe them that are naked, give shelter to them that wander and steadfastly keep the oaths sworn to Us, the Grand Sovereign. You serve Us, you apply yourself with manly courage to Our affairs, you care for combatants, you punish thieves, and you keep watch over the towns of the King of Sweden with a stout heart.

In 1662, Ordyn-Nastchokin was entrusted with a delicate mission. He was sent by the Tsar as ambassador plenipotentiary to John Casimir, King of Poland, charged with averting a new threat of war. Once in Poland, he employed his eloquence to the full, backing it with genuine conviction and an obvious desire for peace. The fruit was not yet ripe, however. Ordyn-Nastchokin was not destined to pluck it until 1666, by which time Russia was victorious in Lithuania, Vilno had surrendered and John Casimir was ready to make peace. On January 30th, 1667, Ordyn-Nastchokin joyfully put his signature to the Treaty of Andrussovo. Let us quote Collins:

> Ordyn-Nastchokin concluded with Poland a peace extremely advantageous to Russia. He allayed the misunderstanding between Sweden and Russia. He has now become Chancellor of Foreign Affairs, Treasurer of State and Governor of Little Russia.[1]
>
> He has restored the market in silk throughout Russia and there is no doubt that he will involve the Indies in it. He is now occupied with elaborating the laws of the country and the decrees of the Tsar's house. Nastchokin is a man who cannot be bought and who never ceases to work. He is extremely reserved. Speaking one day of France and Denmark, who support the Dutch, he expressed himself thus: 'I marvel that the Kings of France and Denmark can act so carelessly

[1] Collins is wrong here. Ordyn-Nastchokin was neither Treasurer nor Governor of Little Russia, but first nobleman of the palace and head of the Office for Little Russia.

> in arming such boors against the King of England. It would be much more to their advantage to ally themselves with all the other sovereigns of Europe in order to destroy all the republican governments, who are nought but generators of heresies and revolts ... Ordyn-Nastchokin is a sincere champion of the English.'[1]

But war and diplomacy were not the sole interests of this remarkable man. Ordyn-Nastchokin organized weekly postal services between Russia, Finland and Courland, and later between Russia and Poland. He founded the first Russian gazette and published information bulletins which came to be known as 'The Cursives'. Written on sheets of paper laid end to end and sometimes several yards long, 'The Cursives' informed the Tsar and government departments of recent developments in foreign affairs.

[1] *The Present State of Russia*, London, 1671.

CHAPTER FOUR

BEYOND the walls of the Kremlin, Russian society was assuming new forms, even though social life was still chaotic and the bureaucracy was attempting to define the rights and obligations of each social stratum.

Nothing could be more complex or baffling than the organization of Russian society in the seventeenth century. Each section of the population had its own legal status, but the subdivisions were almost as numerous as the stars in the Milky Way. Moreover, the lines of demarcation between them were far from rigid, and it was quite easy to pass from one class to another, losing an old or acquiring a new juridical identity on the way.

One important section of the population was composed of 'men of [the Tsar's] service' or State servitors. Boyars, city and provincial nobility, officials, soldiers and courtiers formed a sort of *druzhina* round the sovereign. Their first duty was to obey any call the Tsar might make, fight for him, secure the country's borders and maintain internal peace. This duty, which began at adolescence and ended at death – since neither age nor infirmity conferred exemption – allowed the members of this 'territorial army' only as much private life as their sovereign chose to grant them. State servitors not only served in the army but filled government posts. They could be members of the Duma, officials in the *prikazy* or government departments, governors of town or courtiers, each according to his rank and (sometimes) his merits. Every landed proprietor was a State servitor responsible for local administration and government on the Tsar's behalf, in his name and in the best interests of the nation. Thus the concept of nobility was bound up with the hereditary ownership of land, of which some had belonged to families for generations and some was allotted as a lifetime grant for services rendered.

Before Peter the Great, Russia had no noble title save that of prince, which belonged exclusively to those who had never been ennobled, that is to say, the descendants of Rurik or Russo-Lithuanian princes of the Gedimnas family, such as the Golitsyns and Trubetskoys. Descendants of the Tatar tsars of Astrakhan and Kazan bore the title 'tsarevitch', like the sons of the Tsar, as did the children of the tsars of Georgia, who enjoyed Russian protection. Where a title was lacking, the sovereign conferred various ranks of which the highest was that of boyar. The idea of ennoblement was not a very well-defined one, and the ladder of promotion was not barred even to merchants, who were mostly of peasant stock. By becoming a clerk or official, a merchant might sometimes become one of the Tsar's closest advisers and receive land and rank.

Finally, there were the people of the *possad* (inner suburb), that is to say, clerics, merchants, shopkeepers, craftsmen and townsfolk other than State servitors. Musketeers, who often pursued a trade or profession in their spare time, also belonged to this class. The city, properly speaking, was the fortified centre of the capital, and the possads formed a ring immediately surrounding it. Merchants were divided into three categories of varying status.

Guilds and trade associations did not exist in Russia except in the embryonic form of journeymen's guilds, though armourers, for instance, had quite a highly developed professional organization.[1]

The second and outer ring surrounding the city consisted of suburbs proper, of which some sections were reserved for the foreigners who lived there, practising their own customs and forming small independent communities. The inhabitants of the suburbs were socially inferior to the people of the possads but were, like them, subject to government dues and taxes. They were often grouped according to their occupation: weavers, coachmen, carters or the seventeenth-century equivalent of the long-distance lorry-driver, who traversed the arterial roads of Russia in summer and winter, transporting freight and passengers.

With a few exceptions, all these people had good cause to complain of their lot, for they were so overburdened with taxes that some of them preferred to sell themselves into *kabala*, i.e. pledge their persons to richer men and so avoid paying taxes, while others went off to join the Cossacks and likewise escaped State control by becoming itinerant seasonal labourers.

Almost at the bottom of the social scale came the peasants. In the Middle Ages, Kievan Russia had a singular conception of landed property. A stranger questioning a peasant to discover whose land he was riding over would receive the following reply: 'The land is God's. We have the use of it under the protection of our prince.' By the seventeenth century, all land apart from hereditary appanages or Church-owned estates was implicitly regarded as belonging to the Tsar or Crown, i.e. as State

[1] The Soviet historians Simonov and Speransky rightly state in their article on the possads (*Studies in the History of the U.S.S.R.*, 1955) that the seventeenth century saw the formation of the bourgeoisie. At the time of the Salt Rebellion, popular indignation was also directed against the prosperous inhabitants of the possads.

property. The Tsar could dispose of it as he pleased, with the result that peasants could never become the owners of the land on which they worked. Until the end of the sixteenth century they still had the right to leave their master and take up service with another, though this right could be exercised only once a year on the Feast of St George. Boris Godunov abolished this important privilege, so that under Alexis Michaelovitch the peasant was an integral part of landed property. Nevertheless, his servitude was not complete. He was still a citizen with full legal rights. He could make a will, engage agricultural labourers and, after discharging certain obligations towards his master, dispose of the fruits of his labour by selling them at market or to private individuals.[1] He could also own livestock and was supplied with agricultural implements by his master. His obligations, however, were heavy. He had to supply his master with hay, wheat, provisions, firewood and sometimes 'processed' items such as woven cloth, semolina, wine, etc. It was forbidden to sell a peasant without selling the land on which he was settled. By making a contract with his master and paying an agreed sum a peasant could abandon the land and seek an outlet in trade or commerce. Some ex-peasants managed to amass considerable fortunes in this way, but they were exceptions.

Under the Ulozhenye Code, peasants and their descendants were bound no longer to the land but to the person of the landed proprietor. It was the first step – a giant step – towards the serfdom which Catherine, 'liberal' friend of Voltaire and Grimm, was to carry to extremes. In the old days, a peasant on the run at least had the benefit of a statute of limitations with a ten-year term, after which his owner could neither search for nor reclaim him. The Ulozhenye robbed the fugitive even of this chance. Unjust, stupid and confused though they were, however, the new laws still left the peasant of the seventeenth century a semblance of the legal status which he was destined to forfeit later.

Although the peasant's lot was incredibly harsh, that of the serf was even more so. The word for slave was unknown in Kievan Russia save in an ecclesiastical context (e.g. 'slave of God'), but *kholop-smerd* existed. One could become a *kholop* in one of several ways: by capture in war, by parental sale or by voluntarily pledging oneself. Certain crimes were punishable by serfdom. A merchant, for instance, could become a serf for culpable insolvency. A free man who entered another's service without defining his rights contractually was also considered as such. What distinguished serfdom from all other orders of society was that the serf had no legal status. He could not even be called to give evidence at a trial,

[1] Just as the kolkhozniks can today.

and could be bought and sold like an animal or an inanimate object. Serfdom could be acquired by *kabala*, that is to say, by means of a 'loan contract' freely entered into. However, a man in *kabala* could regain his freedom after paying or working off the loan, whereas a serf could only do so at his master's whim – or by flight.

Russia in the time of Alexis Michaelovitch had yet another social category which defied all classification: that of 'free men'. No one knew who they were or where they came from. They might be men of the possads or suburbs trying to escape taxation, discontented peasants, serfs on the run or boyars' sons who had fallen on evil days. These people hired themselves out to peasants as seasonal labourers or tramped across the vast expanses of the Russian country-side making for regions controlled by the Cossacks, who welcomed them without asking what brought them there.

* * *

The Tsar's subjects included some who were subjects only in name. There were times when they heeded their sovereign's commands and carried them out, but, equally, there were times when they behaved exactly as they pleased. These independent spirits were the Cossacks, a phenomenon as specifically Russian as the 'vagabond' class and one which had its origin in the country's vast tracts of underpopulated territory, where any man with a taste for liberty could lose himself without trace.

Seasonal labourers who had no definite trade or known domicile became known as *volnitsy* (free men), and small agglomerations of them gravitated little by little to the border regions of Russia where the central administration found it hard to penetrate. Some *volnitsy* made their way to the fortified towns along the frontiers while others took to the steppes, where nomadic remnants of the Tatar Horde still roamed; these were subjected to incessant guerrilla attacks by the Cossacks, who harassed them for their own purposes but to the advantage of the nation as a whole. Other Cossacks confined themselves to hunting and fishing and sold the fruits of their skill to the traders with whom they maintained contact. Their ranks were continuously swelled by serfs on the run from their masters, penniless boyars' sons and Tatar converts to Christianity.

According to Klyuchevsky, the original home of Cossackdom extended from the Middle Volga to Riazan and Tula. In the Ukraine, one important group became established beyond the Dnieper rapids. These were the Zaporozhye Cossacks, who were to play a significant role as a 'third force' separating Poland and Russia. Another group, that of the Urals, helped to colonize Siberia Thus, Cossack communities existed almost throughout the Don and Dnieper areas, the most active during the seventeenth century being the Zaporozhye and Don Cossacks. By lending Tsar Michael powerful support in his struggle against the Polish invaders the *dontsy* had obtained important privileges from the government, but their spirit of independence, their indiscipline, their insistence on retaining their own customs and, above all, their flat refusal to extradite fugitives wanted by Moscow often provoked violent conflicts with the central administration.

By the middle of the seventeenth century, the Don Cossacks were divided into two groups, the 'lower' and the 'upper'. Members of the first category were abandoning their nomadic ways, building towns and villages and founding important commercial enterprises. Their area became a centre of trade with Moscow. The 'upper' Don Cossacks owned no property of any kind and were gradually falling under the influence of the 'lower', who sent them off on raids whose proceeds were shared between the men of action and their sleeping partners. The Soviet historian Tchayev remarks that the 'lower' or sedentary Don Cossacks slowly but surely developed into agents of the Russian government. Generally speaking, while refusing to sacrifice their own interests or relinquish their privileges, the Don Cossacks faithfully played the government game. Discounting a few minor incidents, they remained loyal to Russia and the Crown, and it was they who handed over the rebel leader Stepan (Stenka) Razin to the Tsar in 1671.

One branch of the Don Cossacks was traditionally supposed to have settled on the Volga. These were the Yaik Cossacks, who maintained close relations with those of the Don.

As for the Zaporozhye Cossacks, known to the West through Gogol's epic *Taras Bulba*, they had been established on the banks of the Dnieper for some decades. To the Zaporozhye Cossacks, situated as they were between Catholic Poland and Orthodox Muscovy, the seventeenth century was a time of decision. Grouped in 'free corps' and governed by leaders of their own choosing, they hailed from every corner of Russia. Records show that in the time of Stefan Batory one Zaporozhye unit was composed of five hundred men from seventy-four different towns or districts in Western Russia and Lithuania and seven towns in Poland. Among them were men from Central Russia, a few from the Volga, some Moldavians, a Serb, a German and a Muslim Tatar. United by no common ideal, these ill-assorted elements formed a sort of autonomous foreign legion composed of tough adventurers who varied as greatly in social background as in national origin. They were desperadoes and mercenaries, ready to lease their sabres to anyone willing to pay the price.

They went to war to enrich themselves, harried the survivors of the Tatar Horde across the steppes on their own account, fought as fiercely with the Poles against the Russians as they did with the Russians against the Poles, and offered their services to the Emperor against the Turks but did not jib at pillaging and massacring Christians when the Turks paid them to do so.

Like the Zaporozhye Cossacks, the civil population of Little Russia, urban and rural, had no noblemen, although the power and arrogance of the neighbouring Polish *shliachta*[1] sometimes prompted Zaporozhye chieftains and wealthy members of the sedentary population to pass themselves off as such. Properly ennobled families only appeared in the area in the eighteenth century, under Catherine II.

Although the Zaporozhye Cossacks were devoid of any patriotic sentiments, they had retained the idea that they were Orthodox. To quote Adam Kissel, a Polish nobleman (Orthodox, incidentally) who was Polish commissioner to the Zaporozhye Cossacks in 1636: 'They are much attached to the Greek religion, albeit they behave more like Tatars.'

Each man was against his neighbour in the regions of the south-west, Russian against Pole and Pole against Russian, Catholic against Orthodox and Orthodox against Catholic, Polish *shliachta* against Cossacks and Cossacks against the Polish nobility and commons, regular or 'enlisted' Cossacks against free Cossacks, Cossacks and Poles combined against the Jews, who were very numerous in the area, and, finally, the Cossacks against their own freely elected leaders, who were often drowned, slaughtered or hanged by the men who had elected them.

Turbulent, greedy, fickle in their affections and vague in their ideas of patriotism, the Cossacks were at once a valuable source of support and a constant menace. Like immigrants who leave Europe because they are unhappy there but cannot stifle a kind of sentimental attachment to it once they reach the United States, the Cossacks, who equated their wild existence with liberty, were tied to the home of Orthodoxy by the instinctive needs of the heart.

* * *

The Muscovy in which Sophia grew up was rich in natural resources but ill-organized and lacking in cohesion. Yet it was precisely at this juncture that it embarked upon nationhood.

Russia's historic destiny declared itself in every sphere of life during the

[1] Gentry.

reign of Alexis Michaelovitch. The population, though largely Russian, was still an ethnographic mixture of extreme complexity. Since Russia had never possessed an overseas colonial empire, the absorption of the non-European element was a fairly easy matter and the racial question never presented any serious problems. Religion was to prove the only obstacle to the complete Russianization of the assimilated territories. Nevertheless, numerous ethnic groups still had very weak administrative links with the capital at this period because of their remote position.

The Tsar and his advisers had plenty to occupy them. Incessant wars and a process of spontaneous economic expansion demanded resources which the State was incapable of providing, and the government had periodically to cope with severe financial crises.

Alexis Michaelovitch had inherited some grave financial burdens from his father, the first Romanov, most of them attributable to the aftermath of the Time of Troubles, which plunged Russia into such tragic anarchy and misery.

The revenue of the Muscovite dominions was drawn from direct and indirect taxation, private commerce and government enterprises. With the population already impoverished and overburdened with taxes, the administrators found themselves trapped in a vicious circle and did not know where to turn.

Despite all obstacles, however, the country had been making steady progress ever since the year of the first Romanov's election. Constantly developing and gathering strength, Russia was propelled forward by her unconscious vitality like a tree whose roots grope their way across rock towards a life-giving stream.

Factories multiplied in number, many of them powered by water. Metal, principally iron, was processed by thirty or more firms of varying importance, two or three of which were owned by foreigners. Arms manufacture was no longer confined to the Tula district. In about 1650 a Swede named Koet built a glass-works, and thirty years later a number of Russian glass-works were in full operation. Manufacture of textiles, mainly linen, was stepped up in order to satisfy domestic and foreign demand, and there came into being a new, free, working class composed of technicians and female workers, many of whom acquired a remarkable degree of proficiency.

The country became more accessible to the West with every passing day. The Russian Residents appointed by the Tsar to Sweden, Poland, the Netherlands and England were under orders to develop trade between Russia and foreign countries.

The famous 'Muscovy Company of Merchant Adventurers' – an

English association, though many of its members were Scotsmen – had long made a practice of entering Muscovy by the northern route, i.e. via the Arctic Ocean and the White Sea. They have left behind some extremely interesting accounts of their voyages through these little-known regions.

The port of Archangel represented Russia's chief link with the West. In 1618, the Dutch merchant and diplomat Isaac Massa noted in one of his reports that he had seen twenty or thirty Dutch and three English vessels in the harbour there. Traffic continued to mount steadily. In 1630–1, the Dutch envoys Bourch and Feldtril counted no less than a hundred Dutch and several English ships at Archangel.

Ivan the Terrible had dreamed of using the Baltic as a medium of commercial intercourse with the West, and his dream was shared by Tsar Alexis and Ordyn-Nastchokin. As mistress of the Baltic, Sweden had offered Russia the use of it, but Russia declined because it would have made her commercially dependent on her powerful and troublesome neighbour.

What Archangel was to trade with the West, Astrakhan was to the East, where Russia was less geographically constricted. Raw silk, carpets, precious stones and pearls reached her from Persia, Khiva and Bokhara. Towards the middle of the century, Muscovy established direct contact with India. Having crossed the Urals and colonized the virgin lands beyond, the Tsar's subjects were already established on the borders of China. The majority of the Russians in Siberia had settled there of their own free will, for anyone who was dissatisfied with his lot could find freedom on the other side of the Urals. The State owned land there, but few large land-owners existed, so new arrivals settled there as free men in a free country. Isbrand wrote that he often came across prosperous Siberian villages on his travels. The first attempts to exploit the mineral wealth of Siberia were made at Tobolsk, the regional capital. It may be added that Siberia was not lacking in educated men.

Russia's imports from the West included cloth, metal, weapons, colonial produce, chemicals, dyes, ammoniac and arsenic. Some idea of her exports to the West can be obtained from a report by de Rodès, Swedish resident in Moscow between 1650 and 1655. Records of traffic passing through the port of Archangel indicated that in the year 1653 Russia's exports included leather (32 per cent), corn, wheat and barley (21 per cent), bacon (11 per cent), potash (10·4 per cent) and furs (8·5 per cent), the remainder being made up of caviare, meat, tar, mica, pitch and cloth, mainly linen. No less than 30,000 arshines (1 arshine = 28 inches) of woven linen passed through Archangel in a single year.

The country's economic momentum and expansionary tendencies were such that the home market developed with equal vigour, despite the government's fumbling and largely empirical measures.

New men brushed aside the handicap of humble birth and attained prominence, laying the foundations of the country's great commercial dynasties. In the year 1650 alone, 7,000 mink and sable pelts worth 10,000 roubles were exported from Siberia by the Bossii, a family of peasant stock, nor were they the only people to run businesses of this magnitude. Peasants belonging to the boyar Morozov, the Tsar's brother-in-law, took over the management of distilleries at Nizhni-Novgorod and made a fortune out of them. Other peasants were financed by their masters and also became business men on a grand scale. Assisted by his sons and nephews, a man named Antipov succeeded by the end of the century in becoming one of the wealthiest merchants in the country and the owner of a river fleet which he employed to transport salt, cured hides and fish. Enterprising peasants belonging to the Metropolitan of Novgorod, some of whom became personal advisers of the Tsar, engaged in foreign trade and visited Reval and Stockholm in the course of their business activities.

The general picture was still chaotic, but the foundations of an organic structure had been laid.

It soon became necessary to protect Russian merchants from foreign competition. Having no silver of her own, Russia was obliged to import it from abroad. Silver pieces and foreign coins were melted down to provide the metal required for Russian currency. The Treasury, of course, made a good profit out of such transactions, and it was this policy which culminated in the devaluation of copper coinage and the insurrection which was finally crushed at Kolomenskoye. In 1667, the Russian government compelled foreign merchants to pay customs duty in gold and silver coinage. Naturally enough, they in their turn insisted on being paid in similar currency by Russian merchants, an arrangement which hardly appealed to the latter because their own customers paid them in copper.

The government granted preferential tariffs to its own nationals, and, when the 'mad people of England' killed their king, Alexis Michaelovitch revoked their ancient privileges and compelled them to pay the same duties as those exacted from the merchants of Holland and Hamburg and other foreigners.

Undeterred by a host of difficulties, Alexis Michaelovitch obstinately strove to set Russia on the road to prosperity. Describing a journey to Russia made by his father, Patriarch Makarios, Deacon Paul of Aleppo told a friend from Antioch how astonished he had been to find that it was possible to buy every type of essential commodity in Moscow.

The seventeenth century witnessed not only the birth of Russia's territorial, economic, psychological and linguistic unification but also her first steps towards centralization of power.

CHAPTER FIVE

THE woods and forests dividing the belts of arable land round Moscow had been left intact, and it was in these so-called 'islands' that Tsar Alexis used to hunt elk, fox and hare. For a long time, dogs were regarded in Russia as unclean beasts, and packs of hounds were not formed there until the reign of Grand Prince Vasily III, in the first half of the sixteenth century. Alexis Michaelovitch was fond of hunting, but his favourite sport was hawking, and the whole of the country-side round the capital was reserved for his *sokolniky* or falconers.

Tsar Alexis loved Nature as much as he loved entertaining novelties from abroad. He was a country gentleman at heart, and it was only natural that, travel being a slow and tedious business at this period, he did his utmost to restore the existing palaces and pleasure pavilions in the immediate vicinity of Moscow.

At Izmailovskoye, Alexis Michaelovitch carried out a model farming project. In 1663 he ordered a large number of peasants to be transported there from his other estates. Woods were cleared, the ground watered by an extremely skilful system of irrigation, and mills, stabling and stone silos constructed. Russian and Tatar specialists, the latter summoned from Astrakhan, worked wonders in the severe climate of Central Russia. Walnut trees, mulberries for feeding silk-worms, vines and even cotton were grown there. Vegetables of every conceivable variety flourished in the vast market-gardens, one of which was devoted to the cultivation of medicinal herbs. Apiculture and cattle-breeding were introduced on a large scale. Home-grown flax was woven into linen cloth, beer brewed from home-grown hops and honey from the estate's own hives made into mead – and all on the spot, at Izmailovo itself. Lisek, who was attached to the embassy of Emperor Leopold I, did not exaggerate in the least when he noted in his diary:

'Pomona is as generous in Muscovy as Ceres. Gooseberries, cherries, apples and plums, cucumbers and water-melons, melons in great abundance and of the most excellent quality – all are of remarkable size.'

Farming methods at Izmailovo were singularly advanced for the period, and there was even a degree of mechanization. Flour, for instance, was ground in highly efficient mills. In 1665 a clock-maker named Andrey Krik submitted plans to the Tsar for a threshing machine operated by water-power, and another Russian, the musketeer Viasma, invented a thresher driven by air. Factories sprang up at Izmailovo. An Italian called Mignot set up a glass-works where Russian apprentices underwent instruction by master glass-blowers from Venice. (Another glass-works, run by the Russian Bukhanin, was already in operation near Moscow.) Although its glass production was at first absorbed by the requirements of the Court, articles manufactured there were later sold to the population at large.

Sophia was seven years old when Izmailovo came into being, and she no doubt spent many happy hours watching the inmates of the zoological garden which her father had established in the grounds, the largest of its kind in the whole country. Specimens of every beast and bird found in the plains and forests of Russia were assembled there – elk, bear and wolf, fox and boar, mink, marten and ermine – together with animals brought from even farther away, such as reindeer from Siberia, caribou from America, lions and tigers, leopards and cheetahs. The aviary swarmed with peacocks, swans, English hens, Chinese geese and turkey-cocks. Sometimes – a barbarous but commonplace form of diversion – the Tsar's children and his guests were treated to the cruel spectacle of fights between bears, wolves and greyhounds.

In the spacious pleasure-gardens, which were laid out with rigid symmetry in the French style, covered galleries adorned with *trompe-l'œil* murals allowed the stroller to enjoy the view in all directions and in all weathers. Every arbour had its own summer-house. From the galleries, the Tsar and his friends used to watch fights between teams of bare-knuckle boxers, a favourite Russian sport. Also greatly admired for their strength and bravery were the numerous Russian practitioners of the art of unarmed combat with bears. Foreigners stood rooted in amazement at the sight of men wrestling bare-handed with one of these powerful beasts, not only because of the courage they displayed but also because of the sheer physical strength required by this particular sport. Seizing the bear by the ears, the man shook it until it fell to the ground exhausted.

There was, of course, another side to the coin, although gentle Alexis Michaelovitch was probably unaware of the high price paid by the peasants and labourers who worked on his magnificent estate. His overseers did not spare the rod, and in later years human bones and skulls were found in a secret well-shaft beneath one of the towers.

The palace at Izmailovo was built of wood like that of Kolomenskoye, but differed from the latter in its Westernized design. Austere in appearınce and surrounded by moats filled with water, it formed an island vhose inhabitants had to cross a bridge in order to reach the gardens, ields and woods. This bridge, surmounted by a tower, betrayed the first igns of a new style which later came to be known as the 'Naryshkin tyle'.

It was at another of the Tsar's favourite properties, Kolomenskoye, also ituated not far from Moscow on the high ground overlooking the right ›ank of the Moskva, that Sophia first heard the roar of an angry mob and aw bloodshed.

According to tradition, the village of the same name was founded in the niddle of the thirteenth century by the inhabitants of the town of Kolomna during their flight from the hordes of Batu Khan. During the ixteenth century it was the site of a small but compact palace belonging o the Tsars of Moscow, more a hunting lodge than a family residence, hough its orchards and kitchen-gardens were already renowned at that ›eriod. In 1562, Grand Prince Vasily III built a magnificent church close ›y. The Church of the Ascension was quite unreminiscent of the traditional lomed churches of Russia. It was a large tower surmounted by a conical pire of airy, almost magical delicacy. In his book *Art and Architecture*, ›ublished in Moscow in 1947, A. Tsires quotes the following lines by Berlioz, who visited the church in the eighteen forties:

> Nothing impressed me more than the monument to ancient Russian architecture which stands in the village of Kolomenskoye. I have seen Strasbourg Cathedral, centuries in building ... I have stood at the foot of Milan Cathedral ... but here I was confronted by a unity. My entire being trembled. There was a mysterious stillness in the harmony of the exquisite shapes.

In the old days, a look-out used to climb the interior staircase to a point ›f vantage just beneath the great eight-armed Orthodox cross at the ummit of the steeple, where he signalled the enemy's approach by means ›f smoke signals. On the top floor was the 'Tsar's seat', a stone chair from vhich the sovereign could watch parades and manœuvres taking place ›n the plain across the river.

Having inherited a dilapidated palace from his father, Alexis Michaelo-vitch decided to build a new one. In July 1662, however, before he could ›ut his plans into effect, Kolomenskoye became the scene of a sanguinary ncident. Tsar Alexis was spending the summer months there with his vhole family. The country was in bad shape financially and the Polish var of 1656, although successful, had severely depleted the national exchequer. Moreover, the immediate resumption of hostilities against

Sweden demanded fresh sources of revenue. In 1656, therefore, the government began to reconsider the possibility of taking financial measures designed to replenish the Treasury, and someone – it may have been Theodore Rtistchev, the most honest of the Tsar's advisers – proposed a scheme of camouflaged devaluation. This involved putting copper coinage into circulation while at the same time arbitrarily maintaining the existing silver currency. Accordingly, new coins were struck of the same weight and shape as silver pieces. People accepted the measure willingly at first, and the operation might well have succeeded had it not been for some shrewd but unscrupulous individuals who immediately decided to exploit a situation which offered such opportunities for self-enrichment. A large number of people were compromised, notably the boyar Miloslavsky, who was the Tsar's brother-in-law, and Matiushkin, gentleman of the Duma and husband of his maternal aunt. What had happened, in fact, was that 'genuine' rogue money had been put into circulation on a grand scale.

By 1662 the value of copper coins had deteriorated so greatly that people were offering fifteen copper roubles for one of silver. The cost of living reached dizzy heights. Since wage-earners, soldiers and workmen were paid in official currency, it was the common people of the possad who first became restive. Subversive letters and proclamations started to go the rounds, many of them denouncing important men such as the relatives of the Tsar whose names we have just mentioned.

In due course, the great fraud was unmasked. The dishonest merchants and the Treasury's master-coiners were severely punished, some of them by mutilation, but the Tsar's relations by marriage, Miloslavsky and Matiushkin, were spared despite the fact that they were closely involved. Miloslavsky simply had to undergo a long lecture from the Tsar on the subject of honesty, and Matiushkin was relieved of his post. Highly sensitive where justice was concerned, the people were outraged by this display of family forbearance towards the main instigators of the fraud.

The crisis continued to grow until, one night in 1662, unknown hands plastered the walls of Moscow with what were known in the contemporary idiom as 'malefactors' letters'. Other proclamations were nailed to the columns of the Lubianka and to the walls of churches. Men who knew how to read declaimed their contents for the benefit of the illiterate, and knots of people gathered to discuss their implications. Two constables dispatched to the Lubianka by the government tore down the seditious posters, but the crowd, already large and growing with every moment that passed, yelled: 'You mean to take the letter to the traitors because the Tsar is not in Moscow. Leave it there! Everyone ought to read it.' The two officers were unhorsed and the letters snatched from their hands. They fled, pursued by the mob as far as the Spassky Gates. A musketeer named Nagayev then read out a proclamation on the steps of St Theodosia's and called on the crowd for support. They followed him to the 'Court of the Provinces', where, standing on a milestone, he read out the proclamation once more.

In Red Square, groups of people feverishly discussed the day's events and denounced the guilty parties by name. Then the tocsin began to sound. Stalls and shops closed immediately, and shopkeepers who refused to join the movement were roughly handled by the mob. Meanwhile, merchants in the possad who were popularly reputed to have been involved in the currency fraud had their premises looted.

Next, some five thousand people converged on Kolomenskoye, just over six miles from Moscow. The crowd, which was heterogeneous in the extreme, included soldiers and musketeers, people of the possad, a few priests and nuns and a sprinkling of peasants. It was predominantly a townsmen's revolt.

* * *

Tsar Alexis was at Mass when the crowd of Muscovites burst into Kolomenskoye, unceremoniously demanding to see the sovereign. Palace officials informed him of their arrival and the names of the boyars and officials whom they wanted him to punish. Alexis Michaelovitch at once ordered the men in question, among them Ilya Miloslavsky, brother of Tsarina Maria, to take refuge in the Tsarina's apartments. Then, dispatching couriers to Moscow with instructions to the troops of the garrison to march on Kolomenskoye with all speed, he coolly went out to meet the insurgents.

A merchant or artisan from the possad named Luka Zhitkoy presented the Tsar with a petition, proffering it on the crown of his *shapka* as though on a salver. The rioters milled about, yelling coarse insults at those whom they held responsible for their misfortunes but levelling none at the person of the Tsar himself. They demanded justice and insisted that the guilty parties, whom they described as traitors, should be severely punished. Unruffled, Alexis Michaelovitch asked them to return to Moscow, promising that as soon as Mass was over he would return to the capital to deal with the affair in person and see that justice was done. The rioters caught the Tsar by the buttons of his long robe, entreating him to promise that he would punish the culprits, and he swore to, calling on God to bear witness.

Tragedy might still have been averted if another mob had not set out for Kolomenskoye in its turn. This second wave of rioters began by looting houses belonging to noblemen and merchants whose names were associated with the disastrous monetary reform. Angrier and more excited than the first, it proceeded to take a number of hostages with the intention of proving to the Tsar that some of his boyars were in illicit communication with Poland.

The Tsar's orders reached Moscow safely, however, and two companies of musketeers, one of them commanded by Artamon Matveyev, at once set off for Kolomenskoye. Other companies were charged with the task of restoring order within the capital. Prince Ivan Khovansky, who was popular with the commons, harangued the townsfolk, promising them justice in the Tsar's name. Kotoshikhin, an eye-witness of the insurrection, reports that the crowd shouted back: 'You are a good man, Khovansky, and served the Tsar well against Poland. All we want is that the Tsar hand the traitors over to us!' One of the Tsar's couriers alerted the regiments in the German Quarter. General Gordon, still a junior officer at the time, noted in his diary that there was 'great disorder in the quarter'. Mounted and on foot, the foreigners in the Tsar's service made for Kolomenskoye as fast as they could.

On the way to Kolomenskoye the second group of malcontents met the first, which, appeased by the Tsar's guarantees, was returning to Moscow. The latter allowed himself to be talked into joining forces with the former, and the atmosphere changed abruptly. On reaching Kolomenskoye, the rebels reappeared in front of the summer palace waving clenched fists and hurling threats. They no longer asked: they demanded. Punishment of the guilty was no longer enough for them: their initial grievance was now accompanied by other demands, e.g. for a reduction in taxes. The boyar Streshnev, an uncle of the Tsar, had to seek refuge in the courtyard of the palace itself, hotly pursued by mutinous cavalrymen. Alexis Michaelovitch lost patience. Not unnaturally perturbed at the violent way in which the motley crowd had invaded his property and encouraged by the news that reinforcements had arrived, he called on his men to attack the insurgents. The result was a massacre. Large numbers of people, most of them unarmed, were cut down where they stood, while others, sandwiched between converging bodies of government troops, raced for the only remaining route of escape – the river-bank – and were drowned in the Moskva.

Terrible reprisals ensued in the days to come. It has been estimated that seven thousand men were condemned to death. Another fifteen thousand were sentenced to mutilation and had their arms or legs cut off, several thousands were deported, and others had their property confiscated. Only a limited number of the demonstrators had been genuinely guilty of sedition. The majority had simply swum with the stream, some out of idle curiosity and others in order to draw the Tsar's attention to their misfortunes.

* * *

The insurrection and its bloody aftermath were plainly visible from the windows of the Terem, where the objects of popular wrath had taken refuge. Kotoshikhin, who has left us a detailed account of the affair, reports:

'As for the Tsarina, the tsarevitches and tsarevnas, they shut themselves up in their apartments, sorely afraid and filled with apprehension. Tsarina Maria, whose terror was extreme, took many months to recover.'

In 1663 the Tsar published a decree reinstating the use of silver coinage, but the State, whose financial position was still far from sound, played the bankrupt by only allowing its creditors between one and five kopeks for each copper rouble. The copper 'reform' had been a setback for the Treasury and a disaster for the population.

* * *

For all the evil memories which hung over Kolomenskoye from then on, Alexis Michaelovitch did not abandon his plan to construct a new palace there. Building started in autumn 1666 and the bulk of the work was completed within a year. The new palace at Kolomenskoye was built of wood like that of Izmailovo, but seems – in contrast to the latter, with its Westernized appearance – to have been based on tales from Russian national folklore. Its absurd but pleasing lines smacked of Moscow's Church of St Basil, and its onion-domed roofs, towers, turrets, innumerable stairways and maze of interconnecting passages all proclaimed the brilliant workmanship of native joiners.

Visiting the fortress of Archangel in 1586, almost a century earlier, a French sailor named Jean Sauvage had marvelled at the incomparable skill of the local carpenters. 'It is a fortress constructed of tree-trunks,' he noted in his journal, 'admitting neither of nails nor hooks, and its builders had no tools save axes. No architect could have done better.' (Saws did not come into general use until the reign of Peter the Great.)

Perhaps the best way to describe the new palace at Kolomenskoye is to compare it with sets for Russian ballets or the opera *Le Coq d'Or*. It was a building which preserved the traditional elements of the peasant *izba*. The summer of 1668 was devoted to decorating it and adding finishing touches. The palace had two hundred and fifty rooms and three thousand windows. Its carved wooden ornamentation frothed like lace and its roofs were covered with multicoloured wooden tiles painted in delicate colours and gilded with gold imported from abroad. An unusual note was struck by decorative motifs in copper and tin affixed to both the interior and exterior. Apart from traditional ornamentation, the builders employed new methods such as the coloured ornamentation of walls and ceilings – the first application of this technique to a wooden building.

The interior decoration of the palace was entrusted to a team of Russian painters supervised by Simon Ushakov, the artist who had decorated the Kremlin. The portraitist Saltanov was commissioned to paint portraits of historical figures such as Julius Caesar, Alexander the Great and Darius. Jaques Reitenfels, who visited Kolomenskoye, described it in the following terms: 'The palace is worth seeing, even though it is built of wood. Its decoration, which is astonishingly well-executed, is so remarkable and its profusion of gilding so brilliant that it appears to have emerged from a jewel-box.'

It would have been unlike Alexis Michaelovitch not to have busied himself with enlarging and improving the existing gardens and orchards at Kolomenskoye. An inventory of 1701 describes them in detail. One particular orchard contained more than four thousand apple trees and several hundred pear trees, and was bordered on all sides by cherry trees and raspberry and blackcurrant bushes. The entire population of five villages and nine hamlets furnished the labour force needed to maintain the estate. Kolomenskoye[1] was the Tsar's favourite place for receiving foreign ambassadors. Its praises were sung by the Court poet, Simeon Polotski, who likened it to the eighth wonder of the world:

> The world's four quarters are represented there,
> Across the ceiling spreads the celestial vault,
> The four seasons, flowers most marvellous …

Kolomenskoye's three thousand mica-covered windows glittered like stars, and, wonder of wonders, Alexis Michaelovitch's throne resembled that of Solomon himself. It was flanked on either side by two lions made of gilded copper. Stitched into sheepskins painted and dressed 'lion-

[1] The building has disappeared. All that remain are models, of which one now reposes in the Stchussev Museum of Russian Architecture, Moscow. Another, older example is in the British Museum in London, and during the eighteenth century there used to be a third in the Botanical Gardens at Leyden, Holland.

ashion', these figures were connected by means of a complicated mechan-
sm invented by the craftsman Peter Vissitsky to a pair of bellows operated
y a man stationed in a hidden chamber. They rolled their eyes, opened
heir jaws and roared with life-like ferocity.

CHAPTER SIX

In July 1658, the Kremlin's venerable cathedral witnessed an extraordinary scene. Patriarch Nikon, reformer of the Russian Church, was officiating in the Cathedral of the Assumption, where he had administered the sacrament of baptism to Sophia a year before, when an envoy from the Tsar, Prince Yury Romodanovsky, came to tell him that he had incurred the sovereign's disfavour. The official pretext was as ill-founded as the time and place were ill-chosen. The Tsar reproached the Patriarch with having improperly arrogated the title of Grand Sovereign, a royal prerogative.

Reminding Romodanovsky, with complete justification, that he held the title by permission of the Tsar himself, the Patriarch impetuously called on the faithful who were assembled in the cathedral to bear witness to the injustice he had suffered. Then, doffing his cassock, the emblem of his rank, in full view of the congregation, Nikon propped his pastoral cross against the iconostasis and declared: 'From this moment forward, I am Patriarch no longer.'

Turning on his heel, he strode from the cathedral in high dudgeon and drove to a monastery in Moscow, whence he later moved to 'The New Jerusalem', another monastery which he himself had founded.

It was the end not only of the long friendship between Nikon and Tsar Alexis but also of a long series of disagreements between two men who had once collaborated in the great task of reforming the Russian Church.

* * *

In The New Jerusalem, an imposing retreat which reflected the majestic personality of its founder, the Patriarch brooded on his disgrace. Winter came. Ice clothed the river Istra and dispersed again in the spring, leaving its waters free to resume their course. Nikon watched the seasons come and go in a state of self-imposed inactivity which must have been hard to endure for a man whose energy had rocked the foundations of a whole world of prejudice and ignorance. Would he ever emerge from oblivion and regain his prestige?

It is possible that the Patriarch found peace in The New Jerusalem's handsome church, but he can hardly have failed to ponder, when he was alone with his thoughts in the silence of his apartments, on the strange turn of fate which had transformed a peasant boy who once ran barefoot through the mud into the Grand Sovereign Patriarch of the Russian Church and a 'very dear friend' of the Tsar of all the Russias.

Born into an impoverished peasant family but brilliantly self-educated, Nikon chose the priesthood very early in life. As a secular (i.e. non-celibate) priest, he was unfortunate enough to lose his two sons, and having personally experienced the precarious nature of human relationships he decided, in concert with his wife, to embrace monasticism. His wife took the veil and was never heard of again. Nikon, too, asked nothing better than to be ignored by his age, and sought the perfection and peace of God in the austere atmosphere of the monasteries of the far north.

With the accession of Alexis Michaelovitch, winds of change blew across the country. Led by the Tsar, the country's finest minds turned towards the culture of the West, which had been so close to Kievan and Novgorodian Russia but had lost its identity while traversing the vast expanses which held Muscovite Russia a prisoner within its own continent.

Upheavals occurred in every field. Language became freer and manuscripts were no longer written in Slavonic but in the rich, flexible and vivid vernacular of Russia. Icons reflected the new aspect of the national genius,[1] songs became polyphonic, portraits recorded the features of contemporary personalities, the sciences were no longer regarded as a province of the Devil, a wider knowledge of foreign languages spurred men to greater intellectual activity, thousands of volumes poured from the State printing office, would-be reformers sprouted spontaneously in every class of society, and the Church itself awoke to the need for instilling some order into the anarchy which prevailed among religious customs and usages.

Editors of liturgical works printed by the State printing office in Moscow were already aware of the necessity for textual amendment in the time of Patriarch Joseph (1640–52), and both the Patriarch and the Tsar had now sanctioned it. The only remaining problem was to find scholars capable of carrying out the task, that is to say, men with a perfect knowledge of Slavonic and Greek.

[1] The latest works of Grabar, Lazarevsky, Tiulin and other authorities on Russian art consider as obsolete the theory of the decline of Russian religious painting in the seventeenth century.

The great majority of the Muscovite clergy was undoubtedly more ignorant than the Catholic priesthood or the Orthodox priests of the south-west. Priests who belonged to the 'white' or secular clergy, and could therefore marry, formed a class apart, and their sons usually followed them into the Church. The 'black' clergy or monks, who alone were eligible for the episcopacy, were drawn from every social stratum. Peasants and merchants, musketeers and princes all aspired equally to the 'angelic' state.

Brother Nikon very quickly made an impression on his superiors. Intelligent, energetic, erudite and competent, he found himself entrusted with missions of increasing importance. Thus, without personally seeking promotion, he was torn from the peace of the cloisters and thrust into an active life which suited his temperament far better, and it came as no surprise when, on the death of Joseph, Nikon acceded to the vacant patriarchate and at the same time became the 'very dear friend' of Tsar Alexis.

Nothing could have belied the proverb 'birds of a feather flock together' more effectively than the friendship which bound the benevolent tolerant and good-natured Tsar to the new Patriarch, with his generous heart but stubborn and unyielding temperament. Klyuchevsky calls Nikon a man capable of great things but prone to lose himself in details. Little things exasperated him and opposition roused him to cruelty. Nikon has been compared with Popes Gregory VII and Innocent III, and there is no doubt that it was his authoritarian nature and dogmatism which conduced to the personal setback whose extent he had ample time to gauge during his solitary meditations in The New Jerusalem.

What of the past that now seemed so far away? Nikon had enjoyed the sovereign's absolute confidence, so much so that Alexis entrusted him with the reins of government when wars compelled him to leave Moscow for the field of battle.

But his greatest task was yet to come. The order and dignity of the Church had to be restored. Ever mindful that the Russian Church was a branch of the Byzantine Church, the Russians regarded the Greeks with a certain degree of mistrust. The union with Rome concluded by the Greek hierarchy at Florence in 1439 had, in Russian Orthodox eyes, been a betrayal of the true faith, and public opinion was wholly on the side of Grand Prince Vasily of Moscow when, following this event, he expelled the Greek Metropolitan Isidore from the country for preaching in favour of union. The fall of Constantinople, which was regarded as fitting punishment for this apostasy, only reinforced the Russians' vision of themselves as the world's sole surviving depositaries and defenders of

Orthodoxy. When, at the close of the sixteenth century, Patriarch Jeremiah of Constantinople elevated Metropolitan Job of Moscow to the rank of Premier Patriarch of Russia and reminded the Tsar that 'Ancient Rome perished because it had fallen prey to heresy; the second Rome, Constantinople, fell into the hands of impious Turks; Moscow, the third Rome, remains the sole bastion of piety, and you alone in all the universe can call yourself "Tsar of the Christians" ', he was only expressing what the Russians themselves thought.

Nothing penetrates men's consciousness more readily than an idea which in some way enhances their sense of national superiority. Convinced that they were the only people to have preserved the Orthodox faith in all its purity, the Russians allowed themselves to slip, little by little, into a religious particularism which blinded them to the universality of the Church. Local practices grew up, and, although the jealously guarded purity of dogma remained intact, rites underwent certain changes. Similarly, liturgical books, the Bible and works by the Fathers of the Church had been so often copied and recopied in the course of centuries by careless or ignorant copyists that they now contained a mass of errors, and the development of printing had disseminated these erroneous texts on a wide scale.

People had been worried by this anarchy, and it was even whispered at the time of the Tsar's marriage that heresy could be born on the steps of the throne itself. Far from being confined to the old guard, opposition to changes in ways and customs was also rife among younger men who had been sent to places of learning to be trained as successors to the present generation of clergy. For many of them, custom had taken on the force of dogma and practices had become principles.

Once it had turned, however, the tide was not to be halted. In response to urgent pleas, Greek monks hurried to Moscow to restore order to religious affairs.

Ever since the fall of Constantinople, the Greeks had regarded Russia as the world centre of Orthodoxy. But the learned monks no sooner arrived there than they humiliated the Russians by tactlessly preening themselves on their intellectual superiority. After six centuries of Christianity, during which time they had demonstrated their loyalty to the true faith by professing it in the face of Tatars and Poles, the Russians now learned that they could neither pray nor sing Mass decently and that their sacred icons were mere daubs.

Accordingly, a summons went out to the Laure (abbey) of Kiev requesting the presence of monks from the regions of the south-west, notably Epiphany, Arsenius and Damaskin. The authorities took advantage of their stay in Moscow to entrust them not only with the amendment of religious books but also with an entire educational programme. The monks compiled encyclopedias and wrote treatises on anatomy, psychology, pedagogy and even sociology which enjoyed a great success among the more literate boyars. At the same time, orders were given to print a catechism composed by Peter Mohila, scion of a princely Moldavian family and Rector of Kiev Academy.

In the Court itself, a group called the 'Zealots of Religion' was formed on the initiative of the Tsar's confessor. It was composed of a substantial number of well-known clerics and distinguished laymen, the latter including Theodore Rtistchev, the Tsar's friend and associate.

Only Nikon could have carried through the reform of the Church with such vigour, but few could have pursued the task with less Christian charity, and it was his uncompromising severity which gave rise to the distressing schism that later plunged the country into bloodshed and disrupted internal peace.

Unlike that of the West, Russia's great Reformation originated at the top and was sponsored by the Tsar and the Patriarch. It was the outcome not of rebellion but of a high-level decision, and came into being in Russia at about the time when Louis XIV was fulminating against the Jansenists of Port Royal. The men of Port Royal were intellectuals and skilled theologians, however, whereas the 'Old Believers' with whom Nikon had to contend were ignorant and prejudiced men.

Despite the sovereign's support, Nikon had been as isolated on his patriarchal throne as he was in The New Jerusalem. Rightly deploring the national particularism of the Russian Church, he aimed at re-establishing and rediscovering for his flock the concept of the Church's universality. The universality of the Church was, in fact, his overriding concern, and he tried to strengthen the ties with other Orthodox patriarchates at a period when the Russians, in their thirst for dogmatic purity, looked askance at everything which had not been firmly established and implanted in Russian Christianity for seven centuries.

Lacking any understanding of Nikon's breadth of vision, the Old Believers found him highly suspect. The Patriarch had once declared, for instance, during a plenary session of the Russian hierarchy, that although he was a Russian and the son of a Russian his faith was Greek. A few days later, not content with having stirred up this hornet's nest, the Patriarch removed his Russian cassock in the middle of a service and exchanged it for one of Greek pattern. When a rumour spread that the Patriarch was favourable towards the Roman Church and had Popish tendencies, Nikon confined himself to remarking: 'If the Pope does good, why not honour him? There were two great Apostles in Rome, St Peter and St Paul, and the Pope honours them ... '

Nikon was universally disliked. To his implacable foes the Old Believers he was the Antichrist; to the Tsar, a source of bad political advice and a threat to the sovereign's authority; to the modernists, a kill-joy.

Curiously enough, there were two sides to the Patriarch's personality. Though a revolutionary by temperament, he had a reactionary mind. His reforms were not innovations, even though he crossed swords with the Old Believers, who refused to understand that he was, in fact, trying to re-establish the purest and most rigid kind of traditional Orthodoxy. It was Nikon who compelled the Tsar to take action against public entertainers and took up arms against new ways and new styles of art, and it was undoubtedly Nikon to whom the following passage in a letter written by an icon-painter named Joseph Vladimirov to Simon Ushakov (the great exponent of iconography who decorated the Kremlin) referred:

> Where did these men of little intelligence discover the rule which ordains that the faces of saints should be painted always in the same sombre and gloomy way? Was the human race created according to one universal criterion? Were all the saints dark and thin? What intelligent man would not laugh at the absurd notion that gloom and darkness are preferable to light?

* * *

Hours, days and seasons sped by like dead leaves scudding before the wind, or like the waters of the Istra, on which the old man's gaze must so often have dwelt. Yet his determination never faltered. He waited to be recalled, waited to be implored to return and resume his post. Time passed and no call came, and Nikon, resolutely refusing to accept defeat, vented his rage in acrimonious letters addressed to the Tsar and the Patriarch of Constantinople.

CHAPTER SEVEN

FAR away in his apartments in the Kremlin, Alexis Michaelovitch, too, felt his anger mounting. Nikon's high-handed departure had irritated him in the extreme, and the importunate churchman's first letter of 1659 had been followed by a stream of other missives, all equally infuriating. The latest to reach him contained the following passage:

> By your actions you are assembling a great tribunal which will proclaim your iniquities at the Day of Judgment. You call upon your subjects to do penance, yet there is no one here who does not do penance nor keep Lent, bread being scarce. No one is spared! The poor, the blind, the widows, the monks and nuns, all are subjected to heavy taxes. Weeping can be heard on every side, all are cast down. Who would have the heart to rejoice today!

The Tsar angrily rejected this letter like all the rest, asking himself whether he would ever be rid of Nikon's burdensome presence. Alexis Michaelovitch would gladly have let bygones be bygones if only Nikon had given him the chance, but his reserves of patience were dwindling. And he had been very patient in the past. There had been the day when he returned to Moscow after an exhausting campaign, only to be forced by the Patriarch to attend a ceremonial burning of new icons – he, the sovereign, who refused to believe that a good Christian had to renounce everything that was beautiful and alive, every new expression of human activity and everything capable of enhancing human existence.

Why did Nikon not resign himself to oblivion? The past was dead and gone. New vistas of the future were unfolding before Russia and the Russians with every passing day. The Tsar's 'very dear friend' owed him too many apologies to be justified in drawing attention to himself in such a discourteous way.

The Patriarch's intrusions into affairs of State had been equally disastrous. Convinced, ever since Little Russia's reunion with the Russian crown, that Poland was a negligible factor, Nikon had urged the Tsar to conclude a peace with the Poles and so leave himself free to undertake a war against Sweden. This campaign was beset by difficulties, however, and its results were to prove unfortunate.

In the past, the Tsar had too often been forced to contend with the Patriarch's fierce enthusiasms. He gradually came to realize that, obsessed with thoughts of the Church's greatness, the Patriarch dreamed of re-establishing a theocracy in which the Tsar would be no more than the executor of the wishes of the head of the Russian Church.[1]

For all these reasons, Alexis Michaelovitch decided not to conceal his displeasure. The letters which reached him put him out of temper for a while and he sometimes discussed the affair with his intimate friends in the family surroundings of the Terem, but it was soon forgotten in the cares of state, the joys of family life and the pleasures of reading and the chase.

He would listen happily to his sister Irina's accounts of the little happenings in the Terem and enjoyed inspecting the latest addition to his family when it was brought in on the arm of its nurse, though it must have been painfully obvious to him that, while he owed thanks to God for endowing him with so many offspring, his daughters were sturdy and his male children puny and lacking in vitality.

The Tsar spent a great deal of time in his apartments, studying the latest dispatches. The country was large, and the *prikazy* or government departments employed numerous informants to keep them posted on current developments. On the Baltic, in Poland and the Crimea, in the far north and along the borders of China, voivodes (provincial governors) stood guard over the Russian frontiers.

There was, however, a constant flow of reports from The New Jerusalem. The exiled Patriarch was receiving a large number of visitors. His activities began to intrude on national policy, and an official search of his Moscow residence brought to light a portion of his correspondence with the heads of foreign churches.

Alexis Michaelovitch – we are now in 1660 – convened an assembly of Russian bishops and submitted a proposal for the deposition of Nikon, his object being to secure the vacation of the patriarchal throne and pass judgment on the man who had abandoned him so churlishly. In reply to Pushkin, the Tsar's envoy, the Patriarch declared that if he had, in fact, abandoned the patriarchal throne it did not mean that he had renounced

[1] For example, as a reminder that spiritual power took precedence over temporal power, Patriarch Nikon sent to the monastery of Solovetsky in the far north for the mortal remains of St Philip, Metropolitan of Moscow, who was tortured, deported and finally suffocated on the orders of Ivan the Terrible, whose crimes he had denounced. The Tsar, on the other hand, demonstrated his absolutism and his solidarity with all other Christian monarchs by sending envoys and large sums of money to Charles II, who was waiting in exile for the day when he could reoccupy his late father's throne.

the dignity of his office. He went on to say that he would nevertheless be happy to choose a successor and personally invest him with the title of patriarch. That done, he would be prepared to retire to a monastery for good.

The Patriarch's suggestion was coldly received by the Council, which resolved to depose him without more ado and elect his successor. This solution, agreeable though it was to the Tsar, was opposed by the prominent theological authority, Epiphany Slavinetsky, who pointed out that canon law contained no precedent to justify such a measure. And there the matter rested until 1664. Nikon continued to agitate behind the scenes. In particular, he vehemently criticized the provisions of the 1648 code, which curtailed the privileges of the Church, conveniently forgetting that he himself had signed them at the time.

The exiled Patriarch meditated increasingly on the relationships between spiritual and temporal power. 'The priesthood,' he wrote, 'is superior to royalty. It is not the tsars who confer priesthood but the priest who anoints the tsar for his reign.' The Byzantine principle of equality between the two powers was shattered, and with it the 'wise duality' which had governed the relations between the sovereign and the head of the Russian Church.

In February 1665, Nikon sent a letter to the Patriarch of Constantinople, Dionysios, in which he violently denounced the Tsar's seizure of ecclesiastical property and criticized the rulers of Russia in the following terms:

'They take men for the Tsar's service; they take bread and money, too, without pity. The Tsar is crushing the entire Christian nation with taxes.'

Intercepted by government agents, this letter roused the Tsar and his ministers to a new pitch of anger.

They decided to cut the Gordian knot. In 1666 a new tribunal of Russian bishops was convened, this time with the participation of the Eastern patriarchs. Nikon accepted this solution, reflecting that he had friends among them and could bank on the support of the Patriarchs of Constantinople and Jerusalem. By November, however, the only foreign churchmen to have arrived in Moscow were Makarios of Antioch and Paissi of Alexandria.

On December 12th, Nikon's case was heard in Moscow in the presence of the Patriarch himself. Although he behaved with great dignity, his fate was already sealed. He was pronounced guilty of abandoning the patriarchal throne and of trespassing against the Church, the Tsar, the Tribunal and all Orthodox Christians. It was the end of a proud career. Reduced to the status of a simple monk, the Grand Sovereign Patriarch was sent to live in exile at the monastery of Belozersk in the far north, escorted by a company of musketeers.

Having defeated Nikon, the worthy Tsar was stricken with remorse. He never forgot his old friend to the day of his death. Money and gifts, donations of all kinds and objects of religious value flowed from Alexis Michaelovitch to the monastery where Nikon was to end his days, and Tatiana, the Tsar's sister, wrote the exiled Patriarch cheering letters and sent him gifts as well.

* * *

Nikon retired into oblivion, but his disappearance did nothing to extinguish the flames of religious controversy. Controversy raged not only in the country at large but in the Tsar's palace, where opinions were sharply divided.

Sophia's infancy, adolescence and young womanhood were spent in an atmosphere of appalling religious discord. Her tutor was a Latinist who owed his immunity from the attentions of over-zealous champions of Orthodoxy to the Tsar's good offices. As for the Old Believers whom she saw every day in her mother's entourage, the witch-hunts instigated by Nikon and his successors had only succeeded in rekindling their ardour, such was the Russians' deep-rooted conviction that suffering is the reward of the righteous.

One of the most influential and high-minded members of Tsarina Maria's court was a young widow called Theodosia Morozova, whose husband had been the brother of the Tsar's brother-in-law and one of Alexis's childhood companions. Her sister had married Prince Urussov. Widowed in 1662, when she was still under thirty, Theodosia Morozova was a virtuous matron who inspired love and respect in all who knew her. Unlike Tsarevna Tatiana, the Tsar's imperious sister, who supported the Patriarch's reforms and later tried to alleviate the burdens of his exile, Theodosia Morozova devoted herself entirely to the traditionalist cause. In spite of her youth, she enjoyed the sort of independence which only widowhood, an unblemished reputation and great wealth could confer. She fulfilled her duties with the Tsarina, ran her household and cared for the poor. A letter written to her by Avvakum, who was her confessor, contains a description of the life she led before she was martyred for her schismatic beliefs.

> I know, my dear friend Theodosia Prokofievna, that you were the wife of a boyar, an honoured widow and supreme among the Tsarina's ladies-in-waiting. You owned eight thousand peasants;

your fortune was estimated at between 200,000 and 250,000 roubles; you were surrounded in Moscow by a host of relatives and used to pay them visits in a superb coach draped with muslin, adorned with silver and drawn by numerous horses – six or eight of them – harnessed to it with jingling chains. Behind you, guarding your honour and well-being, marched your retainers and serfs, a hundred, two hundred, sometimes even three hundred men. Above them your countenance shone as, in the Israel of yore, did that of the widow Judith, who slew Prince Holophernes. You were as renowned in Moscow as were Deborah and Esther, wife of Artaxerxes, in Israel.

Although she did not enter the religious battle immediately, Theodosia Morozova had made her decision. Living in the splendour appropriate to her rank, she felt stifled by its futile pomp and luxury. At home in her own house, which she had turned into a convent, she lived with monastic simplicity, obeying to the letter the precepts of the *domostroy*, the family code which said: 'You shall gather in your house the clergy and the poor, the afflicted and pilgrims.'

While the persecutions were at their height, Theodosia gave refuge to Old Believers, recalcitrant priests 'wanted' by Nikon, nuns expelled from their convents for having refused to comply with reforms, invalids and 'devout simpletons', to whom she gave food and shelter. Like the strong woman of the Bible, Morozova worked with her hands, stitching clothes for the poor and embroidering altar cloths for churches. Asked by an Old Believer monk to shelter a nun in flight from persecution, Morozova accepted her as the abbess of her convent. At nightfall, the two of them used to roam the alleys of Moscow dressed in rags, distributing alms and visiting prisons.

Had it not been for Avvakum, the worthy woman would probably have ended her days in peace, but the 'Fiery Archpriest' wrested her from the traditional passivity of feminine existence and launched her into the religious fray. She carried the fight into the palace itself, discussing religion not only with the ladies of the Terem but also with male members of the Tsar's circle, notably Theodore Rtistchev, one of the most enlightened men of his day and one of the initiators of the reformation, but so tolerant and generous that he did not hesitate to offer financial aid to Old Believers who had fallen upon hard times. Upstairs in the Tsarina's apartments, Theodosia denounced Nikon's 'heresy' in the most explicit terms, declaring to all who cared to listen, when her confessor was deported for the first time, that 'like a true disciple of Christ, he doth suffer for having obeyed His law'.

Tsarina Maria, who loved Theodosia and looked on her as one of the family because her own sister had married a Morozov, also felt a discreet and tacit sympathy for the Old Belief and did her best to protect Theodosia until her death in 1669. With Maria gone, Theodosia's disobedience, indiscretion and – one might almost say – deliberate courting of the Tsar's displeasure were destined to bring about her downfall.

Sophia was only twelve at this period, and it is unlikely that the religious turmoil in the Terem affected her to any great extent. However, Theodosia Morozova was her aunt by marriage and Theodore Rtistchev had access to the 'upstairs' apartments in his capacity as her brother's tutor and father's friend, so she no doubt witnessed some impassioned arguments. Little though she knew it, they were to equip her for her own disputes with schismatics in years to come.

CHAPTER EIGHT

THE man whose influence prompted the beautiful and virtuous Morozova to lay down her life for the Old Belief was a talented preacher. Surnamed 'the Fiery Archpriest', Avvakum was one of the provincial clerics whom Nikon had summoned to Moscow in the hope that they would support his reforms, only to see them turn into his most determined opponents. Having explored every means of persuading them that his reforms were necessary, the Patriarch decided to exact blind obedience from them under threat of punishment, even though in the Orthodox Church, as Father Jean Meyendorf[1] points out, the episcopal office neither presupposes the infallibility of its incumbent nor renders him immune to human frailties and imperfections.

Avvakum and his friends assembled to study one of the Patriarch's decrees. 'We are gathered together,' declared Avvakum in his florid style, 'for the purpose of reflection. As we plainly see, winter is at our door, our hearts are cold, our legs quaking.' Under his leadership, the Old Believers girded themselves for a struggle which was to end in martyrdom.

Although many of the Old Believers were fanatics with a greater regard for the letter than for the spirit of religion and although they clung to traditional forms of worship with childish obstinacy, they were respectful of dogma and included a number of men who were rich in spiritual experience. Their self-sacrifice and annihilation dealt the Russian Church a grave blow, for its victory over the Old Believers left it in a devitalized condition which Peter the Great later exploited to the full.

Men who refused to accept the reforms stubbornly resisted intimidation, punishment and the voice of reason. While their views carried no weight with theologians – and understandably so – they were heeded by the mob, which was more susceptible to fiery words than common sense. And, because the Old Believers were closely linked with a national past which was striving to ward off the new forces ranged against it, it was not long before their religious intransigence left its imprint on political life.

Avvakum was the most famous exponent of the Old Belief. His

[1] *Le Messager orthodoxe*, 1960.

sobriquet, 'the Fiery Archpriest', was singularly apt, for it not only fitted his ardent and indomitable nature but presaged his subsequent death at the stake. He outlived Nikon, however, and Sophia was to encounter him in the course of her public career.

In deference to his confessor's wishes, Avvakum wrote an autobiography, the first of its kind in Russia. Though a reactionary in the religious field, Avvakum was a bold innovator in the field of literature. He was the first man to write a work not in ecclesiastical Slavonic nor in the bastardized and turgid style introduced into Russian literature by Simeon Polotski and other products of the schools and academies of the south-west, but in the colloquial, uninhibited, sturdy, vehement and highly-coloured language which still provides Russian authors and philosophers with such stimulating reading today.

Avvakum was less erudite than Nikon but he undoubtedly had a touch of genius. He hailed from a village on the Volga near Nizhni-Novgorod. 'Son of a poor priest who was addicted to drink, and of his pious and abstinent wife, who taught me the fear of God,' Avvakum saw an animal in pain at a neighbour's house, 'and the same night I arose and wept bitterly before the icon because I, too, was destined to die.'

Conversion is one thing and temperament another. Even in his young days, Avvakum found it difficult to get on with the people around him. The inhabitants of his native village drove him out. Thinking to instil some sense into him, his mother chose him a wife. The young priest married this 'young and gentle orphan' and set out on his apostolate. 'In churches and houses, at cross-roads, in towns and villages, in the capital and in Siberia,' he wrote, 'I preached and taught the word of God.' But the Devil and his snares lay in wait for him at every turn. Avvakum described the wiles of the Evil One with remarkable candour. To help him resist the temptation that overcame him when hearing a pretty girl's confession, he burnt his hand with a candle and so regained the straight and narrow path. He chastised a bear-tamer with his own hands. He refused to bless the son of the voivode Sheremetev because he had shaved off his beard, and the voivode angrily ordered his men to throw the headstrong priest into the waters of the Volga. As archpriest of Yuriev, Avvakum became so unpopular with his parishioners that a thousand of them, women included, tried to lynch him.

It would take too long to enumerate all the ordeals which Avvakum underwent during his career and which his whole family shared so unflinchingly. 'But God,' he remarked in his autobiography, 'never abandons his servant,' and little miracles helped to console him as he went his difficult way. One of the faithful would unexpectedly bring him money, a boyar would send some flour just when his family was on the point of starvation, or the Archpriest's little black hen would begin to lay two eggs a day.

Avvakum was so strong in the Lord that he remained unshaken either by fear of punishment or the lure of an easier life. He confessed that during his exile in Siberia, where he was brutally persecuted by the voivode Pashkov, he sinned terribly by wishing that Pashkov's son, who was setting off on a campaign against the Mongols in command of a detachment, would be killed in an ambush. Filled with repentance, he subjected himself to the most rigorous forms of self-mortification. Avvakum concludes his description of what he had to endure at Pashkov's hands by saying: 'He tortured me for ten years – or did I, perhaps, torture him? I do not know. God will judge at the end of the ages.'

Avvakum was thrown into a dungeon, put in chains and deprived of food, but he was not entirely without friends. Between bouts of persecution he received gifts of money from the Court itself, sent by Tsarina Maria and by Theodore Rtistchev the Compassionate.

Throughout his trials and tribulations, Avvakum continued to preach resistance to the Antichrist, convinced that before the advent of Nikon 'all was Orthodox in our Russia and the Church at peace under most devout princes and tsars'.

'I fear no one save Jesus Christ,' he proclaimed, and again: 'It were better to burn at the stake than be untrue to Jesus Christ.'

Avvakum loved his family dearly, but he took it for granted that his children would be prepared, like him, to die for what they believed to be the truth. There could be no finer insight into the essential humanity underlying his dramatic and flamboyant existence than the following lines from his autobiography, taken from a passage describing how he made his way back to European Russia from Siberia.

> For five weeks we had been travelling over the bare ice in sledges. Our one wretched horse could scarce pull the clothing and children. The country was wild and its inhabitants unruly. My poor wife hobbled along, stumbling because it was slippery. Once, while walking, she fell down, and a man as weary as she herself fell on top of her. 'Pardon me, my lady, my little mother!' cried the *muzhik*, and my wife cried: 'Why did you crush me, little father?' 'How long shall we suffer thus, Archpriest?' the poor woman asked me plaintively as I approached. 'Unto death, Markovna,' I told her. And she, sighing, responded: 'Well then, Petrovitch, let us walk on.'

Avvakum was both brilliant and persuasive. His very fanaticism invested him with influence over strong-willed men whose sole desire was to cross swords with suffering. Religion was a concrete thing to him and his friends. In the eyes of the Old Believers, nothing in a church could be moved, not a letter in an ancient text nor a note in a liturgical chant altered, without jeopardizing Orthodoxy. All who sought to infringe its purity were, according to Archpriest Avvakum, 'whoresons', 'dogs', 'accursed ones', 'pot-bellies', 'sots', 'coarse mouths', 'twisted noses', 'perverts' or 'murderers', be they Patriarch or Tsar. One day during his exile in Tobolsk, Avvakum entered a church under the Patriarch's jurisdiction and found consolation in prayer. Before long, however, he was tortured with remorse and became convinced that it was the Devil himself who had softened his heart. Nevertheless, he often regretted his quick temper and violence, and did not omit to pray for his enemies.

'I would even have forgiven Nikon,' he wrote, 'had he repented of his sin against Christ; but the bird has flown into an impenetrable forest and is unwilling to turn back.'

While young Sophia certainly took no active part in all this tumult and excitement, she was occasionally present during discussions between the ladies of the Terem. She must have been aware, without understanding the reason for it, of the disgrace which had befallen Theodosia Morozova, her relation by marriage, of the worries inflicted on her father by the Old Believers and of the compassion lavished on the victims of persecution by Theodore Rtistchev. As a pupil of the erudite Simeon Polotski, who flayed the schismatics for their ignorance and obscurantism, she learnt to distinguish the political conflict that lay behind these religious disputes. One day – not that she knew it yet – she would have to grapple with it in defence of her father's work.

CHAPTER NINE

'MEN and youths discuss theology here today, as, in the forests, do those who inhabit them. Horse-copers speak of it in the market-places, not to mention drunkards in the taverns. And, to crown all, women themselves have embarked on the foolish debate, vexing their husbands and the Church.'

The lean, stooping monk who penned these words was Simeon Polotski, venerable tutor of the Tsar's children and a man of great erudition.

Simeon Polotski did not, however, make his first appearance in Moscow until 1667, when Sophia was ten years old. He came armed with a letter of recommendation to Paissi Lagarida, a Greek Metropolitan who enjoyed great influence in the capital, and it was as the Metropolitan's aide and interpreter that he first set foot in the Kremlin Palace. He accompanied his patron to religious assemblies and attended the tribunal which examined the case of Patriarch Nikon. His lively mind and his ability to present erudition in a pleasing, one might almost say, worldly guise charmed Alexis Michaelovitch so greatly that he entrusted him with the education of his children, boys and girls alike. Simeon Polotski was a man of boundless energy. He became the official Court poet, but did not confine himself to singing praises to order. He composed primers for his pupils, wrote plays and supervised the training, in a monastery, of groups of interpreters, a vital necessity at a time when Russia's diplomatic and commercial contacts were expanding both to east and west. Because Polotski was unfamiliar with Greek, Latin was adopted as the main language of the new college. A brilliant dialectician, he took up arms against the Old Believers, buttressing his arguments with written treatises and sermons, a medium of religious expression which had become almost extinct in Moscow.

The advent of Polotski opened a new window on the world for the inmates of the Kremlin. He was not only a consummate theologian but a man with what were, for the seventeenth century, liberal views on education. Grouped round him, the Tsar's children hung on his words avidly, each responding to them according to his or her temperament.

For the first time, girls were considered worthy of instruction. Sophia, who was endowed with a 'high intelligence', was to profit from these lessons more than her sisters, and the likeable scholar in his black robe had lived too long within the confines of the Latin West not to bring a breath of the Renaissance with him into the 'upstairs' apartments in the Kremlin.

The education received by the Tsar's children bears witness to Polotski's excellent teaching methods. A Latin scholar influenced by Poland, though certainly a less profound thinker than Epiphany Slavinetsky, he did all he could to make his lessons entertaining and presented a large number of them in verse form. His two constant preoccupations were morality and political acumen. 'He who governs,' he never tired of repeating, 'must be a good shepherd.'

> Thus must the master
> Right sturdily his subjects' burden bear,
> Not scorning them nor treating them like dogs
> But loving them like children.

Sophia was a gifted and studious pupil like her younger brother Theodore. She learnt foreign languages such as Latin, Polish and French, and, also like her brother, wrote poetry and pieces for the stage.

Simeon Polotski's growing influence aroused misgivings in certain quarters, for he was not universally liked. His patent Latinism was of a kind which the Russians found peculiarly suspect. On leaving Kiev Academy he had completed his studies at centres of higher learning run by Jesuits, and this had left its mark on him. Grecophiles like Epiphany Slavinetsky and Efim of Tchudov were opposed to him. Polotski's theological, moral and didactic works were all branded with the Latinist mark and none of them contained any condemnation of Roman Catholicism. When preaching, he quoted St Augustine and St Jerome in preference to the Fathers of the Eastern Church. His pupil Sylvester Medviedev was later to escape excommunication by a hair's breadth, but for the moment Polotski continued to ventilate the Court's cobwebby interior under the patronage of the Tsar.

* * *

Thus Sophia grew up among her brothers and sisters in the obscurity of the Terem, an insignificant little creature, perhaps, but one who was ready to throw off the wrappings that enshrouded her like a mummy. Working with gold and silver thread under the supervision of her sewing-mistress, she embroidered a chasuble as a gift to the churches. Bent over alphabets whose complexity would terrify any modern child, she discovered the joys of reading. She listened to the tittle-tattle of the Kremlin just as she did to conversations between the Tsar and the Patriarch, who sometimes met in her mother's apartments. No one paid any attention to her. Her future was mapped out in advance, or so her parents thought. But great changes were afoot. Thanks to Alexis Michaelovitch's open-mindedness and lack of prejudice, history was on the move again, and history was something in which Sophia was to have her place.

The face of Russia was changing around her and the old prohibitions giving way. Freed from Nikon's strictures at last, Simon Ushakov and his friends once more took up their brushes to glorify God and his saints in the manner of their age.

The sciences – cosmography, astrology, medicine, geography – all excited interest. The chemist was still something of an alchemist, but the remedies he prescribed must have been of some use because his patients survived them. The Copernican theory, which had been condemned by Rome, was translated and printed in Moscow without any accompanying commentaries. Architecture received a fresh impetus which at the end of the century gave birth to the interesting species of baroque which later came to be known as the 'Naryshkin style'. Stone houses became commoner in the cities, their façades embellished with white and red brick and sometimes slabs of decorated faience. Such was the growing skill of Russian architects that monastery halls increased in size without the necessity for supporting columns.

Whether in Little Russia, the provinces or the capital, the foreign influences which infiltrated from east and west were speedily adapted to the national taste and genius in such a way as to eliminate mere slavish copying. What was more, seventeenth-century Russia very quickly produced a large body of native craftsmen who excelled in every field.

Although the great clock in the Kremlin's Spassky Tower was based on plans drawn up by Holliday, an Englishman, there were already large numbers of clock-makers in the country. Russia's masons and smiths were second to none, and the unrivalled skill of her carpenters was exemplified by houses, palaces, churches and monasteries constructed of wood, the natural building material of a country swathed in forests. The most famous carpenters' guilds were those of Vladimir and Yaroslavl. Equipped only with the axe which they wore in the girdle of their caftan, these journeymen carpenters produced unique pieces of architecture, few of which, unfortunately, have survived the ravages of time.

This period also marked the birth of a passion which was never to desert the Russian people, their passion for reading. Alexis Michaelovitch owned a considerable library, and one which was not composed exclusively of devotional works. Patriarch Nikon, too, owned an important library containing numerous books written in foreign languages, with which more and more people were becoming familiar. Sophia's brothers, the heir apparent Alexis and his younger brother Tsarevitch Theodore, both of them intelligent and thoughtful boys, also possessed growing libraries to which Sophia no doubt had access.

Thousands of volumes were produced by the Printing Office. More and more foreigners were entering the half-open door that led to the unknown land of Muscovy, bringing their native customs and ideas with them. New tides and currents lapped unceasingly round the walls of the Terem, where the little princess remained imprisoned. Styles of dress were swept along with the stream, and many courtiers soon abandoned traditional Russian costume, except on ceremonial occasions, in favour of the Polish style.

* * *

In Russia as in the West, the Church was the primary ingredient of civilization, but the seventeenth century witnessed a new phenomenon: the appearance of lay scholars. The Russians acquired a taste for education very quickly, despite the reserve of some and the abhorrence of others. Boyars, merchants, peasants and serfs all wanted to learn to read and write. If one member of a family knew the alphabet, he taught it to the rest. Children and adolescents who worked as apprentices taught themselves to read at their places of employment. Only women were excluded from the new craze. One primer first published in 1634 was reprinted several times, its low cost (one kopek) bringing it within the reach of the poorest citizen, and a grammar and arithmetic book were also published. The Printing Office had to be enlarged during the second half of the seventeenth century. Its one hundred and sixty employees included four editors, a reader, a copyist, twenty-four compositors, twelve sorters, forty-eight printers and forty-eight colourists. In the year 1648–9 the warehouse attached to the Printing Office contained a stock of 11,450 printed volumes.

If Kotoshikhin could have revisited the country which he decried so bitterly he might not have recognized certain of its features, so many changes had occurred since his departure. In the Terem, the elderly boyar Morozov never tired of telling his royal sister-in-law's children how much he regretted not having enjoyed the benefits of education in his youth, and the children responded by proudly displaying their new-found knowledge, showing the old man their picture books and reciting poems of their own devising. Morozov would then retire to the Tsar's apartments, where dinner awaited. The Tsar had recently discovered the joys of eating to music. A German musician played the organ while the 'gentlemen of the table' served Alexis and his friends with food and wine. Horns blared and drums rattled, drowning the lusty voices of the diners. And when Morozov left the palace at night he no longer travelled in the shabby and uncomfortable coach of yore but in a splendid vehicle, draped in gold brocade and adorned with embossed silver designs, which had recently been presented to him by the Tsar, who bore Morozov no ill will for the disastrous advice he had received from him in the past.

Ensconced in his magnificent residence, the boyar Nikita Romanov played the Maecenas and took foreign émigrés under his wing. The Tsar's uncle was a lively and amiable character – though there was no good reason why he should have been otherwise, considering that he was as rich as Croesus and took no part in public affairs, which had never appealed to him.

The changing habits and new mode of existence gained an increasing hold on the country, not only, it may be noted, among the boyars and more prosperous military men but also in commercial circles.

Artamon Matveyev, who had been the first to go to the Tsar's assistance when he was besieged by the rebels at Kolomenskoye, went from strength to strength. Like Morozov, Romanov and other prominent figures, he was attracted by the Western way of life. His wife was a Russified Scotswoman, née Hamilton. Their residence was furnished in Western style, so much so that the foreigners whom Matveyev welcomed so warmly to his home felt entirely at ease there. Even junior officials and ordinary musketeers adopted the new ways and rearranged their abodes to accord with contemporary taste.

It was the thin end of the wedge, the first symptom of a hiatus between two classes which was to continue to grow until the Revolution of 1917. In the old days, only wealth had separated the privileged from the under-privileged, both groups being united in their strict observance of ancestral customs. But the masses, far from following in the steps of the modernists, recoiled from the new world which was unfolding before their eyes and which, in the opinion of the old guard, bore 'the Devil's mark'.

Under the influence of Greek monks and, more especially, scholars and monks from the south-west, the Russians also developed a taste for literature proper. In 1672 a Kievan monk sent a thousand different books to Moscow, most of them in Slavonic but some in Polish, a language which was coming into particular vogue among the upper classes. In the following year he dispatched another eight hundred volumes. Books published in Little Russia had to undergo censorship because they were often impregnated with Latinist influence. Polish books were not sold to the general public, though the nobility revelled in them.

As profane literature started to gain favour, so translations of foreign works became more and more numerous. Only twenty-six translations were known in the sixteenth century: by the seventeenth century there were one hundred and twenty-seven. Censored copies of Ukrainian and even Polish books were on sale in Moscow, and Russian versions of French and Italian epics circulated among the lower orders of society. It is worth noting that Russia herself had been reflected in foreign literature well before this date, notably in certain passages in Shakespeare, Sidney's sonnets and plays by Fletcher.

In 1668, Alexis Michaelovitch formed a committee to conduct research into ancient musical manuscripts. Linear notation was adopted with the active encouragement of Patriarch Nikon, and Alexander Mezents composed a song primer. Three harmonic systems existed in the country at this period: Kievan, Bulgarian and Greek. Finally, a composer named Titov broke entirely new ground by writing accompaniments to poems by Simeon Polotski, the Court bard. At the same time, Russian books were translated into foreign languages. Between the close of the sixteenth and the middle of the seventeenth century, one hundred and fifty-three translations were published of which a hundred and sixteen were of literary works.

Technical works, for which there was a growing demand, were also published in Moscow. Apart from a few noblemen and a large number of monks, civil servants constituted the best-educated class, even though their education was of a circumscribed nature.

With Nikon out of the way, icon-painters could return to the modern style without fear of reprisals. At Moscow, Yaroslavl, Tchernigov, Uglitch, Rostov and Romanov-Borissoglebsk, Ushakov, Dimitry Plekhanov, Gury Nikitin, Sila Savin and other, anonymous, artists glorified God and His saints in the contemporary manner.

We have already said that Church Slavonic, 'the Latin of Russia', was giving way to the vernacular. Numerous seventeenth-century manuscripts testify to the variety, freshness and vigour of contemporary language, which at times assumed a Rabelaisian exuberance. During Peter the Great's enforcement of Western ways on Russia, the government encouraged a bastardization of the national tongue. Literature became rhetorical, high-flown and studded with foreign expressions, and remained so until Pushkin's genius once more wedded it to popular speech. *The Life of Archpriest Avvakum Written by Himself* was not only the first autobiography to be written in Russian but a literary masterpiece and a document of human and historical interest. The *Life of St Julianna*, written by a son of that remarkable woman, appeared at the same time, together with the biography of a layman, Alexis's friend and confidant, Theodore Rtistchev.

Pharmacies and hospitals existed at this time, and research by the Soviet scholars Mivemnergsky and Tarnovsky indicates that Russian hospital organization was very advanced for the period. Moscow had a school of medicine from 1662 onwards.

It would be wrong to imagine that the fruits of progress were confined to Moscow alone. Baroque was blossoming in the magnificent churches of Little Russia. Archbishop Theodore opened libraries and schools in every town in his diocese, which was based on Tchernigov. Vologda was experiencing a renaissance. At Rostov, Metropolitan Jonah erected churches and civil buildings in the four towns comprising his diocese, aided by Irina and Alexander Mussin-Pushkin. He also conserved ancient monuments and founded the first museum of antiquities in Russia. Great though his interest in building was, however, he did not neglect the humanitarian obligations of his high office and repeatedly defended his flock against abuses of civil power.

The German Quarter, with its motley collection of foreign émigrés, took little part in this intellectual awakening. The denizens of the Western colony included a large number of swindlers on the look-out for easy pickings, but most of them were first-rate specialists in their particular field. Literature and the arts interested them little, however, and their influence on Moscow, save in the technical sphere, was negligible, with one exception: 'Nemetskaya Sloboda' was the birthplace of the Russian theatre.

CHAPTER TEN

THERE were few braver sights than Alexis Michaelovitch's army in battle formation. 'The first of the line', a musketeer regiment composed of elite troops, marched in front, led by a detachment of the same regiment armed with arquebuses. All these men were clad in long green tunics and marched five abreast. Following them came ten richly caparisoned warhorses, their saddles covered with black bearskins or wolf pelts. Then came the voivode with a *nabat* attached to his charger's saddle, the small copper drum with which he signalled an assault or rallied his troops. Behind the voivode, in picturesque disarray, came the remainder of the regiment.

Next came the band, kettledrums rattling and trumpets braying plaintively, followed by 'the great regiment', which advanced in the same order as the first. A detachment of musketeers, this time dressed in red tunics trimmed with ermine, marched past in ranks of five. Then came a single musketeer leading the charger of the Grand Voivode or commander-in-chief, its saddle covered with leopard- or lynx-skin. The Grand Voivode himself marched on foot surrounded by the Russian and foreign advisers who formed his general staff.

Three other regiments – the right, centre and left of the line – were each preceded by a guard of honour and commanded by a voivode before whom marched a man carrying a *shestoper*, the emblem of his rank. Ten or so men from each regiment carried *nabaty*.

At the very rear, in a state of indescribable pandemonium, came the supply train, drivers shouting and yelling at the tops of their voices and horses jostling each other and overturning calashes laden with rations and ammunition. Kotoshikhin stated that the din made by the 'service corps' was so formidable that it sometimes put the enemy to flight before battle was joined.

Regimental colours flapped in the wind, that of the leading regiment embroidered with a picture of Joshua halting the sun, the remainder depicting St George slaying the dragon.

Though Russia did not go to war clad in lace, there was no lack of brocade and fur. Voivodes, who were helmeted and wore long caftans of ermine-trimmed brocade, silk or velvet over their breastplates, carried a sword on one side, a bow and quiver on the other and a finely wrought spear with an ornate haft in their hand.

The Russian army of the period numbered 100,000 men under arms in peacetime and 300,000 in time of war, not including officers' orderlies or the peasants and serfs who were mobilized at moments of crisis.

By the latter half of the seventeenth century the infantry outnumbered the cavalry and constituted the major part of the Russian army. *Strieltsy* (musketeer) regiments were commanded by their own officers and came under a special government department known as the Office of Musketeers. Membership of the musketeers was largely an hereditary honour, and applicants were carefully sifted. Later on, musketeers were sometimes chosen for their height and smart appearance, like the men of the Imperial Guard.

The musketeers, who were to play a vital part in Sophia's accession to the regency, formed an elite corps of infantry. Their numbers rose from 40,000 at the beginning of Alexis Michaelovitch's reign to 55,000 in 1681.

Peasants and serfs were only eligible for the new regular infantry units commanded by foreign officers. However, these new formations soon surpassed the musketeers in fighting efficiency under battle conditions.

The cavalry, which was the arm of service favoured by boyars' and noblemen's sons, who considered it beneath their dignity to serve in a regiment of foot, numbered 100,000, a figure which included 28,000 Tatars and 10,000 Cossacks. Estimates of their strength were only approximate, but the government could easily swell the number of effectives when necessary.

Infantrymen were armed with pikes. Helmets were few and far between and only the more prosperous had swords, but a certain number owned armour. The men's clothing was long and swept the ground like that of their officers, whose silk tunics were lined with wool.

Musketeers carried nothing but a battle-axe on their shoulders and a sword or cutlass at their side.

Most cavalry horses came from Russia, though the Horde of the Nogay Tatars sent several thousand remounts to Moscow every spring. These were wiry geldings of medium build, unshod but extremely fast. Special saddles enabled their riders to turn and fire in any direction, but the fact that they rode in the Turkish fashion meant that they were unseated at the slightest touch of a lance. Spurs were almost unknown. Instead, cavalrymen carried *nogayky* (Tatar whips) attached to the little finger of their left hand. Bows were worn on the right side and the quiver containing arrows beneath the right arm. In addition, each man carried a battle-axe and a *kisten* or heavy iron ball on the end of a thong.

Fire-arms were coming into more general use. The long, clumsy arquebus was being replaced in the infantry by muskets or musketoons and in the cavalry by carbines. Arms factories were rapidly increasing in size and number. State-owned arsenals were in full production at Tula and Kashira and private concerns employing master-armourers were turning out muskets and more traditional weapons elsewhere.

When Kazan was captured in the sixteenth century, Ivan the Terrible's corps of artillery could deploy about 150 field pieces, mortars and light and heavy cannon. During the war of 1669, Tsar Alexis Michaelovitch's army already had 400 mortars and regimental cannon at its disposal. These pieces, which used to be forged in iron, were replaced at this period by guns cast from copper or cast-iron. The factory at Tula produced more than 25,000 cannon-balls between 1668 and 1673 alone, and foreign visitors declared that they had never before seen projectiles of such a size.

To bring the existing armed forces up to strength, the government augmented the territorial guard and the first regiments of the regular army by recruiting several thousand 'free men' each spring. These troops, who were employed as frontier garrisons, were later formed into regular regiments of infantry and mounted dragoons. Between 1642 and 1648 peasants were withdrawn from domanial estates and private properties in the south and enrolled as dragoons, but during the second half of the seventeenth century the infantry was more important than the cavalry and constituted the major part of Tsar Alexis's army. These foot soldiers were controlled by drum-signal and commanded by foreign officers, whose numbers continued to grow steadily.

When engaging a foreign officer or trooper, the Tsar presented him with a horse, uniform and money. Foreigners also enjoyed a far more substantial rate of pay than Russians, but their position was not without its disadvantages. Although – or, rather, because – they were useful to the government and their services were highly valued, the Russians put so many obstacles in their path that it was virtually impossible for them to return home.

Military hospitals were established in Moscow from 1630 onwards, and by the reign of Alexis Michaelovitch each regiment had its own surgeon. Military organization was very advanced for the period. Private soldiers were paid very little (five kopeks a day in war-time) but, like all government employees, they were paid with meticulous regularity. Any money not collected by a soldier on pay-day was sent to his home on the day following. Widows received a pension until they remarried and provision was made for children up to the age of adolescence. If a soldier was taken prisoner, half his pay went to his wife and the other half formed a nest-egg to be given him on his release.

Although supreme command was vested in the Tsar and his Duma, military administration was shared by several *prikazy*, and thus was not fully centralized. Unified command was not destined to become a reality until the beginning of the eighteenth century.

The fighting qualities of this ill-assorted army with its lack of central control were not great, and the idea of military valour as conceived by the West was practically non-existent because the code of chivalry had never found its way into Russia. The Russians considered it folly to go off to war voluntarily, and nothing astonished them more than foreign mercenaries embarking on such a perilous profession. To get killed or maimed fighting for money on behalf of an alien sovereign seemed ridiculous. Besides, half the army was fit only for garrison duty, and the musketeers, intended to maintain order in the interior, lived in the towns. About ten thousand men were assigned to frontier defence.

The *prikazy* kept detailed registers of men liable to service and inflicted severe penalties for evasion, so that willing soldiers and would-be deserters found themselves shoulder to shoulder when war came. The Russians flung themselves fiercely at the enemy, signalling their advance – we learn from eye-witnesses – by a weird din of yells, tattoos and the wailing of fifes and bugles.

The endurance of this army, which had only been in existence since Moscow's liberation from the Poles, was destined to be put to the test on many occasions. Of the seven decades between 1613 and 1682, the year when Sophia became Regent, Russia spent three decades at war, often fighting on several fronts at once. Her permanent foes were Sweden, Poland and Turkey, all of whom abutted on her frontiers, a fact which illustrates the difficulty of maintaining friendly relations with neighbours.

Between Poland and Russia stood a third force: the area known in the seventeenth century as Malorussia or Little Russia, cradle of the Russian nation (known today as the Ukraine, which means 'border' or 'march'). Little Russia formed a buffer state between the two hostile sisters. Although it had never enjoyed *de jure* independence, it possessed a distinctive national character. The population was not descended from the original inhabitants, for fratricidal quarrels between early feudal princes and invasions by Polovets, Avars and Petchenegs had devastated the area during the Middle Ages and forced its people to flee into the Russian interior. By the seventeenth century, Little Russia was populated by men from every corner of the land.

At the beginning of Alexis Michaelovitch's reign, Little Russia asked to be reunited with Moscow at the instigation of Bogdan Khmelnitsky, the hetman whose statue stands in Kiev today. An energetic and pugnacious man of considerable diplomatic ability and boundless ambition, Khmelnitsky had been so irritated by the arrogance of the Polish nobility during the Polish occupation that he decided to prick the bubble of their self-esteem. The outcome of his rebellion surpassed his wildest dreams. After winning two or three victories against the *pany*, or Polish overlords, the hetman suddenly found himself master of Little Russia. Success went to his head. Seeing himself as the future monarch of the Ukraine and master of Poland, but in need of an ally to help him realize his ambitions, he turned to Moscow.

The Russians still had vivid memories of the Polish occupation at the beginning of the century. The lessons of the past counselled caution. At length, after suffering some reverses, Khmelnitsky lost patience with Moscow and was compelled to ask the Tatars for an alliance. He did so reluctantly because while the Tatars supported him, they pillaged and devastated Little Russia more like enemies than allies. Moscow continued to survey the situation. Khmelnitsky now wrote to the Tsar in humbler vein, "what we desire is an autocratic sovereign such as Your Majesty, a Christian, Orthodox Tsar. May the prophecies of ancient time be thus fulfilled." (In other words, let the two Russias be reunited.) It was not, however, until 1653 that Moscow decided to declare war on Poland and admit Little Russia to Russian citizenship. The Rada or Zaporozhsky Assembly swore allegiance to the Orthodox Tsar, but the alliance was precarious and Little Russia continued to vacillate, playing a major role in the Russo-Polish game.

* * *

A few months after Sophia's birth, in June 1657, the Russians embarked on military operations against the Swedes in the districts round the Neva and Lake Ladoga in Carelia, whose inhabitants were better disposed towards the Russians than towards the Swedes or the Teutonic Knights.

A year later the Swedes assumed the offensive. In early September, six thousand men representing the bulk of the Swedish army and commanded by Count Magnus de la Gardie besieged the powerful fortress of Gdovsk, again without success. Although the Russians never hesitated to flee when defeated, their patience and dogged acceptance of the most arduous living conditions made them tenacious defenders. Though racked by hunger and fatigue, Russian soldiers occupying the forts of Livonia resisted the enemy to the last.

Meanwhile, the Swedish-occupied areas of Sub-Carpathian Poland and Lithuania had grown restive, and John Casimir of Poland seized the opportunity to try to recover them. Charles X of Sweden advanced as far as Yaroslavl, but had to retreat when the troops of his ally the Margrave of Baden were defeated by Polish forces. Charles then went to Prussia to ask for assistance from the Elector of Brandenburg. He was in a dangerous position, with the Russians threatening the Baltic area and the Poles trying to liberate their occupied provinces. In 1657 the Poles negotiated with the Elector through diplomatic channels, and by renouncing all claims on Prussia secured not only his neutrality but active support. In 1658, the Holy Roman Empire in its turn concluded a military pact with Poland and Brandenburg.

Greatly strengthened, the Poles stopped humouring Russia and adopted an attitude that compelled Moscow to abandon the war against Sweden and make hasty preparations for war against Poland.

Paradoxically, all Russia had achieved by attacking Sweden, Poland's enemy, was to further Polish aspirations and strengthen Poland. Since Poland was obviously going to recover her lost territories, it would be folly if Moscow continued to fight Sweden instead of defending the territory which Bogdan Khmelnitsky had placed under the Russian Crown.

Accordingly, the Tsar entrusted Athanasius Ordyn-Nastchokin with the task of concluding a peace or armistice with the Swedes, and in November 1658 plenipotentiaries of the two countries opened negotiations at the village of Valiesarsk, near Narva. France offered to mediate, but the Russians declined on the grounds that France had never exhibited any goodwill towards them in the past.[1] Despite this, a treaty was signed under which Russia retained all the territories which she had occupied prior to May 1658.

Having made peace with Sweden, Alexis Michaelovitch hurriedly dispatched troops, arms, ammunition and supplies to the south-west. What with the hard winter and the Ukrainians' vacillating loyalties, the Russians could do no more than guard the majority of the White Russian and Lithuanian towns which were already in their possession.

The fortunes of war continued to fluctuate until 1660, by which time Russia was tiring. Although the pact with Sweden was supposed to last for three years, ominous incidents portended a resumption of hostilities. Once again, the task of averting this threat was assigned to Ordyn-

[1] The Soviet writer V. Preobrazhensky states in his study of Franco-Russian relations in the sixteenth and seventeenth centuries that French influence was responsible for Sweden's intransigence during negotiations and her uncompromising attitude towards all territorial concessions.

Nastchokin. Well before the birth of Peter the Great, Nastchokin was obsessed with the idea of Russian access to the Baltic. He demanded restoration of Ingermanland, which had belonged to Russia since the treaty of 1595, offering Sweden a large indemnity in return. The Swedes, no fools, were perfectly aware of Russia's difficulties and countered by demanding restoration of their pre-war frontiers. Other equally fruitless discussions took place in 1660.

France, meanwhile, was busily encouraging a rapprochement between Sweden and Poland, and in the spring of 1660 peace was signed between the two belligerents. At the same time, Sweden signed treaties with Denmark and the Netherlands, so that Russia found herself isolated and hemmed in by enemies.

At Kardis in March 1661 Prince Prozorovsky, representing Russia, and Bernthorn, representing Sweden, reopened negotiations. This time things went a little better. After three months of deliberation, Sweden finally consented to remain neutral, to refrain from helping Poland against the Russians and attacking the Grand Duchy of Lithuania, Little Russia or White Russia. Moscow paid a heavy price for this neutrality, for the Russians had to relinquish all Swedish territory under their control.

The war with Poland dragged on, and Poland had to experience military reverses before she would accept the idea of peace. Her first set of conditions, put forward at a time when Khovansky's troops had just been defeated near Vitebsk, were – needless to say – extremely harsh and entirely unacceptable to the Russians. Nevertheless, an unofficial armistice came about through force of circumstance, and in April 1666 a Russian delegation led by Ordyn-Nastchokin met a Polish delegation in the village of Andrussovo. This time the Russians had the advantage, for Prince Liubomirski was currently in revolt against the Polish Crown.

The Treaty of Andrussovo was not signed until 1667. It was a monument to Ordyn-Nastchokin's diplomatic skill. The Russians were unable to realize their main ambition, which was to see Little Russia placed permanently under Russian sovereignty, but for a nation exhausted by war the Andrussovo agreement was an exceedingly profitable one. True to his nature and principles, Ordyn-Nastchokin stubbornly defended his country's interests by arguing each point at length. He brought all his intellectual subtlety to bear, all his reserves of diplomacy, all his brilliant statesmanship. With consummate skill he outmanoeuvred his opponents, overcame their opposition, pleaded, persuaded – and won.

Ordyn-Nastchokin had long cherished an overriding desire to establish the closest and most friendly relations with Poland. Although he regarded the Poles as 'an extraordinarily inconstant, inhuman and unstable people',

he believed that Russo-Polish amity could serve the best interests c
Russia in a multitude of ways. Russian access to the Baltic was, in his eye
a prime necessity, but the 'Swedish question' could never be settled as lon
as Russia's relations with Poland remained in a state of flux. A hosti
Poland – Ordyn-Nastchokin was convinced of this – was the mai
obstacle to a union of all Eastern Christians and greater Slav unity.

When Polish envoys arrived in Moscow to ratify the Treaty of Andrus
sovo in 1667, the Prime Minister seized the opportunity to expound th
idea that was so close to his heart. If only it were possible to unite Russi
and Poland under the same crown, as Ordyn-Nastchokin fondly hope
the way would be paved for the formation of an immense ethnic unit
a vast Slav bloc stretching from the Adriatic to the Baltic and even to th
Arctic Ocean.

Ordyn-Nastchokin naturally became one of the most fervent champion
of Tsar Alexis's or his son's candidacy for the throne of Poland. Com
pared with the grand design for a pan-Slav or even pan-Orthodox union
the Russo-Polish dispute over Little Russia held little significance for him
The Zaporozhye Cossacks exchanged one camp for the other so readil
that he commented in his report: 'If they are traitors, is it worth while tc
wage war on their account?'

To the Russian Prime Minister, the Treaty of Andrussovo seemec
reasonable if not advantageous. Not only did it set the seal on a war o
nearly thirteen years' duration and give Russia the whole of the left bank
of the Dnieper and the Smolensk and Seversk districts, but it made Kiev
and the surrounding areas on the right bank of the river a Russian
protectorate until 1669.

With Russia firmly established on the upper as well as the middle
reaches of the Dnieper, Ordyn-Nastchokin felt that he could relax. Such
was his probity, even in the political sphere, that it never entered his head
that someone might break the treaty one day or fail to respect its clauses.
Unqualified integrity was as much one of his characteristics as universal
charity was one of his friend Rtistchev's. 'I would rather,' he wrote, 'bring
my miserable life to an end and gain eternal liberty than act at variance
with the truth.' And by truth he meant a combination of right and justice.

CHAPTER ELEVEN

HE Tsar of Muscovy received foreign ambassadors seated on a throne
. one of the halls in the Granovitaya Palata, or 'Palace of Facets'.
lthough Alexis Michaelovitch had several thrones at his disposal in the
remlin itself, not to mention those installed in each of his other resi-
ences, his favourite since 1659 had been the diamond throne presented to
im by the Persian company of Armenian merchants.

It was a high-backed armchair covered with pierced plaques of gold
nd silver encrusted with precious stones, mainly diamonds, and stood
etween two windows in one corner of the chamber. On the wall above
ne sovereign's head hung an icon of the Holy Virgin, and on the bare
vall, farther to the right, one of St Saviour.

The Tsar used to dress in a long brocade robe glittering with precious
ones and adorned with a large gold cross. His head was bare. On a foot-
ool beside him stood the ancient crown of Vladimir Monomach, a
onical bonnet surmounted by a cross and encircled at its base by a band
f fur symbolizing the continuity of the Russian monarchy from the
urikids to the Romanovs. This crown was sometimes replaced by that of
van the Terrible or by the 'modern' crown which had been made
pecially for Alexis Michaelovitch himself. In his hand the Tsar held a
osokh cross.

To the sovereign's right, on a round gold-embossed table, stood an orb
f solid gold. Stationed on either side of the throne were *ryndas*, pages or
ouths belonging to his personal bodyguard, clad in white and carrying
hort-handled halberds on their shoulders.

Also on the foot-stool supporting the crown was a shallow gold basin
illed with water and covered with an embroidered towel, in which the
Tsar could wash his hands after receiving ambassadors – especially those
f the Catholic persuasion.

European diplomats usually entered Russia by way of Poland and
ithuania, mounting their carriages on skis from Vilno onwards if they
vere travelling in winter. At the beginning of the previous century, the
resence of brigands forced Herberstein to take the dangerous route from

Vilno to Novgorod via Polotsk. The journey took twenty-two days, no
counting another week spent in getting from Novgorod to Moscow.

Diplomats in Moscow fell into three categories: Grand Ambassador
Minister and Envoy, each of which was entitled to certain honours strictl
designated by protocol.

The arrival at their frontiers of any foreign visitor threw Russians into
state of painful confusion. They found it difficult to assess the importanc
of the newcomer at a glance and were fearful, etiquette being strict, o
receiving him with either excessive or inadequate ceremony. To pay
foreigner more respect than was necessary was to lose face and dim th
glory of their sovereign.

Hardly had a foreign diplomat crossed the border when the governo
of the frontier district sent a courier to Moscow to ask for precise instruc
tions. At the same time, another courier was dispatched to meet th
visitor, the rank of the former varying with the relative importance of th
latter. On meeting the foreigner, the courier announced that a person o
higher rank than himself – with a retinue whose size was carefully bu
sometimes wrongly gauged – was on the way to greet him.

The arrival of this second personage heralded the opening of a
elaborate farce which was solemnly performed in all weathers, whethe
under the broiling summer sun or in the rain and swirling blizzards o
winter. The Russian official advanced to meet the diplomat along the roa
taken by the latter's party, successfully barring the route. In some case
the ambassador's party had to squeeze past the group of Russians sent t
welcome them, not always an easy manœuvre because the ruts were dee
in summer and the snow-drifts dangerous in winter.

Regardless of intense cold or heat, the ambassador was obliged t
dismount from his coach and listen to an address of welcome on foo
Jealous of the Tsar's prestige, the Russian envoy took care not to be th
first to dismount, and, since the ceremony was a lengthy one, the dis
comfort to both parties was extreme.

Following established procedure, the Russians never hurried a visitc
along but delayed his progress on any pretext until instructions could b
received from the government.

Voivodes or local governors welcomed diplomats with great deferenc
especially if they belonged to friendly powers, firing cannon in the
honour, showing them round fortifications and generally aggravating th
effects of an already tiring journey by plying them with lavish repas
and ample liquid refreshment.

Once they had set foot on Russian soil, members of a diplomat
mission were entirely in the hands of the Russian government. If the

journey was held up by bad road conditions or a political incident of some kind, the envoys had to grit their chattering teeth and wait patiently, deprived even of the right to buy personal necessities.

The state of the roads was so shocking that the Russians sometimes had to build temporary causeways across open country, leaving their visitors to chafe at the enforced inactivity. This not only caused confusion and delay but frequently aroused violent opposition among the local inhabitants who had been conscripted into building the provisional road.

Throughout the journey, Russians and foreigners stubbornly defended their rights of precedence. The Russians were careful to see that a foreign ambassador was the first to remove his head-dress and the first to dismount, and, conversely, that once compliments had been exchanged he was the first to cover his head and remount or climb into his coach. No holds were barred in the war of precedence. Olearius recounts that at a reception for the Turkish ambassador in 1634 the poor man was purposely assigned such a high-spirited charger that he lost face by falling out of his saddle.

The 'Potemkin village' was known in Russia long before the advent of Catherine II, Potemkin – or, for that matter, the Soviet Union. Like the model *sovkhozy*, these spuriously prosperous villages were created to make a favourable impression on visitors from abroad. Whenever a foreigner was passing the shops were closed and the villagers, dressed for the occasion in their Sunday attire, promenaded through the streets as though they were men of substance.

In 1664, the English ambassador arrived in Moscow with a column of two hundred sledges accompanied by numerous footmen and servants. The route was lined by several detachments of Russian cavalrymen dressed in uniforms of varied colours and a special detachment of musketeers was drawn up outside the gates of the capital. The latter, who were clad in scarlet and mounted on white chargers, excited great admiration among the visitors. The procession advanced slowly along streets lined with soldiers and thronged with eager spectators. Rich and poor, noblemen and serfs craned their necks in curiosity. High-born ladies ventured into the streets and mingled with the jostling townsfolk, their heavily rouged faces hidden behind *fatas*, or veils. The Russians were eternally fascinated by the West.

Alexis Michaelovitch housed visiting diplomats in a magnificent stone building in the immediate vicinity of the Kremlin. It was a vast three-storeyed structure adorned with four decorative turrets. Round the fifth and principal tower ran three tiers of balconies affording a panoramic view of Moscow. Some idea of the building's dimensions can be gauged from the fact that in 1678 it easily accommodated the whole of the Polish ambassador's retinue – more than fifteen hundred persons. The halls and chambers in its interior were furnished in the height of luxury. There were benches and tables upholstered in sumptuous red cloth and tapestries rich with gold thread. One of the latter portrayed the story of Samson and Delilah – not inappropriately, considering that its theme of 'seduction and enfeeblement' was a staple ingredient of diplomatic strategy.

Diplomats accredited to the Kremlin were less likely to suffer from hunger than indigestion, judging by the daily rations allotted to the ambassador of Holstein in 1634: sixty-two loaves of bread, a quarter of beef, four sheep, twelve chickens, two geese, a hare, fifty eggs, a quarter of a bucket of Spanish wine, two buckets of mead, three-quarters of a bucket of beer and unlimited supplies of vodka. In addition, privileged visitors were allocated fifteen kopeks a day to cover routine expenses.

Foreign diplomats have left us numerous accounts of their experiences in Russia. The majority passed stern judgment on the Russians, their government, their mode of life and, above all, their religion, but few of them – if the truth be told – made any serious endeavour to study the strange and often inaccessible world whose guests they were.

A work published at Leyden in 1669 under the title *Journey to Muscovy by the Ambassador of Emperor Leopold to Tsar Alexis Michaelovitch*, by Baron von Mayerberg, sheds an interesting light on conditions in contemporary Russia. Sent to Moscow in 1661 to try to restore peace between Tsar Alexis and the King of Poland, John Casimir, the Baron and his staff experienced nothing but setbacks. Their mission was considered inopportune, and although they were courteously treated their status in Russia was almost that of prisoners and they were not granted permission to return home until 1663.

The Baron took advantage of his journey to gather information about the country's resources and take a rather cursory glance at the Russian way of life. While travelling through the Baltic area he noted the quality of the cattle, commented favourably on hides and was impressed by the abundance of wheat and corn and the quality of hemp, honey, wax and bacon, adding, however, that 'all these riches are shared by the Prussians, Swedes and Danes. Lithuania and Muscovy obtain their gold and silver from abroad, for these countries have no metal save iron.'

Ordyn-Nastchokin, then a voivode, received the ambassador with great civility and made an excellent impression on him at their first encounter, but Mayerberg's opinion of the Russian way of life, even among the upper crust, was far from favourable. When he visited Ordyn-Nastchokin he was placed at a long narrow table covered with a simple linen cloth and laid with a vinegar cruet, a pepper-pot and a salt-cellar. Each guest was given a spoon and some bread but only the most distinguished personages got plates, napkins or cutlery. Plates and cutlery were made of pewter and bore traces of previous meals. After vodka, the travellers ate cold boiled beef served with onions and vinegar, followed by various other dishes, seldom accompanied by sauces but always, to the Baron's great disgust, dressed with onions and garlic.

'No one may leave the dining-room unless he be carried out dead drunk,' Mayerberg noted. 'Ordyn-Nastchokin, who wisely emulates our customs, granted us permission to refrain from drinking ourselves senseless.'

Riding on horseback across the plain which had witnessed the battle between the Teutonic Knights and Prince Vasily I of Moscow, the diplomats were met at Pskov by three hundred horsemen and an emissary from the voivode and boyar Prince Ivan Khovansky. Describing Khovansky, who was actually an excellent general, the Baron remarked contemptuously: 'It is the Russian practice to take noble origin into consideration rather than military experience.'

The ambassador and his companions reached Nizhni-Novgorod just as Lent was drawing to a close. Mayerberg marvelled at the great sugar-loaves on sale in the shops there. When he awoke next morning, it was Easter Sunday. Bells were ringing, joyful crowds thronged the streets carrying coloured eggs, and there were drunkards everywhere.

'The Russians' religion is naught but superstition,' declared Mayerberg, but he took umbrage when, though a good Christian, he was refused permission to enter an Orthodox church. Ignorance and incomprehension reigned equally on both sides.

On reaching Moscow, the diplomats were granted an audience of the Tsar, but only after much wrangling over the respective titles of the two sovereigns and the complex formalities to be observed. Emperor Leopold's embassy presented Alexis Michaelovitch with sable pelts and other gifts, complying with Russian tradition by adding some bread and salt in token of their desire for his favour. The Tsar accepted the symbolic offerings but declined the rest.

As in Ordyn-Nastchokin's case, Mayerberg managed to find a few pleasant things to say about the Tsar:

'He is gentle and good-natured, never meting out punishment save to the guilty. His natural disposition inclines him towards peace. He is greatly attached to the fallacious dogmas of his religion and extremely devout.'

Mayerberg found the Russians vain, arrogant and impolite to

foreigners, but his main bone of contention was their religion, and he constantly returned to the attack on this point. He could never forget for a moment that he was living among people whom his Church termed schismatics. 'Thus,' his account begins, 'we were already in Muscovite Russia, which confesses Jesus Christ only after the Greek usage, which, with the aid of the incontestable and divine grace, has long been condemned by His only true bride, the Roman Catholic Church.' Christian charity was conspicuously absent in the relations between the two Churches and was to remain so in the centuries to come. Nevertheless, while he lashed out at the Orthodox faith and blamed it for what he considered the deplorable state of Russian morals, Mayerberg is second only to Captain Margeret[1] as a source of information about the country. In his anxiety to be impartial, he praised the asceticism of Russian monks but at once thought better of it and concluded by remarking that it could only be 'specious'.

Other travellers from the West who visited the country before and after Mayerberg all pursued this tradition of severe criticism based on total or partial ignorance. Virtually none of them spoke a word of Russian and few had any knowledge of the country's history or any personal contact with its inhabitants. To them, the Russian people were merely 'bearded, long-haired men dressed with barbaric and sordid magnificence, wearing furs in the height of summer, maintaining a horde of lackeys who resemble janissaries and speaking a strange tongue which no one can understand save with the help of a series of interpreters.'[2]

Neither Adam Olearius, who visited Russia between 1635 and 1639 as a member of Duke Frederick of Holstein's embassy to the late Tsar Michael, nor any other foreign visitor could point to a single likeable characteristic in the Russians. To the West, they were never more than 'stupid, wicked and perverse'.

The Russians, for their part, had no hesitation in suspecting the foreigners of moral turpitude. The clergy refused to shake hands with the 'ungodly' and forbade them to enter their churches, and the Tsar himself felt obliged to wash his hands after receiving them. Although no foreigners spoke Russian, the number of Russians who spoke a foreign language was infinitesimal, so it is understandable that each side found it difficult to do the other justice. But, despite all this and despite the obscurity that shrouded contemporary Russia, nothing can dim the fact that she had a virtuous and pious Tsar in Alexis Michaelovitch, an

[1] A Frenchman in the service of Tsar Boris Godunov in 1598.

[2] Alfred Rambaud, *Instructions données aux Ambassadeurs et Ministres de France en Russie*, Paris, 1890.

intelligent, essentially honest and upright minister in Ordyn-Nastchokin, a paragon of disinterested generosity and brotherly love in Rtistchev and a beautiful and virtuous woman in Theodosia Morozova.

Twenty years after Olearius, another foreign visitor described his trip to Russia in totally different terms, though it is true that he was Orthodox. Archdeacon Paul of Aleppo, son of Patriarch Makarios of Antioch, accompanied his father to Russia twice, once to collect gifts for the Church of Antioch and on the second occasion to arbitrate in the dispute between Patriarch Nikon and the Tsar.

Paul of Aleppo, though an Arab, appears to have felt a strong affinity for the Russians. He fitted into the community better, doubtless because he was Orthodox and was able to enjoy privileges denied to other foreigners, who were only admitted to official ceremonies. Neither politics nor religion formed any sort of barrier between Paul of Aleppo and the Russians.

The Archdeacon, who wrote well and with a keen eye for detail, described all he had seen in a letter to a friend of his. Some things aroused his unstinted admiration. He spoke, for instance, of the Russians' profound religious sense, of their patience and of the rigorous acts of self-mortification performed by the faithful. Paul of Aleppo was received by the Tsar:

> The first thing to be offered us was Cretan wine of a marvellous red hue and excellent flavour, followed by a liquor of cherries and mead of various kinds. As for cooked dishes, we were served a fish resembling stuffed lamb in shape, for this country is so abundant in fish that the most diverse dishes, both in taste, savour and appearance, are made from it. All the bones are removed and the meat is pounded to a paste in mortars. This liquid pulp is poured into moulds shaped like lambs or geese, and the moulds fried in a very deep vat of vegetable oil. The flavour is excellent, and anyone who tastes the dish might think that he was eating lamb's flesh. The Russians also make great use of pies stuffed with white cheese.
>
> All these dishes were served to us by the noblemen of the table, forty or fifty of them, who carried them in at a trot. The Tsar was present from the beginning of the meal to the end. We reproached him, for he ate not a morsel.

Paul of Aleppo kept his eyes open during his travels. Everything interested him. Here, for instance, he is describing Tula to his friend in Antioch.

> This town has a stone fortress, for it affords a passage into the land

of the Turks. Magnificent beds of iron ore have been discovered during the reign of Alexis Michaelovitch ... They have amazing furnaces in which they smelt the mineral, which becomes as water, flowing through an aperture into grooves scooped out of the ground and from these into tubes of different shapes corresponding to cannons and cannon-balls. Before each aperture are forty to fifty holes [moulds]. When the moulds are full they are removed without the use of a single hammer, easily and without effort. Thousands of different articles are made in this way. Great numbers of cannon are sent to Astrakhan in winter by sledge, the seven hundred versts being covered in forty days. These cannon are sold to the Franks. They are cast in solid iron.

We are only able to see ministers and important persons very early in the morning. Each one of them possesses, within his residence, a very gracious and marvellous church served by three or four priests who receive clothing and a salary from the boyar. No courtier presents himself before the Tsar without first hearing the priest recite the prayers prescribed by the Church and then attending Mass. We have been chiefly astonished by their humble and modest demeanour towards the poor, and by their piety.

The houses are built of stone and brick. The bricks, which are excellent, resemble those of Antioch in hardness, weight and mottling. The lime is better here than in Aleppo.

Eminent people are not entitled, however important the posts they occupy, to have a retinue of more than three hundred men. When one of them departs for the wars, the Tsar gives him thousands of soldiers. Note the wisdom of this measure: because of it, rebellion never occurs among dignitaries.

Paul of Aleppo had an inquisitive turn of mind. His jottings are a blend of the trivial and the important. He wrote to his friend:

In winter the sledges are draped with white bearskins. Dignitaries' wives have coaches on runners fitted with glass windows. These coaches are draped with red or rose-coloured cloth reaching to the ground. Widows dress entirely in black, even the hangings and cushions of their sledges being of that colour.

Russian children learn to ride on small horses at a very tender age. A large number of servants is assigned to their person, all of them children of their own age. They are very high-spirited and salute passers-by in the street courteously ...

As to the poor, few are to be seen seeking alms in the streets of

Moscow because the Tsar distributes beggars among his dignitaries. Each person of importance is given a certain number of poor people to feed in his house. Moscow also boasts a hostel where food is distributed on behalf of the Tsar and Tsarina, and the same is done for men detained in prison.

In short, Paul of Aleppo noted an abundance of praiseworthy features, although he was equally frank about abuses and commented sadly that 'the peasants are like slaves'. He described Nikon in a wealth of detail, gave sketches of other leading personalities and described the festivals which he attended.

The Patriarch of Antioch's son was alive to contemporary religious trends. Strangely enough, none of the other visitors realized that the entire Russian nation, from princes to serfs, was undergoing a grave crisis of conscience. The people whom Olearius described as animals devoid of reason and morals were sacrificing their lives and worldly goods to defend what they believed in, convinced that their very salvation was at stake.

* * *

It was only natural that Poland, whose forces had occupied Moscow during the Time of Troubles and which was so intimately linked to Russia by historical ties, should be better known there than other foreign countries. Polish diplomatic missions visited the capital frequently. In Ordyn-Nastchokin's time, the Russians and Poles entered into discussions regarding the eventual election of the Tsar's eldest son, Alexis Alexeyevitch, to the throne of Poland. However, Tsar Alexis was unwilling to be separated from his heir, who was still a boy, and put forward his own name instead. This situation was somewhat reminiscent of an incident which preceded the election of the first Romanov during the Time of Troubles. On that occasion, the Muscovites had already sworn allegiance to Vladislas IV when his father, the Polish king Sigismund III, reclaimed the Russian crown for himself.

John Casimir's renunciation of the Polish throne gave rise to a crop of international intrigues. Tsar Alexis's rivals included Emperor Leopold, the Duc de Lorraine and the Prince de Condé, whose candidacy was supported by the King of France. In 1668 the Polish envoys were received in the Kremlin by the young Tsarevitch Alexis, who read them a dissertation in Polish extolling the virtues of Slav unity. In February 1674 (Alexis Alexeyevitch having died in 1670), a new Polish mission arrived in Moscow bearing five petitions, signed by prominent figures in Lithuania and Poland, which they handed to Prince Yury Dolgoruky and Matveyev, who was just beginning his career as the Tsar's favourite. This was the signal for new negotiations aimed at persuading the Tsar's second son, Theodore, who was now the heir apparent, to accept the Polish crown. The signatories stressed the advantages that would accrue to both parties if agreement could be reached on such an alliance, which would effect a close union between two nations with common interests. 'Trade would expand,' they wrote, 'and troublesome neighbours, notably the Turks, would be weakened if His Majesty the Tsar consented to entrust his beloved son to Poland.' But the conditions governing the bestowal of the Polish crown proved unacceptable to Tsar Alexis, for it was stipulated that Poland's new king must be a Roman Catholic. Eventually, in May 1674, the throne passed to John Sobieski, the man who later liberated Vienna from the Turks.

CHAPTER TWELVE

STEPAN RAZIN! Stepan Razin! The whispers rose to a murmur, then swelled to a full-blooded roar as the name sped across field and forest from one town and village to the next, borne into history on the wings of a legend that was half fact, half fiction. Hero of a bloody epic, Stepan Razin was the seventeenth-century catalyst of popular fury and adventurers' day-dreams.

Sophia was now a grown-up girl of thirteen, grown-up because royal children matured rapidly under a rigorous etiquette which was intended to be a constant reminder of their exalted station. The storm-clouds were gathering round her father once more, this time in the shape of a revolt centred on the home of the Yaik Cossacks, hundreds of miles from the capital.

Reforms were under way, but not fast enough to suit the more impatient spirits. The Tsar and his advisers were never given a moment's respite in which to pursue their labours unhampered. Free at last of Nikon's venomous strictures, Alexis Michaelovitch now had to listen with growing impatience to complaints from Athanasius Ordyn-Nastchokin, whose brilliance was gall and wormwood to the many ignorant men round the throne.

There remained the problem of the masses, weary of hardships and overburdened with taxation. Alexis Michaelovitch tried to ameliorate their existence as far as he was able. However, when allied with men who had committed crimes but preferred to take risks rather than face certain punishment, they made inflammable material. It only needed one man to become the symbol of all their aspirations and the country would be plunged into a welter of blood and fire.

Living in quasi-autonomous communities on the Don, Volga, Yaik and Dnieper, the Cossacks, their numbers swelled by a steady stream of fugitives of every description, had become a force to be reckoned with by the central government.

Ever since the Turks fortified the town of Azov in 1642, Cossack excursions along the shores of the Sea of Azov and the Black Sea had become increasingly hazardous, and the 'upstream' Cossacks, deprived of the proceeds of periodic forays, were beginning to feel the pinch.

The 'downstream' Cossacks viewed this enforced inactivity on the part of the Dontsy or Don Cossacks with apprehension because they were afraid that their starving neighbours would raid their own towns and villages. With considerable presence of mind, therefore, they organized raids by the 'upstream' Cossacks in the Volga and Caspian areas. The central government did not remain indifferent to these disorders. It could tolerate the Cossacks as long as they harried the Tatars, fought the Poles and attacked Turkish garrisons, even though their inopportune actions sometimes conflicted with general policy, but their appearance on the Volga and the Caspian was a serious threat to Russian trade and to Russia's long-standing commercial links with Persia. The undisciplined and ever-increasing body of 'free men' was beginning to represent a national danger. Inflamed by success, some Cossack chieftains developed grandiose ambitions. During the summer of 1666, for instance, a hetman named Us ('Moustache') advanced into the vicinity of Tula under the pretext of offering his services to the Tsar, a move which necessitated the dispatch of government troops to protect the town.

In 1670, Us was succeeded by Stepan Razin, whose name was already known among the Cossacks of the Don and Volga. He had been a member of a Russian mission sent to open negotiations with the Kalmucks in 1660. In 1662, the Don Cossacks sent him to Astrakhan to persuade the Kalmucks to join forces with them against the Crimean Tatars. A foreigner named Streis, who met Razin personally, described him as follows:

'He is a man of tall stature, well-built, with an agreeable but haughty countenance. He comports himself with great dignity.'

Stepan Razin had planned to break through to the Sea of Azov and there engage the Tatars or Turks, but his scheme failed and he decided instead to operate on the Volga or the Caspian, an area which he knew well from his previous travels. Having friends among the Yaik Cossacks, a branch of the Don Cossacks, he spent the spring of 1667 in recruiting a sizeable body of fugitives, serfs, artisans and impoverished boyars' sons and then sailed down the Volga with a veritable fleet of boats. Several thousand strong and armed with weapons from a small town which they had sacked, Razin and his marauders scoured the area for plunder, searching merchantmen and boats belonging to the Patriarch.

Thirty-five boats and some fifteen thousand men (a tribute to Razin's recruiting methods) debouched into the Caspian Sea. The government sent musketeers from Astrakhan to intercept the brigands, but they escaped. Razin, who had by now assumed the title of *ataman* (hetman), reached the river Yaik and captured a small town of the same name by a simple stratagem. Pretending to be on a pilgrimage, he was at once admitted into the fortress with a few of his men. Once inside, they opened the gates for their comrades and massacred the whole garrison. Razin was now master of a small stronghold. Fortune favoured him, for the detachments sent to dislodge him by the authorities were attacked en route by Bashkirs and Kalmucks and suffered heavy losses.

In March 1668, after spending the winter in Yaik, Razin embarked his men in twenty-four boats and made a sortie without any preconceived plan. Realizing that he would be unable to recapture his little fortress, he loaded the light cannon on board his craft and dumped the heavy pieces into the river.

Razin was now, if not master of the Caspian, a powerful pirate chieftain. He attacked and plundered Persian coastal towns, scoring one success after another. News of his exploits spread like wildfire and his growing reputation became embroidered with legendary detail.[1]

The Cossacks of the Don, Razin's native district, were growing restive. Unable to control them, their hetman tendered his resignation, announcing that his men were no longer loyal to the Tsar. He was immediately replaced by a more accommodating leader. Stepan Razin continued his exploits on the Caspian and pushed on past Baku. Glutted with prisoners and booty, he disembarked at Rasht, where Persian troops were awaiting him in battle order. This was a setback, but Razin did not lose his head. Hastily informing the Persians that he had only put ashore in order to offer his services to the King of Kings, he sent a few men to Isfahan to discuss the terms of the offer. While Razin's envoys were conducting negotiations with the town authorities, the inhabitants of Rasht grew tired of the deplorable behaviour of his troops and massacred four hundred of them. Razin's Cossacks defended themselves vigorously. They destroyed almost the whole of Rasht and then moved on to the neighbouring town of Afarabat. Here they tried to engage in peaceful trade, but found it unprofitable and sacked the town as they had Rasht. The losses suffered by Razin's Cossacks were more than made good by the impoverished Persians and foreign immigrants who flocked to join his colours.

Razin's private army continued to plunder, burn and slaughter with varying success until the summer of 1669, by which time his headquarters were on a small island on the Caspian known as The Four Hills.

[1] Every Russian knows the song inspired by him, which describes the fate of a Persian princess whom he sacrificed to his companions.

> Stepan Razin's boats are scudding
> o'er the billows from the island...

The apathy of the Russian government was as apparent as its insolvency. Razin's sphere of operations was so remote that Moscow temporized and ordered local authorities to take measures which bore no relation to the gravity of the situation. To underestimate the importance of such an outbreak in a country where the spirit of revolt and the appeal of anarchy were never far below the surface was tantamount to fanning a spark into an uncontrollable conflagration.

Prince Prozorovsky, voivode of Astrakhan, sent four thousand men against Razin under the command of Prince Lvov, but for some reason or other Lvov was ill-informed. Unaware that Razin's numbers had been depleted by his losses in Persia, he prepared to besiege The Four Hills with the maximum of caution and deliberation, thereby allowing Razin to give him the slip. The hetman declined to give battle and evacuated the island. Lvov sent him a courier armed with a letter from the Tsar, who promised to pardon him and his men if they laid down their arms and handed over their prisoners and cannon. Razin would not accept these conditions in their entirety. He insisted on keeping enough boats to transport him back to the Don and added that, although he might consent to release his Russian and Christian prisoners, he hoped to get such rich ransoms for some of his Persian prisoners that he intended to negotiate their sale.

On August 25th, 1669, Stepan Razin decided to accept the government's extremely favourable terms after all. He sent his flags and his commander's baton to Prince Prozorovsky and promised to hand over his cannon and release all prisoners. Furthermore, he humbly besought the sovereign to allow him to retire with his men to the Don and asked Prozorovsky's permission to send a deputation to Moscow to crave the Tsar's indulgence.

Prozorovsky agreed, thinking the affair settled, and Razin and his men marched into Astrakhan more like victors than vanquished, making an ostentatious and impudent display of the ill-gotten gains which the government had so generously allowed them to keep. Razin's exploits had transformed him into a popular hero. He and his companions paraded in glory through the streets of Astrakhan like kings, garbed in robes of silk, velvet and gold thread. Jacob Streis, who was living there at the time, describes the splendour of Razin's men, and his impressions are corroborated by a chronicler of the period: 'The Cossacks are wealthy beyond belief. Even the sails of their boats are made of fine Persian silk.'

Razin passed through the streets, scattering gold ducats on the admiring crowd. The adventurer's open display of wealth was, in fact, a flat contradiction of the popular adage, 'crime does not pay'. Razin's desperadoes had demonstrated only too clearly that crime can pay well, and the psychological effect on the mob was pregnant with consequences.

Attracted by his daring and dazzled by his aura of success, large numbers of men from the lower orders decided to follow him to the Don.

Razin was not slow to exploit this atmosphere of popular adulation. Why should he honour the terms of his surrender when supporters were hourly flocking to his banner? 'We need boats,' he explained to Prozorovsky, 'to help us accomplish the return journey, and cannon to protect us from the Crimean Tatars and Turks during our voyage up the Don. As to the Persian prisoners and the booty, how can they be returned when both have long ago been distributed among the members of my party?'

Although it had not been one of the terms embodied in the Tsar's letter, the voivode tried unsuccessfully to obtain a list of Razin's men, for Razin was proposing to sail up the Don accompanied not only by his original band but also by any members of the local population who wished to join him. Razin preserved the utmost decorum throughout the discussions and the authorities seemed equally determined to behave with tact, though it turned out that both sides were animated by ulterior motives.

At last, the hetman set off for the Don escorted by some fifty musketeers from the Astrakhan garrison and one of the town's leading merchants, who had been assigned to watch him during the journey. Razin was hardly clear of Astrakhan when he evinced the most flagrant contempt for his escort by seizing a convoy of wheat. He bribed the musketeers who had been detailed to guard him, and by the time he reached Tsaritsyn he was so firmly re-established in the role of robber baron that the local voivode had to flee for his life.

Preceded by his reputation, Stepan Razin arrived on the banks of his native Don with all the panache of a returning hero. The 'downstream' or sedentary and prosperous Cossacks hurried to greet him, eager to share in the spoils of an enterprise which they had financed to such good purpose.

In 1670, Tsar Alexis sent an envoy to assess the mood of the Don Cossacks. The freebooters received him in their 'Cossack Assembly'.

'Who sent you?' Razin asked him. 'Do you come from the Tsar or the boyars?' 'I come in the Tsar's name,' replied the emissary. 'Liar!' shouted Razin. 'You are naught but a spy sent by the boyars!' And the unfortunate man was promptly thrown into the river.

Razin's words embodied the nucleus of his future course of action. For the first time, the idea of a great national uprising seemed to take shape in these simple questions. The Tsar's person was so sacred in the eyes of the Russian people and his prestige so great that an assault on his personal authority was out of the question. 'For the Tsar: against the boyars and officials' was a slogan with which Razin was to make great play from then on. Meanwhile, he schemed and conspired.

Emboldened by success and conscious of his popularity, Stepan Razin was planning to be something more than a mere robber chieftain. Proclamations issued by him began to circulate in the Don and Volga areas, carefully couched in traditional phraseology. Razin called upon the people to rally to him in the name of the Patriarch and the Tsar, the Patriarch being Nikon and the Tsar being the late heir apparent, Tsarevitch Alexis Alexeyevitch. The fact that Tsarevitch Alexis had been dead for some months and that the exiled Patriarch was far from contemplating such an adventure did not matter in the slightest. The populace gullibly swallowed these impostures and accepted the improbable in good faith.

Razin was an adroit stage manager. The armada of river boats which travelled up the Volga towards Tsaritsyn and Astrakhan past the towns and landscapes of Razin's youth included two vessels draped in velvet, one red and the other black. Although they carried an imaginary cargo, the people needed no further convincing that Razin was accompanied on his bold venture by the two personages who embodied the two powers on which Russia herself was founded. Gliding along unseen within the scarlet curtains sat Tsarevitch Alexis, while the boat draped in black carried the Patriarch, who had been victimized by the boyars: of this there was no doubt in the popular mind.

In his proclamations, which were known at the time as 'letters of subornation', the hetman opened his summons to the masses to join him with the following preamble:

'He who wishes to serve God and the sovereign, honour the Grand Army and Stepan Timofeyevitch and crush the traitors ... '

The rebel leader's 'fifth column' was already at work in the towns along his route. Outside Tsaritsyn, Razin's men took the opportunity to seize caravans bound for Astrakhan laden with wheat and merchandise of various kinds. The voivode Turgenev barricaded himself inside one of Tsaritsyn's fortified towers with his musketeers and put up a fierce but vain resistance. The tower was taken by storm, the musketeers slain where they stood and the voivode transfixed by a dozen spears and thrown into the river.

Razin made his new headquarters in the captured town and introduced Cossack methods into its administration. Since there was no regular contact between towns in the area, government authorities remained in ignorance of Tsaritsyn's fate for some time and Razin was able to settle in at his leisure, replenishing his supplies by picking off caravans destined for Astrakhan.

Eventually, troops commanded by Prince Lvov advanced from

Astrakhan to deal with the unrepentant rebel once and for all. Unfortunately for Lvov, many of his musketeers had known and admired Razin's opulence and devil-may-care personality when he was living in Astrakhan as a privileged captive. They deserted wholesale. Those of their comrades who resisted were massacred on Razin's orders, and Lvov only just escaped with his life.

This news threw Astrakhan into utter confusion. Feverishly, the voivode of the town set to work to strengthen its defences, assisted by numerous foreigners who lived in the port, some of them being members of the crew of the *Orel* (Eagle), the first sea-going ship ever built in Russia.

At the risk of destroying a popular misconception, it should be stated that the first units of the Russian navy were laid down not by Peter the Great but by Tsar Alexis. His flotilla consisted of a ship, a yacht, two boats and a *shnyak*, and were built in the village of Dedinovo, near Kolomenskoye, under the supervision of two Dutch shipwrights. The largest vessel was christened the *Orel*, and on May 7th the whole flotilla left the banks of the Moskva bound for Astrakhan.

Astrakhan was heavily fortified for the period, but its defences and its four hundred cannon proved unequal to an assault by Razin's desperadoes. As usual, the attackers were greatly assisted by the fifth column, and the townsfolk's morale was not enhanced by their awareness of the ferocious reprisals customarily exacted by the champion of 'Tsar' Alexis Alexeyevitch and Patriarch Nikon. The voivode Prozorovsky was wounded and hurled off the ramparts, his brother and five hundred musketeers slaughtered, and the *Orel* and the other units of Russia's first fleet burnt at anchor by Razin's men.

With a sluggishness which was in sharp contrast to the speed with which Razin was taking fortified and open towns one after the other, Moscow refused to recognize the gravity of the situation. Razin's venture was identical in nature with the bloody gamble taken under Catherine II by another Cossack, Emelian Pugatchev, 'a Russian revolt devoid of sense or mercy', as Pushkin described it. The have-nots were ranged against the haves. It was a venture in keeping with the anarchic character of the Russian people, who always equated liberty with disorder. The fact that Razin's men were accompanied on their forays by the shade of Tsarevitch Alexis Alexeyevitch and the mythical benediction of Patriarch Nikon is sufficient evidence that the revolutionaries could not have pictured Russia without the twin pillars of Tsar and Church.

Thanks to the success and scope of his operations, Razin's forces snowballed. Peasants, released prisoners, renegade soldiers and musketeers and Asiatics from the regions through which he passed all rallied to his side.

It was a blind but potent force, devoid of any consistent purpose and spreading chaos in its wake.[1]

Fortune, which had smiled on the *ataman* for so long, finally deserted him. He encountered his first major reverse at Simbirsk, an already important town situated at the confluence of the Volga and Sviaga and defended by Ivan Miloslavsky, the Tsar's brother-in-law. Mounted attacks by Razin's men and attempts to burn the town by lighting fires round its walls proved fruitless. The insurgents suffered heavy casualties, and, when regular troops trained by foreign officers and commanded by Prince George Bariatinsky inflicted a further defeat on them near the Volga, their leader abandoned them and fled. The great adventure was drawing to a close.

The tide continued to turn against Razin throughout December 1670. Bariatinsky, who was busy recapturing towns taken by the hetman in the Volga region, did not spare the rod. Beheadings, hangings and impalings became a daily spectacle. 1671 was a particularly sanguinary year, and in December Razin's last stronghold was taken by government troops.

Razin was not the sort of man to fight to the death. Realizing that his luck had run out, he abandoned his men and went to earth in a secret hiding-place. Unfortunately for him, a group of Cossacks who had remained loyal to the government arrested him and turned him over to the Tsar. They made a rich haul. Far from being alone in his lair, Razin was accompanied by his whole staff, including his brother Frolka and his chief aides. The latter were hanged on the spot, but Razin and Frolka were sent to Moscow.

Watched by an enormous crowd of spectators – morbidly curious and no longer admiring – Stepan Razin mounted the scaffold. His bearded head rolled.

* * *

The difficulties encountered by Alexis Michaelovitch in his efforts to maintain order in his realm are reminiscent of a popular Russian story entitled *Trishka's Caftan*. In this, the unfortunate hero tries to make the garment more comfortable by cutting the skirt to lengthen the sleeves, then the sleeves to enlarge the collar and then the collar to widen the shoulders – all without achieving a satisfactory result.

While the government was dealing with Stepan Razin's rebellion, trouble broke out at the Solovetsky monastery, in the far north, where

[1] Peter Kovalevsky believes that Razin's revolt enjoyed foreign support, as some Persian records seem to indicate.

the embers of religious strife had been smouldering ever since 1657, the year of Sophia's birth.

The country ruled by Tsar Alexis was too vast, cumbersome and decentralized ever to be entirely at peace. Rebels were always active in some corner of his dominions. Moreover, although insignificant beside the epic deeds of Stepan Razin, the rebellion at the Solovetsky monastery took even longer to quell.

In this case, the affair had a religious origin. During the fifteenth century, three pious hermits – the blessed Zosima, Savati and Guerman – in search of a retreat where they could devote themselves to penitence and spiritual exercise far from the world, had settled on the White Sea island of Solovetsky off the north-west coast of Russia. Its harsh climate and remoteness from civilization suited them admirably, but it was not long before rumours of their exemplary life began to spread. Other monks came to join them, followed by pilgrims from every corner of Russia, all attracted to the new monastery by its pious reputation.

By the time of the Great Schism, the famous monastery had become a maritime fortress guarding the approaches to Archangel. Its material resources were very considerable and a large number of commercial enterprises had been set up there under monastic control, among them salt-works, mines, tanneries, potash factories and fisheries. These enterprises were permanently short of labour, and the monastery gladly accepted potential recruits without demanding references. Thus the Solovetsky monastery, like the Cossack communities, became a place of asylum for considerable numbers of fugitives of every origin and shade of opinion. What was more, the government had, from the sixteenth century onwards, adopted Solovetsky as a repository for intractable monks, fallen priests and citizens whom it wished to deport for political reasons or infringements of common law.

Although the Abbot of Solovetsky accepted Nikon's reforms in 1657, the monastery's Chapter condemned them and refused to abandon Old Belief practices.

Solovetsky remained in a state of siege for eight years. According to a report by a voivode acting for the government the garrison of the ecclesiastical fortress comprised three hundred monks and four hundred peasants, Cossacks and rebel musketeers, the latter including some ex-members of Razin's private army.

Eventually, a monk who had decided to obey the orders of the Orthodox hierarchy and break with the schismatics opened the monastery's gates and admitted the besiegers. In January 1675 the monastery was occupied by government troops. The rebels, monks and laymen alike, were severely punished by the secular authorities at the instigation of Patriarch Joachim, who had been promoted to the patriarchate in 1674 and was persecuting schismatics with an unremitting vigour worthy of Nikon himself.

CHAPTER THIRTEEN

YEAR succeeded year in the Kremlin, and each brought its quota of births and deaths.

Tsarina Maria Miloslavsky died in 1669 at the age of forty-four, and a year later Tsarevitch Alexis Alexeyevitch succumbed to a mysterious ailment, possibly tubercular meningitis, and followed her to the tomb. The death of the young heir apparent, who had shown great promise, was greeted with universal regret. It was a crushing blow not only to Tsar Alexis and his children but also to the faithful Theodore Rtistchev, who had brought the boy up. Deprived of his sole reason for tolerating the pomp and ceremony of Court life, Rtistchev left the Kremlin despite the Tsar's entreaties, taking with him the young Tsarevitch's baptismal cross as a memento of his tutorship. Rtistchev's departure meant that the Tsar had lost his only friend, a man who had never asked anything for himself but had demanded justice and clemency for others.

The future of the royal line now rested entirely on the shoulders of Tsarevitch Theodore, born in 1661, an attractive child but as delicate as his elder brother had been. Describing Tsar Alexis's youngest son Ivan, a chronicler remarked that he had 'a sad head', a polite circumlocution implying that he was abnormal. He was a weakling, mentally retarded and almost blind, and although he was still a babe in arms it was already obvious that he would never be capable of governing. Alexis's daughters, Sophia, Maria and Theodosia, were a sturdy and flourishing trio but – or so it was thought by the Tsar's entourage – a negative factor in affairs of state.

The Tsar was not, however, a man who naturally succumbed to despair. 'The Lord giveth, the Lord taketh away' was one of his guiding principles and he regarded excessive grief as a sin, as he demonstrated in his letter to Prince Odoyevsky. His three most notable friends were no longer with him. Patriarch Nikon still lived in his monastery, supported by donations from the Tsar and his family; Theodore Rtistchev was leading a Christian life outside the palace; and Athanasius Ordyn-Nastchokin, weary of ingratitude and worn out by his unremitting struggle against governmental shortcomings and the defects in the Russian national character, longed for nothing more than the tranquillity of monastic life. Apart from this, Nastchokin's incessant complaints and political importunities had driven a wedge between him and the Tsar. In 1671, on a day which he had ticked in red beforehand, he gave up everything for which he had lived for so many years and asked Alexis to release him from public service. He then retired to the monastery of St John, a few miles from his native Pskov, where, freed from the vanities of the world, he became a monk and was adjudged worthy of the *schima*, the highest and most ascetic form of discipline in the Orthodox Church.

Living in solitude, meditation and silence, the former statesman gave orders that the revenues from his estates should be devoted to the foundation of a hospital in Pskov where the sick could be cared for by monks of his own choosing.

The Tsar was still surrounded by his late wife's relatives, but the Tsarina's death had left them apprehensive about their future. If the Tsar remarried they would be ousted from their privileged position, and their sense of insecurity was further heightened by the fact that a new favourite's star was rising fast.

Artamon Matveyev, like the Tsar's other personal friends, did not come of an illustrious family. In fact, nothing is known of his ancestry and it is probable that he was not even of noble birth. Some of his contemporaries said that he was a priest's son, while others traced him back to a Lapp fisherman. He was a handsome and intelligent man with pleasant manners and a talent for flattering the Tsar, whose admiration for the Western way of life he shared.

Matveyev, who had distinguished himself as Commander of Musketeers during the negotiations with Bogdan Khmelnitsky, later accepted the allegiance of the Little Russian Cossacks in the Tsar's name. By the time Emperor Leopold's second mission arrived in Moscow, Artamon Matveyev was already in the Tsar's favour, but he acted with discretion and did his best to win the boyars' sympathy or at least neutrality. Matveyev's knowledge of foreign languages and his Scottish wife set him apart from the general run of courtiers. His comfortable house with its Western furniture displayed an opulence which must have been rapidly acquired, since he was born a poor man. Its walls were hung with paintings by the German School and its ceilings richly decorated. The iconostasis in his private chapel was composed of icons painted by Italian artists. Like the Tsar, he owned a large number – in modern parlance, a collection – of clocks, which were luxury articles in those days. Each indicated the time in the style of its country of manufacture: German clocks from midday onwards, Italian or Bohemian from sunset and others from dawn onwards 'in the Jewish or Babylonian manner'.

Matveyev's library was remarkable for the period. He himself was an author, though no copies of his works are extant. These included *A History of the Election and Coronation of Michael Theodorovitch*, *A History of the Ancestors of the Great Tsars* and *The Designations, Titles and Seals of the Great Princes and all the Great Christian and Infidel Sovereigns who had Relations with the Grand Sovereign Tsar Alexis*, a work which he presented to Tsarevitch Theodore, who kept it in his library.

Matveyev did not actively strive to westernize the national way of life. He profited from and delighted in Western culture without devoting himself to it as Rtistchev and Ordyn-Nastchokin had done in their endeavours to remould the national way of life. The courtier in Matveyev shrewdly indulged the Tsar's tastes by building a private theatre on to his house and forming a company to play in it. Alexis Michaelovitch visited Matveyev's house with increasing pleasure and frequency. It was an oasis of civilized existence where he could drink without getting drunk and discuss affairs of state with a man of balanced intellect who never presumed to thwart him as Ordyn-Nastchokin had done.

Matveyev made a good companion for Alexis Michaelovitch in the years of his prime. The Tsar still had his healthy complexion and physical vitality. No one dreamt that he had only six years to live, nor that those six years would exercise a profound effect on Sophia's future.

* * *

Artamon Matveyev and his wife had only one child, a boy named Andrei, but they also had a young ward whom they treated as if she were their own daughter. It seems probable that no blood relationship existed between the Matveyevs and Natalia Naryshkin. Tradition had it that her place of birth was Kirikov in the province of Riazan, a small village whose inhabitants were of noble origin but so impoverished that they lived little better than peasants.

While passing through this village one day, Matveyev noticed a young girl crying bitterly. He stopped to ask the cause of her grief and learnt that she was weeping because her serving-woman had hanged herself – or so we are told by Collins in *The Present State of Russia*.[1] The good man was touched by her distress and took her into his household. Collins informs us that Natalia was so poor that she often used to go gathering mushrooms in the woods, but he adds that she was extraordinarily beauti-

[1] Quoted by Tereshchenko, *Survey of Lives of Senior Foreign Office Officials*, St Petersburg, 1837.

ful, timid and devout. (No contemporary of Peter the Great's mother ever claimed that her intelligence matched her beauty!)

The first encounter between the Tsar and Matveyev's young ward is described in highly romantic vein by Tereshchenko. He quotes no sources, but the story has a certain naïve charm.

It seems that the Tsar paid his friend an unexpected visit one day, and, seeing the table laid for the evening meal, declared his intention of staying to dinner. Accordingly, he sat down at table with Matveyev, his Scottish wife, his son and young Natalia, whom he had never seen before. Much to the girl's confusion, the Tsar's eyes never left her face.

'I thought,' said Alexis, 'that you had only a son, yet now you have a daughter. How is it that I have never seen her before?'

'I have naught but a son, Sire,' replied Matveyev. 'My wife is rearing this girl. One day, with God's grace, we shall find her a husband.'

Alone with his host after the meal, Alexis said: 'The girl is comely. She appears to be good-natured and is of marriageable age.'

'True enough,' said Matveyev. 'Natalia is intelligent [an assertion belied by the silence of other writers on the subject] and exceedingly modest. Our whole family love her as if she were their own kin. She takes pity on the poor and would gladly share all that she has with the disinherited, yet she herself is without means.'

'God's mercy is great,' replied the Tsar. 'Perhaps the Lord will send her a betrothed who will think less of a dowry than of the beauty of her soul.'

'Our prayers are not always granted,' Matveyev commented.

Some days later, the Tsar came to see Matveyev again. 'I think that I have found a suitable man for Natalia. He is rich, but there is something about him of even greater import. He fears God and does his best to be a good man.'

When Matveyev expressed his eagerness to know the suitor's name, the Tsar declared: 'It is I. But I wish her to become my wife of her own free will.'

'How can you doubt that she will accept, Sire? But, I beseech you, arrange this marriage in such a way that no one shall accuse me of having contrived it. Many envy me and I have many enemies. If you wish to wed my ward, who does not come of an illustrious family and has no fortune, all will say that I have contrived the affair.'

So much for conversations which no living ear could have heard. We cannot be certain, but there is a possibility that Matveyev may after all have arranged the meeting between his ward and the Tsar. In any case, Alexis had certainly made up his mind already when, to comply with tradition and avert scandal, he summoned sixty girls of noble birth to the Kremlin to make his official selection.

It was a great honour to take part in this competition for the royal couch and crown, but the conditions of entry made it a cruel ordeal. So fierce were the intrigues carried on by the relatives of potential brides and so brutal the methods used to eliminate rivals that one loving father, on hearing that his daughter had been selected for presentation, exclaimed: 'It were better to throw our daughters into the river than send them to the Terem!' This time, rumours of the Tsar's choice had gone the rounds despite all his precautions and the presentation ceremony deceived no one. Nevertheless, the candidates were duly assembled, inspected and interrogated by female members of the Terem staff. The Tsar's two foreign doctors, Samuel Collins and Daniel Gaden, also gave their verdict. Finally, after all the girls had filed past, the Tsar presented his chosen bride with a ring and a handkerchief embroidered with gold, silver and seed-pearls, according to custom.

The presentation ceremony took place in 1669, six months after Tsarina Maria's death, but the marriage was postponed because of some anonymous letters which aroused consternation in the Kremlin. Collins describes the wedding-day in great detail. Very early that morning, several boyars escorted by a detachment of soldiers and trumpeters went by Court carriage to Artamon Matveyev's house to fetch the bride. Waking Natalia, who was still asleep, they conveyed her and some of her serving-women to the palace. The poor girl's clothes were so loaded down with precious stones that she groaned aloud beneath their weight. Then, amid a flurry of drums, the bride was led into the cathedral, where the marriage was solemnized in the presence of a few close friends and relatives. After that, the boyars and officials repaired to the banqueting hall. So great was the fear of poison and the evil eye that the palace was sealed off and isolated from the city for several days as though in preparation for a siege.

Theodore Rtistchev emerged from retirement to make his last public appearance at the Tsar's wedding, but Theodosia Morozova chose this moment to infuriate the Tsar by pleading a non-existent illness to avoid fulfilling her duties as lady-in-waiting during the nuptial rites. Her refusal to compromise with the reformers who were persecuting the Old Believers was to cost her dear. The Tsar, who had hitherto closed his eyes to Morozova's shortcomings to please Maria Miloslavsky, confiscated her property and estates.

* * *

Natalia's promotion to the Tsar's couch made Artamon Matveyev the most important figure in Russia.

Historians of the seventeenth and eighteenth centuries were so anxious to obliterate the memory of all that Sophia and her friends had achieved that they piled Pelion on Ossa in their eulogies of Matveyev. Judging by official testimonials designed to rehabilitate him from the disgrace which overtook him after Alexis Michaelovitch's death, he was a model of generosity and disinterest, wisdom and prudence. For all that, the immense fortune which he accumulated during his palmy days (in company with the new Tsarina's numerous relatives) hardly speaks for his total disinterest. Nor was his generosity as unostentatious as that of Theodore Rtistchev. Matveyev appears to have spent his money with deliberation, obviously determined to build up the support he lacked and win popular favour because the boyars grudged him his privileged position.

The Tsar's favourite could best be described as an amiable man – which was saying a great deal for a Russian courtier of the period. 'Matveyev,' wrote Lisek, Emperor Leopold's ambassadorial secretary in Moscow, 'is an enthusiastic patron of all that is useful. He is very much better educated than his compatriots. He has permitted his son to shave and study foreign languages and literature.' Although this was substantially true, Matveyev's predecessors had so effectively blazed the trail that he never had to fight as hard as they did for the first fruits of Western culture.

* * *

But to return to the Terem, which had just acquired a young and beautiful addition in the new Tsarina.

Sophia was fourteen years old at the time of her father's second marriage, and Natalia nineteen. The haughty tsarevna and her youthful stepmother might well have become friends, but Sophia was a Miloslavsky and the Naryshkin clan represented a threat to her family. Sophia was intelligent, well educated, stubborn and imperious. Natalia had been in the Matveyev household for only three years before she became Tsarina, so her education had been neglected. She was beautiful, charming and lively, but intelligence was not her strong point and, although she welcomed certain novelties and fashions with pleasure, her character inclined her more towards tradition. The Naryshkins, who were all she brought to Court in the way of a dowry, were petty noblemen whose rapacity was all the keener for their long years of penury. Brainless and uninterested in public affairs, they were transformed by their newly acquired wealth into fashionable socialites, the 'playboys' of a court that had never known such a phenomenon before. They never shone as soldiers or statesmen, and the sole point in their favour was their sponsorship of an architectural style, Moscow baroque.

With the advent of the Naryshkins, the Miloslavskys were pushed into the background and had to pin their remaining hopes on Tsarevitch Theodore, now aged ten. Theodore was a precocious boy imbued with a sense of duty, but listless and deprived by ill health of all physical vitality. He merited the surname 'gentle' even more than his good-natured but volatile father. As his elder sister, Sophia already had some influence over him and was old enough to realize that she belonged to the Miloslavsky clan. She wielded a similar influence over the Tsar's other children by his first marriage – even little Ivan, whom she did her best to amuse and entertain.

After years of loveless marriage, the Tsar was finding Natalia the woman of his dreams. Vivacious, merry and easy-going, she exuded such youth and gaiety that the Tsar was constantly devising new ways to please her. He commissioned Matveyev to buy 'lace like that worn by the kings of Spain and France' from abroad and to engage comic dramatists and German technicians capable of making 'mechanical birds which sing in the trees' and 'automatons which blow trumpets'.

To divert Natalia, Alexis Michaelovitch built a secret compartment at the entrance to the audience-chamber in the new palace at Kolomenskoye from which she could watch foreign emissaries being received. The young woman's taste for personal adornment was indulged with the finest materials and rarest jewels. The grille covering the box where she watched theatrical performances was dismantled and the curtains of her carriage drawn back when she was on pilgrimage or travelling to one of her summer residences. In the streets of the capital, passers-by were astonished, if not shocked, when their gaze rested on the Tsarina's unveiled countenance. A foreigner noted that when the common people caught sight of Natalia's face they averted their eyes quickly in awe. Before long, she had boldly taken to riding in an open carriage.

Stahlenberg speaks of the Tsarina's gaiety and love of pleasure, and Reitenfels, who saw her on two occasions, describes her as follows: 'She is a young woman in the flower of her youth, of imposing stature, with dark and striking eyes, a pleasing face, round mouth, high forehead and harmonious proportions. Her voice is clear and agreeable, her manner gracious.'

On St Isaac's day, May 30th, 1672, to crown the Tsar's happiness, his young wife was delivered of a sturdy boy whom the couple christened

Peter. The Tsar's delight was unbounded, and anyone reading a descriptior of the festivities organized to mark the occasion might be forgiven fo thinking that Peter's birth was celebrated with greater pomp than tha of his half-brothers and sisters.

After a baptismal ceremony at the Tchudov monastery inside the Kremlin precincts, tables were laid in the Granovitaya Palata and upstairs i Tsarina Natalia's apartments. A hundred and twenty dishes were serve to the Tsar's guests and a hundred to the Tsarina's. Among the sweetmeat distributed to them were gigantic spiced loaves representing the arms o Moscow and Kazan, a confection of the Kremlin itself complete witl figures of horsemen and musketeers, birds in sugar, an eagle, a swar weighing seventy pounds, ducks, a parrot, a dove, almond pastes of al kinds and the preserved fruits known in Moscow as 'vegetable sugars' Those who could not be seated in the Granovitaya for lack of space wer sent dishes from the Tsar's table. More than eight hundred retainers, no counting the musketeers who mounted guard near the Red Gate and in th Kremlin courtyard, received a distribution of thirteen pounds of suga lozenges, seventy pounds of dried raisins, thirty-five pounds of figs an over fifty pounds of dried plums. Nor were the ladies' maids and seamstresses of the Terem forgotten. June 29th, 1672, might fairly be describe as a day of milk and honey, even though the child whose baptism wa being celebrated grew up to be singularly devoid of tenderness.

The vigorous blood of Natalia Naryshkin, the noble peasant, flowe more strongly in the boy's veins than the blood of the Romanov dynasty whose burden of heredity weighed so heavily – despite its recent foundation – on the male offspring of Alexis Michaelovitch and Mari Miloslavsky. Nevertheless, it is reasonable to assume that Peter got hi genius from Alexis. Although none of the Naryshkins ever displayed an brilliance, there is abundant testimony to the intellectual precocity o Tsarevitch Alexis Alexeyevitch and the intelligence of Theodore an Sophia.

The birth of Peter, the focus of all the Naryshkins' hopes, was a bitte blow to the Miloslavsky party. The Court seethed with intrigues. Sophia' relatives gloomily compared the sturdy boy with his sickly stepbrother watched the growing influence of Artamon Matveyev and envied th Naryshkins, who were cutting themselves large slices of the rich cak which was the Tsar's favour. Sophia was a conscious ally of the Miloslav sky clan long before she placed herself at its head.

Peter was a high-spirited, restless child of Herculean build. He was thre years old when Leopold I's envoys were received at the Kolomenskoy palace in 1675. Lisek gives a detailed account of their reception.

We arrived at the mansion at last. In the two courtyards, which were quite large, stood men-at-arms with numerous flags and all manner of weapons, among them two cannon known as 'serpentines'. The Tsar, his son Theodore and his boyars watched our arrival from the windows. This was the first occasion on which his son was officially presented as heir to the throne. A senior official standing by the ceremonial staircase bade us welcome on the Tsar's behalf.

The envoys replaced their hats and mounted the steps. At the top they were greeted by another nobleman who conducted them to the audience chamber, where two princes inquired after their health. His Majesty the Tsar was seated on an uncanopied throne with his august son on his left. Each of them was holding a sceptre surmounted by a crescent. On the Tsar's right stood Dolgoruky and Matveyev, Grand Voivode and Prime Minister respectively. On his left sat a large number of boyars and in front of him stood four *ryndas* of his personal bodyguard dressed in white and carrying axes with concave, sickle-shaped blades on their shoulders. The sole illumination in the audience chamber came from four windows decorated with gilded portraits.

The ambassadors then presented the Emperor's gifts to the Tsar, each article being called out in turn by an official. After that, the presents were carried one after another into an adjoining room. Finally, an interpreter announced that the envoys were invited to dine at the 'House of Ambassadors', and the audience was at an end.

'We had been told,' Lisek goes on, 'that the Tsarina was watching us from her hiding-place with her son Peter, who was not yet three.' The inquisitive child pushed the door of the closet open before the envoys had left the audience chamber, and Lisek reports that he caught sight of the Tsarina.

Outside, the envoys had their swords returned to them and set off for Moscow again. Mounted lackeys lit the road with torches when night fell, and the cavalcade reached Moscow at one o'clock in the morning.

CHAPTER FOURTEEN

HAPPINESS reigned in the Kremlin once more – or at least in the hear of the doting Tsar. Matveyev shielded him from all unpleasantnesse diplomatically smoothed over any difficulties that arose, carried out hi orders and indulged his whims.

Alexis Michaelovitch was an ardent lover of the theatre. Two yea after Patriarch Nikon had pressed him into issuing a decree directe against 'wearers of masks' we find him avidly reading a report fron Likhatchev, his ambassador in Florence, the city where Bishop Abrahan of Suzdal had marvelled at a performance of a mystery-play in 1437 Likhatchev was well aware of his master's passion for the theatre and wen out of his way to give a detailed description of what he saw at the Prince' court in 1658. It was the first time that the ambassador had seen a profan play.

> Rooms appear. One room appears and then vanishes below, to be replaced by another. There are six changes of scene in all. We are shown a sea disturbed by waves, and, in the sea, fish with men riding upon them. Above is the sky complete with clouds and people seated on them. Then a man with white hair descends from a cloud in a coach, and a most beautiful maiden descends from the other side. The horses harnessed to the coaches seem to be alive and move their limbs. The Prince explains that the man represents the sun and the woman the moon. In another scene, a man enters accompanied by fifty others, all clad in armour. They begin to fight with swords and sabres and to fire muskets. At the close three men are well and truly dead, or so it would seem. Then a number of handsome young men and comely maidens emerge from behind the curtain and dance. And we were able to see many other marvels as well.

It was fortunate for the Tsar, his family and Russia as a whole tha his confessor did not veto this quite unobjectionable hobby but modelle his attitude on that of the Byzantine emperors, who were not onl defenders of Orthodoxy but patrons of the arts. Like Artamon Matveyev Simeon Polotski encouraged the Tsar's fondness for the theatre. Every hing combined to soothe the Tsar's scruples, even Kiev Academy, which naugurated performances by its students. Foreigners living in Moscow lso enjoyed amateur theatricals. Describing his sojourn in Russia as English ambassador, Lord Carlisle recorded that a performance was held t his house in Moscow in 1664.

Learning that Johan Gregory, a former Polish cavalryman and now pastor of the Lutheran church in the German Quarter, had formed a troop of actors, the Tsar, who may even have attended one of their performances, commissioned him to form a company for his own theatre. The actors were at first recruited from among the children of soldiers and foreign merchants resident in the German Quarter.

A theatre was hurriedly erected at Preobrazhenskoye. It was a vast hall with walls swathed in emerald-green and raspberry-red cloth and floors covered with thick carpets. The seats, which were hardly the height of comfort, consisted of benches arranged in a semicircle with 'the Tsar's eat', upholstered in red, in the foreground. The stage was enclosed by curtains and illuminated by a multitude of tallow candles marshalled in ows flush with the floor of the proscenium.

On October 17th, 1672, Tsarevitch Peter's birth was celebrated by an entertainment of an unusual kind. It was a memorable moment for the Russian theatre when, to the thunder of organ music, the curtains were drawn back to reveal the stage for the first time. The wings were decorated with fir trees, the boards covered with red cloth. The vivid blue of the back-cloth or 'sky' had been achieved with the aid of more than three hundred yards of material. An actor read the prologue, the 'per-spectives', or scenery, were brought on, and finally the actors made their entrance clad in cloth of gold, satin, velvet and tin armour. The play, *Esther*, was clumsily acted and full of glaring anachronisms, but what did it matter!

Gregory, who staged the first play, went on to produce *Judith*, the comedy *Joseph the Pure* and the tragedy *Adam and Eve*. These pieces, which hailed from Germany, bore no resemblance whatsoever to theatrical works by the Fathers of Kiev Academy or St Dimitry of Rostov, or even the worldly Simeon Polotski. Despite the Biblical majesty of their subject-matter, they were imbued with a lay spirit which often expressed itself in terms of the utmost vulgarity. The audience was sometimes confronted by scenes worthy of Grand Guignol. People were shown being tortured and killed. Sound-effects, which were ear-splittingly realistic, included actual cannon-shots. The Jester, an obligatory character, popped up inopportunely in the middle of the action and amused or scandalized the public with coarse jokes of a highly scatological nature.

The new Tsarina and the princesses watched the entertainment fron boxes screened by grilles, but soon even these were to disappear, markin yet another stage in the Terem's emancipation.

During the intervals, when the spectators were temporarily exhauste by scenes of bloodshed and dismemberment, conjurers provided lighte entertainment. The Tsar was so enthralled that he refused to budge fron his seat for ten solid hours.

The first performance was given in German, a language which th majority of the audience found as unintelligible as the elaborate plot, bu it was such an enormous success that a dramatic school was opened i Moscow. It took only six days to improvise a winter theatre in th Kremlin. Cleaners dusted the decorations with swans' and pigeons feathers and all the windows and doors were carefully sealed to preven precious warmth from escaping. Young commoners from the Mestchan skaya and the *possads* were recruited to replace the German actors, togethe with some young civil servants. These first official members of th Russian theatre gave performances of *Judith*, *Tobias* and *Holophernes*. I 1672 the troop consisted entirely of foreigners and numbered sixty. In 167 the Russian company numbered twenty-six and in 1776 seventy-eight

Ringubern, one of Gregory's assistants, was right when he forecast a the time of the first performance of *Esther* that it would prove 'the makin of our fortune'. Foreigners received handsome salaries, whereas Russia actors were paid a mere pittance. In 1675, without actually going o strike, they addressed a large number of petitions to the Office of Foreig Affairs, which was responsible for the Russian theatre. Actors, technicians painters and carpenters all lodged complaints, but it is not recorde whether they received satisfaction. Theatres multiplied, among then popular establishments such as The People's Theatre, which stood in th Novodievitchy Field not far from the monastery of the same name. A large number of boyars emulated Artamon Matveyev and built privat theatres of their own.

One thing led to another, and the Russians discovered ballet: firs *Orpheus*, then *Holophernes* and *Artaxerxes*, performed to an orchestra accompaniment of organs, kettledrums and flutes.

Audiences were deeply impressed by the realism – not as yet 'socialist' – of dramatic performances, and were quick to shed tears when their heart were wrung by scenes of horror and bloodshed. As for clever stage effects simple folk tended to regard them as the result of a compact betwee actors and the Devil, and the more superstitious among them hastily made the sign of the Cross when they met performers, to ward off evil spirits.

Dramatic realism was accompanied by dramatic symbolism. The
idience knew in advance, for instance, that a white-clad woman with
ishevelled hair represented Mercy and that a woman carrying a sword
as Vengeance. The Lover was invariably melancholy, the Warrior
oastful.

Sophia not only shared her stepmother's and sisters' enthusiasm for
atching plays but performed in them herself in company with young
oys and girls from noble families. This was yet another indication of how
odernized life in the Terem had become in the closing years of Alexis's
ign. Sophia employed her knowledge of French to translate Molière's
e médecin malgré lui and wrote a tragedy of her own, *Catherine*, in which
ne of Tsarevitch Peter's playmates, Prince Alexis Schakovskoy, later
erformed, as he records in his memoirs.

* * *

The storm-clouds seemed to have dispersed, enabling the Tsar to look
ack and take stock of his career from the day when he ascended his
ther's throne as a youth.

Death seemed incredibly remote, but despite his new-found happiness
'sar Alexis found time to think of it. On September 1st, 1674, New Year's
)ay by contemporary reckoning, the sovereign solemnly proclaimed his
on Theodore heir to the throne.

There was no form of legislation governing the order of succession to
ie throne. Without convening a national assembly, Tsar Alexis appeared
efore the large crowd which had gathered in Red Square and pro-
laimed his eldest son heir to the throne. Tsarevitch Theodore's poor
ealth undoubtedly gave cause for anxiety and he might secretly have
referred to see the crown pass to Peter, but Peter was only a child.
'heodore's thoughtful nature, his virtues and sense of duty were well
nown to his father. He was now of an age to govern, and had he been
tronger he would have made an ideal monarch. Alexis Michaelovitch
id not consult public opinion. His father had been created by the boyars
nd was supported by the people through its representatives. In Michael's
lay, even the Duma had been subjected to a measure of democratic
ontrol by a national assembly representing all classes of society. Tsar
Michael had accepted certain conditions imposed by those who elected
im. Alexis Michaelovitch was Tsar by right of birth, and he never
orgot it.

When he presented Theodore Alexeyevitch to the people it was merely
o inform them of a *fait accompli* and also, perhaps, to cut short family

intrigues at Court. Once the announcement had been made, life returne to normal both inside the palace and out. No one either expected or hope for the demise of such a happy and likeable sovereign.

At Kolomenskoye and Izmailovo, surrounded by his children, laughin with Natalia or chatting with Matveyev, Alexis Michaelovitch sti looked forward to many years of life. The greatest ordeals of his reig were behind him. Peace had been established, after a fashion, with Swede and Poland. The Old Believers were still active, but the Church had th situation well under control. The only remaining threat was Turke Accounts would have to be settled with her sooner or later, but not b Tsar Alexis Michaelovitch. In January 1676 he was struck down by a unidentified disease, and on January 30th he realized that he was going t die. Lying in state surrounded by his friends, courtiers and retainers, th forty-seven-year-old Tsar still had time to prepare for his final journe in the manner befitting a Christian monarch. He blessed his eldest son i the presence of numerous witnesses and reaffirmed that he was leavin him the crown. Then, composedly and in full possession of his facultie he received extreme unction at the hands of Patriarch Joachim.

When the Tsar's testament was opened, it was found to contain th last preoccupations of a just man. Alexis Michaelovitch declared h unshakeable devotion to Orthodoxy and his desire for Christian perfe tion. He had not wished to leave the world without becoming reconcile with those whom he had wronged, and many of his bequests, not only t friends but to those from whom life had separated him, amounted t tokens of gratitude.

'Of my spiritual father, His Holiness Grand Sovereign Nikon, blesse prelate and pastor, although he no longer occupies the patriarchal thron God having willed otherwise, I ask pardon and forgiveness for my sins

The death-bell tolled. People everywhere were smitten with sorrow but nowhere more so than in the Terem, where the air was rent by cri of lamentation. The Tsarina's very genuine grief was tempered wit anxiety for herself and her children, but the presence of her old frien Artamon Matveyev reassured her. The palace prepared for a new reig and the people watched and prayed. For all his human failings, not voice was heard to accuse the dead man of cruelty or greed. Eve foreigners, usually so quick to criticize everything Russian, placed the verdict on record in terms more glowing than any monarch, king o tsar, had ever evoked. Mayerberg, the Austrian ambassador who was contemporary of Tsar Alexis and knew him well, wrote: 'He neve coveted another's possessions nor violated any man's life or honour

PART TWO

TSAR THEODORE ALEXEYEVITCH

(1676–82)

'Behold, how good and how pleasant it is for brethren to dwell together in unity! ... Praise the Lord, O my soul. I will sing praises unto my God while I have any being. The Lord loveth the righteous.'

Psalms 133 and *146*, translated into Russian verses by Tsar Theodore

CHAPTER FIFTEEN

HEMMED in by the furious activity which broke out among circles close to the throne almost before Alexis Michaelovitch had breathed his last, young Theodore presented a noble and pathetic figure, already dimmed by the shadow of death.

The power wielded by the Tsars of Muscovy was vested in them by God, and the sumptuous coronation ceremony was there to remind Theodore Alexeyevitch of that fact. Prayers were said in every church in the land throughout the night preceding the event. In the Cathedral of the Assumption workmen had already erected the dais and the five steps leading up to it. A carpet of scarlet cloth flowed from the threshold of the cathedral like a trail of blood. On the left of the sovereign's throne, a resplendent affair of gold-embroidered velvet set with precious stones, stood the Patriarch's throne, almost but not quite as magnificent. Noblemen marched solemnly from the palace bearing the imperial regalia and a pectoral cross set with a fragment of the True Cross.

Alone with his confessor, the young Tsar had been praying in his private chapel since dawn, and when the crowd of assorted dignitaries came to conduct him to his coronation he was ready to assume the heavy responsibilities of his new status.

Capped and dressed in gold brocade, decked out with pearl and diamond necklaces and wearing heavy, jingling chains of enamelled gold on their broad chests, boyars, noblemen, generals and senior officials led Theodore to meet his appointed destiny. Musketeers lined the route from the palace to the cathedral, and the impressive cortège was preceded by *ryndas* carrying silver axes on their shoulders.

Weighed down by imperial finery far too heavy for his frail form, Theodore Alexeyevitch bowed three times on reaching the doors and entered the nave, where the Patriarch greeted him, gave him his blessing and sprinkled him with holy water. The two men embraced and ascended the steps of the dais side by side. Having taken his place on the throne, Theodore listened to a lengthy address by the head of the Russian Church, to which he responded. Then two boyars of the highest rank wrapped the sovereign in the imperial cloak.

This done, the Patriarch laid his hands on the Tsar and hung the pectoral cross, with its precious relic, about his neck, reciting prayers specially composed for the occasion. Archimandrites then carried the crown, sceptre and orb from the altar and gave them to an archbishop standing at the Patriarch's side, who in turn handed the emblems to the Patriarch. Setting the crown on the Tsar's head, the Patriarch placed the sceptre in his right hand and the orb in his left while the clergy intoned the *Te Deum*.

Even then, the long ceremony was far from over. It was now time for Mass, in the course of which the Tsar received Communion 'in two kinds', as was customary in the Orthodox Church. After the consecration, the Patriarch approached Theodore and anointed his forehead, ears, neck, shoulders, arms, lips and hands, accompanying each unction with the words: 'This is the seal and gift of the Holy Spirit.' The pieces of tow with which the holy Chrism was applied were immediately burnt, and the Tsar was forbidden to wash the anointed places for seven days.

After Communion, the Tsar, who had not broken his fast since the night before, was allowed to partake of the *prosphora*, a small consecrated loaf. Then, High Mass concluded, the procession devoutly set off on pilgrimage. Theodore went on foot to the Cathedrals of the Archangel and the Annunciation, which stood inside the Kremlin precincts, pausing in the Cathedral of the Archangel to meditate beside the tombs of his father and other former Russian monarchs.

Throughout the tour, the Tatar tsarevitch of Kasimov showered 'abundance' on the Tsar's person from a bowl of gold pieces carried by Alexis Likhatchev, for whom the new reign portended growing influence and material prosperity.

Lavish and interminable banquets in the Granovitaya Palata and Terem palace rounded off a day which might have exhausted more robust men than the pale and youthful Tsar.

* * *

The people were still unfamiliar with the new Tsar, for Theodore's childhood had been almost as shielded from the public gaze as that of his sisters.

During 1674 and 1675 Alexis Michaelovitch often took his second son, then heir presumptive, on hunting expeditions at Izmailovo, Alexeyevskoye or Kolomenskoye. In October and December 1675, Theodore, together with the rest of the Tsar's family, attended the theatrical performances at Kolomenskoye. On December 13th of the same year, Alexis Michaelovitch left Kolomenskoye to hunt at Sokolovo, while Theodore accompanied Tsarina Natalia, the Tsarevitches Ivan and Peter and their sisters on a pilgrimage. Forty-eight days later, during the night of January 29th–30th, Alexis Michaelovitch met his untimely end, and the timid and reserved boy became Tsar of all the Russias. Then came the coronation, with its two days of festivities and public merrymaking, after which the coloured lanterns were extinguished and the boy was left alone with the unfamiliar problems of his new status.

The Tsar was only just fifteen. He had inherited not only his father's love of literature and the sciences but his devout and benevolent nature. Less imperious and hot-tempered than Alexis Michaelovitch, Tsar Theodore may not have had much taste for power, but he applied himself to his duties conscientiously, choosing the right advisers to interpret his intentions rather than carrying them out in person. Fortunately, his tutor Simeon Polotski was still alive at the beginning of his reign and continued to wield considerable influence.

Theodore Alexeyevitch preferred the gentle pleasures of humanism to the fierce joys of war and the chase. He knew Latin and Polish, wrote verse, patronized painters and singers, delighted in literature and the sciences, practised meditation and enjoyed intellectual pursuits. Being endowed with a highly developed aesthetic sense, the youthful Tsar compensated for the lack of exercise to which his failing health condemned him by concentrating his attention on beautiful clothes and fine furniture, the noble horses in his stables and the flourishing gardens which he maintained with even greater care than his father had done. Tanner, who came to Moscow in 1678 as treasurer of the Polish embassy, records in an account of his trip[1] that he saw two gardens near the German Quarter, of which one had been laid out in the Italian style and was extremely beautiful. 'The Tsar,' he noted, 'takes such pleasure in it that he comes to walk there at least once a week.' Not far from the gardens stood a glass-works and a paper-mill. Theodore was equally interested in technical subjects. Russian and foreign master-craftsmen employed in the Kremlin's workshops received very high salaries for the period and their work was closely followed by the Tsar.

* * *

For a while, nothing stirred in the palace. Artamon Matveyev was still Minister of Foreign Affairs and had retained all the other posts which the late Tsar had entrusted to him, among them that of administrator of

[1] Quoted by Tereshchenko, *Survey of Lives of Senior Foreign Office Officials*, St Petersburg, 1837, p. 225.

the Palace pharmacy. Then everything started to happen at once. Theodore Alexeyevitch's various relatives pushed forward, elbowing their rivals out of the way. No quarter was given in the scramble for the power and favours that would flow from the hands of the young monarch from then on.

The Miloslavskys were kings of the castle once more. Ivan, the Tsar's maternal uncle, an alert and cunning man with a gift for intrigue, was more than a match for the Naryshkins. Tsarina Natalia's father was devoid of intelligence and subtlety and her brothers were hare-brained young men who had been dazzled by their sudden rise in the world. All of them were heartily detested for their garrulity and arrogance by boyars and commoners alike. The only member of the Naryshkin camp who represented any threat to the Miloslavskys' ambitions was Matveyev, who was as well-versed in public affairs as in palace intrigues. Did Matveyev hope to place little Peter on the throne so that he could govern in his name and in the name of the Tsarina, who would thus become regent and owe him everything? There is no historical evidence of such a plot at this juncture, though it is probable that the idea had crossed Matveyev's mind. Theodore was delicate and had not yet married. Ivan was universally acknowledged to be incapable of acceding to the throne. But between planning for a time when the throne would be vacant and poisoning a legitimate Tsar lay a gulf which Matveyev's conscience would probably have forbidden him to cross.

Miloslavsky, on the other hand, was not a man to shrink from slander, especially when it could serve his purposes so effectively. The superabundance of honours enjoyed by Matveyev during the latter years of Tsar Alexis's reign had aroused great antipathy, and his rivals were only too happy to back any plot hatched by the Tsar's uncle.

Since the Minister of Foreign Affairs was not unpopular with the masses, the conspirators began to play on people's credulity and superstition by spreading rumours that he practised black magic and consorted with demons. A more plausible pretext had to be invented for Theodore's benefit. The Tsar's health had continued to decline since his coronation despite his doctors' efforts and the medicines which they poured down his throat, so it was only too easy for Ivan Miloslavsky to point out that all these medicines had been prepared in the Palace pharmacy under Matveyev's direction.

Miloslavsky was not, as we have said, the only man to yearn for Matveyev's downfall. He was abetted in his endeavours by personal enemies of the Minister such as Volynsky, a senior official in the Office of Foreign Affairs whose wife was greatly sought after by the recluses of the

Terem for her skill at embroidery with gold thread, and two former tutors of the Tsar, Prince Theodore Kurakin and the nobleman Khitrovo, whose wife was a lively woman with a well-oiled tongue and a deep dislike of Tsarina Natalia.

It was impossible for Theodore Alexeyevitch to disbelieve Kurakin's and Khitrovo's insinuations. He had known both men from his infancy, and since he felt himself growing weaker every day it was easy for them to persuade him that the medicines supplied by Matveyev were nothing less than slow poisons calculated to consign him to one of the sarcophagi in the Cathedral of the Archangel. Once the Tsar was convinced, Matveyev was lost. He was officially accused of having enriched himself by dishonest means, of having taken bribes, sold favours and ruined a large number of noblemen by extorting land from them by blackmail – charges which probably had some basis in fact.

Only a few months after Alexis Michaelovitch's death his friend Artamon Matveyev was an exile, the true reasons for his disgrace camouflaged by an appointment as voivode of Verkhoturye in Siberia.

At the same time, a report from the secret police indicated that Ivan, one of Tsarina Natalia's brothers, had told a musketeer named Orel (Eagle): 'You are an eagle, but there is a still larger eagle. If you rid us of him, Tsarina Natalia will know how to reward you.' Only a man of Ivan Naryshkin's unbelievable stupidity could have made such an imprudent remark.

Ivan was summarily tried and condemned to be 'flogged with the knout, burnt by fire, torn apart by pincers and tortured to death.' This, however, was only a formula. The Tsar commuted Ivan's terrible sentence to one of banishment in perpetuity and sent his brother Athanasius to keep him company.

Matveyev left Moscow to take up his post at Verkhoturye, putting a brave face on his abrupt fall from favour. Since he was still a wealthy man, his cortège consisted of a hundred or more servants and a large quantity of baggage. Accompanying him were his wife, his ten-year-old son Andrei, his almoner and his son's faithful tutor, a Polish nobleman named Poborski.

On reaching the town of Kazan he was overtaken by an official from his former department, Ivan Gorokhov. Being an old enemy of his, Gorokhov was the willing bearer of evil tidings. This time, Matveyev was officially accused of trafficking with the Devil and practising black magic. Gorokhov took great relish in humiliating his former chief. He rummaged among Matveyev's possessions for a full month, making an inventory of them under the pretext of searching for books on sorcery.

The former favourite was then informed that he had been stripped of the title of boyar, that his possessions had been confiscated and that he was to be taken under heavy guard, like a common malefactor, to a place of perpetual exile, namely Pustozersk, a wretched little town on the shores of the Arctic Ocean. His wife returned to Moscow with a party of servants, but his son, his almoner, Poborski and some fifty servants accompanied him in simple peasant carts across the icy wastes which were the home of Samoyedes and savage Hennis.

Life was hard for the exiles in Pustozersk, and Matveyev and his son were both stricken with scurvy. Moscow was bombarded with letters and petitions from the Tsarina's adoptive father and protector. To Prince Yury Dolgoruky he wrote:

> He through whose valour Oriental Greece resounded with glory went his way begging, blind Belisarius entreating passers-by! Give alms to Belisarius! Be moved by the misfortune of him who conquered the Empire's foes and himself fell prey to calumny ... Though I shed tears, I never cease to trust in God. And you, Prince Dolgoruky, have you abandoned me? I know not my crime ... I trust in God. The sovereign's heart is in the hand of the Lord.

Matveyev also wrote to the Tsar:

> The sixth summer of my suffering is at hand, Tsar, yet you have never lent ear to the voice of your servant, who cries out to you ... Be as merciful as Emperor Titus, who would weep whenever a day passed without his doing good. I am imprisoned at the confines of the sea, I suffer from the bitter cold and can expect no mercy or intercession except it be from you, Sovereign. Bid them examine my case.

But these missives never reached the Tsar. Miloslavsky and his friends had a finger in every pie, and Tsarina Natalia's lack of influence over her stepson may be gauged from her inability to melt his normally compassionate heart in Matveyev's favour.

CHAPTER SIXTEEN

MILOSLAVSKY had cunningly succeeded in ousting Matveyev, but it was now his turn to be outmanœuvred. Fearing that his influence over the young monarch was becoming too complete, Bogdan Khitrovo and the Prince Dolgoruky to whom Matveyev was addressing his pathetic appeals from the Arctic Ocean started to encourage Alexis Likhatchev, the nobleman who had carried the bowl filled with gold pieces at Theodore's coronation.

Like the favourites of the preceding reign, Likhatchev did not belong to an illustrious family, although Alexis Michaelovitch had sent one of his relations on a mission to Florence to thank Grand Duke Ferdinand of Tuscany for the welcome which he had given Muscovite envoys in Venice and to negotiate customs exemption for Russian traders, offering Tuscan merchants a caviare concession in return.

Alexis Likhatchev was an eminently respectable man. He was not young, having been one of Theodore Rtistchev's friends and associates and having, like him, belonged to the Zealots of Religion, the group dedicated to religious reform and public education. Studious and cultured, Alexis Likhatchev later wrote a life of Tsar Theodore, to whom he remained deeply attached throughout his life. In 1677, Theodore appointed him a 'gentleman of the table'. He was held in great esteem by all parties, and Matveyev himself described him as 'a man of great integrity, full of intelligence and virtue'.

Another newcomer to the Tsar's circle was Ivan Yazykov, sponsored by Khitrovo and at first supported by Miloslavsky. Yazykov was also intelligent and well educated, but he was above all a shrewd courtier and as ambitious as his patrons – so much so that, according to a contemporary, Khitrovo very soon 'felt the hardness of the bit which his protégé placed in his mouth'.

These two men, who became loyal and competent advisers of the young Tsar, were joined in 1681 by a third, Prince Vasily Golitsyn, who belonged to one of the most illustrious families in the land and had virtually grown up on the steps of the throne. He had been a member of the palace staff since the age of nine and held senior rank at fifteen. Tsar Theodore invested him with the title of boyar when he was thirty-three.

Likhatchev, Yazykov and Golitsyn handled affairs of state between the three of them, since the post of Minister of Foreign Affairs remained vacant for five years after Matveyev's dismissal. Volynsky was appointed to the post in 1681, but he was never more than a pawn in the hands of the men who really governed Russia – and competent hands they were. Even though we must deplore the injustice done to Artamon Matveyev, we can only admire the young sovereign for having accepted as his advisers three men of such great merit and liberal views.

* * *

Russia was slowly emerging from economic stagnation at this period. Her exchequer was still in a depleted state and her sorely tried inhabitants still as heavily taxed.

Miliukov, an historian who made a very exhaustive study of Russia's finances in the seventeenth century, tells us that her gross revenue amounted to a million and a half roubles, though it would be risky to assess the present-day equivalent of that sum. He also notes that taxes on liquor accounted for the bulk of government revenue. Direct taxation produced only 44 per cent of total revenue, 16 per cent of which came from special imposts. As for outgoings, half the budget was earmarked for military expenditure, the Tsar's Court took up 16 per cent, and transport and postal services had to make do with 5 per cent. When Theodore Alexeyevitch came to the throne in 1676, tax receipts were more than a million roubles in arrears, and the government had to solve a new economic crisis in 1681 without resorting to supplementary taxation, the country having already been squeezed dry.

Although plans for reform were born in the minds of the three men whose advice the Tsar accepted so willingly, the Duma or Council of State continued to be a consultative body of some importance. Its members included boyars and other dignitaries, gentlemen of the Council, almost all of whom belonged to the petty nobility and died without ever attaining more senior rank, and clerks of varied origin, who were often educated men and formed the lynch-pin of the whole organization. As for the National Assembly or Zemsky Sobor, which Klyuchevsky describes as having played an essential role at the time of the first Romanov's election, its story during the seventeenth century was one of gradual disappearance. What made this even more regrettable was that the Zemsky Sobor, having come into being immediately after the Time of

Troubles, was really the embryo from which parliamentary democracy on Western lines could, and should, have grown.

* * *

The first national assembly was a symbol of the sacred unity of the ntire Russian nation and genuinely represented all classes of society. Its owers as a consultative and legislative body were great enough to enable t to give Russia an elected monarch, but the first appearance of the people n the political scene was destined to be a democratic phenomenon of hort duration. Alexis Michaelovitch steadily curtailed the role of popular onsultation by strengthening the sovereign's authority and weeding the ower classes out of the Assembly. The peasants were virtually un-epresented on the National Assembly convened in 1649 to work out the ew legal code, and its periodical meetings after that date dispensed with heir presence entirely. Henceforth, it was only convened sporadically n times of crisis and in a purely consultative role, the major problems f government being handled by the Tsar after discussion with the nembers of the Duma and the Church Council.

During Michael's reign the National Assembly played such an impor-ant role that it was convened on ten separate occasions. Under Tsar Alexis t met only five times, all at the beginning of his reign. Under Theodore t was convened only twice, each time in committee form, the participants eing limited strictly to representatives of the class directly concerned in he matters under discussion.

Apart from one extremely important reform – the abolition of the ight of precedence – the measures proposed and implemented by Theodore Alexeyevitch's government were hardly spectacular, but they vere all of practical value and put an end to some piece of barbarism or onfusion. The reforms which had been initiated under Alexis Michaelovitch proceeded without clashes or violence. Tsar Theodore ontinued to grant privileges to the nobility on the very eve of abolishing he secular right of precedence, but he simultaneously tightened up the egulations governing their liability to State service.

'The Tsar's service' does not seem to have held any particular appeal for oung noblemen, who did their best to get out of it. In 1678 the Tsar rdered a census of all landed estates together with the exact number of peasant homesteads' owned by each proprietor. Young noblemen and oyars' sons were called upon to join the armed forces by special decree. Those who owned less than twenty-three peasant homesteads were nrolled in the cavalry and received an annual salary of twenty-three roubles. Young noblemen who owned no land or peasants were also drafted into the cavalry, but without pay. Wealthier individuals who owned more than twenty-three homesteads had, whether they liked it or not, to join the urban regiments, whose prestige was greater than the cavalry even though they formed part of the infantry.

Another decree of 1678 specified that:

> Many noblemen and boyars' sons have children, nephews and grandchildren fit for the Tsar's service, but do not enrol them. The sovereign ordains that they be enrolled for service as soon as they be of suitable age; and, should you shield them from this service, the sovereign ordains that they be excluded from the list of promotion and that all those of junior families be enrolled in the urban nobility.

This threat to deprive high-born youths of advancement and honorific rank and to enrol those from less industrious families in the urban, or inferior, nobility apparently failed to achieve results, since the government was compelled to revive the subject each year and devise new penalties for non-compliance.

In 1679 another decree appeared. 'The Grand Sovereign commands men holding rank at Moscow to enrol those of their sons, nephews brothers and kinsmen who are of an age to enter service. Should they fail to do so, the census-takers will conduct the aforementioned to the county town and enrol them in regiments of cavalry.'

It is a little difficult to understand the nobility's reluctance to fulfil an obligation which still carried so many prerogatives, particularly if the 'novice' came of a wealthy or illustrious family. In fact, State servitors were rewarded not only with rank but also with grants of land, and the distribution of domanial land to the nobility survived until the reign of Peter the Great.

* * *

Serfs had no juridical or social status in national life, but peasants were of great importance to the country's economy, and noblemen who owned a large number of them were more or less assured of a successful career because they brought a certain number of men-at-arms with them into the Tsar's service when they reported for duty themselves.

Agricultural labour being a source of wealth, peasants on the run from one landed proprietor could easily find refuge with another, who regarded them as manna from Heaven. Tsar Alexis had already issued a decree discouraging this abuse in 1671. Anyone who harboured a fugitive had to return him to his owner and hand over four of his own peasants in compensation. The illicit practice continued despite this, and in 1681 Theodore Alexeyevitch issued a new decree under which the guilty party had to pay the rightful owner an indemnity of ten roubles a year for the 'absence' of each peasant harboured on his land, plus ten kopeks for every day that intervened between the lodging of the complaint and the return of the peasant to his original master.

In 1680 the government inaugurated a register of landed property, thereby putting an end to the sanguinary feuds which often existed between neighbours. It also took the opportunity to make a census of the peasants living on each estate.

* * *

In 1681 Theodore made a half-hearted attempt to revive the use of the National Assembly. All he really did was to form a committee of interested parties to examine the problem of taxing land and real estate, though it may be noted that a few peasant representatives attended its meetings. Little was achieved, incidentally, because the committee members failed to master the complexities of the problem.

During Theodore's six years on the throne his government drafted several amendments to the Ulozhenye laws. The Tsar rescinded the practice of cutting off hands and feet (the penalty prescribed for certain crimes, notably theft) and replaced it by deportation to Siberia. It might be noted that in contemporary England thieves were being condemned to death. The punishment of quartering was not implemented under Theodore, although it was still prescribed for crimes of a particularly grave nature.

In general, Theodore merely followed the path taken by his father, though in a somewhat less forceful manner. Nothing precipitate, no revolutionary reforms, steady progress along humanitarian lines: such were the hall-marks of Theodore's reign over his vast and cumbersome dominions. It was the reign of a wise and worthy monarch in whom thoughts of personal glory were subordinated to the will to do good, and we can only wonder that the frail youth managed, without provoking violence, to abolish the right of precedence that had weighed so heavily on public life.

CHAPTER SEVENTEEN

THE Great Schism was far from being resolved. Among other surviving leaders of the *raskol* was Avvakum, the Fiery Archpriest. Flogged, chained, imprisoned and banished, the obstinate cleric may have been ready to die for his cause but he still hoped to see it triumph during his lifetime. Having waited in vain for Tsar Alexis to repent and return to the Old Belief, Avvakum now pinned his hopes on young Theodore.

Like most men, Avvakum was sometimes inconsistent. He summoned his co-religionists to martyrdom because, according to him, it was their duty to become expiatory sacrifices for the iniquities perpetrated by Nikon. He also deplored the fact that his own children had confessed their sins before the 'heretics' when threatened with death rather than submit to the ordeal of purification – that, as he so succinctly put it, 'they lacked the courage to grasp the martyr's crown'. Yet Avvakum himself strove to evade the Kingdom of Heaven just when – the phrase is again his own – it was falling into his mouth like a choice morsel.

Avvakum was in a monastery in the far north when he learnt of Alexis's death and Theodore's accession – very belatedly, for news travelled slowly in the seventeenth century.

'I am a dog, yet I aspire to a morsel of your grace,' the Archpriest wrote to the new sovereign. He begged Theodore for clemency because he was 'anointed with the chrism of joy and his servant was shivering in chains'. Pleading not only for himself but for his co-religionists, the Old Believer soon abandoned his moving pleas in favour of threats.

> If you do not help us in the name of the Lord, it is He who will help us. The Pillars of the Temple [bishops] are shaken by the stratagems of the Fiend, the patriarchs are enfeebled, the Holy Fathers failing, the whole clergy scarcely alive. God knows if it be not already dead! ... Pour out wine and oil upon them, that they recover their spirits. If, Sovereign Tsar, you gave me liberty, I should confound them all within the space of a day. It would not soil my hands, but rather sanctify them. And if, in addition, I could have the

> assistance of a wise and powerful voivode such as Prince Yury Dolgoruky [Theodore's former tutor] ... To begin with, we should cleave the dog Nikon in quarters, and then the others, the Nikonians ... Never fear, Prince Theodore Alexeyevitch, it were no sin. Rather, we should win celestial crowns ...

It was a lengthy missive. Patriarch Joachim, too, came in for some brickbats. 'Tell Joachim, the Patriarch, that he must abandon the Roman laws. The cause is an evil one. He is a simple man, that Joachim. Secret agents from Rome have given him viper's venom to drink. Pardon me, Father Yakimoishka!'

* * *

Born in 1620, Patriarch Joachim belonged to a family of Muscovite noblemen called Savelov. He had been married, but his wife and children died before he was thirty-five, and in 1655 the widower entered a monastery. Two years later, for no good reason that anyone could see, Patriarch Nikon took the illiterate monk into his entourage, and it was then, at the age of thirty-seven, that Joachim embarked on the studies which he was never to pursue very far.

At a period when an intellectual elite was evolving and gaining ground, Joachim's ignorance made him a sitting target for the gibes of the circles in which he moved. He was not devoid of influential patrons, however, and led an exemplary life. In 1664 he was appointed Archimandrite of the Tchudov monastery in the heart of the Kremlin. Its proximity to the palace enabled him to win a number of friends among the boyars and noblemen of the old guard, and it was probably they who drew Alexis Michaelovitch's attention to the abbot. Promotion followed rapidly. Elevated to the rank of Metropolitan of Novgorod, Joachim soon displayed a personal initiative which confined itself to the efficient management of religious ceremonies and an almost exclusive preoccupation with the outward forms of religion.

In 1674 the Metropolitan mounted the patriarchal throne, which had been vacant since Nikon's dismissal. He was to remain on it for sixteen years, playing an important though not always opportune role in the nation's religious life during Theodore's reign and Sophia's regency.

Joachim was not of the same calibre as Nikon. He figures in Russian history as a narrow-minded and ungenerous man whose virtues were as inconsiderable as his shortcomings. His attitude towards anything he could not understand was characterized by distrust. As Patriarch, he pursued the policy of anti-schismatic repression initiated by his predecessor and urged the government to take even firmer and more definite action thereby solving nothing and jeopardizing the chances of a reconciliation between the two opposing parties.

While Simeon Polotski was still alive, the Latinist movement was tolerated in Moscow despite the new Patriarch's hostility, and Joachim was compelled to allow monks and scholars who had received their training in the academies of the south-west to continue their role in public education.

Although Joachim used the Greeks in his campaign against the Latinists he had no great admiration for them either. Where Nikon had tried to instil a spirit of universality into the Russian Church, Joachim forced it into a narrow, national framework.

* * *

As for Avvakum's letters to the sovereign, which the exiled schismatic always concluded with a blessing, it need hardly be said that they contributed nothing towards resolving the differences that existed between himself and the Church and government. They also displayed utter confusion of mind. Avvakum was no doubt right in accusing the Patriarch of naïvety, but anyone who could think him amenable to foreign influence, be it Greek or Roman, was not being very perspicacious himself. However, Avvakum was far from Moscow at the time and rumours from the capital took a long time to reach him.

Between imprisonments and deportations, Avvakum found time to return to Moscow on several occasions. Other leaders of the *raskol*, though they may have lacked Avvakum's stature and great literary talent, were no less energetic, determined and fanatical.

Dissent spread, gaining support in every class of society and penetrating the remotest corners of the land. Spiritual colonies of Old Believers came into being and grew, evading control and playing a political role. Champions of the Old Belief were recruited from the ranks of those who opposed the new spirit and persisted in thinking that education was pernicious, that Western influence corrupted the mind and that the least disturbance of established tradition threatened the salvation of the soul.

Before long, this amorphous mass entered the clandestine gloom of religious anarchy. Sects were formed, some of a vile nature. Their promoters got out of hand and rejected all spiritual authority, each believing in his own personal revelation, and a dispute which had once been confined to the sphere of dogma now engendered the strangest heresies. The leader of one religious community, an unordained peasant-turned-monk, decreed that priests were worthless and that the sacraments could be administered by anyone, women included. Another taught that marriage was a sin and that children born of concupiscence should be thrown into the forest as fodder for wild beasts and expiatory sacrifices. A third declared that nothing on earth was holy, and that it was up to God, as the sole repository of holiness, to redeem men in His own way without their having to work for their salvation.

Even Avvakum and other Old Believers who had not fallen into such heresies eventually forgot that the Orthodox Church regarded suicide as a mortal sin. The Fiery Archpriest and his friends started to preach self-destruction by fire, declaring that deliberate martyrdom was blessed in the eyes of the Lord.

Flames sprang up in the Russian forests as, chanting psalms, whole communities of fanatics lit enormous bonfires and flung themselves into the inferno. Appalling scenes occurred when mothers threw their own children into the flames, or when wretched men and women changed their minds at the last moment and tried to escape, only to be forced by their co-religionists to undergo an agonizing death which they no longer wanted.

Passions ran so high and mental turmoil was so intense that the government, egged on by the Patriarch and powerless to stop the scandal, lit bonfires of its own, but it failed to improve the situation despite all the resources at its command.

Gentle and respectful of Patriarch Joachim's authority, Theodore Alexeyevitch did not venture to oppose the measures which the churchman deemed it necessary to take. The Patriarch, an illiberal man who never forgot a grudge, continued to persecute his predecessor, whose moral authority he resented. Nikon had long ago relinquished all political authority, but for some reason Joachim ordered him to be retried and consigned to another monastery where he was treated with the utmost harshness. Neither the Tsar, his aunt Tatiana nor the other members of the royal family ceased to show their affection for the former Patriarch and continually sent him tokens of moral and material support.

In 1680, after Nikon had spent five miserable years in the far north, the monks of the Monastery of the Resurrection, founded in Moscow by the former Grand Sovereign Patriarch, made representations to Theodore Alexeyevitch with a view to obtaining Nikon's transfer to the capital. By now more conscious of his authority, Theodore at once consented to the transfer despite Joachim's opposition.

When the news reached the exile, he immediately made preparations for his long journey. All along the way, the Grand Sovereign was acclaimed by respectful but enthusiastic crowds. Peasants vied with each other for the honour of hauling his boat along rivers, and weeping devotees flocked to kiss his hands.

The old man's heart must have been gladdened by his triumphal progress, but he never reached Moscow alive. At Yaroslavl he called a halt, realizing that he was about to die. Having rested, he combed his long hair and beard and summoned his confessor. Then he confessed, received Communion and asked the priest to administer the last rites. Finally, hands folded on his breast, Grand Sovereign Patriarch Nikon, indefatigable crusader for the universality, authority and doctrinal purity of the Orthodox Church, closed his eyes for the last time. It was August 17th, 1681.

His remains were transported to Moscow amid scenes of popular lamentation. Tsar Theodore requested the Eastern Patriarchs to reinstate the dead man in his patriarchal dignity, which they did, and his obsequies were celebrated with due pomp and ceremony. Later, Tsarevna Tatiana made several gifts to the Monastery of the Resurrection, notably a precious reliquary containing the right hand of St Tatiana.

* * *

In the same year, a Church Council met at the Kremlin to consider proposals put forward by Tsar Theodore and take the requisite action.

Patriarch Joachim's failings were considerable, and his narrow-mindedness and intolerance made him an unendearing personality, but he was far from colourless. He was autocratic, obstinate and endowed with great energy. Like his great predecessor, he sought to obtain the clergy's independence of temporal power and secure personal control over the management of religious affairs. He always knew what he wanted but, being almost completely illiterate, he could only express himself through a secretary or 'ghost-writer' who drafted pastoral letters and various treatises directed against the Old Believers.

When admonitions and threats proved ineffective, Patriarch Joachim nudged the government into applying more brutal measures. The irrepressible Avvakum and a large number of the more prominent Old Believers were sentenced by the secular authorities to undergo the death which they had so often commended to their initiates.

On April 14th, 1682, some days before the death of Tsar Theodore, the Fiery Archpriest entered the wooden cage which was to be his last abode. Legend has it that when the sinister contraption was deposited in the flames four white doves rose from it, symbolizing the souls of Avvakum and his three companions ascending into Heaven.

* * *

The Old Believers were not, as we have seen, Patriarch Joachim's only source of worry in his capacity as the man responsible for the destinies of the Russian Church. Fear of Rome and 'the Roman schism', which he was inclined to regard as a heresy, made him distrust everything that bore the imprint of Latinism. Simeon Polotski's standing at Court and the affection and esteem shown him by two successive Tsars rendered his position impregnable.

Polotski died in 1680, leaving his magnificent library to his favourite pupil, Sylvester Medviedev, who later paid homage to Polotski's memory by publishing a complete edition of his works. In the same year, Tsar Theodore appointed Medviedev principal of the Zaikonospassky School. Theodore had a high regard for his old tutor's protégé, who had been bound to Polotski by ties of mutual esteem and enduring affection. Like Polotski, Medviedev was a Latinist, although he had first seen the light of day at Kursk in Great Russia and was not of Little Russian origin.

Sylvester Medviedev was born in 1641. He must have received an excellent schooling, for he was only twenty-two when, in 1663, he first made his mark as deputy head of a department in the Office of Secret Affairs.[1] In 1665 he was sent to the school which had been recently founded by Rtistchev and his friends in the Zaikonospassky monastery, where he lived in the shadow of his master, Simeon Polotski, until 1668. Medviedev's intelligence and eloquence made him the school's star pupil. He studied rhetoric, history, philosophy and theology and knew Latin, Polish, Greek and German.

Medviedev was still a layman when he accompanied Ordyn-Nastchokin to Courland in 1668–9 and assisted the Minister of Foreign Affairs during his negotiations with the Swedes and Poles. He might very easily have made a brilliant career in the civil service and become a senior official – perhaps even a minister – but in 1672 he went into retreat at a hermitage near the ancient city of Putivl. There he underwent a moral crisis, possibly inspired by the temptations of the age. However, his reputation for wisdom and morality was already so great that he was inundated with visitors seeking advice and consolation. Unable to pursue his meditations

[1] Of the thirty-nine *prikazy* or government departments the most important was the Prikaz of Secret Affairs, set up by Tsar Alexis and presided over by the sovereign himself. The weighty matters discussed there were never raised in the Duma.

in peace, Medviedev fled to another monastery where, in 1674, he took his vows. Three years later, in 1677, he was recalled to the capital at Tsar Theodore's request and transferred to the Spassky monastery, where the ageing Simeon Polotski prepared to hand over the reins to him. In 1678, Patriarch Joachim appointed him editor of sacred literature, and by 1680 his position was firmly established.

* * *

Although Russia had no direct contact with Rome, the continual influx of monks and scholars from the south-west served as a link between the two great but estranged religions.

At the beginning of the seventeenth century, the authorities in Polish-occupied Little Russia had waged a vigorous and brutal campaign against Orthodoxy, as the number of Orthodox martyrs testified. The hetman Nalivaiko was boiled alive in a copper cauldron. Another hetman, Pavligoga, was martyred with a large number of companions, and many priests, monks and laymen died because they refused to be converted to Catholicism and accept union. It was not until 1650, when John Casimir had mounted the throne, that an agreement signed by the Polish authorities and the Orthodox community established some semblance of religious peace. Uniate churches in Orthodox communities in Poland and Lithuania were closed, the Orthodox Church became independent of the State, and secular property belonging to the Church received official recognition. Jesuit colleges in Kiev, seat of the Polish Senate and still in Polish hands at this period, were shut down. In 1654, when part of Little Russia was restored to Russia, the position of Orthodox Christians improved still further. The Orthodox Church lost more members in Lithuania and White Russia than in the Volhynian and Little Russian areas of Red Russia, where conversion under duress proved a failure.

However, monks and scholars in these regions were in a dilemma. Starved of education, they were faced with two alternatives: either to abandon their studies, or pursue them in Polish academies run – and brilliantly so – by the Jesuits. A certain number of them embraced Catholicism in order to gain admittance and, having completed their studies, returned to Russia and asked to be readmitted to the bosom of the Orthodox Church, attributing their conversion to papist trickery. Naturally enough, some of these men never entirely threw off their Catholic instructors' influence, and the 'Latin spirit' so distrusted by Patriarch Joachim and many other Russians continued to live on in them.

There was also a new factor to be reckoned with. At a time when scholarship and theology were being rent by conflicting trends, men appeared at the helm of government who were comparatively indifferent to spiritual values, who dissociated themselves from or at least took no active interest in the faith of their ancestors, and who possessed what we should now call the lay spirit. It is impossible, for instance, to tell where Yazykov's or Likhatchev's sympathies lay, and although Prince Vasily Golitsyn displayed goodwill towards the Latinists, he seems to have been prompted solely by the attraction which the Western way of life held for him.

CHAPTER EIGHTEEN

THE six years of Tsar Theodore's reign were unmarred by any form of internal unrest save the religious conflict which still raged with such unremitting fury. On the other hand, the young monarch had to face a grave military situation arising out of the war with Turkey, which Alexis Michaelovitch had begun but did not have time to conclude satisfactorily.

Having settled his disputes with Sweden and Poland with varied success, Alexis had found Russia threatened by her old and powerful enemy, the Sultan. The Sublime Porte was in a favourable position because it had just signed trade agreements with France and England, highly advantageous to both countries, which effectively precluded the possibility of their joining any alliance directed against their new partner. In 1664 Turkey negotiated a pact with the Holy Roman Empire; in 1669 another, with Venice, under which Crete was ceded to her; and in 1672 she succeeded in acquiring Podolia and Kamenets, a Polish town of strategic importance.

Even where Sweden was concerned, the position was far from being as satisfactory as it had been towards the end of Alexis's reign. After signing the treaty linking them with France, the Swedes marched into Brandenburg, where they were defeated by the Elector, Frederick William. Denmark turned against Sweden and the Diet of Ratisbon declared her an enemy of the Empire. The Netherlands, the Bishopric of Münster and the Duchy of Limburg all followed suit. In normal times, Moscow would have profited by a situation which was so fraught with danger for the Swedes but so favourable to Russian aims, and Alexis Michaelovitch would no doubt have exploited it if his hands had not been tied by a new threat from the opposite quarter.

Little Russia, which was divided between Russia and Poland and had been partially occupied by the latter's forces, was arousing the Sultan's appetite.

* * *

In 1675, a Cossack colonel named Doroshenko, who had been elected hetman of the Polish-occupied right bank of the Dnieper, was seized by an ambition to become ruler of an independent Little Russia. The rebel leader over-estimated his strength, however, and was soon forced to place himself under the Sultan's protection, whereupon the Turks immediately occupied his territory and laid claim to the whole of the Ukraine.

Tsar Alexis had foreseen the possibility of a war with Turkey and made every effort to avoid it, but the series of Russian ambassadors sent to Constantinople with orders to settle matters on an amicable basis returned empty-handed. Turkey asserted her claims not only to Little Russia but the Caucasus as well, and in 1673, having invaded part of Poland, she seized upon the Tsar's protests as an additional pretext for war.

A year before, Russia had sent emissaries to several countries in Western Europe to try to form a coalition of Christian nations against the Porte. These emissaries had been well chosen. A Scottish Catholic named Menezius, who had been in Russian service for many years, visited Vienna in 1673; another foreigner, Vinnius, was sent to negotiate with England, France and Spain; and a Russian, Shetsov, made approaches to Sweden, Denmark and the Netherlands. Moscow knew that an alliance with France, England and Holland might still avert war, but the latter, foreseeing that Louis XIV's policies could well lead to a new war in Europe, were reluctant to commit themselves elsewhere. Pleading the importance of their trade with the countries of the Levant, France and England refused to lend their support.

However, France was interested in forming ties with Sweden, Poland and Turkey in order to strengthen her position vis-à-vis the Empire, and tried to secure Russian support in the event of a conflict with Sweden. In 1675 a treaty was signed between Russia and the Holy Roman Empire under the terms of which Moscow promised, in exchange for an undertaking from Austria to help her in the event of a war with Turkey, to send troops to the Swedish border after the close of hostilities in Europe, thereby preventing the Swedes from denuding their frontiers of men and sending them to the Austrian front.

Later on, in 1679, the Russian ambassador took care to stress the advantages which had accrued to the Empire from Russia's action and made new and insistent demands for the creation of a coalition against Turkey. As for Poland, her value to Russia as an ally was uncertain. In 1676, while negotiations for Russian military aid were still in progress, John Sobieski's government tried, unbeknown to the Russians and possibly on French advice, to reach an understanding with the Sultan. The result of this unfortunate piece of double-dealing was that Poland had to hand over Podolia and Kamenets to the Porte and undertake to support the Sultan against the Russians.

The immediate consequence of Doroshenko's submission to Turkey was an invasion not only of the right bank but also of part of the left bank of the Dnieper by Janissaries and Tatars. Their looting, extortion and crop-burning inspired such terror among the people under Doroshenko's jurisdiction that they abandoned him and fled to Russian-protected territory.

Discarded by the Turks and aware that he had been hoist with his own petard, the imprudent hetman belatedly repented and implored Moscow to come to his aid. He made his submission to the Russians by surrendering to Samoilovitch, hetman of the right bank of the Dnieper, who had remained loyal to his oath to the Muscovite Tsar. Alexis Michaelovitch ordered Samoilovitch to send Doroshenko to Moscow, a summons which Samoilovitch obeyed with great reluctance and only after it had been repeated several times, probably because he had given certain undertakings to Doroshenko at the time of his surrender.

'May God pardon Samoilovitch!' Doroshenko exclaimed on learning that he was to be handed over to Moscow. 'A condemned man is informed of his sentence, but he never told me of this threat.'

Doroshenko's fears were groundless. When he was brought to Moscow under escort in 1676 and led into the Tsar's presence, the Tsar confined himself to saying:

'Your crimes and errors are pardoned. You shall remain in Moscow to assist us in our parleys with the Crimea and the Turks.'

When his services were no longer required, Doroshenko was appointed voivode of Viatka, a town as devoid of charm then as it is today. Disguised exile was a lenient punishment for a man whose ambitions had provoked a murderous war.

Russia was, therefore, in a critical position when Tsar Alexis died. In response to a summons from Theodore, Ordyn-Nastchokin, now a monk, emerged from retirement and performed his last public duty by returning to Moscow and giving the government the benefit of his advice.

Samoilovitch, loyalist hetman of the left bank, and Prince Romodanovsky, voivode commanding the government troops, advanced toward Tchigirin, a town of strategic importance in Polish Little Russia. Tchigirin had been besieged since June 1677 by a substantial Turkish force commanded by Ibrahim Pasha. This comprised fifteen thousand of the proverbially ferocious infantrymen known as Janissaries, ten thousand Wallachian and Moldavian auxiliaries and forty thousand Tatars. Doroshenko's defection had compelled the Turks to look for another collaborator, and the Sultan had appointed as hetman of the right bank Yury Khmelnitsky, son of the same Bogdan who had offered Little

Russia to the Russian Crown. Khmelnitsky had no authority and was little more than a useful, and therefore privileged, captive, but Ordyn-Nastchokin's remark that Russia would be better advised to reach an understanding with Poland than place any reliance on the vacillating sympathies of the Little Russians had been vindicated yet again.

Tchigirin's garrison consisted of only twelve thousand men, but the army hurrying to its relief numbered twenty-five thousand Little Russians and thirty-two thousand Russians. Most of the Russian troops belonged to newly formed regiments and were well armed. Moreover, the Russians had brought a hundred and twenty-six pieces of artillery with them, whereas the Turks had only thirty-five.

The fortress of Tchigirin continued to hold out while the Tsar's army approached the Dnieper, and the river-crossing was effected in twenty-four hours.

On August 28th, one wing of Ibrahim Pasha's large army was defeated by the Russians and a number of Turkish officers killed, among them the Pasha's sons, the sons of the Khan of the Crimea and some Tatar princes.

During the night of August 29th, the Turks evacuated their positions outside Tchigirin and the Russians and Little Russians hurried in pursuit, only to be halted by lack of fodder and provisions. The fields and villages through which they passed had been burnt and devastated by the Tatars, making it impossible for them to feed either men or horses.

The army commanded by Romodanovsky and Samoilovitch withdrew along the left bank of the Dnieper and disbanded for the winter.

A year later, in June 1678, the Turks and Tatars reappeared before the walls of Tchigirin. The second-in-command of the fortress at this juncture was Patrick Gordon, the Scottish Catholic who had been one of the first foreign officers to go to the Tsar's aid at Kolomenskoye during the Copper Rebellion.

Having re-formed his army, Romodanovsky advanced on the Dnieper once more, but as soon as his troops crossed the river on July 20th twenty thousand Turkish soldiers commanded by the vizier Kara Mustapha and supported by Tatar horsemen attacked them in force. Russian losses were considerable, but thanks to his artillery Romodanovsky managed to establish himself on the opposite bank. There followed a number of sporadic engagements in which the Russian forces failed to gain any decisive advantage. In the circumstances, Romodanovsky and Samoilovitch thought it wiser to await the promised arrival of Kabarda (Caucasian) reinforcements under Prince Kapulat Tcherkassky.

One important factor in the Russians' favour was the support lent them by the Zaporozhye Cossacks, who sided with Moscow and embarked on

guerilla operations against the enemy, harassing their lines of supply by
seizing Turkish caravans and killing their escorts.

Tcherkassky's men attacked the advance guard of the Turkish army an
pushed it back into the mountains, but this did nothing to clinch matters
Straddling the heights, the Turks controlled the plain and made i
impossible for the Russians to cross the Tisamin.

Romodanovsky was under orders from Tsar Theodore to burn Tchigirin if he could not relieve it. The commander-in-chief of the fortress
Rzhevsky, having been killed, Patrick Gordon was now in sole command
The original garrison had been replaced in 1667 by Romodanovsky'
regulars and Samoilovitch's Little Russians, none of whom was used t
being commanded by foreigners or had any experience of siege warfare
The Turks had made meticulous preparations for their assault on Tchigiri
by driving long saps beneath the town. When the day came, they attacke
the fortress and the lower town simultaneously through breaches blow
in the walls by explosives. The hard-pressed Cossacks broke and fle
towards the Tisamin. One group of Russian troops made for the onl
remaining bridge across the river and were drowned when it collapse
under their weight. A few Cossacks, who were still holding the wei
which served as a bridge to the fortress, made a stand beneath the wall
of a church and thus enabled Gordon to evacuate the remainder o
the garrison. The town went up in flames, but isolated groups of Russia
soldiers fought on in the burning streets. On August 16th, 1678, afte
receiving written orders to abandon Tchigirin, Gordon led the survivin
defenders from the smoking ruins, noting in his diary that 'Tchigiri
was abandoned but not vanquished'. He estimated the losses suffere
during the defence of the fortress at over thirteen hundred killed and
larger number wounded.

This marked the end of the war proper. There were only occasion
clashes between the two sides in the years 1679 and 1680, and the lu
spurred the Russian government to renewed diplomatic activity. Buturli
was sent as the Tsar's ambassador to Vienna, where he employed h
eloquence to the full in an effort to convince the Imperial and Roy
Government that the Tsar's enemy was also the enemy of Christendo
and that to abandon Little Russia to the Sultan was tantamount t
unleashing a wave of Turkish expansion which would have serio
consequences for all concerned. The Empire turned a deaf ear to his plea
however, and a similar scene was enacted in Poland.

John Sobieski agreed to break the treaty of 1676 binding Poland t
Turkey and to take sides against the Sultan only on condition that th
terms of the Treaty of Andrussovo were revoked and that Russia returne

1 Tsar Alexis Michaelovitch, 1672

2 Tsar Theodore

4 Peter the Great in Youth

3 Tsarevna Sophia

6 Boyar Artamon Matveyev

5 Boyar Athanasius Ordyn-Nastchokin

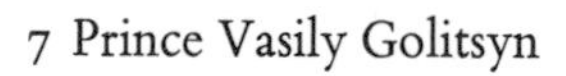

7 Prince Vasily Golitsyn

8 Hetman Bogdan Khmelnitski

9 Patriarch Nikon

10 Simeon Polotski

11 The Terem Palace (Kremlin)

12 Interior of the Granovitaya Palace

13 The Palace of Kolomenskoye

the left-bank areas of Little Russia and the cities of Kiev and Smolensk – in other words, on condition that she renounced everything which she had gained hitherto. Naturally enough, Moscow was unable to accept.

John Sobieski next attacked Tiapkin, the Russian Resident in the royal city of Cracow, for the tone of his reports to the Tsar, on the grounds that they were jeopardizing Russo-Polish relations. After compelling him to leave Cracow and assigning him a new residency in Warsaw, the Poles threatened him with imprisonment in the fortress of Marienburg. Tiapkin defended himself with courage and dignity. He protested vigorously that the nature of the negotiations which Poland was conducting with the Porte and the Tatars had never been conveyed to Tsar Theodore, either via himself or the Polish Resident in Moscow, and insisted on being officially informed about the secret discussions of whose existence he was fully aware.

'I shall remain neither blind nor deaf nor dumb,' Tiapkin declared, 'and I shall acquaint my sovereign with the whole truth.'

The volte-face is one of the oldest rules of politics. A year after threatening Tiapkin, John Sobieski was treating the Russian Resident with the utmost friendliness and the two men spent many hours together in amicable and animated conversation. In April of the same year, 1677, the Seim voted for peace with neighbouring countries and Tiapkin, having obtained satisfaction, returned to Moscow.

In 1678, John Sobieski's ambassadors, Tchartorisski and Sapeha, arrived in Moscow to sign a thirteen-year armistice which was to come into effect in June 1680. Among the Russian statesmen who took part in the discussions was Prince Vasily Golitsyn, who had emulated Ordyn-Nastchokin, now back in cloistered tranquillity, by becoming an enthusiastic champion of peace and friendship with Poland. The thirteen years of the armistice were intended to pave the way for a 'perpetual peace' between the two countries.

The conditions imposed on Moscow by the Poles were extremely harsh, but Poland was sailing before the wind at that moment and could hardly be expected to forgo the advantages of her diplomatic position. Russia was still at war with Turkey and it was reasonable to suppose that she would not raise any undue difficulties. The Russians were prepared to sacrifice a great deal in order to retain the purlieus of Kiev on the right bank of the Dnieper, which Ordyn-Nastchokin had so astutely obtained under the Treaty of Andrussovo. They had to cede three towns and their surrounding districts and pay an indemnity of two hundred thousand roubles, an enormous sum for the period. However, they refused to cede western Little Russia and rejected a Polish proposal for a military alliance because Poland's conditions for entering the war against Turkey were that Russia should pay her an annual fee of two hundred thousand livres and consent to a merger of the two countries' armed forces.

Tsar Theodore's diplomatic missions had been an almost total failure. In France, Louis XIV's sole ambition was to see the Empire and Turkey wear each other out, thereby furthering his designs on the Rhine and maintaining his influence in the Near East. Discretion, therefore, dictated that Russia should negotiate with the Porte.

In 1680, Moscow made tentative approaches to the Vatican through the medium of the apostolic nuncio in Poland, begging the Pope to withdraw his objections to the formation of an alliance between Russia, Poland and the Empire, and reminding him that such an alliance would be directed against the enemy of the Holy Rood.

However, the Christian front was no more united now than it had been at the time of the fall of Constantinople, and Russia's potential allies melted away. In August 1680, with all hopes dashed and all illusions shattered, the Russians took the only course still open to them. Tsar Theodore sent his plenipotentiaries Tiapkin and Zotov – the latter being Tsarevitch Peter's tutor and a man whom Yazykov was currently trying to remove from Court – to the Tatar Khan of the Crimea to obtain his recognition of Russian rights over Kiev and the Zaporozhye area. The Turks were also sounded, but since they held the whip hand at this stage they imposed so many awkward conditions that Moscow shelved the question of its rights over the Zaporozhye region.

The treaty between Russia and the Porte was signed at Bakhchisaray on the shores of the Black Sea, the town whose fountains were later immortalized by Pushkin. The frontier between the two belligerents was to follow the line of the Dnieper, but Kiev and other ancient Russian cities on the right bank were to remain in Russian hands. One clause of the treaty stipulated: 'The territories between the Dnieper and the Bug shall not be populated; the Tatars are entitled to roam [nomadize] on both sides of the Dnieper; the Cossacks and the Russians are entitled to fish in the Dnieper and its tributaries. They may also gather salt and hunt the length of that river as far as the borders of the Black Sea.'

It is probable that in consenting to terms which were comparatively favourable to Russia, considering the awkwardness of her existing position, the Sultan was taking into account the potential dangers of a Russo-Polish coalition.

Russia was not obliged to pay any form of indemnity and retained intact all the territory previously under her jurisdiction. The Porte contented itself with the Polish right bank of the Dnieper, a region which had not only been devastated and impoverished by civil war but was largely depopulated, the Little Russians of the area having taken refuge in Russian territory.

Unsatisfactory though they were from the Russian point of view, the terms of the Treaty of Bakhchisaray (ratified in 1682) were not only honourable but set the seal on a war which had already lasted far too long.

* * *

The war with Turkey showed up certain defects in Russian military organization. The crossing of the Dnieper under enemy fire, for instance, had demonstrated the superiority of regular troops, i.e. Muscovite regiments of recent formation, and the inferiority of the musketeers, who were hidebound by tradition and unable to adapt themselves to new tactics. The musketeers were still elite troops under Alexis Michaelovitch, and the upheavals caused by their eclipse were destined to have political repercussions.

The musketeers were a special formation which dated in its present form from the reign of Ivan the Terrible and had steadily grown in importance under his successors. They were used both as armed police for maintaining internal order and as shock-troops in time of war. By the end of the seventeenth century, however, their combat methods had become archaic and their peculiar way of life had gradually destroyed their unity and sapped their morale. Following established tradition, the musketeers combined a military career with a civilian trade or profession. Craftsmen and shopkeepers in their spare time and resident in quarters specially allocated to them, they remained preoccupied, even on the battlefield, with the financial losses which their workshops and businesses might suffer as a result of their absence. They had become 'spare-time' soldiers who submitted to military discipline only with extreme reluctance, yet when they returned from campaign they brought home the rough manners and habits of the barrack-room. Their ancient privileges and the fear which they had inspired in the population – and sometimes the government – for two hundred years had made them arrogant and undisciplined. They had been a power in the land, and they could not forget the fact.

The officers who commanded them were not among the better elements in the Tsar's service and often accepted their commissions solely from a desire to enrich themselves rapidly and by every available means. Disorder and prevarication reigned in the Prikaz of Musketeers itself, even though it was directed in Tsar Theodore's time by two eminently respectable men, Prince Dolgoruky and the boyar Yazykov. Their contemporaries, usually so quick to blacken anyone's name, never cast aspersions on their honesty, but Dolgoruky was too old to be able to exercise effective control and Yazykov was too preoccupied with cementing his influence over the sovereign, who now entrusted him with tasks of major importance.

Profiting by this lack of higher supervision, the officials in the Prikaz of Musketeers made hay while the sun still shone. Confident of their impunity, officers made their men do personal chores for them, an abuse of authority to which the spare-time craftsmen and merchants took great exception. Despite the mounting discontent, men of higher rank continued to force subordinates to work in their houses like domestic servants, repair their roofs, chop wood and carry water for them. Some officers pocketed depreciation allowances and made musketeers repair regimental drums, cannons and muskets at their own expense, while others were not averse to withholding part of their men's pay.

Although well-to-do musketeers evaded fatigues by paying substantial bribes, the rank and file were so exasperated by ill treatment, extortion and excessive penalties for minor military offences that by 1680 the general spirit prevailing among the musketeers bordered on mutiny.

They at first expressed their discontent by lodging complaints which the authorities firmly ignored. Conscious of the valuable assistance which their corps had rendered the Tsar and government in past decades, the musketeers expected some gratitude in return. Having re-established order in the country after the Salt Rebellion and crushed the Copper Rebellion in 1662, they now saw their military glory eclipsed and their privileges and concessions threatened by men who took care to see that their voice no longer reached the Tsar's ears.

Musketeers from the various Moscow regiments lodged collective complaints twice during Theodore's reign. The result of these complaints, though logical enough, was not exactly what had been intended by those who lodged them: the innocent were punished and the guilty left in peace. The signatories of the petition were sentenced to a dose of the knout, which did nothing to soothe their spirits. Further agitation ensued, this time in the form of a more strongly-worded petition in which the musketeers, while complaining of their conditions of service, uttered threats not only against the men directly responsible for their misfortunes but also against the government itself.

The powers-that-be confined themselves to half-measures, as they had done at the time of the Copper Rebellion. Sylvester Medviedev describes the musketeers' state of mind as follows: 'They began to fear that they would be unjustly punished for their just demands, and from that time forward the men in each regiment began to discuss secretly among themselves how to avert such a disaster.'

Although there was never any open mutiny among the musketeers while Tsar Theodore was alive, the mounting anger and tension in the various regiments was soon to be translated into violent action.

CHAPTER NINETEEN

APART from honorific titles, of which the highest was that of boyar, Russia had inherited a burdensome legacy from feudal times in the so-called right of precedence. Even though Alexis Michaelovitch and Theodore Alexeyevitch had chosen their friends and associates without regard to family background, and even though – to the displeasure of more illustrious families – they had promoted Artamon Matveyev and Ivan Yazykov to the rank of boyar, they were both hampered by incessant squabbles over precedence, which had nothing to do with the ranks and distinctions conferred by royal decree.

Records which had been sedulously maintained for centuries not only showed the relationships between princely houses and noble families, but also listed every post held by each member of those families under every preceding reign. Proud of the command held by one of his ancestors at the battle of Kulikovo in the fourteenth century, or of the role played by another ancestor at the marriage of Grand Prince Vasily to Sophia Paleologa in the fifteenth century, one of Tsar Theodore's voivodes would refuse to serve under another voivode who, though more competent, had to defer to him in the matter of precedence. Homeric feuds broke out between courtiers in the Kremlin itself. A nobleman who had been assigned a less honoured seat at a banquet in the Granovitaya than another whose great-grandfather had been seated at the foot of the table in the reign of Ivan the Terrible considered it a stain on his honour to comply with the demands of protocol, his protests rendered all the more violent because in accepting an 'inferior' seat he would be degrading all future generations of his family. The fact that, say, a Sheremetev was placed lower than a Saltykov on one particular occasion was immediately noted in the annals, and from then on the Saltykovs would always be one up on the Sheremetevs.

Before we dismiss this as a primitive Russian foible let us remember that, according to Saint-Simon, French dukes of the same period were just as jealous of their prerogatives and that duchesses' tabourets were the object of much intrigue. Besides, protocol still raises ticklish problems today when it comes to seating politicians round a table or organizing a ceremonial procession. Human vanity feeds on little things.

There was an element of tragi-comedy, nothing more, in the picture of a bearded and dignified personage lying rigid on the floor, being carried back to his bench by force and braving the sovereign's displeasure by promptly leaving the room, or of a healthy man feigning sickness to avoid having to tolerate such a disgrace. What was more serious was that precedence weighed heavily on the conduct of military operations and public affairs as a whole. A competent general might have to obey the orders of an incompetent superior because one of the latter's ancestors had commanded an army two hundred years earlier. Military commands, like the best seats at table, were always a hereditary prerogative of the same families, whatever the merits of the individuals in each generation.

Prince Vasily Golitsyn's superior in the Tchigirin campaign was the elderly Prince Romodanovsky. Romodanovsky was a brave man but a poor general, and certainly not an ideal instructor in the art of warfare. Although Golitsyn seems to have had little taste or inclination for generalship, he was too intelligent not to concede that the reverses suffered by the Russian army were due to the archaic right of precedence, which compelled the government to entrust the supreme command to an incompetent old man because his noble birth and high priority on the lists of precedence entitled him to it.

Once the Turkish war had dragged to a close, Tsar Theodore nominated a committee of State servitors to work out some salutary army reforms. At its head was the young boyar mentioned above, Prince Vasily Golitsyn.

After studying the setbacks experienced in the recent campaign, which were ascribed to the 'new stratagems' of the enemy, the committee began by suggesting some structural reforms. 'Hundreds' were to become battalions commanded by lieutenants and captains instead of 'heads' and 'leaders of hundreds'. When the Tsar accepted this proposal, the committee members set about drawing up a list of future officers and found themselves brought up short by the right of precedence. They at once decided to forward a petition to the sovereign, telling him in plain terms that the only way to ensure military success and profitable relations with foreign countries was to abolish the right of precedence and make all office-holders dependent for their appointment on the sovereign's wishes alone.

The man who conveyed this historic petition to Theodore Alexeyevitch was Prince Golitsyn himself. As the husband of a Dolgoruky and a descendant both of Gedimnas, the sovereign prince of Lithuania, and of the house of Rurik, Vasily Golitsyn belonged to one of the most illustrious families in the land and had never personally suffered from the rule of precedence. By sponsoring this reform he was, in a sense, acting against his own interests, so no one could suspect him of hoping to benefit by it.

On January 12th, Theodore called his Council together to condemn the right of precedence. Those present included boyars, *okolnitchy*, noblemen and clerks of the Duma, the Patriarch, the high clergy and a few representatives from the world of commerce. The Tsar opened the proceedings.

'Our forbear, Tsar Michael Theodorovitch,' he declared, 'ordained in his time that boyars and other dignitaries, as well as soldiers of all ranks, should not take account of precedence, and our father decreed during the campaigns against the King of Poland and the King of Sweden that rank should not be allotted according to the right of precedence.'

The Patriarch, who also gave an address, had hardly finished speaking when the whole assembly broke into shouts of:

'May precedence perish by fire, accursed begetter of enmity and destroyer of fraternal affection, and may its memory vanish for ever!'

The registers of precedence were summarily burnt in a fireplace in the antechamber, and the ledgers which for three hundred and fifty years had provoked hatred and jealousy, malice and misunderstanding, family feuds and military disasters, were soon reduced to a heap of ashes.

Highly delighted, Theodore Alexeyevitch expressed his gratitude to the men who had supported him in his task. He ordered that the genealogical relationships of every princely house and noble or ennobled family should be entered in four books without delay, so that the destruction of the registers of precedence should not rob future generations of a record of their origins and their ancestors' exploits. The first book was reserved for Rurikid, Georgian and Tatar princes and for families whose date of ennoblement was lost in the mists of time, the fourth for obscure families or those, like Matveyev's, which had been ennobled during the last two reigns. But, although each family was inscribed in a different book according to its fame and antiquity, the sovereign emphasized that genealogical status conferred no privileges in respect of service or rank. Ability was to be the determining factor in Russia from now on, not birth.

The reform was made official by a royal decree. 'Theodore Alexeyevitch, by the grace of God Tsar and Grand Prince of all the Little, Great and White Russias, in confirmation and implementation of this collective measure, and in order that accursed precedence be abolished for ever, I hereunto set my hand. Theodore.'

The Tsar's signature was followed by those of Patriarch Joachim, the metropolitans, archbishops, archimandrites, boyars, gentlemen of the Duma, generals, cavalry colonels and elected citizens.

Relics of the right of precedence persisted for a time, and members of the old guard lodged several complaints on the subject – to their cost. Before the right of precedence was abolished, the sovereign used to examine a complaint and then punish the party whose claim was unjustified. From now on, Theodore Alexeyevitch merely punished, without review, anyone who refused to serve in the capacity assigned him by royal command.

With the evils of precedence banished for ever, a decree governing the foundation of a new Academy signed and sealed, and the army reforms put into operation, the balance-sheet of Theodore's brief reign revealed substantial assets. Tsar Alexis's achievements had in no way been impaired by his youthful successor.

* * *

Russia continued to attract foreigners, and enterprising individuals knew how to exploit the fact. The existence of capitalism at this date is vouched for by the career of the Marcelis family, who had settled in Moscow with their relations, the Kellermans, Frencels and Marcelises, before the accession of the first Romanov. They were the first foreign entrepreneurs to exploit the commercial, not to say industrial, potential of a large country which was still unaware of its own wealth. The sons of Peter Marcelis I leased the right to develop postal services between Moscow and the Western borders, and their descendants had played an important role in national affairs ever since.

The Russians drew a distinction between 'new' *nemtsy*, or foreigners who had recently arrived in Russia, and 'old' *nemtsy* or Russified foreigners who had been born there. It was said of the latter that 'their German blood has evaporated' – though it did not evaporate so completely as to deprive them of the efficiency which native Russians so often lacked.

During the lifetime of Tsar Alexis, Matveyev sent a colourful character named Nicholas Spafari on a mission to China. Spafari was a Wallachian Greek and a kinsman of the Hospodar of Wallachia, though family feeling did not deter the Hospodar from cutting off his nose for informing the Sultan of the text of a secret agreement signed between himself and the King of Poland. Disgraced and disfigured, Spafari fled to Russia, where his knowledge of Russian, Greek, Latin and Italian soon gained him employment as an interpreter in the Office of Foreign Affairs. Theodore was on the throne by the time Spafari returned from his two-year trip to China.

He brought the Russians precise details of a route from Tobolsk to the Chinese frontier, which greatly facilitated commercial relations between the two countries.

* * *

Numerous foreign officers continued to play an important part in the reformed army. Although the majority confined themselves strictly to their professional sphere, three of them served the Russian State in a wider capacity.

The first of these was Patrick Gordon, whom we have met before. At the age of thirty-six, the Scottish Catholic soldier received two offers, one from Moscow and the other from Vienna. He opted for Russia and signed a three-year contract, but remained in the country for thirty-eight years, becoming a general and an ambassador in turn. If the truth be told, Gordon had no choice. Whenever he requested permission to go home, successive governments assured him that his services were greatly appreciated and intimated that if he persisted in his desire to abandon Russia he would be deported to Siberia. It is fair to assume, however, that Gordon could not have been too dissatisfied with his lot because he did not defect when he was appointed ambassador to England.

Gordon was an honest man. He possessed unusual strength of character and common sense, and his native phlegm prevented him from losing his head in awkward situations. His steadfast refusal to be embroiled in political intrigues enabled him to serve Russia without becoming the tool of any one faction. Respected by Tsar Theodore, held in high esteem by Sophia and Prince Vasily Golitsyn, and later an invaluable associate of Peter the Great, he survived the vicissitudes of Russian politics without losing an iota of his prestige.

His friend Paul Menezius, likewise a Scottish Catholic, knew French, English, Latin and German and represented Russia at a number of foreign courts. Menezius was related to Artamon Matveyev through Matveyev's wife, Eudoxia Hamilton, who was a kinswoman of his, and was thus on close terms with the Naryshkins.

The third man was François Lefort, a Swiss born at Geneva in 1653. Lefort had begun his military career in Holland and did not arrive in Russia until 1675. For the time being he remained in the background, waiting to enter the political arena. His moment came when Peter broke with his sister, then Regent, and the erstwhile Swiss soldier ended by becoming not only admiral of the fleet created by Peter the Great but an ambassador as well.

CHAPTER TWENTY

THE libraries of Tsar Theodore and Prince Vasily Golitsyn each contained, among many other highly interesting manuscripts, a work by Yury Krizhanitch, who came to Russia in the reign of Alexis Michaelovitch.[1]

Krizhanitch was a lonely and tragic figure. Croat by birth and Catholic by creed, schooled in theology, philosophy and, to a lesser degree, political economy, a gifted philologist and a fervent champion of the Slav unity so dear to Ordyn-Nastchokin's heart, Krizhanitch was never appreciated by his contemporaries and his life was consequently a series of bitter trials.

His career was as chequered as his knowledge was wide. He was born under Turkish sovereignty, studied for the priesthood in seminaries at Zagreb, Vienna and Poland, and after being ordained was appointed to the College of St Athanasius, or *Congregatio de propaganda fide*, in Rome.

Being a Slav, Krizhanitch was sent by Rome to do missionary work in Russia. The great country had always haunted the young man's dreams, its attraction for him deriving partly from Slav patriotism and partly from his conviction that Moscow was the only conceivable centre of Pan-Slavism. In an age when the West obstinately refused to foresee Russia's political future and regarded her as a purely Asiatic power, Krizhanitch felt that her destinies were linked with, or at least parallel to, those of Europe.

Krizhanitch realized that anyone who wanted to understand Russia must go there equipped with a language that was intelligible to the Russians, rather than a thorough but valueless command of Latin. As a philologist, he believed that the Slavic language could become the lingua franca of all the countries originally converted by St Cyril and St Methodius. While studying in Rome, he kept up his Slavonic by compiling grammars, philological treatises and dictionaries which would be useful to him in his future activities.

Krizhanitch yearned so fiercely to see Russia and grew so impatient of

[1] Krizhanitch may fairly be regarded as the precursor of the Slavophile movement which blossomed in Russia two centuries later.

the work set him by his superiors (the preparation of a polemic for us
against the Greek 'schismatics') that he left Rome for Moscow withou
asking permission. Realizing that anyone who entered Russia as a Roma
Catholic priest would find it impossible to settle there, he represente
himself to the Russian authorities as a Serb named Yury Ivanitch who wa
anxious to offer his services to the Tsar. Krizhanitch arrived in Moscow
his mind seething with vast projects, only to be faced with the problem o
earning a living. He applied successfully for the post of librarian to th
Tsar, but the government curbed his enthusiasm and offered him littl
encouragement. Although his pay was meagre, Krizhanitch was a man o
ideas, not money, and discomfort was the least of his worries. Undeterre
by pangs of hunger, the incognito priest worked away happily at hi
Slavonic dictionary and grammar.

'I am called a vagabond,' wrote Krizhanitch in one of his numerou
works. 'It is not true. I have come to place myself at the disposal of th
Tsar of my race, to rejoin a people to whom I belong, to live in my
native land, the only country where my labours may be of some worth.

In a place where even semi-educated people found well-paid jobs, the
erudite Krizhanitch, with his wealth of ideas and wild schemes, failed to
achieve the recognition he deserved. There was no one to share his hopes
and dreams.

After working in obscurity for a year, Krizhanitch was deported for
some unknown reason to Tobolsk, where he spent fifteen years. Curiously
enough, they were not the unhappiest years of his life. He was extremely
well treated in Siberia and received a comfortable allowance. No one
bothered him or forced him to work, and he was fed – to use his own
expression – 'like a beast destined for the slaughter-house.' He began to
enjoy his exile. At Tobolsk, he was able to complete his life-work, the
Slavonic grammar at which he had been toiling since the age of twenty-two.

When Tsar Alexis died, Theodore, who knew Krizhanitch's work,
allowed him to return to Moscow. Abandoning all hope of seeing his
dreams materialize, the unfortunate man revealed that he was really a
Roman Catholic priest or, as the Russians would say, 'a tonsured priest',
and received permission to leave Russia for ever. His subsequent career
remains as much of an enigma as the reason for his deportation, but some
sources indicate that Yury Krizhanitch, the champion of Slav unity, was
killed before the walls of Vienna in the ranks of Sobieski's army.

When speculating on the failure of Krizhanitch's mission, we must
remember that the idea of Pan-Slavism had already been broached by
Ordyn-Nastchokin and that the Russians had displayed little enthusiasm

r it. Tsar Alexis was more concerned with the liberation of all Orthodox hristians living under the Infidel yoke, and his interest in the reunion f small Slav nations with Russia was limited to that context. The eorgians, for example, interested him far more than the Poles, for whom e seems to have had little sympathy, judging by the letters which he xchanged with Ordyn-Nastchokin, who was always urging him to oncentrate on achieving better relations with Poland at the expense, if ecessary, of the Little Russians.

To sum up, although Russia saw herself as the religious centre of rthodoxy, she was unwilling to become the political centre of a vast lav bloc. Even before the time of Peter the Great, she was already trying o integrate herself into the European community and become a Western ation in her own right.

The champion of Pan-Slavism bequeathed his works to Russia despite he lack of recognition which his adopted country had shown him. Like otoshihkin's accounts, they afford us a valuable picture of seventeenth-entury Russia.

Krizhanitch went into Russia with his eyes open. He felt a great affinity or the Russians, but he also knew the West and could therefore compare he two worlds. Kotoshikhin, who spied for his country's enemies and was man of questionable morality, did his best to denigrate the *status quo*. rizhanitch, while criticizing life in Russia, thought only of the progress which Russia could make. He wrote:

> No other people under the sun has been so humiliated and so wronged for centuries as have we, the Slavs. Foreigners cheat us, tread us down, climb on our backs and gallop along on us as though we were cattle. They call us pigs and dogs. They regard themselves as gods and us as imbeciles ... All that can be extracted from the taxes, oppression, tears, sweat and fasting of the Russian people is squandered by foreigners, Greek merchants, German merchants and settlers, and Crimean brigands. This is because we are infatuated with things from abroad. All that comes from beyond our frontiers we esteem, and all that we have at home we despise ...

Krizhanitch was well aware of the faults and failings of the Russians, i.e. the Slavs, and regarded ignorance as the mainspring of all their troubles. He declared:

> In the West the nations are shrewd and capable. The West is organized: Russia is not. She is imprisoned in the interior of a continent and, on that account, minds are slow. No one understands

> anything of agriculture, commerce or domestic economy ... It is you, honoured Tsar, whom fate has destined to think for the entire Slav people. You have been given us by God as a helper of all those who dwell beyond the Danube, the Czechs and Poles ... Our great failing is our unawareness of moderation. We are incapable of setting ourselves on the path of the golden mean and seek to walk above precipices.

Prompted by didactic motives to paint a gloomy and exaggerated picture of national shortcomings, Krizhanitch outlined measures designed to correct the situation, notably the development of public education and the re-ordering of political life and liberty by the creation of a body in which representatives of every social stratum could express their views and requirements, thus eliminating misunderstandings and administrative abuses. Finally, the author of the memorandum stressed the need for technical training and suggested the establishment of vocational schools for girls as well as boys.

Krizhanitch was no extremist democrat. He approved of the Tsar's absolute power because it would enable him to introduce sweeping reforms. He also believed that national reorganization would permit the development of the country's natural resources and of 'modern' industries, notably metallurgy.

Yury Krizhanitch was undoubtedly a man of genius, but he was a Slav genius, and therefore passionate, impatient and unmethodical, despite the inner logic of his grand design. The unwieldy jumble of his writings seethed with revolutionary ideas, some of which were adopted by the Slavophiles of the nineteenth century.[1] He asserted in one of his essays:

> Other nations are handsome, hence their pride. As for us, we are neither handsome nor ugly: our looks are commonplace. We are not grandiloquent and cannot express ourselves, whereas they are glib talkers and capable of expressing themselves pungently and with sarcasm. Our minds are slow and our hearts simple. They are filled with guile. We lack the spirit of economy and are extravagant. We do not know how to keep accounts and squander our possessions heedlessly. Other nations are close-fisted and greedy, thinking night and day of means to fill their purses. We are lazy: they are industrious and do not let a day pass in vain that can bring them a profit. We are the inhabitants of a poor land: they are born in rich and beautiful lands, and they catch us in the toils of what their lands produce as a

[1] The Eurasians in the twenties followed Krizhanitch's example by emphasizing that the Slavo-Russian East and the European West are two separate worlds with disparate civilizations.

hunter catches game. We think and speak simply, and act likewise. We put an end to our disputes by making peace. As for them, they are ungenerous, deceitful and malicious, never forgetting a word that has injured them; and when they enter into disputes they seek revenge rather than make peace sincerely.

If we are dwelling on the ideas and personality of Yury Krizhanitch it is because, in spite of everything, some of his ideas were reflected in the life of the seventeenth century. Although the 'tonsured priest's' writings were not widely known, they were read by Tsar Theodore's circle and found some measure of expression in the Russian attitude towards the West.

* * *

Tsar Theodore, who realized the value of technical training and encouraged its growth, was naturally disposed in favour of humanistic education. In 1679 a Greek school was attached to Moscow's great Printing Office. Simeon Polotski dreamed of enlarging it and turning it into a Graeco-Latin-Slav academy. In fact, the text of an imperial decree creating such an academy was drafted by Polotski, but the Tsar did not sign it until 1682, the year of his death, so the worthy monk, who died in 1680, never had the joy of seeing his project materialize nor the chance of defending the spirit in which he had conceived it. Theodore's old tutor was hardly in his grave before Patriarch Joachim hastened to add some amendments of his own to the academic statute.

It was intended that the academy should become a genuine university capable of equipping young people, regardless of their social background, to assume senior positions in the Russian government. Tsar Theodore opened the pertinent decree with a preamble which was not only touching but patently inspired by his former tutor's sermons:

'Having ascended the throne in my boyhood, as did King Solomon, no thought is more precious to me than the thought of Wisdom, which lies at the origin of royal dignity and is the creator and executor of all good things. Through it, men receive the gifts of God.'

The Principal of the Academy, who bore the title 'Guardian', was to be assisted by Russian and Greek professors whose role was not only to instruct their pupils but to protect the Orthodox faith and defend it against other creeds and heresies.

The Academy enjoyed a surprising measure of independence, since neither staff nor pupils could be tried by ordinary tribunals unless delegates from the Academy itself were present. Grammar, rhetoric, dialectics and philosophy – logical, natural and juridical – were to be taught there. No professor could be accepted without the Patriarch's recommendation and without being interviewed by his colleagues. This citadel or Vatican of the Russian Church was, in Soloviev's expression, a veritable court of inquisition. The Academy did not begin to function until after Theodore's death, but its foundation was his work and proved that the trend towards education which had evolved in the preceding reign did not lose momentum during his six years on the throne.

To provide funds for the Academy, Theodore Alexeyevitch donated a whole district belonging to the royal domains and ten other non-urban properties. He also encouraged donations from individuals. From the Church, the Academy received seven monasteries and the land adjoining them.

Wishing to supervise the printing of his works, the indefatigable Simeon Polotski had, in 1670, sought Tsar Alexis's permission to instal a small printing office in the Kremlin palace. Two of the works printed there in 1679 were a reading primer for use by young Tsarevitch Peter and a rhymed psalter by Polotski which included two Psalms (133 and 146) put into verse by Tsar Theodore himself. Alexis Likhatchev urged the Tsar to write a *History of Russian Sovereigns*, but the book never went beyond the planning stage because Theodore was too ill and preoccupied to devote the necessary time to it.

In 1680, a miscellany composed of old Slavo-Russian manuscripts and chronicles was printed at the monastery of Kievo-Petchersk. Theodore Alexeyevitch was dissatisfied with its brevity and ordered it to be amplified by the inclusion of other works by ancient and contemporary historians in Russian, Greek and Latin. This enlarged edition, which remained in Likhatchev's archives and was never published, may even have survived the passage of time and be stored away in some Soviet record office.

* * *

Uninterested in refined literature and syllabic verse by erudite poets, common folk continued to create popular literature and poetry. Story-tellers still sang their ballads to circles of appreciative listeners. Drunkenness was still a very topical subject and a large number of satires flayed it unmercifully, taking as their theme *The Apocrypha of the Devil and Noah*, in which the Devil teaches Noah's wife how to prepare 'a drink of hops' for her husband so as to find out where the Ark is being built. In one of these stories, the Hop boasts: 'And since that time, I, the Hop, have become renowned throughout the earth and my name is known to all men.' Describing the progressive evils of alcohol, 'the arm of Satan' continues: 'I make a man courageous and violent, proud and vain, careless, boastful and immoderately talkative. He enters into quarrels and fights unto bloodshed and death!'

All efforts by virtuous men to turn the hard-drinking Russians into a nation of teetotallers encountered stubborn resistance, and other story-tellers passing through the same villages represented drink as the least of the world's sins. Inspired by a French story, *The Drunkard's Tale* is a somewhat irreligious attempt to rehabilitate the vice of alcoholism. This relates how, after his death, a drunkard knocks at the Gates of Heaven. When St Peter asks him why he is knocking, he announces: 'I am a drunkard, and I wish to live with you who dwell in Paradise.' To which St Peter replies: 'Drunkards are not admitted. You will have to suffer eternal torment with the adulterers and sinners.' 'Remember, Peter,' counters the drunkard, 'that when the Saviour was led away to his torments you denied him thrice, whereas I, a drunkard, have drunk wine each day of my life but have never denied our Lord.'

Folklore is a hardy thing, and Russia had to wait until the October Revolution before the links between the people and their past were finally broken. Meanwhile, folklore continued to develop concomitantly with the new trends in literature, comparatively unmolested since Nikon's disappearance from the scene. Mourners keened over their dead, ritual songs rang out at weddings, and at night whole villages would gather round their old women and listen to ancient legends which each generation had transformed and enriched in turn.

While scholars were discussing dogma and instructing their pupils in scholasticism and philosophy, blind minstrels were wandering among the clamorous crowds with which Red Square was always thronged.

'The Tale of the Book of the Dove' told of a cosmogonic book which contained answers, phrased in the light of the Christian faith, to all the questions that had troubled men since the Creation. This tome, which fell from enormous clouds, was so large 'that no one can hold it in his arms nor place it on a lectern'. It was called 'of the Dove' because the wisdom contained in it was a revelation of the Holy Spirit.

> Our free Universe proceeds from the Judgment of God,
> The red sun from the Countenance of God
> And from Christ Himself, King of Heaven,
> The bright young moon from the Bosom of God,
> The black nights from the Thoughts of God,
> The blithe winds from the Holy Spirit.

Our spirit is that of Jesus,
Of Jesus Himself, King of Heaven.
Our thoughts come from the celestial clouds.
We men are born of Adam,
Our sturdy bones of rock,
Our bodies of damp earth,
Our red blood of the deep sea ...

The men who, according to legend, came to consult 'the Book of the Dove' were a very mixed assortment. They included kings and princes, priests, monks and humble folk, but none dared turn the pages except King David, who answered questions put to him by the others. 'The Tale' closes with a dream in which Prince Vladimir sees two beasts, one from the East and the other from the West, fighting savagely. King David interprets the dream thus:

These are not two beasts that confront each other,
Not two wild beasts that contend together.
'Tis Truth and Injustice that are at grips,
That fight each other and attack.
Injustice tried to triumph over Truth,
But Truth had the last word.
It ascended into Heaven beside Christ, the King of Heaven.
And Injustice traverses our land,
Our land, our Russian world,
And all the universe inhabited by Christians.

CHAPTER TWENTY-ONE

THEODORE ALEXEYEVITCH'S aunt Irina, who had dominated the Terem for so long, died in 1679 and was buried with fitting ceremony. Her sister Tatiana at once stepped into the breach. Self-willed, but intelligent and energetic, Tatiana was particularly fond of her niece Sophia. Tsar Theodore's sisters, who were unmarried, played a not inconsiderable role in various events which had far-reaching effects upon the Terem.

The Tsar's aunts and sisters were solidly united against the intruder, Tsarina Natalia, whose position had been a lonely one since the banishment of her brothers and Matveyev's deportation. Her father, Cyril Naryshkin, had been left unmolested, but he was a nonentity and could not be of any assistance to her.

Largely composed of Miloslavskys and seething with intrigues concocted by the wily Khitrovo and the treacherous Volynsky, the Terem spurned and despised the young widow. The Tsar's sisters were no longer children. Eudoxia was thirty in 1680, Martha twenty-seven, Sophia twenty-three and Theodosia seventeen. They were women in the flower of their youth, frustrated women in whom virtue was imposed but not accepted, embittered women who could never hope to emerge from their living grave. Sophia, the most enterprising of them, was helping her aunt to weave the meshes of a net which would keep her father's youngest son far from the throne.

The existence of that lively and flourishing child was never far from the Tsarevnas' thoughts whenever they unburdened themselves to poor Theodore, whose chances of survival were obviously so slim, or when they were in the company of Ivan, their gentle and listless brother, who had a chronic eye complaint and spent his whole time prostrating himself in church – Theodore and Ivan, two small flickering flames whose extinction would sentence the princesses to a lifetime of dependence on Natalia's whims.

* * *

Since Theodore's health demanded careful nursing, Sophia and her sisters often visited him in his apartments, where they met his friends Yazykov, Likhatchev and Golitsyn. The Miloslavskys and other relations of the Romanovs always had free access to the Terem, and Simeon Polotski kept Sophia informed of current developments until he died. After Polotski's death, his pupil Sylvester Medviedev became Sophia's chief source of intellectual consolation because her sisters, who accepted her supremacy, were not her intellectual equals and could never share her secret ambitions. As for Tsar Theodore, he also bowed to his elder sister's influence and the requests of his aunt Tatiana, who had never ceased to devote herself to Patriarch Nikon and protect him from the attentions of his successor.

In 1680 the recluses of the Terem received a new and welcome addition to their ranks. Observing a time-honoured favourite's tradition, Alexis Likhatchev had decided to reinforce his influence over the sovereign by choosing him a bride: Agatha Grushevsky, the daughter of an Orthodox and Russified Polish nobleman whom no one had ever heard of before. The Terem was beside itself with joy. What mattered was not the bride's identity but that Theodore should have a son and so bar Peter from the Muscovite throne for ever.

Girls of good family were probably summoned to attend a 'selection board', as in Natalia Naryshkin's case. If so, the ladies-in-waiting and the doctors must have made their reports and Theodore Alexeyevitch must, without reading them, have handed Agatha the gold- and pearl-embroidered handkerchief and the engagement ring.

Although customs had changed somewhat, it is probable that the marriage ceremony was still much the same as it had been in the time of the first tsars of Moscow. After it was over, the young couple seated themselves on two thrones of velvet and gold-embroidered satin covered with sable and marten skins, which were believed to have the property of warding off the evil eye. As a further precaution, one of the Tsar's intimates sat on each of the thrones in turn to transfer to his own person any curse or spell that might have been placed on them by disappointed competitors. Agatha, who was designated a tsarevna before the marriage, was dressed in the Terem by the ladies of the palace and then conducted to the ceremonial chamber, preceded by two boyars carrying large and weighty candles. When the nobleman in charge of protocol had seated the guests in accordance with their rank, the Tsar appeared, accompanied by his *druzhkas* or pages of honour. Finally, the bridal pair took their places on the thrones, the bride's face carefully hidden from the eyes of the guests by the *fata* that fell from her crown. The young couple listened to some preliminary prayers, and the cortège then moved off towards the cathedral across the red damask that carpeted the courtyard.

Bride and groom did not take part in the ensuing festivities but were conducted to the bridal chamber, where a light meal was brought to them. Nuptial candles were placed at the head of the bed, each in a silver-gilt bowl. Following ancient custom, sheaves of rye were spread beneath the bed as a symbol of fertility and grains of wheat scattered beneath the coverlets. Above the bed hung two icons, one representing the Nativity and the other the birth of the Virgin Mary.

Next day the young couple visited the steam-baths, and on their return one of the foremost boyars raised the bride's veil with an arrow, thus revealing the new Tsarina's face to those privileged to be present. On the following day, clergy, nobility and merchants came to present the Tsar and Tsarina with gifts, though since Tsar Michael's time this had been no more than a symbolic ceremony at which the royal couple graciously refused the various offerings.

Theodore's wedding was celebrated in July 1680 without the customary pomp. Ceremonial was cut to a minimum, and for several days the court remained isolated from the rest of the world. We do not know the exact reason, but it is probable that the Tsar's state of health already precluded his exposure to undue fatigue. No reception or banquet was held after the marriage.

* * *

Theodore was nineteen in 1680 and Agatha probably younger still. Little is known of the appearance and character of the new Tsarina, who lived at Theodore's side for only just a year. Since she was probably as poor as Natalia had been, Agatha must have received her share of the clothes and jewellery in the hereditary wardrobe which was at the disposal of royal brides. The house of Romanov was still comparatively poor. Michael had ascended the throne at a time when Russia was utterly ruined. The 'false' Dimitry and the Poles of his entourage had ransacked the Kremlin before fleeing from Russia's resurgent might, so the Romanovs were only three generations down the road from penury to the splendour on which future Russian monarchs were to base their prestige. Each new Tsarina received her share of the robes and jewellery of her predecessors, and Agatha was able to benefit from what had been left of Maria Miloslavsky's possessions after some of them had been passed on to Natalia.

With the advent of Agatha, Polish influence at Court became pronounced, if not predominant. Theodore was the first Tsar to dress in Polish style. According to a contemporary report, etiquette became impregnated with 'Polish civilities', which in turn affected the Russians' manners, way of life and human relationships.

Although the young Tsarina's personality was of secondary importance to the aunts and sisters of Theodore Alexeyevitch, she soon became pregnant and was pampered by the whole of Terem, whose sole concern was the birth of a new heir who could protect the Miloslavskys against the Naryshkins.

On July 11th, 1681, Tsarina Agatha was duly delivered of a son, the Tsarevitch Ilya, but the Terem's jubilation was short-lived. Three days later, Agatha died. The Tsar, who loved her dearly and was prostrated with grief, could not summon up enough energy to attend the funeral and accompanied his wife's body only as far as the Red Gate. On July 20th, the little Tsarevitch followed his mother to the tomb. Once again, Theodore Alexeyevitch only accompanied the small coffin to the Red Gate and did not attend the funeral, which was held in the Cathedral of the Archangel.

* * *

But what of Tsarina Natalia while her stepson's Court was being gripped alternately by hope and despair? The young widow seldom visited Moscow, but spent most of her time at Kolomenskoye and Izmailovo with her son Peter and her daughter Natalia, two years his junior. Peter, who was Tsar Theodore's godson, had everything he needed and was well cared for by his mother and tutors. A number of children of his own age or older were chosen to keep him company. Alexis Michaelovitch's youngest son had a marvellous constitution. He began to walk at six months, and his lively intelligence, alert mind and robust health were a constant source of amazement. The child was always on the move. He loved energetic games, and his father indulged his passion for the army by appointing him, at the age of three, commander of a detachment of children older than himself. Prince Dolgoruky presented him with a miniature cannon, and his collection of warlike toys – bows and arrows, musketoons, sabres and axes – grew with the passing years.

There are conflicting accounts of Tsar Theodore's relationship with his stepmother. Some chroniclers report that Theodore Alexeyevitch behaved coolly towards the Tsarina, others that he was devoted to her and treated her with respect. Knowing Theodore's kind heart, it seems improbable that he would ever have maltreated his father's widow, even though he was forced to show severity to Matveyev and the young Naryshkins. Peter was his godson as well as his half-brother, and Theodore knew how much Alexis Michaelovitch had loved the last of his offspring.

Though cautious and preoccupied, no doubt, with the actual or naginary conspiracies of Matveyev and the Naryshkins, Theodore was a ıst man and endowed with a sense of duty. Simeon Polotski was too old) take on the task of educating Peter. His pupil, Sylvester Medviedev, 'as both competent and erudite and would have made an ideal tutor had not been for Patriarch Joachim, who was violently opposed to the atinist influence of which Medviedev was a leading exponent.

In 1677, hearing the Tsar express a desire to find 'a good master for eter' ('a gentle man, humble and well-versed in the Holy scriptures' vere Theodore's exact words), the boyar Sokovnin put forward the ame of Nikita Zotov, a clerk from the Office of Requests and Favours nd 'a man full of virtues'.

The Tsar summoned Zotov to the palace. The petty official arrived, vercome by this sudden mark of royal favour. After Simeon Polotski ad interviewed him and found his knowledge adequate (admittedly, he id not have to be a great scholar to teach a child of five!), Theodore lexeyevitch introduced him to Tsarina Natalia without delay. Natalia ook her son by the hand and led him to his new master with the words: Accept my son and teach him divine wisdom; instruct him in the fear of God, a worthy life and the Scriptures.' Alas, all these things were beyond oor Zotov, and he knew it. Terrified, the clerk fell at the Tsarina's feet, rotesting that he was unworthy of such favour, but finally yielded to oyal insistence.

Peter started his lessons on May 12th, 1677. Patriarch Joachim recited a pecial office, then sprinkled the unruly child with holy water and onfided him to Zotov's care. Zotov received a number of lavish gifts. The Patriarch presented him with a hundred roubles, the Tsar a house and Natalia two sumptuous robes. Thus, though feeble and timid by nature, over-fond of the bottle and indifferently educated, Zotov was entrusted vith the education of the most gifted of Tsar Alexis's children and robably the one most devoid of any moral sense.

Despite his failings, Zotov worked hard and was not a bad teacher, and is instructional methods were almost revolutionary for the period. Apart from reading his primer, the Psalter and Books of Hours in the raditional way, Peter received instruction on practical subjects. Zotov sked Tsar Theodore to send abroad for engravings and pictures of iouses, cities, rivers, military installations, ships and various articles whose ıses he could explain to his pupil. The child was also given amusing books vhich corresponded to the 'comics' of today.

This was all very well, but Zotov's greatest defect was that he had no uthority over his royal pupil. When Theodore told Sokovnin that he was looking for a humble man he was probably thinking of someone lik Theodore Rtistchev, who practised humility as a virtue and not as a forr of servility. Zotov's humility sprang from lack of personality and fear c his superiors, with the result that, in this case, the master – pupil relation ship was dominated by the pupil.

Peter had not inherited the intellectual leanings so evident in his hal brother Theodore. Literature and ideas never interested him. He had practical mind, plenty of common sense and a natural bent for action. H favourite subject as a child was history, and Zotov, noticing this, dwe on the great military encounters of the past. Peter's lessons were frequentl interrupted by his inability to keep still. He fidgeted and refused to pa attention to any subject that bored him. Since Zotov was no disciplir arian, his pupil turned out to be the worst-educated of all Alexis's childrei His imperial correspondence displays an unfamiliarity with even th rudiments of syntax and spelling.

The brilliant little savage developed a bizarre affection for his tuto coupled with an utter contempt which was not untinged with sadism. I fact, Peter's life-long contempt for his fellow-men and his persistei violation of human dignity may well have dated from his time wit Zotov.

* * *

As she watched her children playing in the lovely gardens at Kolomer skoye, Natalia no doubt thought bitterly of happier days, when the pom and luxury of the Terem was reserved for her. Meanwhile, the Tsar sisters and aunts began to develop a taste for self-adornment. The Tere consumed enormous quantities of red and white cosmetics, and false ha and eyelashes were enlisted as aids to Nature, even though the princesse enhancement of their charms was pointless at this date and could nev have led to marriage or even amorous intrigue.

For the moment, no one was living in the apartments which Tsar Alex had redecorated for Natalia and which Agatha had occupied during h brief sojourn in the palace. No banquets were given in the room whic Peter's mother pictured so often during her retirement, a gilded roo with mural paintings on 'bucklers' (canvases stretched on wooden frame depicting the baptism of Grand Princess Olga and the legend of Quee Dinara, the Iberian king's daughter who waged war on the Persians.

The Kremlin palace was being continually enriched and embellishe It now contained two reproductions of that marvel of marvels, th 'celestial vault' in the palace at Kolomenskoye. Stars, planets and come shone with astronomical precision on the ceilings of Tsar Theodore

remonial chamber and Sophia's dining-room – which proved how high
position the sovereign's sister occupied in her family circle. The paths of
nets and wandering comets were indicated by grains of gold, and the
n's position during the four seasons and at the equinoxes was plotted
th incomparable skill. A Russian named Karp Zolotarev was com-
ssioned to copy the miraculous thing on to a large sheet of Alexandrine
per in colours and gold, so that Zotov could explain the movement of
lestial bodies to the young Tsarevitch.

Theodore, now a widower, lived in the shadow of death. The paintings
his room included one of Tsar Alexis on his death-bed and portraits of
s mother, Maria Miloslavsky, and his elder brother Alexis, all of them
tter reminders of the young monarch's past ordeals. Sometimes, too, his
ze alighted on a painting of the Good Shepherd. To Theodore
exeyevitch it was a call to duty, for though he knew his days were
mbered he was determined to fulfil his obligations to the very last.

The Terem whispered and plotted uneasily. Although she loved her
other dearly, Sophia refused to make allowances for his grief at losing
gatha or his poor state of health: Theodore must have an heir. Yazykov
vised the Tsar to marry again and helpfully provided him with a new
ide. She was a fifteen-year-old girl of obscure family called Martha
praxin, who happened to be a relative of Yazykov and a godchild of
tamon Matveyev. Who knows? Perhaps the adroit courtier in Yazykov
as trying to secure his future by establishing good relations with the
aryshkin clique. Sophia and her party could not understand his choice,
t the bride's identity was of little importance provided that she bore
eodore a child.

Just six months after the death of his beloved Agatha, Tsar Theodore
fied medical advice and bowed to the entreaties of Yazykov and his
hole family. Emerging from the sovereign's study one fine day in
bruary 1682, Patriarch Joachim announced to the assembled boyars that
artha Apraxin had been designated Tsarevna and Grand Princess. Three
ys later, all the gates into the Kremlin precincts were closed once more,
d the palace, which remained cut off from the outside world for several
ys, saw yet another wedding celebrated with the minimum of pomp.
It was the Miloslavsky faction's last hope, and Tsar Theodore's last
tempt to discharge his duties as sovereign and head of his house. The
lls that pealed at his wedding were about to toll a knell for the peace of
s soul.

CHAPTER TWENTY-TWO

THEODORE's days were already numbered before his marriage to Marth
Apraxin, and time was running short. The twenty-one-year-old monarc
was faced by a problem which would probably have defeated the wisest o
older men. To whom should he leave the throne? To his brother Ivan
who could neither reign nor rule, or to his half-brother Peter, a ten-yea
old child who would bring the Naryshkins – of whose incompetence ar
venality the Tsar was only too well aware – back into power?

As head of his family and son of Maria Miloslavsky, Theodo
Alexeyevitch was concerned about what would happen to his sister
aunts, uncles and cousins when he was no longer there to protect them
But he was also Tsar of all the Russias, and it was his duty to safeguard th
patrimony of the young house of Romanov for the sake of the men ar
women who inhabited his dominions. Such were the two loyalties, th
two duties and the two great anxieties that haunted the ailing monarch
dreams.

Theodore guessed that Tsar Alexis would have wished him to leave th
throne to Peter, but Peter had not yet come of age. 'My father wou
rather have crowned Peter himself, and named me heir only because
his youth.' These outspoken words, which several contemporary write
attribute to Tsar Theodore, are probably apocryphal, since we know th
Alexis not only made a point of proclaiming his eldest surviving son he
to the throne in front of the crowds assembled in Red Square, b
reaffirmed that decision on his death-bed. Only one man in Peter's can
could have governed Russia until the boy came of age, and that w
Artamon Matveyev. However, the former favourite was old now and st
far from Moscow, although his position had substantially improved sin
Tsar Theodore's marriage to his kinswoman Martha Apraxin, so astute
arranged by Ivan Yazykov. After that event, Matveyev left Pustozer
for Lukh on the Volga in the Kostroma district, where he awaited com
plete rehabilitation and nursed high hopes for the future.

Confusion reigned in the Kremlin. Ivan Miloslavsky, wily and circum
spect as ever, worked away behind the scenes, ably assisted by Sophi

ıose authority was now generally acknowledged by the Terem. The revna visited her ailing brother's apartments with increasing regularity, ending long hours at his bedside and occasionally attending meetings his privy council. Her lively mind began to grapple with affairs of .te, although, if the truth be told, her ambitions were of a family rather an a personal nature. She was fighting for her brother Ivan, the only lwark behind which the Miloslavsky clan could shelter from the aryshkins.

Fear, greed, jealousy and ambition poisoned the atmosphere in the lace and cast an even heavier shadow on the young Tsar's last few days earth.

Tsar Theodore's favourites, Yazykov and Likhatchev, remained loyal him until his death, but they were shrewd and prudent men. Alexis khatchev had decided on a rapprochement with the Naryshkin party cause, in all conscience, he believed that Ivan's accession would do ıssia nothing but harm and that the country's future could be guaranteed Peter alone.

Yazykov, who shared this point of view, was also taking precautions r the future. He was ambitious, as the whole Court knew. While nversing with Tsar Theodore in 1679, Peter, who was only seven at the ne, had compared the boyar Yazykov to Boris Godunov, another ıbitious man who had opened up a path to the Russian throne by minating the mind of another Theodore, the son of Ivan the Terrible. ızykov's immediate reaction was to suspect Zotov of having inspired e remark, which was a little too perceptive even for a child of Peter's ecocity. He managed to get rid of the Tsarevitch's tutor for a time by nding him on a mission to the Khan of the Crimea in 1680, which kept otov away from Moscow for a year.

Although the new Tsarina was his kinswoman and protégée, Yazykov uld never hope to rule the country. Reflecting that if Ivan became Tsar would be surrounded by Miloslavskys and that his uncle would doubtedly revenge himself on the man who had replaced him in ıeodore Alexeyevitch's good graces, Yazykov hastily made overtures to ter's camp, ignoring Sophia on the principle that a woman could never dangerous.

Of the Tsar's three favourites, Prince Vasily Golitsyn was the only one whose support Sophia could rely. She knew him well, perhaps better d more intimately than her brother's other advisers. We do not know if e amorous relationship between the prince and the tsarevna was actually nsummated at this stage, but it is possible that Sophia was already in ve with the handsome boyar whom she met every day.

Golitsyn was capable of giving sound advice, but his nobility of mi
coupled with a certain weakness of character, completely unfitted him
the role of conspirator. The prince was not a man of action but of ide
He abhorred violence and despised intrigue, thought like a statesman
lived like a sybarite. He was a dilettante, a *grand seigneur* in the classi
mould and devoid of the personal ambitions proper to little men w
yearn for success. Handsome, erudite, intelligent, wealthy and married
a wife whom he loved, Princess Theodosia Dolgoruky, he was satisf
to be himself.

The senior nobility were for Peter and the Naryshkins almost to a m
the most active partisans being Tcherkassky, Troyekurov, Lyk
Urussov and the Streshnevs. Patriarch Joachim, Metropolitan Jonah
Rostov, the abbot and 'elders' of the monastery of the Holy Trinity a
St Sergius were also for Peter. Ivan's party (Sophia's name was not
mentioned) included old Ivan Miloslavsky, the aunts and sisters of T
Theodore, Prince Vasily Golitsyn, the boyar Khitrovo, Peter and Iv
Tolstoy and, representing the clergy, the erudite Latinist monk Sylves
Medviedev.

For the moment, the people dissociated themselves from the strug
for the soon-to-be-vacated throne. As for Tsar Theodore, he continued
ponder on his duty, and, not knowing what decision would be fairest a
most beneficial to the country, took no decision at all.

Before long, the meshes of an intrigue which was destined to end
bloodshed became hopelessly intertwined. Spread by the tsarevn
nurses and the male and female dwarfs who were so much in vogue at t
palace and in boyars' residences, stories of what was being hatched in t
Tsar's entourage began to circulate among the lower orders. Rumou
went the rounds in the booths and workshops of the musketeers' quart
always a hive of discontent. On all sides, people began to reconnoitre t
ground, evaluate possibilities, tick off potential allies. The two Tolsto
got to work on the musketeers and approached an officer named Iv
Tsikler, who was to prove useful to them.

* * *

The Tsar's second marriage was solemnized in February 1682. C
April 16th of the same year, Theodore Alexeyevitch went in state to t
Uspensky Cathedral to celebrate the joyous festival of Easter. On h
return he retired to bed, never to rise again. Sophia did not leave his sid
She ministered to his needs with deft efficiency, and everyone who h
access to the Tsar's apartments praised her devotion and affection. Th

ung Tsarina was worse than useless. All she could do was weep, and r sobs only aggravated the dying man's distress.

On April 27th, the great bell in the Uspensky Cathedral – known as 'the essenger' – began to toll. The death-knell was at once taken up by : bell of Ivan the Great, and soon the whole capital was flooded th the melancholy sound. Sylvester Medviedev, who as Court poet d written some high-flown verse to commemorate the sovereign's :ent wedding, now composed some for his obsequies.

Moscow being aware of the Tsar's illness, the death-knell came as a :prise to no one. Crowds choked the streets and squares, converged on : Kremlin and poured in through the gates. Sophia returned to the rem, to be greeted with tears and lamentation. She was bombarded th questions. The tsarevnas' grief at losing a beloved brother and phew concealed an undercurrent of apprehension as to their own future. ıe ladies-in-waiting donned mourning. The die seemed cast. Closeted in : late Tsar's apartments, the boyars and the Patriarch consulted in secret. ıe outcome of their deliberations was easy to forecast, but Sophia was t the sort of woman to lose her head or bow to the inevitable. Milovsky followed his normal procedure in moments of crisis and feigned ıess. Prince Golitsyn, too, declined to give battle and went off to visit wife in their country mansion. Tsarevitch Ivan, indifferent to everyng save the loss of his brother, immersed himself in the prayers that :re his only consolation in life. Tsarina Natalia saw her dream taking ıpe: her son would be Tsar at last.

In the streets, the populace grieved at having lost so good a monarch. ith Theodore Alexeyevitch solemnly installed – dust to dust – in his nb, virtue deserted the Kremlin. Ancestral tradition failed to withstand : onslaught of the new spirit. The laicization of daily life brought not ly material progress but moral corruption, and Sophia's and Peter's ssions were subject to no moral restraint. Dark clouds piled up in the ıssian sky as the Furies prepared to unleash the horrors of internecine ife.

'According to the testimony of all his contemporaries,' Berg concludes biography of Tsar Theodore, 'Theodore repurchased a large number of soners and personally received anyone who had a favour to ask of him. .e Russians used to say: "Tsar Theodore lived for the joy of the people d is dead to the sorrow of all." '

In a hall in the Kremlin, Patriarch Joachim conducted the boyars in :ir oath of allegiance to Tsar Peter, but a young woman of twenty-five used to submit to what seemed an inevitable personal disaster. The uggle for power had only just begun.

PART THREE

REGENT SOPHIA

(1682–9)

'The administration of the Tsarevna Sophia Alexeyevna began with every sort of diligence and right judgment unto all, and to the satisfaction of the people, so that never did such wise government abide in the Russian State; and during the seven years of her rule the whole State came to a flower of great wealth, and commerce and all handicrafts multiplied, and the learning of the Latin and Greek tongues began to be established, and the people rejoiced in their sufficiency.'

Notes by Prince Boris Kurakin

CHAPTER TWENTY-THREE

PATRIARCH JOACHIM wasted no time. Even before Tsar Theodore had been laid in his coffin he hurriedly convened an assembly. Time was short, and the only way of averting trouble was to set Alexis's youngest son on the throne as quickly as possible, while at the same time paying lip-service to tradition. The assembly which was to elect Peter included a majority of men favourable to his candidacy. As so often in history, considerations of urgency precluded the attendance at these 'popular' elections of representatives from the provinces, and the assembly consisted almost exclusively of citizens of the capital: boyars, noblemen, merchants, officers and a few commoners from the suburbs.

Patriarch and boyars were so anxious to give the impression that the National Assembly had been properly convened and that Peter had been elected Tsar by the will of the entire nation that an addition to the records carefully stated that all classes of Russian society including the Don Cossacks had been consulted. A document dated May 3rd, 1682, noted that 'The Don Cossacks are at present in Moscow. Regional *ataman* Sergeyev and his comrades swore allegiance.' Taking into account distances and slowness of communication in Russia, it would have been impossible to convene a regular assembly within a fortnight.

The Patriarch stood on the steps by the Red Gate, surrounded by members of the Duma and the Orthodox hierarchy. The electors were scattered everywhere, on the balconies and terraces of the palace, in the square and in front of the Church of St Saviour. The head of the Russian Church proceeded to give a speech, in the course of which he made special reference to the physical handicaps of the elder Tsarevitch, his weakness and mental incapacity. 'Whom will you have for Tsar?' he concluded. 'Peter!' came the unanimous response. The Tolstoys and a man called Shaklovity-Sumbulov vainly shouted 'Ivan!', but their voices were drowned by those of their opponents. 'Judge according to your conscience,' the Patriarch went on. 'Is it your wish that two Tsars reign conjointly, or that Russia shall have but one Tsar?' Another roar went up: 'Let Peter reign alone!' It was rumoured – probably with justification –

that Ivan had no wish to rule and had voluntarily waived his rights i
favour of his younger brother.

'Thus it was to Tsarevitch Peter, Grand Sovereign,' wrote th
chroniclers, 'that his subjects, the Tsarevitch of Kasimov and Siberia
boyars and dignitaries, members of the Duma, clerks, merchants, "boyars
children", petty nobility, generals and colonels, voivodes and notaries
musketeers and tax-payers swore allegiance.'

The Patriarch and his retinue went at once to the young Tsarevitch an
asked him to accede to his subjects' wishes. Peter was ten years old
Although he had been carefully schooled for this occasion, he seeme
confused. Remembering, however, that repetition would lend additiona
weight to the request, he began by refusing the crown. The delegatio
insisted, reminding him of his elder brother's illness and his wish t
renounce the burdens of government.

'Sovereign, reject not the entreaties of your subjects,' the Patriarc
adjured him. The child accepted, the prelate blessed him and proclaime
him Tsar of all the Russias, and a dignitary hurried off to the Red Gate t
announce the accession of Tsar Peter Alexeyevitch.

It seemed a rapid and decisive victory, and no one could have bee
blamed for accepting it as a *fait accompli*. But history is shaped more ofte
by passion than reason. Determined to preserve her own freedom and th
interests of the Miloslavskys, Sophia refused to abandon the struggle an
fought on, even though she knew herself to be powerless and almost alone

Tradition demanded that the obsequies of Tsar Theodore be celebrate
on the day after his death. The only people admitted to the ceremony b
protocol were the new sovereign and the widow of the deceased. Othe
members of the family paid their last respects to him in the palace. At th
funeral of Maria Miloslavsky in 1669, Tsar Alexis followed the funera
cortège alone except for the heir apparent, while his younger sons
Theodore and Ivan, remained behind in the palace with the members o
the Terem. When Alexis Michaelovitch was laid to rest, Theodore walke
alone behind his bier, followed by Tsarina Natalia in a litter draped i
black and carried by her lords-in-waiting.

According to protocol, therefore, Tsar Theodore's mortal remains
should have been followed by Tsar Peter and a litter containing Tsarina
Martha Apraxin. Peter being only a child, Natalia accompanied him at a
distance as far as the cathedral, also in a litter. While this shocked no one,
what did cause a scandal was the Terem's determination to attend the
funeral on foot and thus parade itself in front of the watching crowds. No
one had dreamed that the Terem would break with established tradition
or that Tsar Alexis's daughters and sisters would risk flouting public

opinion in this manner. It was Sophia's way of proclaiming with startling clarity that she did not accept a decision which unjustly deprived Maria Miloslavsky's son of the throne that was his by right.

The tsarvena's gesture was, by contemporary standards, an act of great courage. Not content with shocking the Court and capital, Sophia took care to invest her outing with an aura of regal splendour by surrounding herself with an entourage as numerous as that of the new Tsar's mother. Tsarina Natalia saw this as an affront to her dignity. Impulsively, she showed her anger by sweeping out ostentatiously almost before the bier had been deposited in the centre of the cathedral. After embracing the late Tsar's body once more and kissing her son, the Dowager Tsarina returned to the palace without waiting for the Requiem Mass. Only Tsarina Martha and Tsarevna Sophia remained in their seats until the end of the ceremony.

But the scandal did not end there. One can well imagine Natalia's rage and resentment. Hardly had she won the day and begun to relish the fruits of revenge when her stepdaughter again flung down the gauntlet. However, Natalia's untimely exit from the cathedral had displayed a lack of respect for the person of the late Tsar and afforded the Terem a welcome opportunity to be scandalized in its turn. The elder princesses acted as spokeswomen for the family's displeasure and reproached Tsarina Natalia vehemently for her unseemly behaviour.

Sophia, who remained in control of the battlefield, exploited her advantage to the full. Having braved public opinion by her unprecedented act, she decided to appeal to it in an equally spectacular fashion.

Returning from the funeral on foot, as she had come, the tsarevna raised her voice in cries of lamentation strident enough to be overheard by the crowds.

'Wicked persons hastened our brother's death,' she wailed. 'Behold us orphans, bereft of father, mother and protectors. Our brother Ivan has been deprived of the throne. Take pity on us poor orphans. Should you judge us to be at fault in your eyes, let us go to live with Christian kings in foreign lands.'

These lamentations were partially in accord with tradition and closely resembled those uttered by kinswomen or guests at the funeral of the head of any ordinary family, but the allegation that 'wicked persons' had brought on Tsar Theodore's death prematurely and the request that Tsar Alexis's children by his first marriage should be allowed to leave the country were a blatant bid for popular support.

Having made its demonstration, the Terem relapsed into an outward calm which belied the fact that it was deliberately circulating an assortment of rumours designed to permeate the capital, spread to the provinces and sow the seeds of national unrest. It was whispered that Tsarina Natalia's brother Ivan had not long returned from exile before he donned the coronation robe and crown, seated himself on the Tsar's throne and declared: 'This crown becomes no one better than myself.' Tsarina Martha and Tsarevna Sophia had actually found him in this garb, so the story ran, and there was yet another rumour that Ivan Naryshkin had assaulted his royal namesake and nearly strangled him.

The Naryshkins were still extremely unpopular with the masses, and rumours of this kind found a ready reception. Besides, Natalia's family had been less than discreet in exploiting its return to favour. Six of her relatives were promoted to high rank and the universally detested Ivan was appointed a boyar at the age of twenty-three, which alienated a large number of the boyars who had originally supported Peter's claim to the throne.

Meanwhile, Matveyev was leading a peaceful existence in the town of Lukh, where he learned of Tsar Theodore's death on April 27th. The expected summons from the Kremlin soon arrived in the person of Almazov, one of Tsarina Natalia's lords-in-waiting, who reached Lukh early in May. Matveyev's former ward sent news of Peter's accession, which was exactly what Matveyev had hoped for, and assured him of her undiminished affection. She also mentioned the plot which Sophia was hatching against the new Tsar and stressed that she was in urgent need of his advice.

Strangely enough, although Matveyev set off at once he travelled at a leisurely pace, savouring his triumph. The population gave a warm welcome to the man who would probably become co-regent of the country. Artamon Matveyev halted now and again for an official dinner or an informal meal with old friends, and it was not until May 10th that he and his son reached the gates of Moscow. There he was met by seven loyal musketeers who also talked of a conspiracy. Once more displaying a casualness which was uncharacteristic of a man usually so cautious, Matveyev listened to their forebodings with only half an ear. Natalia's brother Athanasius hailed him as the saviour of the Naryshkin family and rode at his side. The former Foreign Minister paused for a moment outside his own mansion, now bereft of its treasures and dilapidated by four years of neglect, and then made his way to the palace, where Natalia and the young Tsar greeted him with tears of joy and lavished endearments on him.

Matveyev did not leave the Dowager Tsarina's apartments for two days. His presence reassured Natalia. Prominent figures thronged the antechambers and hastened to pay court to the future regent. Natalia's spirits gradually rose as support flowed in from all quarters. The only missing face was that of Ivan Miloslavsky, who developed a sudden inflammation of the legs which confined him to his room and prevented him from welcoming his life-long enemy. In fact, the old fox was 'at home' to members of the Miloslavsky faction, including the two Tolstoys, the musketeer officer Ivan Tsikler and many others. As the evil genius of the anti-Naryshkin conspiracy, he had taken it upon himself to draw up a list of those who would have to disappear in order to pave the Miloslavskys' way back to power, and the first name on the list was that of Matveyev.

Yet another figure was active behind the scenes. Prince Ivan Khovansky, 'the Braggart', was also drawing up a list of enemies, but the Miloslavskys did not enter into his calculations. His ambitions were personal and founded on a grave error of judgment, on a wild dream which was destined to ruin him once he had unwittingly brought Sophia to power, for Sophia feared him instinctively but knew how to make use of him.

Moscow prepared for a blood bath. Unrest was widespread, and every day saw the birth of a new plot. Heedless of approaching disaster, the Naryshkin clique – Matveyev included – blissfully shut its eyes to the threat that loomed ahead.

Out of the nineteen musketeer regiments in the Moscow garrison – a force of fifteen thousand well-armed men – only two had sworn allegiance to Tsar Peter, the 'Stirrup' Regiment and the Guards, but even they did not take long to rally to the Miloslavsky faction. Unmanageable as ever, the musketeers were gaining a new awareness of their power. Sophia's agents moved among them spreading skilful propaganda, reminding them of the injustices they had suffered in Yazykov's time and insinuating that the Naryshkins would be even worse. 'But, should Ivan become Tsar, you would enjoy the patronage of boyars who wish you well.'

Possibly to test the new government, the musketeers, supported by a number of regular regiments, addressed a petition to Tsar Peter complaining yet again of their ill-treatment by certain officers, notably sixteen colonels and a general commanding one of the regular regiments. Clumsily seeking to court the malcontents' goodwill, the Naryshkins condemned the officers to be handed over to their subordinates without even ordering an inquiry. The complaint was lodged on April 30th: the decision, with its implication of surrender, was taken in the first few days of May, even before Matveyev's arrival in the capital.

Feeling vaguely that, even if the officers were at fault, there was something iniquitous and immoral about the government's decision to abandon them to the fury of the soldiery without a hearing, the Patriarch sent personal emissaries to the various regiments in an attempt to persuade the soldiers and musketeers to hand over the unfortunate men for trial by a regular tribunal. The priests' efforts met with success and the accused were released for trial, but the new government showed its weakness once again. Still without a hearing, the officers were dismissed from their posts, deprived of their rank, sentenced to have their property confiscated, compelled to pay damages and, finally, bastinadoed in the public square.

This concession turned out to be an error of judgment. On the one hand, the Naryshkins had demonstrated to the nation their contempt for justice and the laws, and, on the other, they had endowed the musketeers with a sense of omnipotence. The soldiery's arrogance knew no bounds. Musketeers and soldiers no longer hesitated to criticize the government openly in taverns and booths. Far from expressing gratitude towards the men in power, they announced their intention of murdering the Naryshkins and putting Tsarevitch Ivan on the throne.

Discipline had completely collapsed. Other officers followed Colonels Tsikler and Ozerov into the Miloslavsky camp and canvassed for support for Ivan. Sophia's former nurse became one of her most valued agents. She was entrusted with large sums for distribution to the mutineers and kept Sophia informed of developments among the people. Finally, the last musketeer regiment loyal to Peter, the Butyrsky, went over to the tsarevna *en bloc*.

Sophia was unaware of her uncle's 'black lists', and there is no indication that she ever contemplated a massacre of her enemies. She probably hoped that the palace revolution would come about through pressure of public opinion and that the threat of insurrection would be enough to send the Naryshkins packing.

The forthcoming trial of strength gave Sophia time to mature. Her personal ambitions, which were limited to the regency since the throne itself was as yet beyond her scope, alerted her to the responsibilities of a head of State. It was clear that a government dominated by the Naryshkins could do the nation nothing but harm. All the men in her late brother's entourage, some of whom had also enjoyed her father's confidence, were now out of the picture. Sophia had great faith in their political judgment and the wisdom of the measures which they prescribed, but she alone could ensure that Russia travelled the road pioneered by the last two Tsars. Even Alexis Likhatchev and Ivan Yazykov had been removed from public life, despite their support of Peter's camp at the time of Theodore's death. Sophia's interests and those of Russia were identical. If the Terem obeyed her in the belief that it was preserving its own freedom, public opinion ranged itself behind her because it was sentimentally attracted by her defence of the gentle Ivan, who had been deprived of the crown despite his right of primogeniture.

The only man capable of reversing the tide of events was Artamon Matveyev, but his five-year absence from public life had divorced him from reality and blinded him to the gravity of the situation. The Naryshkin party slept on, gorged with success. Almost incredibly, in spite of signs that a revolt was imminent, the government took no countermeasures whatsoever. Only five days had passed since Matveyev's return to Moscow when the storm broke in earnest.

CHAPTER TWENTY-FOUR

MAY 15th, the anniversary of the presumed assassination of Dimitry, Ivan the Terrible's son, by Boris Godunov's myrmidons, was the day selected for the Naryshkins' removal. The night preceding this bloody enterprise was marked by an unusually violent storm which impressed itself on the popular imagination. At a given moment – no one knows who gave the order – the awesome clangour of the tocsin rang out from every belfry in the capital. Immediately, the streets reverberated with the sound of drums and the musketeers hurried to the headquarters of their respective regiments in full battle array. While they were forming up, Peter Tolstoy and Ivan Miloslavsky's son Alexander galloped from one regiment to the next shouting that the Naryshkins had strangled Tsarevitch Ivan. The great belfry of the Kremlin burst into life as though to lend weight to the lie, and the musketeers, long subjected to anti-Naryshkin propaganda by Khovansky and the Miloslavskys, accepted the news without demanding evidence. Yelling 'Death to the traitors and murderers of the royal family!', they joined the ever-increasing mob that was marching to storm the palace, hauling their cannon behind them.

Like all revolutions, the musketeers' owed its success to the pusillanimity of those in power. The Naryshkin party allowed itself to be captured with astonishing ease. Artamon Matveyev was on the point of leaving the palace and going home to dine when Prince Theodore Urussov, pale and distraught, came to warn him that the musketeers were marching on the Kremlin. He was too late, however. The musketeers manning the gates had already been bought over by the Miloslavskys.

Amid scenes of indescribable confusion, the courtiers trapped in the Kremlin precincts scurried towards the palace, some seeking refuge from popular fury and others in an attempt to defend the royal family.

Surrounded by terror-stricken boyars and hugging her son tightly to her, Tsarina Natalia heard the roar of the mob grow louder as it invaded the Kremlin's roads and courtyards and massed in front of the palace, demanding vengeance for the assassination of Tsarevitch Ivan. Natalia was forced to step out on to the terrace of the Red Gate and confront the sea of angry faces below, holding Peter by the hand. Then, to scotch the rumour of the elder Tsarevitch's death, Ivan himself was led on to the terrace. Some musketeers who had clambered up the columns of the Red Gate questioned him.

'Are you truly the Tsarevitch Ivan?'

Ivan assured them that he was. The Patriarch appeared and urged the musketeers to disperse peacefully, but his intervention did nothing to pacify them. Then Matveyev came out to harangue the mutineers, but his measured words had no effect except on the few men who were close enough to hear them. At that moment, Prince Dolgoruky, the autocratic chief of the Prikaz of Musketeers, decided to re-establish discipline by backing up his order to clear the square with threats and physical violence. The demonstrators, some of whom had not seen for themselves that Tsarevitch Ivan was alive, at once became transformed into a demented and irresistible mob.

It was a spontaneous, savage fury, deaf to the voice of reason and impervious to everything save hatred and the lust to kill. The musketeers who had reached the Red Gate dragged Dolgoruky from the platform by his arms and legs and threw him on to their comrades' pikes. Next, they fanned out inside the palace and ran Matveyev to earth in Tsarina Natalia's apartments. The young Tsar witnessed an appalling scene as his mother tried to protect her old friend but was brushed aside by the musketeers, who unceremoniously tore Matveyev from her arms and dragged him into the forecourt of the Church of the Annunciation, where they tossed him into the air and caught him on their pikes. Prince Michael Tcherkassky, who went to his aid, was killed in the same manner. The musketeers proceeded to savage Matveyev's body until all that remained of it was a bleeding mass of flesh. Inside the halls and chambers of the palace, the soldiery hunted down all those whose names appeared on Miloslavsky's and Khovansky's lists. Athanasius Naryshkin, Natalia's brother, hid under the altar of the Cathedral of St Saviour, but was betrayed by his dwarf and dragged out to be murdered. His brother Ivan lay down beneath the quilts on Natalia's bed and escaped detection. Prince Romodanovsky, the unfortunate voivode involved in the Tchigirin campaign, Theodore's friend Yazykov and several other members of the Duma were also massacred in the Kremlin. Meanwhile, other musketeers in Moscow itself murdered various prominent personalities and looted their houses.

The mutilated corpses were left in the open for the night because the musketeers would not allow them to be buried. One of Matveyev's retainers, a Negro convert called Ivan, courageously claimed his master's remains, and the musketeers were so impressed by his loyalty that they agreed to hand them over. Collecting the fragments of mangled flesh in a cloth, Ivan carried them home and later had them buried near the Church of St Nicholas, asking to be buried there himself after his death.

As they were returning from the Kremlin through the streets of Moscow, the group of musketeers who had killed Prince Dolgoruky passed his father's house and, yielding to the Russian propensity for remorse, felt impelled to go in and offer their apologies. Old Dolgoruky listened to their condolences without flinching, but after the murderers had left he uttered threats against them. 'They have eaten the pike, but its teeth are still sharp,' he growled. When a servant passed on this remark to the musketeers, who were continuing on their way with consciences appeased, they flew into a fresh rage and rushed back to the house to kill the defenceless old man.

Matveyev's son Andrei and several other intended victims had been concealed in cupboards in the Terem apartments. Andrei and two of his companions were saved by a palace dwarf who disguised them as grooms and took them under cover of darkness to a priest, who gave them sanctuary. Theodore Yazykov was mistaken by the mob for Ivan Naryshkin and so owed his death to what might be termed a tragic misunderstanding.

Finally, in a bid for popular support, the musketeers methodically destroyed the records of the Prikazy of Serfs and Justice, thereby offering a chance of freedom to men who could never have hoped to obtain it in the ordinary way. Oddly enough, the population did not join in the disorders, but rejected the musketeers' blandishments and held aloof from bloodshed. The military revolt was supported neither by merchants nor craftsmen, nor serfs, nor even by those who lived on the brink of the law. Common folk were heard to censure the musketeers for their misconduct, and in several provincial cities, notably Novgorod, where concerted outbreaks of violence took place, prisoners refused to leave their cells, shouting: 'Let those who put us here free us!'

As for the other protagonists in this drama, all the most authoritative historical sources agree that Sophia cannot be held responsible for the murders committed in May 1682. She was ignorant of the 'black lists', and, although her intrigues certainly played a part in the insurrection, her only fault lay in thinking that the threat of revolt would prove sufficient to oust the Naryshkins and set Tsarevitch Ivan on the throne. Nevertheless, her name was so well-known to the musketeers that it had become a rallying cry, as the Danish Resident Rosenbusch discovered two days later when the tsarevna's intervention saved his life.

While searching for Ivan Naryshkin on May 16th, the musketeers kept their eyes open for several other people, among them Ivan Gutman and Daniel Gaden, two foreign physicians who had treated Theodore Alexeyevitch. Daniel Gaden was the Terem's official doctor and numbered Vasily Golitsyn among his patients. Golitsyn's correspondence, now in the archives of the Lenin Library, includes a letter which Gaden sent his patron while on the run. Tsarina Natalia would have liked to save him, as would Sophia herself, but they were two women against a horde of angry men. Natalia, who had just lost Matveyev, did not even know whether her brothers and father would escape death. Apart from her brother Ivan and her father Cyril, her surviving relatives were roaming the outskirts of Moscow in fear of their lives. Having failed to find Gaden, the musketeers decided that the next best thing was to arrest Rosenbusch, another of the missing doctor's patients, on suspicion of having paid Gaden to poison Tsar Theodore.

It was then that Sophia's new-found authority first declared itself, for she pleaded the Danish diplomat's case with the musketeers and had him brought to her. Rosenbusch managed to reach his house unmolested because the mutineers who escorted him through the Kremlin for his own protection told their accomplices: 'He is an ambassador. He has spoken with the tsarevna, let him pass.'

Rosenbusch also recalled hearing some mutineers seeking instructions from Prince Khovansky, who asked them: 'Should we make Natalia take the veil?' Upon which, apparently, the musketeers clamoured: 'Yes, yes! To a nunnery with her!'

Natalia escaped the veil, but Gaden was eventually caught and murdered.

Ivan Miloslavsky, the man who had sparked off the whole affair, reverted to his old fence-sitting tactics and missed the Kremlin massacre by alleging that he was sick. Prince Vasily Golitsyn, who was not a party to the conspiracy, went off to visit his family in the country, as he had done after Tsar Theodore's death. Khovansky played on the musketeers' passions from the side-lines and then, the day after the first massacres, appointed himself their commander, as though to prove that he was a *deus ex machina*.

* * *

Just as the force of an explosion sometimes extinguishes the fire that has caused it, so revolutionary ardour is often quenched by its own excesses. On May 16th, 1682, however, passions were still running high.

Still armed, the musketeers poured into the Kremlin once more, not using the Red Gate this time but converging on the entrance to the private apartments giving on to the inner courtyard of the palace. Their object, said the annals, was to 'demonstrate their devotion to the Terem'.

The tsarevnas came out to speak to the musketeers. They reminded them of their oath of allegiance and told them not to approach them with such 'discourtesy' in future. 'Some discourtesy,' comments the historian Belov. 'The musketeers had come to demand that Ivan, Tsarina Natalia's brother, be handed over to them.' The princesses, playing for time, managed to put them off for twenty-four hours.

This delay did not have the anticipated result, for next day the musketeers were back in the inner courtyard once more. Moscow resembled a besieged city. Doors were bolted and shutters tightly closed. At each gate in the city, or rather the three cities which comprised the capital (Kitay Gorod, Bielogorod and the Kremlin), pickets checked incoming and outgoing traffic. The cautious townsfolk seldom ventured into the streets, and the only people who could circulate freely were Ivan Miloslavsky's couriers.

On May 17th, then, the air was again rent by the tolling of bells and the thunder of drums as the Kremlin was invaded once more. Now that law and order had collapsed, all eyes in the palace turned to Sophia, who, though alone and deserted by her advisers, felt it incumbent upon her to act.

Sophia was with Tsarina Natalia when someone announced the arrival of the musketeers, who could be heard shouting: 'We shall not budge from here until Ivan Naryshkin and all the traitors have been handed over!'

The unfortunate young man whose life they had hoped to save was again in mortal danger. The boyars, members of the Duma and noblemen of Natalia's entourage feared the worst for themselves and cravenly urged the Dowager Tsarina to abandon her own brother to certain death. 'Sacrifice him, Sovereign, to save the lives of the royal family and of us, its devoted servants,' they implored her. Their fears were not unfounded, for the musketeers, exasperated by the delay, were now patently capable of slaughtering everyone in the Kremlin. The situation had got so out of hand that even Sophia was powerless. Coldly, she supported the boyars' demand, refusing to risk the lives of her brother Ivan and her sisters in a vain endeavour to save that of an enemy.

Stunned and bewildered by the pleas of her entourage and the murderous cries of the mutineers outside, Natalia was conscious only of her weakness and the inevitability of impending doom. Even she understood that by refusing to hand over her brother she was jeopardizing the life of her son. Time was running out. As a last resort, Sophia put forward a plan which offered a slender hope of saving Ivan Naryshkin's life. She suggested that Natalia herself should accompany her brother to the Church of St Saviour in the hope that the musketeers would be touched by the sight of her and shrink from profaning a holy place.

Faced with the inevitable, Ivan Naryshkin showed greater courage and dignity than anyone would have believed him capable of. He confessed, took Communion and, accompanied by his sister and the few noblemen who dared to come with him, entered the sanctuary, surrounded by vociferous soldiers but outwardly calm.

'My sister and Sovereign,' he told Natalia, 'I go to my death without fear. My only wish is that my blood shall be the last shed here.' We are told that all those present were deeply moved, including Sophia, who gave Ivan an icon depicting the Virgin Mary before he went out to meet the musketeers – hoping, perhaps, that even they would not lay hands on a man carrying a likeness of the Mother of God.

Meanwhile, the soldiers' impatience was mounting and their cries growing more and more menacing. Old Prince Jacob Odoyevsky, trembling with fear, begged the Tsarina to hurry.

'Saving your grief, Sovereign, you must deliver him up. And you, Ivan, must go forth with all speed lest we be all slain on your account.' (Andrei Matveyev attributes these words to Odoyevsky in his account of the uprising.)

The doors of the church were flung open and Natalia and her brother stepped out into the forecourt. Immediately, a score of hands shot out. Seizing the luckless man by his ankles, the musketeers dragged him down the steps, through the Kremlin and finally to the torture-chamber, where they tortured him for many hours before hacking him to bits in Red Square.

Satisfied at last, the musketeers trooped out of the Kremlin and resumed the task of looting their enemies' houses, leaving the palace to mourn the past and tremble for the future. The sight of his relatives and his mother's friends being slaughtered by the jeering soldiery before his very eyes must have made an indelible impression on Tsar Peter.

'Behold Prince Dolgoruky! Make way for the voivode!' yelled the musketeers, dragging the body of their victim along, or again: 'Make way for the mighty boyar!'

The musketeers had invaded the Tsar's private quarters, playing havoc and turning the boy's world upside down. It is said that the facial tics which afflicted Peter the Great all his life dated from the events of May 1682. A hatred of Moscow, the old Russia and all that reminded him of the tragic past must have become rooted in his subconscious, for he never threw it off, and the callous contempt for human life which he displayed on various occasions during his reign was probably engendered by the traumatic experiences of his youth.

* * *

The flames of rebellion were slow to subside. Unarmed this time, since victory was now theirs, the musketeers came to the palace on May 18th to beseech Tsar Peter – 'humbly', as their official petition phrased it – to persuade his grandfather Cyril Naryshkin, who had survived the massacre unscathed by hiding in Tsarina Martha's apartments, to enter a monastery. Although addressed to Tsar Peter, the petition was, in fact, passed on to Sophia. No one thought of protesting this time, least of all the party in question, who fled to a distant monastery, thankful to have extricated himself on such favourable terms. Natalia's surviving brothers also succeeded in escaping from Moscow and went to ground elsewhere.

On May 19th, the musketeers called at the palace to claim – still 'humbly' – the price of their devotion to the Crown, namely ten roubles per head and a share in the general distribution of property belonging to the boyars and other persons who had been assassinated.

On the 20th came a fresh request: 'Would it please the Tsar to remove Alexis Likhatchev and his relatives, together with the boyar Yazykov's relatives, from the capital?'

On the 23rd, probably reflecting that it might, after all, be advisable to show a little consideration for the sovereign's family – or at least the Miloslavskys – the musketeers returned and requested the princesses, through the medium of Khovansky, to see to it that Russia was governed by two tsars. The boyars at once fell in with this proposal, and Sophia was disposed to accept it on her brothers' behalf as one of the first fruits of victory.

On May 25th, the musketeers suggested that Ivan should be the first or elder tsar and Peter the second or junior. The princesses (i.e. Sophia) at once convened a meeting of the Council of State to study the proposition.

The Duma, with the Patriarch and clergy in attendance, deliberated at length. Its members were perplexed both by the situation and the proposed solution, which was entirely without precedent in Russian history. However, since the musketeers were threatening to resume their mutinous activities in the event of a refusal, some formula for the re-establishment of peace had to be found. Several speakers suggested that it would be difficult to share sovereignty and define the two tsars' prerogatives, but Sophia's men argued that, on the contrary, two tsars were better than one and that it would be a very convenient arrangement. While one tsar was away on campaign (that meant Peter, since Ivan could not sit a horse), the elder tsar would attend to affairs of state.

History was quickly scanned for examples of a similar division of power. It was recalled that Egypt had Pharaoh and Joseph, that Byzantium was ruled simultaneously by two emperors, Basil and Constantine, and that the two sons of Theodosius the Great, Honorius and Arcadius, had also reigned conjointly. The dominating feature of the discussions was, however, a tacit acknowledgment of the fact that the Terem's voice was backed by the musketeers, and it was not long before all the members of the Council allowed themselves to be talked over.

The only problem was that Ivan declined with gentle obduracy to become tsar, and that the elder princesses, Sophia's aunts, thought it senseless to put an invalid on the throne. As to the manner born, the musketeers strode to the palace to tell Khovansky that, having heard from one of Tsarevna Martha Alexeyevna's serving-women that Ivan did not want the crown, they wished to see him personally to ascertain the truth.

Accordingly, chosen representatives from each regiment were received in audience by Ivan, who gave them his hand to kiss in the presence of his sisters. After praising the musketeers for their devoted service, the princesses inquired where they had gained such a mistaken impression of Ivan's intentions. Reassured, the musketeers again affirmed their desire to have Ivan as 'first Tsar', which greatly delighted his sisters. Ivan murmured that he had no wish to be tsar, but that 'If such is the will of God, let Him do according to His Holy Will' – to which the princesses hastily added: 'Truly, it is the Lord's Will, for the chosen members of the regiments speak not of their own accord but because God hath inspired them so to do.' Tsar Ivan's seniority would automatically confer seniority on his sisters, being daughters of Tsar Alexis's first marriage, and Natalia Naryshkin's children would be relegated permanently to the younger branch.

On May 26th, the Patriarch and the boyars came to ask Ivan officially to accept the crown, and the Tsarevitch, as usual, bowed to the will of others 'so that peace shall reign in the land'.

Since the Tsars were too young to rule, it was natural that the regency should be offered to the senior Tsar's elder sister. Observing a time-honoured tradition, Sophia declined the honour and feigned reluctance before finally accepting the role of her dreams. Court, government and people – in other words, public opinion – all took readily to this arrangement, especially as it was the only possible solution now that Natalia had lost her supporters and was alone in the world. On taking over the reins of government, Sophia commanded officials and members of the Duma to present themselves before her 'without dread' to submit affairs of state for discussion.

On May 29th, the Princess Regent announced that, to be valid, all documents or decrees must bear her own name below that of the Tsars.

Sophia was virtually head of State. The Terem had triumphed, sweeping away the obsolete *domostroy*, or family code, and trampling on masculine pride.

CHAPTER TWENTY-FIVE

THUS, from events in which the leading role had been played not by her but by Ivan Miloslavsky and Prince Khovansky, Sophia emerged as the true head of the Romanov family. Bereft of relations and supporters, Tsarina Natalia was entirely in her stepdaughter's power and could offer her no resistance. The days of bloodshed had taught Sophia some valuable lessons, the most important being that her uncle Miloslavsky and her friend Vasily Golitsyn, though useful, had a knack of vanishing at crucial moments. Meanwhile, another man had entered her life, Theodore Shaklovity, a junior civil servant of obscure parentage. No one knows if he was in love with the Princess at this stage, but his devotion to her was absolute and unconditional. He was intelligent, energetic and ambitious – an adventurer, in fact, but someone on whom Sophia already knew that she could rely under any circumstances.

As official Regent, Sophia had to employ all her unusual gifts in order to assert her authority over the country. People were astonished to find themselves being governed by a woman, for not since the tenth century, when Princess Olga of Kiev ruled in her grandson Vladimir's name, had a Russian princess openly ventured to assume the functions of head of State.[1]

Sophia's triumph was not without its problems. Although her name was already known in Moscow and the provinces, she could only govern effectively if she had an army at her disposal. The musketeers were proving hard to control and their demands, which were invariably supported by Khovansky, exasperated and irritated her. Nevertheless, political intuition told her to feign gratitude to the ill-disciplined horde and grant all its requests until she was strong enough to bend it to her will.

In the meantime, the musketeers were ruining the country's finances. Not content with their large gratuity, they claimed thirty-five years' back pay totalling 240,000 roubles, an immense sum for the period.

[1] It is true that during the Time of Troubles the crown was offered to Tsar Theodore's widow, but this was merely a symptom of dissension among the boyars, and the Tsarina did not take it seriously for one moment.

Inwardly furious, Sophia agreed, and added a further substantial bonus which the musketeers, according to Sylvester Medviedev, hurried off to squander in the taverns. Having established a precedent, they pursued their extortions until monasteries and merchants were bled white.

Still uneasy and fearful that the government would one day call them to account, the musketeers sought to protect themselves against the possible consequences of their insurrection by 'humbly' requesting that the Tsars, the younger of whom had watched them massacre members of his family, should sign a declaration of gratitude for their outstanding services to the Crown. The palace duly consented to the publication of the manifesto, which conferred on the musketeers the resounding title of 'Infantry of the Court' and granted them extraordinary privileges. No musketeer, ran the text of the declaration, could be sentenced or deported except after a special inquiry and by royal decree. To complete their rehabilitation and silence popular criticism of their part in the uprising, the musketeers further demanded that a stone column be erected in Red Square on which the text of the manifesto could be engraved and their feats of arms glorified for the benefit of posterity.

Meanwhile, Sophia was forming her government. Ivan Miloslavsky was appointed Treasurer of State and Khovansky confirmed in his self-appointed role as head of the Prikaz of Musketeers, but the highest honours naturally went to Prince Vasily Golitsyn, despite his modest part in the events which brought Sophia to power. He replaced Volynsky, the Minister of Foreign Affairs, who had been unnerved by the revolt, submitted his resignation and retired to his country estate. Vasily Golitsyn also received the specially created title 'Grand Guardian of the Seal of State', which made him a sort of Lord Protector and first gentleman of the Court, it being impossible for him to become Prince Consort. The boyar Sokovnin, formerly deported by Theodore Alexeyevitch and brother of the boyarina Morozova and Princess Urussov, the two women who had been martyred for the Old Belief, was put in charge of the Department of Justice. For the rest, Sophia called upon former associates of Tsar Theodore, though she did not as yet venture to reinstate the most respected of them, Alexis Likhatchev, who, having seen his house ransacked and his collection of valuable manuscripts looted, had been sent into enforced retirement at the musketeers' bidding. The senior officials of the Duma and government departments, apart from those who had been killed during the riots, remained at their posts. The brothers Tolstoy and the two musketeer officers Tsikler and Ozerov were appropriately rewarded. Sophia's nurse Theodosia was not forgotten, either. She eceived a handsome dowry and married Ozerov, who was promoted o colonel.

Where the Church was concerned, Sophia treated the Patriarch with espect but could not forget his support of the Naryshkin party. She was encouraged in her attitude by the Latinist monk Sylvester Medviedev and by Theodore Shaklovity, her confidant and 'watch-dog'.

In general, the Princess Regent's choice of advisers was sound. Only one man in her entourage gave cause for anxiety, and he had been forced on her by circumstances. Khovansky was the real threat to her dynasty, and Sophia knew it.

Vain, lacking in intelligence and unendurably conceited, Prince Khovansky had been a voivode during the reign of Alexis Michaelovitch. As a scion of the kings of Lithuania, Poland and Hungary, 'the Braggart' cherished limitless ambitions and was even contemplating a plan to put his son Andrei on the throne, having previously married him to Catherine, the youngest and prettiest of Sophia's sisters. The people did not like him, but by flattering them and indulging their every whim he had managed to win the majority over to his side. Moreover, during his governorship of Pskov, where the Old Belief was secretly but firmly rooted, he had been converted to the *raskol*. The movement, which had taken advantage of current conditions to go over to the offensive, now regarded him as its principal hope.

The trial of strength between the Regent and the pro-Khovansky forces was inevitable. Sophia took stock of her allies. Her spies assured her that the seditious elements had no popular backing apart from a few young hot-heads. Merchants, men of the *possads* and tax-payers were tired of the musketeers' extortions, and even the serfs tried to reason with them and soothe their inflamed feelings. The musketeers themselves lacked cohesion. They included as many adherents of Orthodoxy as Old Believers, and Sophia had taken the precaution of contacting officers and other ranks who were ill-disposed towards Khovansky. These malcontents often came to see her at the palace, and so the Princess Regent, for all the difficulties of her position, was no longer without support.

Sophia's first concern was to see the two Tsars crowned quickly, and she worked wonders to get it done. The whole coronation ceremonial, which was a complicated one, had to be modified to suit the unprecedented circumstances. Russian sovereigns had always been crowned with the same historic symbols of the continuity of power, and although the palace treasury contained a number of ornate crowns the one traditionally used at the coronation itself was the comparatively modest *shapka* that had once belonged to Vladimir Monomach. Sophia achieved the impossible by getting goldsmiths to copy the crown, sceptre and electrum globe, down to the smallest detail, within the space of a single month.

Bidding farewell to the tragedies of the past few weeks, the Muscovites prepared to celebrate the accession of Ivan and Peter with unrestrained enthusiasm.

The Patriarch and clergy spent most of the night of June 25th–26th, 1682, praying in the cathedral. Then, after snatching two or three hours' rest, the head of the Russian Church returned to the scene of the coronation. The boyar Sheyin and Prince Troyekurov arrived with the crowns, the noblemen Pushkin and Tchaadayev with the sceptres, the treasurer Toltchanov and the gentleman of the seal Bashmakov with the twin orbs, preceded by the premier nobleman of the land and Guardian of the Privy Seal, Prince Vasily Golitsyn.

The bells that had sounded the tocsin a month before began to peal joyously. Prince Golitsyn went to fetch the Tsars from the palace. Clad in gold, with fur shapkas on their heads despite the heat of summer, Ivan and Peter entered the cathedral surrounded by a swarm of dignitaries. Mounting the ramps in the centre of the church together, the youth and the child seated themselves simultaneously on their identical thrones. Then, dressed in their coronation robes, the two Tsars returned to the palace beneath a rain of gold and silver pieces, halting on the way to make obeisance before the relics in the Cathedral of the Annunciation and the tombs in the Cathedral of the Archangel Michael.

* * *

The first rubber was over, but Sophia was a long way from winning the game. Recent surrenders to the musketeers' demands had dealt royal prestige a hard knock, the Patriarch's authority had been weakened by the defeat of the Naryshkins, whom he had unwisely supported, and Khovansky had not backed down when confronted by a *fait accompli*. Sophia remained on her guard.

The coronation, which took place on June 26th, was preceded by a psychological campaign on the part of Sophia, who stepped up the frequency of the two Tsars' public appearances and took care to be present herself.

On June 11th, when a sacred icon was sent to the regiments of the Kazan garrison, the Princess Regent accompanied her brothers to the dedication ceremony.

On June 16th, the Tsars, the princesses and Tsarina Natalia, humiliated and submissive, went on foot to the new Convent of the Virgins. This ime, the real focus of the demonstration was the princesses with Sophia t their head, not Tsarina Natalia and the two Tsars. Natalia could no loubt have absented herself, but she was still so fearful for her son's life hat she had scarcely let him out of her sight since May 15th.

It cannot be disguised that the bold behaviour of Tsar Alexis's daughters ιad shocked the common people, who regarded the feminist movement s brazenly impudent and lacking in dignity. Sophia was not worried bout scandal at this stage, however, and was prepared to go even further.

* * *

Moscow was experiencing a great influx of Old Believers, who had left heir hiding-places and were pouring into the capital to settle accounts with those whom they regarded as heretics and apostates. The time was ipe, for Khovansky, their patron, had assured them of his support. In the treets and squares, preachers of the sect – among them a fanatic by the ıame of Nikita 'Devoid of Sanctity' – openly professed their faith and hreatened 'the breed of Nikon' with violence. They were heard adjuring passers-by to 'Fight, Orthodox Christians, for the Old Belief, which is dying in Russia, among the Greeks and elsewhere besides!'

Patriarch Joachim did not venture to take action against them and no one dared to interrupt the orators since they were usually surrounded by musketeers who were loyal to the sect and ready to deal with any ıecklers.

On July 5th, 1682, emboldened by their impunity, the Old Believers nvaded the Kremlin in force. Setting up their lecterns opposite the fore-court of the Cathedral of the Assumption and beneath the windows of the royal palace, lighting candles and opening the ancient tomes which they had brought with them, the dissident priests heaped the Patriarch with insults and curses, poured scorn on the new icons and vituperated against the revised versions of liturgical works.

The Patriarch, who was officiating in the cathedral, sent a priest to ask the demonstrators to leave the square, but he failed to get a hearing and retired hastily to avoid being stoned.

Sylvester Medviedev, who was at the very hub of the religious controversy, described it in great detail. Khovansky proposed a public debate between the adherents of Orthodoxy and the Old Belief, un-perturbed by the advantage which the established Church, with its wealth of learned theologians, would enjoy over the fanatical but ignorant devotees of the Old Belief because his musketeers were prepared to silence the opposition by force.

Another writer who recorded a description of this memorable day wa
Savva Romanov, a member of the opposing camp. According to him
Tsarina Natalia, still fearing for Peter's safety, sent no less than three
messages to the Old Believers, unbeknown to Sophia, urging that the
debate should take place in Red Square or one of the Kremlin courtyard
and begging them not to come to the cathedral or the palace itself. In
fact, the schismatics did not insist on holding the meeting in the palace
but the Patriarch supported Sophia's decision to do so, pointing out tha
if the debate had to take place in a public square the princesses would be
unable to attend. The Old Believers protested that the tsarevnas should
not mix in matters which more properly concerned the Tsars, but they
finally yielded to Sophia's wishes.

Supported by Sophia, the Patriarch therefore rejected a public debate
and proposed an official discussion in the great hall of the Granovitaya
Palata in the presence of the royal family and delegates of the people. The
Church was represented by the Patriarch, eight metropolitans, five
archbishops, two bishops and a large number of abbots and priests.

There could be no better illustration of Sophia's new-found authority
than the place allotted her at this extraordinary debate. She arrived
accompanied by the noblemen of her court, the two Tsars, Tsarina Natalia
her sister Maria and her two aunts Tatiana and Anna. The Tsars were
seated on twin thrones, while Sophia and her aunt Tatiana took their
places on two other thrones set on a raised dais. In an armchair slightly
below them sat Sophia's aunt Anna, and lower still stood the armchairs
reserved for Tsarina Natalia and Tsarevna Maria. It was a reconstitution
of Byzantine customs in which women had pride of place. The Tsars
being only mute figures on this occasion, Sophia presided over the
assembly, and there is little doubt that this active feminine participation in
matters which had hitherto been an exclusively male province shocked
and irritated the Old Believers profoundly.

A wave of Old Believers swept in, and took the remaining space by
assault. They were a motley and undisciplined crowd – many of them, so
we are told by eye-witnesses, in an advanced stage of inebriation. Yelling
at the tops of their voices, they set up their benches and lecterns and lit
their candles, their whole attitude proclaiming that they had come not to
discuss theology but to impose their will.

Omitting to ask prior permission of the Patriarch and Tsars, their
spokesman at once began to read out a list of demands, so phrased as to
sound like an ultimatum. While the list was being read, Nikita 'Devoid
of Sanctity' interjected comments of his own, hurling insults and coarse
epithets at the Patriarch. When Archbishop Athanasius took him to task

r his unseemly remarks, Nikita threw himself at the prelate and had to : hauled off by members of the Patriarch's retinue.

'How dare you endeavour to strike a holy bishop before our eyes!' ied Sophia. 'You are not worthy to open your lips in our presence!' hen, turning to her followers, she said: 'Take their petition and give it to ıother to read.'

Patriarch Joachim attempted to instil some decorum into the proceed-gs by explaining the purpose underlying the revision of liturgical books ıd, texts in hand, launched into a comparative analysis of correct and roneous translations. Nikita interrupted him:

'We are here to speak of dogma, not grammar!' he shouted, but the Old elievers evidently lacked confidence in their own erudition, for they fused to listen to explanations. Raising their right hands, fingers ɛtended, towards the ceiling, they yelled: 'Thus should ye make the gn of the Cross and no wise else!' Hearing the fanatics accuse Patriarch ikon of being a heretic, Sophia cried: 'If Sovereign Patriarch Nikon was heretic, my late father Alexis was one also!' Angrily, she rose and ıstigated the Old Believers for their ignorance and discourtesy.

They answered her rudely, and the Princess Regent, realizing the futility f further discussion, was threatening to leave the hall in high dudgeon hen above the tumult she heard the musketeers shouting: 'It is indeed me for you to depart, Highness, and retire to a convent. We are content ıat the Tsars are in good health. The palace will not be empty without ɔu!'

Turning pale, the Princess retorted: 'If you will, we can all leave the ɔuntry together. We shall see what the people think of that!'

This threat struck home, though uproar persisted. The noblemen, ɛrgy, officials and delegates in the Tsars' suite declared they were ready ɔ die for the reigning house, the Patriarch persuaded Sophia to resume ɛr seat, and the debate continued amid scenes of chaos until vespers. he Old Believers finally left the palace shouting, 'We have won! We ave won!', but in fact their fate and Khovansky's was sealed from that ıoment onwards.

*   *   *

Ever mindful of public opinion, Sophia could not forget the voices ıat had urged her to retire to a nunnery. Abruptly, she discontinued her ublic appearances with the object of disarming critics until she felt rong enough to ignore them. Her immediate goal was the removal of van Khovansky. As long as 'the Braggart' was alive, the Princess Regent's osition would remain precarious, and she was well aware of that fact.

The atmosphere in Moscow was still ominous. The government an the boyars anticipated fresh trouble from the musketeers, and th musketeers feared the government reprisals which they had so richl merited. Khovansky never ventured forth without a bodyguard of hundred men, but his arrogance remained unabated. He still looked dow on Sophia as a girl who aspired to man's work, and his insolence, like th contempt in which he held her, grew with each passing day.

CHAPTER TWENTY-SIX

Y the strange logic of history, the same forces which had brought
phia to power were those which threatened her and the whole
omanov dynasty as soon as she became Regent.

Like many a king faced by the problem of safeguarding his life and his
rone, Sophia sought to escape her enemies by launching her family on
. itinerant existence. The Tsars and the Terem, accompanied by their
overnment and loyal retainers, journeyed incessantly from one summer
lace and one monastery to the next in an effort to foil the schemes of
hovansky and his musketeers.

Moscow had become Khovansky's private domain. Whenever he
ssed through the streets of the capital, the musketeers ran ahead of their
ther's' horse, calling: 'Make way, make way! The Great One comes!'
reward for their devotion, Khovansky did his best to satisfy all their
ishes. He lavished honours and public money on them and punished
ithout trial any officers who were unlucky enough to have earned their
spleasure. Boyars and commoners alike trembled for their lives and
ssessions. Khovansky's popularity with the musketeers was founded on
magogy alone. He deluded himself that they liked him, but they merely
und him useful. The musketeers supported him because they enjoyed
nmunity under his command, the Old Believers because he had promised
restore the Old Belief. Every other section of the community hated
m. Before her departure from Moscow, Sophia had taken the precaution
leaving behind several loyal agents who could keep her informed of
nditions in the capital. Khovansky had felt uneasy when the royal
mily first departed for the fortified Monastery of the Trinity and St
rgius. However, Sophia risked a brief visit to Moscow during which,
preparation for the *coup de grâce* which she meant to deal Khovansky
hen the moment came, she pretended to further her enemy's schemes by
nsenting to a marriage between young Khovansky and her sister
atherine. Having allayed the foolish man's suspicions in this way, she
ft for Kolomenskoye, taking her whole retinue with her.

In his account of these events, Andrei Matveyev stresses Ivan Milo-

slavsky's part in Sophia's decision to go over to the offensive. Far fro
slumbering on his estate near Moscow, as might have been imagined, tl
old man was keeping in touch with Khovansky's every move through h
spies. There was, in fact, no secret about Khovansky's wish to proclai
himself monarch of all the Russias, having cleared the ground beforehar
by exterminating the entire royal family and a large number of boyar
Realizing that the only means of bringing off this coup was to plunge tl
country into anarchy first, Khovansky energetically set about creatin
disorder.

News of his activities spread from Moscow to the provinces. It w
reported that he intended to have the royal family murdered during tl
traditional procession to the Donskoy Monastery on August 19th. Soph
hastened to spread these rumours, using them as an excuse to leave fc
Kolomenskoye. Her sudden and ostentatious departure provoked
massive exodus from the capital by all citizens of any prominence, so th
by September 1st, the date celebrated as New Year's Day prior to tl
reign of Peter the Great, only one functionary was left in Moscow
attend the official ceremonies.

Khovansky disregarded the warning.

One morning, on emerging from the ornate palace at Kolomenskoy
to make a tour of inspection, Colonel Danilov of the musketeers notice
a letter nailed to the main door. Seeing that it was addressed to th
Tsarevna Sophia Alexeyevna, Danilov at once delivered it to her. Tl
missive was unsigned, but its anonymous authors declared themselves t
be two men of the *possad* and a musketeer who were loyal to their oaths c
allegiance and wished to warn the Princess Regent that Khovansky ha
assembled them, together with other men, to command them in his son
presence to invade the capital and kill Sophia and the Tsars, the Tsarin
Natalia, the Patriarch and members of the government.

Many historians have doubted the existence of any organized con
spiracy and assume that this anonymous letter was the work of Sophia
friends. Be that as it may, it provided the Princess Regent with a satis
factory pretext for vigorous action.

* * *

Accompanied by her family, court and government, the Regent hur
riedly left Kolomenskoye and went to seek refuge on another estate a
Vorobyevo. Finding it too close to Moscow for comfort, the royal famil
moved on to yet another estate at Pavlovskoye and thence to th
monastery of St Savva, whose stout walls gave promise of greater securit

ophia then went over to the attack. Her couriers galloped off, bearing spatches and orders addressed to the provincial cities in the name of the vo Tsars. Soldiers, noblemen, boyars and their servitors were called on muster at the monastery of St Savva to defend their sovereigns' ves.

These messages no longer referred to the musketeers in the glowing rms engraved on the obelisk which was erected after their victory. ophia now called them traitors, thieves and rebels. The boyars who had caped their fury in May were now the Regent's surest allies and dearest iends. This reversal of policy shocked no one. Khovansky was in disrace, and Sophia represented the only hope of disposing of him and ving the Tsars' lives.

While State servitors were converging from all directions in answer to er summons, the Princess Regent and her followers left the monastery f St Savva and made for the monastery of the Trinity and St Sergius, voiding the main roads. Ten versts from its destination, the cortège alted in the village of Vozdvizhenskoye, where the Tsars owned a odest rest-house.

There, the government received further denunciatory letters. Without asting time, Sophia called a session of the Duma to examine Khovansky's ase. The bill of indictment was a lengthy one. Khovansky was charged, mong other things, with having distributed public funds to the usketeers, with having relaxed discipline, with having allowed the usketeers to demand 'discourteously' (a feeble description of what had appened in the Kremlin) that they be received in audience by the Tsars, ith having tortured people without trial, with having appropriated oney wrongfully requisitioned from monasteries and private domains, ith having boasted of his services in the sovereigns' presence, with aving insulted the boyars and threatened them with spears, with having onspired with Nikita 'Devoid of Sanctity' and fought with him against e Church, with having failed to pay his respects to Tsar Ivan on eptember 1st. The list of charges continued, a blend of the trivial and the agic, until it reached the principal count: intended regicide.

Without further ado, the indictment repeated the terms of the anonyous letters and alleged that Khovansky had planned to annihilate the uling house, kill the Patriarch and boyars, foment a popular insurrection nd exploit the ensuing chaos in order to usurp the throne. By a unaniious decision, the Duma summarily sentenced Prince Ivan Khovansky nd his son Andrei to death. The trial was, of course, a mockery, for the ondemned men were not present and had no chance to defend themselves. ophia was later censured by historians for this breach of justice, but she

knew the true extent of the danger which threatened her country a
must have realized that no other course of action was possible.

Sentence having been passed, 'the Braggart' was summoned in the mo
courteous terms to join the Court at Vozdvizhenskoye. It is not clear w
Khovansky accepted this suspicious invitation – unless he was so blind
by conceit and stupidity that he no longer feared anyone. Escorted
his personal bodyguard, Khovansky set off with his son for the Ho
Trinity. Their intelligence service must have been non-existent, for th
were apparently unaware that the Regent was now protected by a lar
number of State servitors.

Warned by courtiers of Khovansky's approach, Sophia sent a sizeab
detachment of loyal musketeers commanded by Prince Lykov to me
him. Lykov surprised Khovansky in the village of Pushkin and arrest
him and his escort without a struggle.

Several hours later, Prince Lykov and his prisoners reached the gates
Vozdvizhenskoye, where the latter were read the bill of indictment a
the verdict. Khovansky protested, demanding to be retried in his accuse
presence and promising to denounce the person really responsible for t
projected revolt. As might have been foreseen, his pleas were brush
aside. The authorities were so anxious to settle the matter that they d
not even wait for the arrival of an executioner from Moscow but behead
Ivan and Andrei Khovansky on the spot, together with thirty-sev
musketeers of their bodyguard.

Khovansky's second son, also called Ivan, managed to escape a
informed the musketeers of their 'father's' death. To the beat of drun
armed musketeers poured into the Kremlin once more. But Moscow w
a dead city, bereft of rich and powerful men on whom they could ve
their spleen. Once inside the walls, the musketeers posted sentries, seiz
the powder-magazines and trained their cannon on the approaches to t
Kremlin. No one made any attempt to dislodge them, however, and the
rage gradually gave way to fear. Their leader was dead, the populati
loathed them and the boyars and State servitors supported the Rege
Their ardour quenched by the prospect of such an unequal struggle, t
musketeers called on Patriarch Joachim in penitent mood to request h
intercession and ask him to secure the Regent's pardon on their beha

The Patriarch, who was engaged in writing – or, rather, dictating –
work directed against the Old Believers, yielded to their entreaties a
sent a metropolitan to ask the Princess Regent and the Tsars to pardon t
mutineers, who declared themselves ready to hand over their ringleade

Krekshin and several others have left us a description of the stran
scene which ensued as almost three thousand men from the ranks of t

usketeers processed along the road leading to the monastery of the Holy :inity. After confessing their sins and receiving Communion, they bade eir families a last farewell. Then, placing running nooses round their cks and carrying blocks and axes, they went to make their atonement ith heads bowed. Their families followed them, lamenting loudly.

The gates of the monastery opened at their approach and a detachment government troops came out to meet them. After being searched to sure that none of them carried concealed weapons, the luckless men ere led into the monastery courtyard, where they erected gibbets and affolds with their own hands, still surrounded by their weeping relatives, ives and children.

Sophia could be magnanimous in victory. She pardoned all the usketeers after strictly enjoining them to refrain from agitation in the ture and forbidding them to take part in conspiracies or bind themlves by secret oaths. They must not 'intend harm', to quote the phrase ed by the Princess Regent.

* * *

On November 6th, some six weeks after the beginning of this distressing fair, the Tsars and the Regent left their retreat and returned to the capital triumph, banners streaming in the wind.

The musketeers had been utterly routed. As a further token of their bmission, they requested the Tsars – this time with genuine humility – order the monument which had been erected in Red Square at their sistence to be demolished.

Tempering leniency with caution, Sophia prudently took steps designed avert the possibility of future trouble and published a decree forbidding e musketeers to carry arms except on official duty. Since Moscow was ll of State servitors, who were armed to the teeth and regarded the usketeers with hatred, this regulation brought home to them the full easure of their impotence. As the royal cortège passed through one reet, the musketeers along the route knelt as a sign of repentance.

With order seemingly restored, Sophia attacked her new tasks with isto while Tsar Peter, his mother and the princesses left the Kremlin d moved with their retinues to Kolomenskoye. Tsar Ivan remained in e palace, praying and discoursing with his friends on edifying subjects, ppy to have passed the burden of public affairs to his sister.

Russia was on the verge of better things.

CHAPTER TWENTY-SEVEN

It would be preferable if contemporary reports of the Princess Regent physical appearance were less contradictory than they are. Some descril her as hideous, others as charming and beautiful. Whom are we to believe

La Neuville, whose verdict on the Russian people, later confirmed b Custine, was to prove the delight of every Russophobe in the Wes described her as follows:

'Horribly ugly, monstrously fat, with a large head resembling a barre bristles on her face, scabs on her legs, and aged at least forty.'

It is hard to understand how La Neuville, who overstates her age at th period by a good ten years, can have seen scabs on the legs of a prince who never appeared in public except in ankle-length robes – unless, c course, he claims to have been her lover, which he does not.

At all events, even if descriptions of Sophia's physical appearance ar conflicting, her contemporaries, enemies included, are unanimous on th subject of her intelligence.

Even Prince Kurakin, the Russian Saint-Simon who was one of Tsa Peter's associates and friends, sang the praises of his 'sister-enemy'. 'Ther were bestowed on her a miraculous intelligence and judicious vision of th mind, so that she might labour for the good of the Russian people Artamon Matveyev's son Andrei, who left a painstaking and detaile account of the events which he witnessed in his youth, treated most of th figures whom he held responsible for the massacres of May 1682 wit understandable bitterness. But, while he abused Ivan Miloslavsky ('tha Muscovite Cromwell, that scorpion, that Jewified chameleon'), describe Khovansky as a contemptible creature and vowed that he would like t see his enemies paraded on hogs' backs, he was forced to admit – thoug he had no soft spot for Sophia – that she was 'a woman of very grea intelligence and the most subtle discernment, a virgin with a mind mor virile than feminine'.

La Neuville rejoins the main stream at this point. 'Her mind,' he wrot of the Regent, 'is a good one and perspicacious, and although she ha never read Machiavelli she knows the precepts of government by nature

ambitious and thirsty for power, impatient, vehement and quick-
empered, the Princess combines resolution with courage and a lively and
nterprising mind.' Here again, La Neuville's psychological portrait is
narred by inaccuracy. If Sophia was vehement, the records disclose no
race of impatience or irascibility. She invariably acted without haste and
never displayed anger unless it was logical or advantageous to do so.

Finally, in a message addressed to the Tsars in 1686, Patriarch Dositheus
of Jerusalem called the Regent 'a model of virtue and a guardian of
aternal nobility'. That, of course, was sheer exaggeration. Whether one
ikes her or not, Sophia was certainly no paragon of all the virtues, even
hough she possessed one or two. On the other hand, she was far from
eing the monster that admirers of Peter the Great have tried to
aint.

We are left, therefore, with the fact that a young woman of indeter-
ninate appearance but high intelligence had virtually assumed control of
Russia. Although the removal of Prince Khovansky and the defeat of the
nusketeers allowed Sophia to breathe more freely, her position was not
et consolidated. Effective government entailed armed support, but Sophia
nd her few personal friends were confronted by a vast country in which
nrest had only just been quelled. The Old Believers persisted in sowing
iscontent, and the boyars who had supported Sophia against Khovansky
vere not all on her side. The abolition of their former privileges under the
ight of precedence had left them with a grudge against Golitsyn's liberal
iews. Moreover, they jibbed at having to obey a woman, with the
esult that the tide began to turn in favour of Peter and Natalia and the
urvivors of the musketeers' purge. Lastly, there were the people,
raditionalist by nature and far from enthusiastic about being governed by
Virgin Tsar, which was a phenomenon known to them only in tales
rom national folklore.

Although they were autocrats, the Tsars had retained their paternalistic
nks with the people. Tsar Theodore used to receive in person anyone
who had a favour to ask of him, and the Kremlin was not merely a venue
or official banquets but also a centre where food was distributed to the
eedy. Thus, in Alexis Michaelovitch's time, the Victuallers' Court
istributed a hundred buckets of wine and up to four hundred buckets of
eer and mead each day. The royal kitchens made a daily distribution of
hree thousand dishes and four times as many on public holidays. Although
he Tsar's stables housed some forty thousand horses, we are told by
Kotoshikhin that they not only met the needs of the royal family and
alace staff but were distributed to State servitors too poor to buy a
nount. They were also used for hauling pieces of artillery in war-time.

A very large number of prisoners and paupers were fed at the expense c
the Tsar, Tsarina and princes. By providing a place where people coul
participate in the family celebrations that were held in the Kremlin, th
palace served as a sort of link between the nation and the Crown, a fra
and sentimental link which Sophia studiously avoided breaking. It was th
people to whom she had directed her pleas when she followed Tsa
Theodore's bier, and it was the people whose wishes she now proposed t
indulge, encouraged by her liberal friend Golitsyn. Nevertheless, althoug
Sophia's measures were implemented without brutality, they were applie
firmly, and she took care not to court popularity by means of the chea
demagogy which Khovansky had used.

The outstanding features of Sophia's reign were the spirit of logic tha
guided her reforms and the methodical manner in which she straightene
out the country's tangled affairs. The tsars who reigned before her fre
quently used empirical methods: Sophia followed a plan, assigne
priorities and applied remedies with remarkable precision.

Her position was still precarious. Sophia knew that there was an elemen
of ambiguity and impermanence about her status, and that she could onl
retain power until Peter came of age; but, being a practical woman, sh
refused to be discouraged, and tackled the more immediate problem
without wasting time.

The musketeers were temporarily subdued, but no one could tell whe
they would grow restive again. Although Zmeyev, who had replace
Khovansky as their commander, was taking them firmly in hand, Sophi
remained on her guard. After disarming the musketeers, she entruste
sentry duties at the Kremlin to the State servitors who had protected he
from Khovansky, and shortly afterwards she replaced Zmeyev with he
faithful friend Theodore Shaklovity.

The new government's first task was to regulate communal life. Unde
a decree dated December 30th, 1682, only seven musketeer regiments o
proven loyalty were to stay in Moscow, while the twelve remainin
regiments were posted to the Swedish and Polish frontiers. This step
though dictated by caution, was not intended as a punitive measure, eve
though it caused consternation among the city-bred musketeers. Sophi
showed her concern by allocating substantial bounties to enable them to se
up their households and businesses in their new place of residence. Thei
families, too, were transferred at government expense. The meticulou
preparations for this enforced resettlement of thousands of individual
showed how greatly times had changed. The itineraries of the variou
columns were carefully plotted so that no bottle-necks would occur e
route, and accommodation and supplies were arranged in advance. Th

whole operation went through without a hitch, which was little short of a miracle in view of the chaotic state of contemporary Russia.

With the same organizing skill and lack of violence, the Princess Regent took measures against a widespread and peculiarly Russian phenomenon: vagabondage. She began by ordering a census of musketeers, and found that a large number of vagabonds had joined them in recent months. Regimental lists were scrutinized for tramps, fugitives and thieves, elderly musketeers pensioned off and musketeers' sons called up for service in regular units when they came of age.

Although the disturbances in Moscow had not given rise to any serious popular unrest on a national scale, a certain number of serfs and peasants had taken the opportunity to run away from their masters or coerce them into granting them their freedom. The musketeers' destruction of the records kept by the Departments of Serfs and Justice made it difficult to track fugitives down, for some of them had settled in the suburbs and were now working for craftsmen and shopkeepers in the *possads*. Once again, the government acted with discretion. Under pressure on the one hand from merchants and craftsmen, who argued that they could not let their workmen go without jeopardizing their trades and businesses, and on the other from landed proprietors, who declared that labour shortages would prevent them from fulfilling the country's agricultural requirements, it issued a non-retrospective decree which stated that, in future, fugitives and those who harboured them would be prosecuted.

At the beginning of 1683, the Regent revived Tsar Theodore's unpopular land-registration scheme. Although her government did not have time to complete it, part of the census was carried out. Government agents, protected from the wrath of landowners by companies of musketeers (a necessary precaution), traversed Russia measuring land. Meanwhile, the government temporarily suspended the distribution of land for services rendered to the State and the sale of land acquired from the Tatars.

Sophia and her government applied themselves to major and minor matters with equal enthusiasm. Anyone examining some of the new regulations governing life in the capital might imagine himself to be reading the by-laws of a modern municipality. The 'parking' of horses was prohibited in certain streets, fighting and brawling in public places carried severe penalties, and police constables had to be obeyed to the letter. Streets were kept clean, at least in the centre of the city. Several steps were taken to render Moscow less vulnerable to fire, and three thousand new stone houses were built at Vasily Golitsyn's instigation. Golitsyn was also responsible for the capital's new stone bridge, whose twelve arches were high enough to withstand the break-up of the ice on the Moskva. Finally, to illustrate the modernity of the Regent's preoccupations, a campaign against noise was launched in the capital.

It was in these peaceful labours that Prince Golitsyn's co-operation proved most valuable, and the association between the humanitarian idealist and the Regent with the practical mind and masculine will-power would undoubtedly have changed the course of Russian history had it been less short-lived.

The laws were pervaded by a spirit of liberalism. Sophia officially abolished the death penalty – already seldom imposed – for 'those whose words incite disorder'. Women who had killed their husbands were no longer buried alive, though this penalty was restored immediately after Peter's seizure of power.

Russia did not have a national budget, properly speaking, until 1860. Sophia tried to balance the national finances, but this was a virtual impossibility in a country which was just emerging from a handicraftsman's economy.[1] Golitsyn developed industry and protected foreign and domestic trade. There was a spectacular growth in the home market. As urban trade increased, so villages began to specialize in the production and sale of textiles, metals and other commodities. A need arose to balance imports and exports and to reconcile the interests of Russian and foreign traders, the latter having hitherto been granted preferential treatment because Russia was dependent upon imports for a large number of products.

When it finally dawned on the Russians that the English had been supplying them with high-priced textiles of inferior quality, they made arrangements to manufacture their own. In November 1682, a German from Hamburg named Abraham Paulus was granted government subsidies to enable him to set up a factory for 'velvet, satin and other silks'. In 1684, a Dutchman named Matthew Tarvet was encouraged to open a spinning-mill in Moscow and teach the trade to Russian apprentices. His fortune made, he returned home in 1688, leaving behind trained Russian operatives who opened businesses of their own.

Production expanded in other fields as well. In about 1684, Christian Marcelis, son of the great entrepreneur whose family had been established in Russia with their kinsmen the Francels for so many years, was able to supply the government with two thousand seven hundred sheets of iron which had been rolled not only in the famous foundry at Tula but also in new undertakings of the same type established in other provincial cities.

[1] As the historian Miliukov says: 'Throughout the seventeenth century, the exploitation of national resources proceeded at a much slower rate than the political development of the Russian State.'

Sophia's government was distinguished for its swift decisions. At the beginning of 1683, Charles II complained of restrictions imposed on English merchants in Russia. The Dutch expressed similar grievances. They were tired of having to entrust their ships to drunken and incompetent pilots when entering the port of Archangel, and equally tired of appeasing the appetites of corrupt and greedy voivodes. In June 1683, Sophia granted them permission to choose their own pilots. She also withdrew privileges from the local voivodes who had made illegal profits out of their contacts with foreigners and transferred them to reputable merchants unconnected with customs administration.

Sophia and her associates did their utmost to iron out the anomalies and remedy the deficiencies in national life. The Augean stables were cleared, if not cleaned. Measures were taken against administrative corruption and obsolete practices. Local tolls and the internal frontiers between Great Russia and the Ukraine were abolished. Vasily Golitsyn took a personal interest in commercial affairs, and within four years he had succeeded in strengthening commercial ties with England, the Low Countries, Saxony and Brandenburg-Prussia. The most important of the new trade agreements were, however, signed with Russia's neighbours, Sweden and Poland.

* * *

Although, like Golitsyn, Sophia preferred to direct her gaze westwards, both she and her chief adviser took a lively interest in Asia. Thanks to the expeditions by Pozharkov (1643–6) and Khabarov (1649–51), the Russians had been able within thirty years to establish three important centres on the route to China: Nertchinsk, Albazin and Aigun. However, China viewed the Russians' steady progress towards Asia with a jaundiced eye, and in September 1682 the Emperor of China sent an armed detachment (ostensibly a 'hunting party') to reconnoitre Russian installations on the Amur and in Northern Manchuria.

Ivan Semenov, the voivode of Albazin, at once sent a report to Moscow warning the government of the threat and predicting an attack before the year was out. Contact between Russia and China had always been sporadic, and although the Russians expressed a keen desire to establish regular commercial relations with their great Asiatic neighbour, their various missions to the Bogdychen had been unsuccessful. Asiatic tribes resident in the areas of Russian penetration recognized the sovereignty of the Son of Heaven, and the fact that some of them had entered the service of Russia naturally irked him. Spafari, who was sent off on a mission to China by Alexis Michaelovitch and Matveyev in 1675, returned to Moscow without having concluded a treaty with the Emperor. While there was a strong possibility of a Chinese attack in 1680, by 1682 the danger had become very real and demanded urgent action. However, the government did not send reinforcements to Albazin because the internal situation forbade any dispersal of strength. Semenov then sought help from Saltikov, the voivode of Nertchinsk, but the latter was equally short of men and horses and could not answer his appeal. It may be added that the situation of these small fortified towns was not enhanced by the petty jealousies of their governors and the lax discipline of their garrisons.

A Chinese ultimatum addressed to Albazin in December 1682 called upon the Russians to abandon the Amur valley for ever. The following is an extract from the Emperor's letter:

> Thus I shall not permit your excursions up the Amur ... And I have commanded all those who see you to kill you or take you prisoner. O Russians of Albazin, renounce all mischief. Return home and we shall let the matter drop and live in peace. But, should you fail to understand this message, neither heaven nor earth will afford you protection, and I shall not shrink from killing you ...

Even then, Sophia and her government failed to act. Although Vasily Golitsyn's many vast schemes included that of populating Siberia with Russians, he was not yet in complete command of the situation. Besides, he preferred to negotiate rather than fight. While encouraging the Siberian garrisons to resist, the government did nothing to help them, with the result that the Russians' position on the Amur remained critical throughout 1684. Trappers were compelled to abandon their activities and Russian settlements lived in constant fear of a Chinese attack. The governors hurriedly strengthened their defences and prepared for the inevitable.

It was not until May 1685 that the Chinese abandoned threats in favour of direct action. Six thousand men under General Lang-tan advanced towards Albazin, whose new voivode, Tolbuzin, had only four hundred and fifty men, three hundred muskets and three cannon at his disposal. The Emperor's emissaries urged Tolbuzin to surrender, but he refused. The bombardment of the town began immediately and lasted for ten days, by the end of which time the Russian garrison was decimated and its ammunition exhausted. With all hope of outside help gone, Tolbuzin eventually surrendered on honourable terms. The Chinese allowed him to march out of the fortress with full military honours and authorized him to lead the survivors to Nertchinsk.

Lang-tan was not only generous but imprudent. After the evacuation of Albazin he ordered his men to destroy the fort and then marched home, confident that the Russians would never dare to reappear on the eastern bank of the great river. Being short of supplies and learning that the sowed fields round the demolished fortress had been left untouched, Tolbuzin and his men made their leisurely way back to Albazin. To fill in time while the harvest was ripening, they rebuilt the fort and installed themselves in it once more, so that in July 1686 Lang-tan and his cavalry were obliged to attack the place for the second time. The indomitable voivode was killed, but his place was taken by a Colonel Belton and the defence of the fort continued. Meanwhile, in default of military reinforcements, the government dispatched a diplomatic mission which reached China in October 1686.

Albazin held out courageously under appalling conditions. Extant letters sent by Tolbuzin to Nertchinsk before his death contain phrases such as: 'The enemy is attacking us furiously ... I am besieged ... I have few men and little ammunition ... '

Golitsyn may have been an indifferent general, but he was a brilliant diplomat who firmly believed that chestnuts could always be pulled out of the fire by negotiation. Undeterred by an initial setback, he sent a second mission to Peking in 1687 under the Grand Ambassador Extraordinary Theodore Golovin, the young and talented son of the governor of Tobolsk. Golovin's task was to settle the dispute with China, and his instructions from Golitsyn ran: 'Bloodshed must be avoided. If the Chinese reject our proposals they must be made to accept the idea of fresh negotiations, but we must secure the Amur for Russia.'

Thanks to sundry difficulties which were aggravated by the intricacies of protocol, talks did not open until 1689, a crucial year for the Princess Regent. When they did start, new difficulties arose. The precise delimitation of the Sino-Russian borders was of vital importance to both countries, and the discussions sometimes took a dramatic turn. The clauses of the treaty were drawn up in three languages, Russian, Manchu and Latin, of which the last was to be the authoritative version in the event of any subsequent dispute.

Despite their stubborn haggling over details, the Chinese were so negligent that the Manchu version of the Nertchinsk agreement, which was eventually signed on August 27th, 1689, did not embody the amendments which they had insisted upon, while the Latin version, translated from the Manchu by two Jesuits, contained ambiguities which left the door open to future Russian territorial claims. However, once frontiers had been fixed and neutral zones defined, agreement on the other terms of the treaty, which concerned hunting rights and extradition of fugitives, was reached without undue difficulty.

This marked the official establishment of commercial relations, and the treaty concluded by emphasizing that friendly ties between the two countries would remove any grounds for disagreement provided that all its clauses were strictly observed. In fact, the Russians had sustained a short-term defeat. While averting a war which they would inevitably have lost, they had been forced to sacrifice most of their territorial aspirations. Most historians consider that the Russians' forfeiture of the banks of the Amur, where they had been established for thirty years, was disastrous. Could Sophia's ambassadors have done any better? Considering that Asiatic Russia was defenceless at the time, this seems unlikely. Since 1683, Golitsyn's attentions had been focused on another problem: that of strengthening European Russia's position, forging the closest possible links with the West and ousting the Tatars from the Crimea so as to gain access to the Black Sea.[1]

It is worth noting that the treaty with Peking was signed on August 27th, 1689, the very day on which Peter seized power and Sophia lost not only the rank of Regent but her freedom as well. The Russians' withdrawal from the Amur was compensated by the establishment of regular and mutually profitable commercial relations. Russia was the first European power to sign a treaty with China which conferred strictly equal advantages on both parties. From then on, Russian caravans could cross the frontier without let or hindrance. A merchant named Nikitin, for instance, was able to sell a considerable quantity of Russian, Persian and German merchandise in China and bring back Chinese silk, gold, porcelain and pearls to Moscow.

[1] C. Bickford O'Brien wisely remarks that Sophia's government had made the most of a desperate situation and so averted a war which could only have proved a national disaster.

CHAPTER TWENTY-EIGHT

IT was not in Sophia's nature to wield her newly acquired authority in an unobtrusive manner or act solely in the Tsars' name. She very soon began to couple her own name with those of Ivan and Peter and demand that the honours due to them should also be accorded to her. Contrary to established practice, she admitted 'to her hand' not only boyars and senior officials but metropolitans as well. During religious services in the Cathedral of the Assumption, the tsarevna did not conceal herself behind the pierced grilles of the compartment reserved for the Terem, but seated herself at a spot which she ordered to be specially set aside for her, the third 'sovereign's place'. When officiating clergy came down from the altar and incensed the Tsars according to custom, the Regent demanded that they swing the censer in her direction an equal number of times, and was furious when they inadvertently omitted to do so. This was not mere petty-mindedness. Sophia clung to her authority, but she knew that it was based on etiquette as well as official status.

Sophia never sent ambassadors abroad without giving them precise instructions. She told them to inform foreigners that Russia was ruled by two Tsars, 'that they are both handsome, intelligent, universally endowed, well-disposed towards foreigners, generous towards their subjects, and that their sister reigns with them'. In 1684 the Princess Regent commanded that her likeness be engraved on medals and coins. In 1686 she assumed the title of Autocrat and proclaimed the feast of St Sophia an official holiday. Her friend Shaklovity commissioned an engraver to produce a portrait of Sophia wearing the imperial cloak and crown and holding a sceptre and orb in her hands. Another engraving, commissioned in Holland, depicted Sophia at the centre of the two-headed Russian eagle. Her Latin titles ran: '*Sophia Alexeyevna, Dei Gratia Augustissima ac praepotentissima Magna Domina, Careva ac Magna Kniasna totius ac Magna Parvea ac Alba Russia autocratix ...*' Seven allegorical medallions surrounding the eagle proclaimed her virtues: '*Prudentia, Pietas, Pudicitia, Liberalitas, Justitium, Magnanimitas, sep divina.*' The original was entrusted to Vinius, who sent it to Holland, where the burgomaster Nicholas

Witsen ordered a hundred copies from the engraver Blotterling.

Another version was engraved in Moscow by the Circassian artist Tarassevitch, who worked on it in Shaklovity's house. Here, the Regent was depicted as one of the members of an imperial triad consisting of herself and the two Tsars. The group was surrounded by allegorical figures and portraits of Prince Vasily Golitsyn, Theodore Shaklovity and the hetman Samoilovitch. Sophia was delighted with the engraving and ordered it to be reproduced on paper, satin and taffeta. Sylvester Medviedev composed the following legend for one of the versions:

> Marble speaks of her generosity,
> Churches glorify her munificence.
> Like Semiramis who dwelt on the Euphrates,
> She excels in a notable work.
> Thus did Elizabeth of England hold the sceptre,
> And Pulcheria received the same gift of wisdom.

* * *

The tsarevna's agents did public relations work among the people by explaining her measures and extolling her virtues. In reality, her status went far beyond that of Regent and became truly regal, which naturally irritated Tsar Peter's mother a great deal. 'How dare you communicate with the Grand Sovereigns?' fumed Natalia. 'We have men who will not leave the matter there.' Needless to say, the Dowager Tsarina's fury only increased the Princess Regent's vigilance.

There were two chinks in Sophia's armour, and she was too wise not to be aware of her own vulnerability. Even at the zenith of her power, she never forgot that it would be terminated by Peter's coming of age. Whatever she achieved, whatever acumen she displayed in affairs of state and whatever titles she assumed, she was slowly but steadily advancing up a cul-de-sac: she could never be crowned Tsar. In addition, her conscience pricked her, not because she had seized power in order to save the dynasty, but because she was the first to violate the tradition of virtue that had reigned in the Kremlin under Alexis and Theodore. With the transfer of power to a woman, moral laxity had infiltrated not only the palace but the cloistered confines of the Terem, as if emancipation were a passport to all other forms of liberty. At court, the atmosphere of sanctity and devotion became no more than a hypocritical tribute paid by vice to virtue.

At this stage, however, a good reputation was still the prerequisite of authority, and Sophia did her utmost to keep up appearances. She undoubtedly retained a memory of the moral precepts in which she had been reared as a child, so the edifying lives of her late parents and brother must have been a constant reproach to her own less admirable mode of existence. Golitsyn the aristocrat and Shaklovity the plebeian shared the same mistress and served the same sovereign. Golitsyn was handsome, but he was an intellectual dreamer. Although Sophia appreciated his intelligence, advice, conversation and manners, she was well aware that he was in love with his wife and may not have found him ardent enough to satisfy her passionate temperament. Theodore Shaklovity was young, courageous, decisive and utterly devoted to the tsarevna, and it was probably not long before he started to 'understudy' Golitsyn in her private quarters. Sophia could never hope to marry either of them, of course, since Golitsyn was too much of a gentleman to make his wife take the veil (a proposal attributed to the Princess Regent by La Neuville) and Shaklovity was precluded by his very origins from becoming the husband of a tsarevna.

The Regent's secret was an open book to her sisters and the boyars, and even she was aware that the Dowager Tsarina's clique referred to her as 'the whore'. Men came and went freely now, and the Terem began to gain the reputation of a house of ill fame. By her own emancipation, Sophia had opened the door to her sisters, who felt that if they could not have power – which they had no wish for anyway – they had won the right to live their own life. Not being endowed with the same intelligence, the princesses soon fell prey to all kinds of adventurers. Sophia's sister Martha took a deacon called Ivan as her lover, and the pretty but avaricious Catherine came under the spell of an insignificant provincial priest named Gregory Alexeyev, who convinced her that the stars had told him where great quantities of treasure were buried. Holes were secretly dug all over the capital on her orders, but nothing came to light except a few bones belonging to people who had been executed or murdered in times gone by. Alexeyev was the only man to find an easily exploitable gold-mine!

The princesses observed tradition by receiving young choristers, pilgrims, elderly people and paupers in their apartments, on the principle that sins could be redeemed by good works. In return, these spongers and hangers-on provided the Terem with a political intelligence and propaganda service, and it was through them that the palace made its influence felt among the masses.

While the boyars whispered, no doubt with good reason, that the princesses were 'carrying' or 'bringing up' illegitimate children, the common people were deeply moved to hear that the tsarevnas were taking in little orphans and rearing them out of the goodness of their hearts.

The Old Believers were another source of malicious gossip. 'The Tsarevna Sophia is a whore,' they declared, 'and lives in sin with boyars, as does one of her sisters. The boyars visit them and they have children by them.'

The Regent's family life was dominated by the hatred that existed between her and Tsarina Natalia, a feminine feud which fed daily on the little snubs and insults which camouflaged the real issues at stake. Powerless in the face of Sophia's intelligence and the role which she was playing in the Kremlin and the country as a whole, Natalia drew her only strength from the love which she bore her son.

Realizing that authority depended on discipline, Sophia never omitted to show official consideration to Peter and the Naryshkins. When a Prince Kozlovsky failed to appear at a State banquet in the Kremlin on the grounds that he had been assigned a less honourable seat than Ivan Naryshkin, Tsar Peter's uncle and a sworn enemy of the Regent, Sophia had him brought in and forcibly seated in the place which she had allotted him. In private, however, she had no hesitation in humiliating Natalia. In 1683, when a great fire destroyed the apartments of Tsar Peter and the princesses, Sophia had new and luxurious stone apartments built for herself and her sisters, but set aside a very modest wooden residence for the use of the young Tsar and his mother. Tsar Ivan was entitled to eighty-nine lords-in-waiting: Tsar Peter only had sixty-four. When Mazeppa, hetman of the Zaporozhye Cossacks, presented the Tsars with two dwarfs, Sophia made a gift of them to Vasily Golitsyn.

Although Sophia took care to see that her youngest brother was well provided for, everyone in Natalia's entourage knew that the tsarevnas dipped liberally into palace funds and withdrew substantial sums for their private use, whereas Natalia had to keep strictly within her allotted budget. It could not be said that Sophia persecuted the Naryshkins. Rancour was foreign to her nature, as she demonstrated when, having triumphed over the musketeers, she did no more than take protective measures against them. Probably assessing the Naryshkins at their true worth, she tolerated them without liking them, but kept them under surveillance because she knew how much they detested her.

The boyars who supported Peter did not bother to disguise their contempt for poor Ivan. On October 22nd, 1684, the boyars Saltykov and Buturlin and the Princes Khilkov and Zirovoy-Zassekin, together with several noblemen, received orders to escort the elder Tsar to a religious ceremony. They refused, whereupon the Regent promptly punished them for disrespect.

Determined that the right of precedence should not linger on after its abolition by Tsar Theodore, Sophia meted out the same justice to all, regardless of class. When Peter Kikin, a nobleman, and Korobin, a commoner, committed an identical crime, the rape of a young girl, they both received the same punishment, a public flogging. Prince Peter Kropotkin and the musketeer Khvostchinsky were both flogged for shifting boundary stones on their estates.

Although they led an active life during the years 1682–5, the members of the Terem contented themselves with the joys of private freedom and did not show themselves in public, no doubt because they remembered the outcry provoked by their first venture into the outside world.

On the ground floor of their new residence, Sophia installed a large audience-chamber where she could consult boyars and hear their reports. The walls of this room were covered with portraits of the tsarevnas. The princesses at first wanted to be shown carrying the emblems of sovereignty and wearing the imperial purple, but they thought better of it and had themselves painted in pearl-encrusted pelisses bright with lace. Their apartments were furnished in the height of luxury. In hers, Sophia displayed an ode dedicated to her some years before by Simeon Polotski:

> O Most Noble Tsarevna Sophia,
> Who seek divine wisdom
> And order your life according to your name,
> Speaking with wisdom, acting wisely ...

Tsar Alexis's other daughters spent money like water, but Sophia did not allow herself to be distracted from her self-appointed task. Her family was no help to her. Ivan Miloslavsky died in 1685, but his niece had treated him with a certain reserve ever since the Khovansky affair because he cautiously steered clear of her at the vital moment. Her real family circle was composed of three men with absolutely nothing in common save their devotion to the Regent and their views on government.

The first was Vasily Golitsyn, of illustrious origins and impressive appearance. Judging by his interests and mode of life, the Prince would have been more at home in the gracious, epicurean and philosophical atmosphere of the eighteenth century. His personality was so appealing that even his enemies were unanimous in acknowledging his exceptional qualities and statesmanlike brilliance. Golitsyn did not merely have the Western veneer which Catherine II's courtiers were later accused of: he was a Westerner to his finger-tips. Not only did his questing mind apply itself to literature and the arts and sciences, but – not that this was exclusive to the West – he possessed a generous nature. His manners were exquisite, his erudition great and his views liberal. La Neuville paid homage to him in the following terms:

> Prince Golitsyn was incontestably one of the most gifted men in Muscovy, which he wished to raise to the level of other countries. He spoke Latin and was happy to converse with foreigners without making them drink. Besides, he himself did not drink vodka and derived his pleasure from conversation. He esteemed the virtues and scorned important figures because of their ignorance.

Golitsyn's house was one of the finest in Europe. The great halls where he received ambassadors and visiting foreigners were furnished not only with luxury but in the most refined taste. Mirrors gleamed on the walls between the windows, and his gold and silver plate bore the hallmarks of great Russian and foreign craftsmen. His friendship with the royal family was apparent from the many portraits that hung on the walls: Alexis Michaelovitch and Maria Miloslavsky, Tsar Theodore, Tsars Ivan and Peter and three equestrian portraits of the kings of Poland, a country for which the Prince entertained the highest regard. The ceiling of one of his reception rooms was adorned with a copy of Kolomenskoye's celestial vault, and his study was furnished with German maps, a globe and engravings. An impressive library, one of the best in Europe, testified to his love of books, and he collected numerous manuscripts in Polish, Russian, German and Latin. He also had a collection of the rarest and most intricate clocks and watches, porcelain vases, gorgeous materials and magnificent carpets. It was in this setting that he welcomed guests and conversed with them on subjects ranging from the political, economic and social life of Europe to poetry, philosophy and religion.

Golitsyn's head was filled with vast schemes. La Neuville assures us that he discussed them with him but gives only incoherent glimpses of them. Since Golitsyn became the target of posthumous persecution by champions of Peter the Great, these plans have only reached us in fragmentary form. Enough of them has survived, however, to show how amazingly liberal they were in conception – and this at a time when the word 'liberal' had not yet gained currency. Klyuchevsky says that Golitsyn was not only more forward-looking in his plans than any other statesman prior to the accession of Peter, but more so than the Russian statesmen who succeeded him during the next two or three reigns.

Some of his projects were not only daring but downright utopian. The 'political dreamer', as Platonov called him, even contemplated freeing the peasants from servitude and exempting them from military service. The emancipated peasants would then have been subjected to a special tax, the revenue from which would have been used to finance an army composed entirely of noblemen. Golitsyn favoured something which Peter later implemented in quite another spirit: the dispatch of young Russian noblemen to foreign countries to form a cadre of educated men who would act as the spearhead of Russia's technical and cultural progress.

All Vasily Golitsyn's plans, judging by what we know of them, were components of a complex design which embraced economic, social, technical and cultural goals. 'If I were to attempt to write all that I have heard concerning this prince, I should never reach the end thereof. Suffice it to say that he strove to people deserts, to enrich the needy and to transform savages into civilized men, cowards into heroes and cottages into stone mansions ... '

This flattering testimonial deserves qualification. Vasily Golitsyn's schemes were admirable and bore the imprint of a great mind, but the vague and fanciful side of the prince's nature often transported him into a Cloud-Cuckoo Land of his own. There was something about him which calls to mind the great-hearted but unrealistic young aristocrats whose abortive plot against Tsar Nicholas I came to light on December 18th, 1827. Like them, Golitsyn allowed himself to be dominated by dreams.

Golitsyn's role in Sophia's administration was considerable, but his influence was less than might be supposed. The Regent's powerful personality could not be influenced except along lines which corresponded with her personal aspirations. If she listened to Golitsyn's advice and applied liberal measures when they seemed justified, it was because her own nature prompted her to inject as much humanity into her relations with the masses as circumstances and the requirements of her position allowed – never more.

For Golitsyn, the West which Russia needed was essentially the Latin, Mediterranean West which appealed to his humanistic and aesthetic inclinations.

There is no doubt that Sophia loved her handsome adviser – passionately at first and later tenderly. Golitsyn's feelings towards the imperious tsarevna are less easy to analyse. He must have admired her intelligence and mental versatility. What was more, she was the medium through which he could promote the ideas close to his heart and continue the work which he had begun under Tsar Theodore. Yet contemporaries tell us that he lived in 'great harmony' with his first wife, Princess Theodosia

Dolgoruky, and was equally in love with his second wife, Eudoxia Streshneva, who was related to the Romanovs by marriage.

* * *

Theodore Shaklovity was quite another proposition. Apparently a bachelor, since contemporary records never credit him with a wife, he turned up at the Kremlin in 1673 as a junior clerk in the Prikaz of Secret Affairs. By 1682 he had risen in the world, thanks to the patronage of the tsarevna, who had been impressed by his devotion and bravery during the musketeers' revolt and the Khovansky affair. A man of action, but gentle, well-educated and intelligent, Shaklovity was loaded with honours and promoted to a senior rank immediately below that of boyar. His practical mind contrasted sharply with that of Vasily Golitsyn. Although he was a parvenu, a self-made man without background or family influence, his ambition never degenerated into venality and he never betrayed the Regent, even under torture. Golitsyn soared above parochial feuds and palace intrigues, but Shaklovity was always prepared to face immediate dangers and attack the problems of the moment without losing himself in the vast and imponderable problems of the future. Whenever the Regent was in peril she found Shaklovity not only at her side but, unlike Golitsyn, ready to act and expose himself to danger.

We do not know exactly when Shaklovity first became Sophia's lover but it was probably during the first Crimean campaign, if we are to believe Prince Kurakin.

> At the time of Prince Vasily Golitsyn's departure for the Crimea with the army, Shaklovity profited greatly from his affair with the Tsarevna Sophia and entered into nocturnal pleasures, more than the prince although less overtly. It is likely that, had Sophia's government endured, Prince Golitsyn would have fallen into disfavour – unless retained as Prime Minister for appearances' sake – and that it would have been Shaklovity who possessed the real power and directed affairs.

Serving the same cause through the same woman, the two rivals became close friends. Both were heartily detested by the boyars, whom they in turn despised. Shaklovity called them 'withered trees', while Golitsyn simply kept his distance from 'those great dunces'.

* * *

The third member of Sophia's chosen team was the monk Sylvester Medviedev, a methodical, faultless, even pedantic bureaucrat, but a man whose learning and intelligence distinguished him from his sworn enemy Patriach Joachim. Medviedev was Russia's first biographer and the author not only of numerous theological polemics but also of a *Detailed Catalogue of Books published and of the Authors who wrote them,*[1] and the leader of the Latinists. He acted as Sophia's Minister of Public Education and was responsible for reviving the plans for a new academy which had been evolved in Tsar Theodore's reign. Medviedev poured out erudite and flowery panegyrics dedicated to the Regent, whom he compared to Elizabeth I and other great queens of the past. As a friend of Golitsyn and Shaklovity, he represented the third member of the triumvirate which was to share the Regent's triumphs and stand by her when final disaster struck.

For the rest, Sophia recalled her brother Theodore's friend Alexis Yazykov to Moscow as soon as she could, honoured young Golovin by promoting him to ambassadorial rank and selected her other advisers from among the former associates of her elder brother, appointing them to senior posts on the basis solely of personal merit and never of birth, even though some of them happened to be enlightened members of the higher nobility. As for the Patriarch, Sophia invariably showed him consideration, but never forgot that he was a member of Peter's party.

[1] The first Russian bibliography.

CHAPTER TWENTY-NINE

SEVENTEENTH-CENTURY RUSSIA at the time of Sophia's regency was a tightly knit complex of interrelated factors. Political and religious questions were closely linked, and the Regent could not, as a former pupil of Simeon Polotski, remain indifferent to the fate of the Church.

Patriarch Joachim was still at the head of the Russian Church, but his severe and often brutal methods had not succeeded in eliminating the *raskol*. The new feature of Russia's religious life was a growing conflict between internal factions. There were still three trends among Russian churchmen: Russian, Greek and Latinist. A fourth trend, the Protestant, was beginning to make itself felt but had not yet emerged into the open. When Louis XIV's revocation of the Edict of Nantes scattered the Huguenots to the four winds, Sophia generously left the doors of Russia open to them. The countries of Northern Europe and Holland, with whom Moscow maintained friendly relations, all exercised considerable influence. Sophia granted foreigners permission to practise their faith freely, with the proviso that they were responsible under Russian law for any crimes and misdemeanours they committed.

Confronted by this Protestant influx, Rome – including the Catholic monarchies – did not remain inactive. Moscow became, on both the political and religious plane, the scene of a battle between Catholicism and the Reformation. Underlying the conflict between the Protestants and the Jesuits was a struggle, not only for influence but for all the benefits which could accrue from the 'patronage' of a large and disorganized country, between the Germanic and the Latin West. To put it bluntly, each power was trying to get its hands on the potential wealth of Muscovy – each power, that is to say, except France. Louis XIV persisted in regarding Russia as of no significance and his political attentions were never directed farther eastwards than Poland. Nevertheless, since His Most Christian Majesty could hardly remain indifferent to religion, he did his best to support the efforts of the Jesuits, who took an active interest in Russia and, through Russia, in her Chinese neighbour.

Knowing Louis XIV's interest in religious affairs, a Saxon who was passing through Paris in 1681 addressed the following petition to him:

> Sire,
>
> Laurent de Reinufer, who has been secretary and interpreter to sundry embassies and physician to the Grand Duke of Muscovy, having completed certain public affairs for which he was sent to His Holiness by the Catholic Christians of Muscovy, casts himself at Your Majesty's feet and presents unto Your Majesty, with profound respect, certain proposals touching the affairs of that country and the means wherewith not only to promote religion there but to procure considerable advantages for France.

We do not know what these advantages comprised. The King apparently thought little enough of them, for he never went further than the innocuous trade agreement which he had signed with Alexis Michaelovitch in 1668. He did not, however, remain unmoved by the religious appeal, and several times gave Catholic missionaries bound for China letters of recommendation to the Tsars.

Like Vasily Golitsyn, Sophia was known to be sympathetic towards the Latin world. A report written in 1682 by two Jesuits, George David and Tobias Tikhanovski, claimed that Tsar Theodore not only showed great respect for Roman Catholicism and the Jesuits, but was contemplating the establishment of a Jesuit college in Moscow at some later date. They added that the Tsarevna Sophia and Prince Golitsyn were prepared to carry on his work, but in secret, '*ad admodum occulte*'.

There is no evidence on the Russian side to support these claims. It is probable that the missionaries were guilty of wishful thinking and mistook politeness for promises. Vasily Golitsyn seems to have held aloof from religious disputes, for he never displayed any pronounced interest in either the Orthodox or the Roman Church. It is quite unthinkable that Sophia would have wished to coerce the Russians into a union with Rome. Orthodoxy was already an integral part of national life, although, to give La Neuville his due, the religious situation in Russia was so confused that the 'Russians themselves were losing their Slav'. Thanks to general confusion and lack of training in theological matters, the least infringement of time-honoured practices assumed catastrophic proportions.

The Patriarch had long regarded the growing influence of the Latinists, upheld at first by Simeon Polotski and later by Medviedev, with a blend of anxiety and irritation. Although certain Russian bishops and priests espoused the heresies of which Medviedev was the mouthpiece, the bulk of the Latinists came from the Ukraine. Bustling, enterprising, intelligent, eloquent and better-educated than their Great Russian cousins, the Little

Russians poured into the capital and infiltrated every corner of society. As learned monks, lay schoolmasters, wine-growers, distillers and tutors to the children of boyars, the southerners wielded a not inconsiderable degree of influence. In 1686, Patriarch Dositheus of Jerusalem, the man who had paid unmerited homage to Sophia's virtue, addressed a message to Tsars Ivan and Peter enjoining them to 'preserve the ancient ways' and ensure that abbots and archimandrites were of Muscovite rather than Cossack origin.

Devoid of new ideas on how to encounter the Latinist onslaught and still encumbered with the Old Believers, Patriarch Joachim turned to the elder sister of the Russian Church, notwithstanding his low opinion of the Greeks, for help against adversaries whose learning surpassed his own.

Such were the circumstances that led up to the arrival in Moscow of the Likhuda brothers. These two monks, one of whom had been married before taking holy orders and had children to whom he was deeply attached, originally served on the staff of Patriarch Dionysius of Constantinople. In response to Patriarch Joachim's earnest request for experienced theologians who could help him in his struggle against the Latinists, the head of the Greek Church personally examined the Likhudas on points of doctrine and dispatched them to Moscow in 1683. They did not arrive there until two years later, 'after many sufferings and ordeals both on land and sea'. They were at first delayed by the war between the Austrians and the Turks and later detained in Poland by the Jesuits, who moved heaven and earth to prevent them from reaching their destination. Three days after their arrival in Moscow they were presented to the Tsars and took part in a theological debate in which they won a resounding victory over their opponents. Ever suspicious, Patriarch Joachim submitted the Likhudas to a fresh examination on Orthodoxy, and in 1687 he thwarted Medviedev by appointing them directors of the Zaikonospassky Academy, a brand-new three-storeyed building. Seventy-six pupils had already been enrolled.

The Likhudas' career in Moscow was brilliant and meteoric. In 1688, Vasily Golitsyn sent Johanny Likhuda to Venice with orders to secure the Republic's assistance against the Tatars – not that he was any more successful than other Russian ambassadors charged with similar missions to other countries. His brother Sophrony stayed behind at the Academy. The curriculum was so exacting that there was a steady drop in attendances, and by 1688 there were only sixty-four pupils left, among them Prince Boris Golitsyn's son and a number of grooms' and footmen's children.

Nothing illustrates Vasily Golitsyn's religious eclecticism better than his protection of the Likhuda brothers, who were foes and doctrinal opponents of his friend Sylvester Medviedev.

Although the Likhuda brothers undoubtedly rendered useful service to Orthodoxy and education, they were not, unfortunately, paragons of virtue. One scandal proved their downfall. Sophrony, Johanny and the latter's children tried to flee the country, but were arrested en route. Men of education being a valuable commodity, the authorities confined themselves to transferring the Likhudas from the Academy to the State Printing Office. They eventually set up as teachers of Italian, which enabled the two young Princes Prozorovsky and eight well-to-do merchants' sons to learn a language that was not only beautiful but of advantage to them in their subsequent careers.

Though we have strayed from religious questions, they were of great importance and invested this period with intense theological animation, giving rise to some fine literature and rousing the Russians, clergy and laymen alike, to a livelier religious awareness. For five years, men, women and even children discussed problems such as 'Does religion depend on faith or reason?' with the same impassioned fervour which people of today expend on football matches or horse-racing.

Sylvester Medviedev was defeated and his writings condemned as heretical despite the Regent's support. He was dismissed by the Patriarch from his editorial post at the Printing Office, and a year later, in 1687, he was forced to give up his lecturership at the Academy which he had been instrumental in founding. As the historian Belov points out, the increasingly critical spirit of Russian society was demonstrated by the very diversity of the trends within it. The Russians were determined to shake off their passivity and choose the path that most suited their inclinations.

* * *

The Regent generally showed great tolerance in religious matters, in spite of Patriarch Joachim's opposition. The Church at Kiev was allowed to go on teaching in Latin as it had done during the Polish occupation. We are entitled to assume, therefore, that the terrible persecutions to which the Old Believers were subjected during Sophia's regency – persecutions instigated by the Patriarch but vigorously supported by Sophia's government – were dictated by considerations of internal policy.

The historian Andreyev suggests that the preservation of ancient usages was only a pretext employed by the Old Believers and that, in reality, the birth of their movement coincided with the measures taken under Alexis Michaelovitch to bind peasants more closely to the land and those who owned it. By this reckoning, the Great Schism formed part of the peasantry's self-defence movement. The provinces were more affected by the *raskol* than the capital and villages more so than towns, which also accounted for the intellectual poverty of its adherents – 'ignorant men, knowing nothing', as Medviedev called them.

In April 1685, the government took stringent measures against the Old Believers, who had organized themselves into rural communities or gone into hiding in the forests. Provincial governors received orders to stamp out these schismatic communities, one of which later ventured to launch an armed attack on a monastery, and draconian decrees were promulgated against 'those who insult the Church and corrupt the people'. Although these measures did not extinguish the movement, which underwent further persecution of a less sanguinary but still rigorous nature in the reigns that followed (the Old Belief still exists in the U.S.S.R. today), its role was never as politically decisive as it had been in Khovansky's time.

As for Patriarch Joachim, although he played an important part in religious and political life during Sophia's regency, his lack of discernment and narrow-mindedness caused him to make a number of mistakes. There can be no doubt that he was filled with good intentions and that he sincerely believed himself to be acting in the best interests of the Russian Church, yet he aroused little sympathy and seemed strangely intent on confirming Sylvester Medviedev's poor opinion of him. He refused to sit at the same table with Catholics and forbade his congregations to go to German physicians. When Polish envoys expressed a wish to attend divine service in the Cathedral of the Assumption, he prohibited them from entering the building despite pleas from the Tsars and the Regent. Finally, he inveighed with a fervour worthy of a better cause against 'the vicious, Hellenic and nauseous custom of cutting one's hair and shaving one's beard'.

Of all the men with whom Sophia had to work during her regency, Patriarch Joachim was certainly the least congenial and most useless.

CHAPTER THIRTY

CHILDREN grow up quickly. When Sophia came to power Tsar Peter was only a ten-year-old child whose existence she could conveniently ignore; yet even at that period he was the central figure and rallying-point around which the opposition forces were grouped.

Preobrazhenskoye, where Natalia and her son most frequently sought refuge from the strain of life in the Kremlin, became a hotbed of derogatory rumours aimed at destroying the Regent's reputation. At fifteen, Peter's build and appearance were those of a twenty-year-old. The young Tsar was highly intelligent but less mentally precocious than Tsar Theodore had been at his age. He still refused to settle down to regular work and would only study subjects that interested him, so the worthy but colourless Zotov kept his job as tutor purely because Peter was attached to him and Natalia had faith in his loyalty.

Sophia and Vasily Golitsyn had introduced Prince Boris Golitsyn, the favourite's cousin, into the Tsar's circle. Boris was intelligent, courageous, and almost as erudite as Vasily, but because the Muscovites had nicknamed him 'the wine-bottle' scandalmongers whispered that the Regent wanted to turn her half-brother into an alcoholic – even though he was in good hands with Zotov in that respect. Instead of supervising Peter on Sophia's behalf, the new tutor went over to the Naryshkins, who, being short of able men, soon came to regard him as the leader of the anti-government party. Natalia's influence over her beloved 'Petrushka' was slight, but her constant harping on the subject of Sophia's misdemeanours formed the backcloth against which he grew up.

The young Tsar ran wild in the summer palaces where he spent his boyhood. Untrammelled by Court etiquette and free to do as he pleased, he was at once spoiled and humiliated, absolute monarch of his own little world, yet conscious that, although his entourage bowed to his every whim, the Kremlin was ruled by a hostile sister whom he had to obey. From his earliest childhood, Peter enjoyed the company of retainers' and junior officers' sons. Although he was now emerging from childhood, he still revelled in the *poteshny* or regiments of cadets whose war-games he directed according to rules taught him by Boris Golitsyn, Gordon and other distinguished officers. Sophia did not discourage this hobby, which she considered childish, and allowed the relevant government departments to supply the boy-soldiers with arms and ammunition. Peter conducted miniature expeditions and mock battles. In 1685 his 'soldiers' built a small fortress on the Yauza. He christened it Pressburg, which revealed how strongly he was influenced by Germany even at this stage.

Having discovered one of Alexis Michaelovitch's boats in an outhouse at Izmailovskoye one day, the Tsar listened ecstatically to the story of the first Russian fleet's voyage down the river to Astrakhan, where it was destroyed by Stepan Razin. Though born and bred in a land of plain and forest, Peter was irresistibly attracted to the sea which he had never seen. In 1687, Prince Yury Dolgoruky brought him back an astrolabe from abroad. Unfortunately, no member of the Tsar's staff knew how to use it. He continued to pester them until they found a Dutchman from the German Quarter, Franz Timmerman, who taught him the secrets of geometry and the art of building fortifications. Timmerman explained that it was possible to sail against the wind with the English boat which he had discovered at Izmailovskoye, and introduced Peter to a compatriot of his, Karsten-Brandt, who taught him how to handle the sails. Having learnt the rudiments of seamanship on the Yauza and various small stretches of water, Peter began to construct ships on a lake sixty or seventy miles from Moscow, assisted by Dutch specialists. He developed a lifelong interest in navigation, the art of warfare and – since gunnery and seamanship demanded a knowledge of it – mathematics.

The sturdy youth soon discovered the pleasures and distractions of the German Quarter in the company of the uncouth adventurers who lived there. Their boisterous camaraderie and free-and-easy behaviour came as a welcome antidote to the official ceremonies and lengthy religious services which he sometimes had to attend and which he found so intensely boring. For him, the rest of the capital was peopled by ghosts, and he unwittingly came to regard everything that made up Russia's traditional way of life as a threat to his life and liberty. Bearded boyars, undisciplined musketeers and fanatical Old Believers had no place in his world. What Peter liked was the snug little houses of the German Quarter where, pipe in mouth and glass in hand, men could chat freely in the presence of women who were neither coy nor prudish. The world to which Peter wanted to belong was a world of back-slapping, coarse laughter, broad oaths, sturdy Dutch wenches and the sort of carousals depicted by Jordaens.

The young Tsar led such a riotous life that his debauches would have ruined a less robust constitution than his own. We are told that he con-

acted an unfortunate disease which affected his health for the rest of his
fe, but what with his little fleet, his miniature army and the delights of
e German Quarter, Peter had no time to think of the future.

'Birds of a feather flock together.' Trite though it is, this saying sheds
ght on the essential difference between the Tsar's nature and that of his
alf-sister. The Regent was surrounded by Renaissance personalities; Tsar
eter by men who would have been at home in a People's Republic.
ne of his intimate friends was a journeyman pastry-cook named
lexander Menshikov, a shrewd and intelligent scoundrel who later rose
the rank of admiral – not that this deterred the Tsar from thrashing him
requently for his misuse of other people's money, as well as public funds.
nother was François Lefort, the Genevese soldier of fortune whom
urakin described as 'unintelligent but good company'. Lefort was an
ntertaining hedonist, 'in short, a true French debauchee. He diverts
imself day and night with suppers, balls, cards, female companionship
nd everlasting drinking-bouts, all of which will bring him to an untimely
nd.'

The young Tsar's other companions were cut from the same cloth.
ntelligent but uncouth men of action, they were the very antithesis of the
Ioly Russia which Peter abhorred. His following was composed of
lebeian adventurers, pleasure-seeking boyars, noblemen who had
bandoned their ancestral beliefs and youths who were preparing for a
nilitary career. None of the Tsar's intimates except Boris Golitsyn had
ny political acumen or definite views on government. While Polish
tiquette flourished at Sophia's court, Peter's entourage was dominated
y a sort of *bürgerlich* uncouthness.

Natalia watched her adored son with apprehension as he grew away
rom her and reached premature manhood. As a devout woman, the
owager Tsarina was not only disturbed by the future monarch's lack of
nterest in politics but convinced that he was endangering his immortal
oul by consorting with the harlots and heretics who populated the Ger-
nan Quarter. She decided to remedy the situation by marrying him off,
nd Peter agreed purely to please his mother. Vasily Golitsyn suggested his
iece, Princess Trubetskoy, but since Natalia regarded everything that
ame from the Kremlin as suspect she chose the future Tsarina herself –
nd chose badly. The daughter of an obscure State servitor, Eudoxia
opukhina was a pretty girl who had received a traditional upbringing –
vhich meant that she was totally uneducated. She was submissive,
pathetic and greedy. Peter was seventeen and his bride twenty when the
narriage was celebrated on January 27th, 1689. The unfortunate girl failed
o win her new husband's affections. Peter, who had no intention of

mending his ways, soon developed a boundless aversion to her, and
month after their marriage he deserted her for the things and people tha
interested and amused him most – among them a wine-merchant'
daughter, Anna Mons.

Tsar Peter's marriage was just another reminder to Sophia that he
power was transient. Only one thing could save her from the inevitable
and that was the birth of a male child to Tsar Ivan. In 1684, four year
before Peter's marriage, Ivan docilely married Prascovia Saltykov a
Sophia's insistence. He never seems to have been tempted by the pleasure
of the flesh – indeed, people who came into contact with him doubte
whether he was physically capable of having children – but four daughter
were born of his marriage.

This gave rise to all kinds of speculation. There was an unconfirme
rumour in Moscow that Sophia and Vasily Golitsyn had introduced
groom into Tsarina Prascovia's bed in order to guarantee the hoped-fo
event which would banish Natalia Naryshkin's son from the thron
permanently and enable Sophia to retain the regency for an indefinit
period. Moscow, however, was a hotbed of unfounded rumours, judging
by the backstairs gossip which was retailed with such relish by La Neuville
who described the Regent's dynastic plans in great detail. According t
him, Sophia intended to make Golitsyn put away his wife and then marr
him herself, but Golitsyn dissuaded her, 'for he loved his wife deeply an
preferred the children which she had borne him to those which he ha
begotten on the Tsarevna Sophia'.

La Neuville went on to allege that the Regent played her hand s
cleverly that Princess Golitsyn agreed to enter a convent of her own fre
will. Still reluctant, Golitsyn came up with another scheme. If the groom
succeeded in producing an heir to the throne, Peter could be forced to
enter a monastery. All that need then be done was to depose Patriarch
Joachim and replace him by Sylvester Medviedev, who, to the delight
of the whole civilized world, would send a mission to Rome to negotiate a
union of the Churches. The people would then be informed of Tsarina
Prascovia's adultery, which would effectively deprive the groom's
children of their right of succession. In recognition of Sophia's services to
religion, the Pope would legitimize the adulterous son of Sophia and
Vasily Golitsyn, who would reign over Russia after Sophia's death ...

La Neuville's tittle-tattle reads like a prurient novelette, and its
implausible complexity gives credit neither to Sophia's wisdom nor
Golitsyn's moderation.

Religious peace was far from restored in Russia, and we have no
grounds for believing that Sophia or Golitsyn, or even Sylvester

ledviedev, was prepared to desert Orthodoxy. Sophia, who was fully formed of the religious climate prevailing in the country, would never ave contemplated braving the people's anger in this way. Pope or no ope, enforced conversion to Roman Catholicism would have cost her ot only her power but her life.

The real element of drama in the situation was that the Regent could see o way out of it. Brought to power by a combination of exceptional rcumstances, she could maintain her position while Peter was too young reign effectively, but knew that, if Ivan had no heir, Peter's coming of ge would spell her downfall. The only guaranteed method – and one hich many a Christian monarch had employed in the course of history – as assassination. Peter's murder would have presented no problem to a oman with someone as resolute and devoted as Theodore Shaklovity her command, yet no attempt was ever made on the younger Tsar's fe. Recoiling from the crime which alone could have saved her, Sophia rned this way and that, searching for some way out of the trap. Her nly other hope was a coup d'état in her favour. No woman had ever een crowned sovereign of Russia, so the prospects of success were bleak, ut, although such an idea would have been unthinkable earlier on, seven ears of successful rule, enlightened government and moderate, unprecipi-te reform had enhanced the Regent's prestige.

The Naryshkin clique called Sophia a whore, and Sophia herself knew at according to the *domostroy* she merited the description. They also leged that she was not Tsar Alexis's daughter, although no one had ever st aspersions on Maria Miloslavsky's morals during her lifetime. Sophia ever flaunted her immorality, however, and her public 'image' was one f regal dignity. Her two lovers were discreet enough not to boast of their ood fortune, nor had anyone ever seen the Regent drunk or in low mpany. She had always treated the Church with great respect and set an lifying example by attending religious services and ceremonies. Here y her advantage over Peter, who had never rendered any public service d was known only for his disorderly life and irascible temperament. he Princess, whom La Neuville accused of being Machiavellian by ture, refused to commit the crime which would keep her in ower.

What really made it impossible for the Regent to reach an understanding ith her half-brother was the people who surrounded him. Tsar Peter was, ter all, of the same stock, and his inexperience and lack of interest in olitics might well have prompted him, if not to submit to the Regent's fluence, at least to consent to her retaining a share of power. However, phia's and Golitsyn's personal enemies continually set the young man

against her, and any chance of compromise was ruled out by the old feu
that existed between her and the Dowager Tsarina.

Theodore Shaklovity subtly prepared public opinion for a coup d'éta
while Sylvester Medviedev bolstered up Sophia's determination b
reminding her of the great queens of the past and assuring her that he
name was hallowed in Russia and well known abroad. The problem was
whom could the Regent rely on when the moment came? There wer
always the musketeers, who owed their lives to her clemency and knev
that the Naryshkin party would never forgive them for the Kremli
massacres. But, although Sophia's administration may have met with th
nation's approval, the one jewel missing from its crown was militar
success, a virtual necessity in an age when war was still invested wit
glamour. Sophia decided that there might still be time to enhance he
prestige in this respect and at the same time enhance that of her advise
and friend, Vasily Golitsyn.

CHAPTER THIRTY-ONE

INCE the attentions of the Regent and Prince Vasily Golitsyn were onstantly focused on the West and it was impossible for them to engage ı hostilities on all fronts simultaneously, it was only natural that they had ıcrificed Russia's Asiatic interests to a certain extent. Though a mediocre eneral – a fact which hastened his downfall – Golitsyn's talent for iplomacy put him on a par with the great Ordyn-Nastchokin himself. Ie can scarcely be reproached for his 'modernity' in preferring negotiation ɔ the dubious advantages of war, and his name is permanently linked vith the political phenomenon known to history as the 'Perpetual Peace vith Poland'. The West has always regarded any transaction between the wo great Slav countries with a certain prejudice and without bothering ɔ study the reasons for the enduring and reciprocal mistrust that has always haracterized Russo-Polish relations.

In 1682, though in immediate and deadly peril from the Turks, Poland till hankered after the territories which she had ceded to Moscow under he Treaty of Andrussovo. Although Poland was officially a republic, the ountry was really governed by a weak form of elected monarchy whose owers were persistently curtailed by the so-called Pacta Conventa. Gallant and romantic by nature, the Poles were still living in a 'Gothic vorld', as Rambaud expressed it. Anyone arriving in Poland from Russia elt that he had entered Western Europe, but any traveller who entered he country from the West realized that he had reached Eastern Europe.

At the period in question, John Sobieski was demanding a revision of he Treaty of Andrussovo and the return to Poland of territory ceded to Russia – the Little Russian areas on the left bank of the Dnieper. This was ɔ be the price of his intervention against the Porte – an intervention, it ıay be pointed out, which was dictated by Poland's own interests. At the ame time, Sobieski strengthened his ties with the Habsburgs and in 1683 gned an alliance with the Empire. On April 21st, 1683, he formally ıvited the Tsars to join this alliance. Having only just dealt with Khovansky, the Regent's government was not prepared to take on any ıternational obligations before it had consolidated its internal position.

With a nice sense of timing, the Sultan chose this moment to ratify th
Treaty of Bakhchisaray, which he had been in no hurry to do earlie
Emperor Leopold found himself in an awkward situation. Emerik Teke
invaded Silesia, the Pasha of Buffa seized Tokay, and in spring 1683 th
Turks launched an attack on Austria.

Leopold called upon John Sobieski to honour the terms of the allianc
and come to his aid. Sobieski did so, but the Emperor showed him s
little gratitude for his epic relief of Vienna and treated him with suc
arrogance that the Poles, who had always been fonder of the Hungariar
than the Austrians, were highly incensed and would have retracted if the
had not already been too deeply involved. Militarily exhausted and sti
faced by a formidable adversary, Poland urged Russia to come to her ai

Moscow was in a favourable position. The Emperor was courting th
Russians, Sobieski was offering them his friendship and Sultan Mahom
had gone to the lengths of dismissing his vassal, the Khan of the Crime
merely to please them. They would have liked to retain their advantag
but neutrality was a precarious status and, besides, Russia's almo
instinctive groping for political and economic expansion impelled her t
find an access to the sea without delay.

Russia was still the prisoner of her continent, her only maritime outl
being the Arctic Sea. The Baltic tempted Sophia just as it tempted Peter i
later years, but the Regent's government was chary of starting a new wa
with a nation whose military strength was only too well known to th
Russians. What was more, the Swedes were keeping abnormally quie
Weighing up their chances, the Russians turned their attention to th
Black Sea, less convenient than the Baltic but more accessible because a
that lay between it and Moscow was the Crimea and its ever-turbuler
Tatar inhabitants. What was more, victory in the Crimea woul
guarantee peace in Little Russia.

In early 1684, rightly distrusting his own judgment in military matter
Vasily Golitsyn sought the great Gordon's advice.

'You will not be the initiators of the conflict,' Gordon wrote in h
report to the Prime Minister. 'The Tatars have attacked your country o
various occasions and carried off prisoners; they have perverted tl
meaning and the terms of the peace treaty and dishonoured your envoys

He was right. Despite the ratification of the Treaty of Bakhchisaray the
were frequent border clashes, and the Pasha of Azov was threatening
invade areas occupied by the Cossacks.

The time seemed ripe for a campaign. Gordon's prestige was immens
and there is little doubt that his favourable verdict on the Regent's ar
Golitsyn's scheme carried a great deal of weight. The Scottish gener

ated that a military operation whose only real difficulty lay in crossing ie arid steppes could be undertaken without undue risk. By following ie course of the Dnieper, the Russian army would never be without vater for more than two days at a time.

Having decided on a Crimean campaign, the Russian government ought to reach an understanding with its future allies and derive benefits rom the assistance which it proposed to lend them.

The first Russo-Polish meeting took place at Andrussovo on January 7th, 684. Vasily Golitsyn's instructions to his subordinates were clear and oncise. While extremely anxious to conclude a treaty with Poland, he vas adamant on three points. First, there was no question of giving back iev and the Zaporozhye district to Poland; secondly, he would not ndertake to enter the war against the Turks; and, thirdly, Orthodox hristians in Poland must be guaranteed protection and Russia's contribu-ion to the alliance would be strictly limited to a war against the Crimean atars.

The Poles also made stipulations. They refused to settle the frontier uestion before signing an alliance against the Porte and insisted that Little ussia should become an autonomous state. In February, highly dissatis-ied with one another, the two sides broke off the talks without signing ny form of agreement. The Cossacks added fuel to the flames by omplaining that the Poles were violating their territory and had thus nfringed the Treaty of Andrussovo.

The proposal to create an independent Little Russia made the Russians rick up their ears. From February 1684 onwards, Golitsyn had been eceiving reports of a separatist movement inspired by Polish agitators in ittle Russia.

The Russians were being subjected to constant irritation by Polish ctivities among the Kalmucks and the Cossacks, whose fluctuating oyalties were a never-ending source of worry. Golitsyn maintained an fficient intelligence service which kept the Russian government informed f all that took place among its untrustworthy allies. At the end of summer 684, twelve thousand Cossacks placed themselves at Poland's disposal, nd one of their colonels warned Golitsyn that forty thousand more would hortly be offering their services to the Poles. Golitsyn protested vigorously gainst this violation of the terms of the Treaty of Andrussovo. The Poles egan by rejecting his charges but, when confronted with evidence, laimed that if they had indeed violated the treaty they were justified in loing so by the steady deterioration in Russo-Polish relations.

In spite of this, a new Polish mission arrived in Moscow in 1686 and alks were reopened, though still in the same atmosphere of mutual

suspicion. The Poles attended a military review and were lavishly entertained at the Kremlin, but the long-drawn-out discussions degenerated
into stubborn bargaining. Russia's insistence on the permanent annexation
of Kiev was the main stumbling-block.

'During these laborious discussions,' Kurakin tells us, 'the Russian
statesmen became divided into two parties. Although the Regent and
Vasily Golitsyn, together with their friends, wished to continue negotiations with the Poles despite all disappointments, a sizeable group led by
Prince Peter Prozorovsky and Theodore Saltykov demanded that they be
broken off and recommended war against Poland instead of the Crimea.'

The talks continued. Representing the King of Poland were Senator
Grzymultowski, the two Princes Oginski and Count Potocki: representing
Russia, Prince Vasily Golitsyn, the boyars Buturlin and Boris Sheremetev,
two gentlemen and four officials of the Duma. The bases of discussion
were, needless to say, the two previous treaties of 1667 and 1678. In
negotiating with the representatives of a country which, despite his
affection for it, had given him so much trouble in the past, Golitsyn
displayed his political genius to the full. He satisfied every one of his
requirements. The Treaty of Andrussovo was maintained intact except
where modified by the concessions which Moscow had been compelled
to grant by the treaty of 1678.

The terms of the new treaty stated that the territories in dispute – the
Seversk district and all its accompanying towns, the Smolensk district,
Kiev, the 'Mother of Russian cities', together with a slightly increased
enclave, and the Zaporozhye region – were annexed to Russia 'in
perpetuity'.

Having settled the frontier question, the plenipotentiaries reached
agreement on the respective titles of their sovereigns, on commercial
relationships between the two countries and on freedom of religious
worship both for Catholics living in areas ceded to Russia and for the
Orthodox Christians domiciled in Poland whom Russia would henceforth
take under her wing. This was a great victory for the Russian Church
which had long been distressed to see the Orthodox minority in Poland
subjected to oppression and persecution. The delegates then passed on to
the subject of a military alliance proper. The Poles demanded an immediate attack on the Crimean Tatars and the dispatch of Russian troops to
Poland to speed the liberation of Kamenets, which was still occupied by
the Turks. Golitsyn pointed out the difficulties of such an operation.

The treaty was ratified on May 6th, 1686. John Sobieski is said to have
signed it with tears in his eyes and an oath on his lips, whereas Sophia
rewarded Vasily Golitsyn and his colleagues handsomely and hastened to

ıblicize the outstanding advantages of the document which she and the ,ars had just signed.

It was a very real diplomatic victory, and one which safeguarded Russia's tal interests. Whatever the disasters in which Russia's obligations towards oland subsequently involved her, the advantages of the 'perpetual peace' ıtweighed them all.

The Russians undertook to abrogate the Treaty of Bakhchisaray and nd an army against the Tatars of the Crimea. Each party swore not to nclude a separate peace with the Porte. In addition, Russia paid Poland e substantial sum of 146,000 roubles to compensate her for the loss of iev, making it clear that she was doing so not in return for territorial ncessions but solely 'out of love and amity'.

Once the treaty was signed, preparations for the Crimean campaign ere speeded up. In September 1686 State servitors received orders to in the colours, and in November new taxes were levied to cover fence commitments. It should be noted that, while Sophia, Golitsyn d the Regent's other associates were delighted with the new ties of iendship which were – or so they hoped – to bind Russia to Poland from enceforth, their boundless enthusiasm was not universally shared. As e have mentioned, a number of boyars, headed by Prozorovsky and ltykov, would have preferred the forthcoming military operations to be rected against the Poles rather than the Tatars. The Russians had suffered much from the Poles in the past and their resentment was so deep-oted that Dolgoruky and Stcherbatov even proposed to adopt mourning token of their disapproval, and some prophesied darkly that Poland ould betray her trust and end by signing a separate treaty with the Porte ter all.

While making active preparations for the campaign, Sophia canvassed r the support of other Christian nations. Her ambassadors combed ırope for potential allies but were rebuffed everywhere. Even the npire and the Venetian Republic, who were at war with the Porte, nfined themselves to wishing the Russian armies well and refused to gn anything that would commit them. Charles II of England offered oscow his prayers for success. Charles XI of Sweden congratulated the ars on their decision but regretted that he could not assist them 'in ew of the great distance that separated Turkey from his country'. The rand Duke of Tuscany (or Florence) could not offer them financial d because he proposed to help Venice. King Christian V of Denmark as the only one who actually promised to support the Russian venture, ıt only with his navy and 'only in case of absolute necessity', which as vague enough in all conscience. Sophia did not hesitate to send a

delegation to Pope Innocent XI. Her overtures to Louis XIV on
succeeded in irritating him.

Despite their universal lack of success, these missions did achie
something of importance. Western Europe abruptly awoke to the fa
that Russia existed and that she belonged to the European communi
of nations.

CHAPTER THIRTY-TWO

)F all the countries in Western Europe, France was the least well known n Russia and the one with which Moscow had least contact. Sophia's nterests revolved around the Empire, Poland, the Low Countries, England nd the Republic of Venice. Since her European policy was dictated nainly by a wish to deal with the Turkish and Tatar threats as speedily s possible, she limited her approaches to countries which could help her n such a venture. Russia maintained the *status quo* with Sweden during he regency, while Holland and England continued to occupy an mportant place in her commercial relationships.

Immediately on coming to power, Sophia sent ambassadors abroad to nform other Christian monarchs of the two Tsars' accession and her ssumption of the regency. Being unprejudiced towards the Vatican, ophia also sought the aid of Pope Innocent XI, and although her brother heodore had never received anything but Platonic encouragement from ouis XIV she decided to seek the French king's support as well – at a noment when circumstances were least favourable to approaches on er part.

'Louis XIV,' writes Rambaud, 'was ever torn between two trains of hought, the political idea which made him desire a Turkish alliance, and he idea of chivalry, the Crusade and Christian solidarity.'

The King's unwaning interest in the East and the Islamic world is ttested by the Battle of St Gothard in 1664 and the Candia expeditions of 1668–9. It was to Louis XIV that Leibniz addressed his memorandum on the conquest of Egypt. However, France had concluded some xtremely advantageous trade agreements with Turkey, and by remaining on good terms with the Sultan the King of France had become the *de facto* protector of all Christians resident in Near Eastern countries. What was nore, by presenting a constant threat to his enemy the Emperor, the Sultan was doing Louis XIV a welcome service. In short, Louis had xcellent reasons for remaining neutral.

Tsar Alexis had sent a mission to Versailles in 1673 to ask His Most Christian Majesty to support him against the Turks. Pleading the war

in which he was currently involved and the threat represented by France
neighbours, Louis XIV rejected the entreaties of his 'dearly belove
brother, The Most Excellent, Most Powerful Alexis Michael, Emper
of All the Russias', and declined to come to his aid on the grounds th
he would be hazarding the security and commercial interests of h
subjects. The King did not, of course, admit that he needed the Sultan t
weaken the Empire. In fact, he officially expressed the hope that th
Infidels would be defeated and urged Tsar Alexis to 'persevere in h
generous designs'.

In 1681, a new Russian mission headed by Ivan Potemkin disembarke
at Calais. This time, on the pretext of seeking a trade agreement, Ts
Theodore was looking for an assurance that Louis would remain neutr
in the current Russo-Swedish dispute.

On this occasion the Russians were welcomed with extreme courtes
Louis XIV's tactics were the same in 1681 as they had been in 1668. H
treated his 'dear and perfect brother and friend' with a civility that mea
absolutely nothing. The Roi Soleil could not bring himself to take Russi
seriously, but he had no wish to fall out with her. As we shall see, h
attitude had changed by 1687.

In fact, Sophia showed a lack of discernment in sending a mission t
the King of France in 1687. Times had changed. Louis XIV's power ha
waned perceptibly since 1683, and Europe, irritated by his pretension
had reacted against them. The business of the Palatine succession and th
siege of Luxemburg had precipitated the formation of a coalition. Throug
her alliance with the Emperor, Russia was a member of the Holy League
nor could Louis ignore the fact that the Regent had sent emissaries t
Pope Innocent XI, a sworn foe of France. When Sophia's mission arrive
in France the Roi Soleil's only ally was the Sultan, and Charles d
Lorraine's victories over the Turks were tantamount to French defeat

Thus it was a singularly inopportune moment to ask for the King's hel
against the Porte. The two Russian ambassadors, Prince Yakov Dolgoruk
and Prince Ivan Myshetsky, could not have landed at Dunkirk at a wors
time, for it was Kara Mustapha who prompted the formation of th
Augsburg League, and it was the Augsburg League which later force
Louis XIV into the Peace of Ryswick.

Everything went badly between the two parties from the outset, an
the succession of tragi-comic encounters which took place are describe
in detail by Solovyev in his *History of Russia*.

The man sent to meet the Russian princes was Stolph, the sam
Gentleman Ordinary to the King who had been assigned to greet Potem
kin at Calais in 1681. This time, however, the King's instructions wer

quite different. Stolph was to communicate his royal displeasure at their arrival. There was to be no more meaningless cordiality, no more slightly ironic courtesy. Versailles was annoyed. Versailles was France, and France was Louis XIV.

The ambassadors disembarked at Dunkirk with a retinue fifty strong, of which twelve were halberdiers dressed in the Persian style. Stolph at once expressed the King's displeasure and his own surprise that Louis had not been informed of the size of the Russian delegation. In fact, a Russian nobleman had been sent on in advance to act as a courier, but since he insisted on delivering his message to the King in person the French had churlishly sent him away unheard.

'Should they display unwarrantable presumption,' ran Stolph's instructions, 'they must be informed that it is useless for them to continue their journey. In that case, Stolph shall entertain them in taverns until new orders are received.'

Stolph began by telling the ambassadors, on His Majesty's orders, that unless they were prepared to conform strictly to the procedure laid down for foreign ambassadors, the King had no wish to receive them into his kingdom.

Astonished by this opening gambit, the ambassadors assured Stolph that they were only too ready to conform with custom. What they did not realize was that the King, knowing that the Regent's envoys had instructions to ask him to join the Holy League, was only looking for an excuse not to receive them. They soon supplied him with one.

Customs officials at Dunkirk having sealed their coffers so that they could be opened only on reaching Paris, the ambassadors or their staff promptly broke the seals. A constable who came to stop them selling some merchandise was insulted by Russian servants, and one of the diplomats went so far as to threaten him with a dagger.

The King at once refused to receive the ambassadors and ordered his Minister of Foreign Affairs to inform them that it would be useless to open negotiations. The Minister added that he had been charged by the King to return their credentials. Dolgoruky fumed and raged, protesting that he also had his instructions and refusing to take back his credentials from anyone except the King – and that during an official audience. He was told that the King was extremely annoyed by his obstinacy. Dolgoruky repeated that neither the King's displeasure nor his own death would make him take back his letters of credence. The French tried to coax the Prince by offering him gifts, which he haughtily refused. When they threatened to stuff them into his baggage by force, he declared that he would abandon both baggage and coaches, and that he had no fear of the King's anger because he was a servant of the Tsars. The affair degenerated into farce. The French tried to starve the Russians into surrender. They stopped the grant which was supposed to cover their expenses, withdrew all the officers who had been placed at their disposal and even stripped the envoys' lodgings of furniture. Dolgoruky remained adamant, and it was the Roi Soleil who finally yielded, though with an understandable lack of good grace.

Colbert de Croissy represented France at the preliminary talks, which were held at Saint-Denis. Replying to the proposal that France should enter the anti-Turkish league, de Croissy said: 'In the present state of things, His Majesty would have to be as imprudent as he is wise to wish to declare war on the Turks. He is not accustomed to declare war unless given just cause for doing so and accorded the greatest share of the glory.' He added that: 'The King has no wish to join the alliance, since imperishable and perpetual enmity exists between himself and the Emperor, whereas between himself and the Sultan there is perpetual peace and enduring amity.'

Louis XIV had been forced to reveal his underlying motives, which at least had the merit of dispelling any illusions the Russians may still have cherished. Dolgoruky and Myshetsky then sought an assurance that the King would not actively oppose their government's schemes, quoting the commercial potentialities of Archangel as an indication that the advantages of the bargain would not be entirely one-sided. Colbert countered by saying that His Majesty would be pleased if the Tsars made it easier for Jesuits and other Catholic missionaries to pass through Siberia on their way to China. Dolgoruky replied that although he had no instructions on the subject he was sure that the King's wishes would be favourably considered.

The last act of the political farce opened when the day of the audience arrived. New difficulties arose at Versailles. The title '*Grands Seigneurs*' did not appear in the Russians' credentials, and they were told that it had never been granted to anyone before. Russian insistence met unyielding French resistance. After that, the Regent's obstinate and luckless ambassadors were subjected to fresh indignities. Friendless, deserted and once more deprived of financial support, the Russian diplomats asked to be given visas for Spain. They were granted them, but forbidden to cross France and told to sail from Le Havre. On reaching the port, they were presented with two alternatives: either to accept the King's gifts or be refused permission to embark. Weary of the struggle and eager to leave a country which had treated them so badly, the ambassadors complied.

In Spain, where 'Don Pedro' (Potemkin) and the magnificent gifts which he had brought the young King Charles were still remembered, the Russian delegation received a cordial welcome. Its success was purely Platonic, however, for when the ambassadors suggested a loan of two or three thousand thalers they met with a polite refusal, Spanish finances being in a pitiable state at the time.

* * *

A French account of this diplomatic episode mentions that: 'Sieur Ogourouki [*sic*,] whom the Tsars Jean and Pierre sent to Paris in 1687 with the rank of ambassador, conducted himself so ill during his sojourn in France and made himself so little agreeable to the King and the entire French nation that he did not further his cause.' In reality, responsibility for the unpleasantnesses seems to have been shared equally between the Russians and the French.

Sophia's government nursed a grudge against France for her maltreatment of the Russian ambassadors. In April 1687, Louis XIV gave two Jesuits bound for China a letter of recommendation addressed to the Tsars. On reaching Poland, one of these missionaries, Father d'Avril, urged a foreign diplomat to send a letter of introduction to Prince Vasily Golitsyn. The letter remained unacknowledged, so Lazinski, the King of Poland's envoy, conducted the two Jesuits to Moscow in person. They were promptly expelled and escorted to the frontier by a constable. It seems that the missionaries may, after all, have secured at least one interview with Golitsyn, who had received a letter from the King of Poland calling for his support. However, the Protestants were on their guard. The Resident of Brandenburg reminded the Russians how their envoys had been snubbed by France, and Keller, the Dutch Resident, thought it appropriate to comment, on the subject of the Jesuits, that 'this crafty and turbulent sect makes a great din at present'. Golitsyn tried to arrange matters despite opposition, but the missionaries were still refused permission to cross Russia, and when they managed to reach Moscow a second time they were once again expelled. Keller declared that 'the Russians' hatred of the French increases from one day to the next'.

CHAPTER THIRTY-THREE

IT was quite understandable that Sophia should take advantage of a combination of favourable circumstances to engage in a military venture which her father and her brother Theodore had contemplated before her. Since victory over the Crimean Tatars would give Russia access to the Black Sea and restore peace in the Ukraine, any sensible government might have made the attempt. Sophia's mistake lay in entrusting the supreme command of the Russo-Ukrainian army to Prince Vasily Golitsyn. The Grand Chancellor himself would gladly have dispensed with this high honour, being too intelligent not to know that his natural aptitudes were for politics and diplomacy rather than generalship. He must have accepted the dangerous assignment with considerable reluctance. 'Golitsyn,' reports La Neuville, 'did all in his power to decline this appointment, reflecting that he would be blamed in the event of failure.' A general who has no confidence in victory seldom brings home the victor's laurels.

The campaign was supposed to open in February 1687, but only the main army, with Golitsyn in command, was in position near the Altyrka on the appointed date. The other units were late in arriving, and operations did not commence until May, after a series of postponements.

At last the Russian army moved southwards, forming a large rectangle two versts long and more than one verst wide. The musketeers marched in the centre, flanked by regiments of regular troops. The supply train followed on one flank and the artillery on the other, protected by a screen of cavalry which also performed reconnaissance duties. According to Gordon, the Russian army comprised 20,000 infantry and 40,000 cavalry. Near the river Samara, the Russian forces were joined by 50,000 Zaporozhye Cossacks commanded by the elderly hetman Samoilovitch. Their numbers were further augmented by the Don Cossacks, who brought the total up to a figure variously estimated at between one and four hundred thousand men. Kurakin puts it at 200,000, La Neuville raises the score to 400,000, and Ustryalov cuts it down to 100,000, though he was probably counting Russians alone.

It was a strange campaign conducted against an invisible enemy. The Tatars made themselves scarce, and when the Don Cossacks succeeded in attacking the flank of an enemy unit on the Dnieper they gained the Russian army's first and only real success.

The Russians had no sooner crossed the Konskie Vody than they found themselves in a living hell. The steppes in their path had been burnt to tinder by the early summer heat, although recent storms and downpours had left deep morasses in which men and beasts floundered helplessly. Before long, fires lit by the Tatars transformed the Russians' route into a sea of flames. Rations were cut and water carefully husbanded, while horses and cattle sank to the ground and died for lack of fodder. When the exhausted Russians finally reached the Nogayskaya Steppe, 'all they could see,' wrote Ustryalov, 'were wild boar fleeing through the tall grasses, which burnt with a dry crackle.'

Shebalsky, Sophia's nineteenth-century biographer, gives the following eye-witness description of a steppe fire:

> The flames run along the ground and raze the grass to its roots. The fire writhes like a nest of serpents, only clouds of smoke and tumbling swaths of grass marking the progress of the dread scourge as it leaves nothing but charred and blackened plain in its wake. Fiery serpents arise at every breath of wind, rearing up and writhing across the tall grasses and stunted bushes of the steppe. Black clouds speed along like harbingers of destruction, spreading an acrid smell and covering everything with ashes. The wall of flame tirelessly pursues the birds and beasts who flee from it and never fails to catch them unawares. All that it touches – whether tree or cottage – disappears. Streams dry up and marshes become like the steppe.

How far was Vasily Golitsyn responsible for the disaster which ensued? In his anxiety to make up for lost time and cut the route as originally planned in Moscow by some thirty miles, the commander-in-chief appears to have decided not to follow the course of the Dnieper after all. Having made this blunder he failed to remedy it. Short of water and nearly asphyxiated by a rain of ash, the men and surviving horses trudged across the blazing steppe for another two days. On June 16th a downpour slightly cleared the air without extinguishing the fires. The army was now doing less than two miles a day, the horses found it hard to haul carts and cannon in their weakened condition, and there was a risk of sparks igniting the powder-wagons.

Golitsyn's army reached a point some sixty miles from the Crimea and twenty miles from the Zaporozhye district without coming to grips with the enemy, and by the time the Russians reached the mouth of the Dnieper they were in no fit state to undertake a military operation.

With a characteristic regard for democratic procedure which amounted to weakness, the commander-in-chief sought to share his responsibilities by calling councils-of-war with such frequency that his indecision and lack of initiative soon produced a detrimental effect on discipline. Each discussion degenerated into a fruitless and sterile war of words.

The Regent grew uneasy at the news that filtered back to Moscow. Knowing her friend's tendency to become easily discouraged, she sent him affectionate letters in cipher. 'Light of mine eyes, friend of my heart,' she wrote, 'may you remain in good health for many years, and may the Lord give you victory over the infidels. I can scarce believe, my light, that you will return to us ... Why do you aks me to pray for you? Though I am a sinner and unworthy, I trust in the mercy of God.'

Golitsyn had already given the order to withdraw. He had been entrusted by the Regent with a task for which he had no relish, but he was haunted by thoughts of the shame which he had brought on her by his incompetent generalship. Knowing how much Sophia had counted on a victory, the man whom all his contemporaries esteemed a man of honour was so gripped by panic that he descended to a sordid and uncharacteristic manœuvre. The idea of a scapegoat was probably mooted to him by Shaklovity, a man of fewer scruples but greater realism. The Regent's two lovers got on well together, and Sophia had no hesitation in sending Shaklovity to Golitsyn to cheer him up and spur him into positive action. However, it was now too late for action, so Golitsyn allowed himself to be persuaded without much difficulty that his lack of success was due to treason. This refinement was actually suggested to him by an historical figure who turned up later at the side of Peter I, namely Ivan Mazeppa, the renegade who went over to the enemy during the Russo-Swedish war. Since Mazeppa was subsequently transformed into a literary figure by Pushkin and Voltaire, he is worth a closer look.

Ivan Mazeppa was born in Podolia and is assumed – though no evidence is forthcoming – to have been the son of a minor Polish nobleman. He became a page to King John Casimir and received a first-class education. Mazeppa was an excellent horseman, a graceful dancer and a skilled duellist. He was also a handsome young man and much in demand with the ladies, and it was one of his amorous escapades that indirectly brought him to Russia. Having seduced the daughter or wife of a Polish aristocrat who did not allow people to trifle with his honour, he was tied to the tail of a wild horse and turned loose. The horse, which happened to be Cossack-bred, galloped towards the south, where its battered human appendage was nursed back to health by the Cossacks. Mazeppa remained with his hosts and won such a reputation among them for his spectacular bravery during skirmishes with the Tatars that he was soon given a senior rank in the Zaporozhye army. His contemporaries described him as being 'neither miserly nor extravagant' but, although he was shrewd enough to amass a considerable fortune, one report states that he 'showed no regret at losing all that he possessed'. In common with all truly ambitious men, his only real passion was for power, and to satisfy it Mazeppa turned traitor as readily as a Cossack would drain a glass of vodka. He began his new career as an aide to the hetman Doroshenko. When Doroshenko rebelled against the Poles, Mazeppa blithely accompanied his leader into the Sultan's service, dreaming even at that stage of offering his services to Russia and grimly determined to dispose of anyone who got in his way. One of his contemporaries described him as 'of above middle height, with an emaciated face and a slender, supple frame. His gaze is hard and haughty. He always wears a pensive air.'

At the time of the first Crimean campaign, the only obstacle to Mazeppa's ambitions was the hetman Samoilovitch, who had rendered Russia great service by obtaining Doroshenko's surrender. Samoilovitch had taken on Mazeppa as his aide, but Mazeppa was now angling for the post of hetman.

As it happened, Golitsyn did not get on with the old Zaporozhye leader, a fact which Gordon noted in his journal. Samoilovitch had opposed the ill-fated operation from the start because he foresaw disaster, and had been indiscreet enough to say triumphantly, when proved right, 'Ah! If they had only listened to me!'

Golitsyn was far from displeased, therefore, when Mazeppa accused Samoilovitch of firing the steppes and claimed that the Cossacks were dissatisfied with his leadership. The latter statement was probably true, few leaders being popular with their men after a disastrous campaign. Without instituting an inquiry, Golitsyn accepted Mazeppa's charges at their face value and thus tarnished his reputation as a gentleman and man of honour. The scapegoat was providentially to hand: forwarding the Cossacks' petition and Mazeppa's denunciation to Moscow, the commander-in-chief immediately arrested Samoilovitch, who was no saint but – as history affirms – certainly no traitor.

On July 11th, the Russian army made its ignominious way back into Great Russian territory. On July 22nd, a dispatch reached headquarters from Moscow. The Regent's decision was: 'If Samoilovitch is unpopular with the Cossacks he must be deported to a suitable spot.'

Next morning, as Samoilovitch was emerging from Mass with his son, not dressed in his ceremonial costume but still carrying his *bulava* or commander's baton, he was arrested. He was then led into the presence of Cossack colonels and Russian dignitaries. Golitsyn charged him with having betrayed Russia, misappropriated public funds and abused his authority. Samoilovitch tried to exonerate himself but was forbidden to speak. No one bothered to produce any evidence of the old man's guilt, and he was placed in the custody of musketeers prior to deportation.

The hetman's departure paved the way for fresh disorders among the Zaporozhye Cossacks, whose discipline deteriorated so badly that Russian troops had to be called in to restore order and enforce a postponement of the new hetman's election.

On July 25th, Prince Golitsyn attended the traditional election ceremony in state. The proceedings were lively, but, when Golitsyn asked the Cossacks whom they wanted as hetman, Mazeppa reaped the benefits of his machinations by winning a majority of the votes cast. And while this dangerous character, who still maintained secret contact with the Polish nobility, solemnly accepted the *bulava*, Samoilovitch, disgraced and deprived of his worldly goods, was travelling to his place of exile in a peasant cart.

* * *

Hard though it was to present this disastrous campaign to the people as a victory worthy of acclaim, Sophia set about the task with great determination. Since it suited the Regent's book that Vasily Golitsyn should be awarded the victor's laurels, she prepared to welcome her incompetent general with all the honours due to a hero. Moscow rang with tales of his imaginary triumph, and the tsarevna persuaded the Tsars to issue a decree proclaiming the conspicuous services rendered by her favourite.

The members of the expeditionary force had hardly entered the capital before they received tokens of official gratitude. Golitsyn, his generals and officers were awarded a gold medal bearing likenesses of the two sovereigns on one side and on the other a portrait of the Regent, dressed in the imperial cloak, crowned and holding the sceptre. Lower ranks and private soldiers received medals of silver gilt or silver. The decoration designed for Golitsyn himself was made from three hundred ducats of gold studded with diamonds, and was attached to a heavy gold chain which the Grand Chancellor wore round his neck.

These medals were only symbols of the gratitude due to those who had rendered great services to the Crown. Sophia distributed other awards as well. All unit commanders and every functionary who had taken part in the ill-starred expedition – down to the last 'boyar's son' – received mink pelisses, gold or silver goblets, grants of land and large sums of money. Nor were the lower orders forgotten. For good measure, the Regent allotted land even to junior officers who had been punished at the beginning of the campaign for being slow to join the colours. Vasily Golitsyn's tangible prizes included a thousand peasant families and a large gold cup.

Tsar Ivan naturally raised no objection to these rewards for failure, but Peter, though he was only fifteen and had to bow to Sophia's wishes, made no secret of his disgust at Vasily Golitsyn's setback and castigated the Prince for having 'irritated the Tatars to no purpose' and exposed the country's frontiers to enemy attack.

While Shaklovity was working out bold schemes for crushing the opposition, Sophia doggedly prepared for a second Crimean campaign. She was probably right in thinking that a rapid and resounding victory would be enough to keep her in power for a long time to come, but her affection for Vasily Golitsyn led her to commit the same psychological error twice. She still believed that her gentle prince could be transformed into a great captain of war.

The Polish King's urgent appeal to the Russians in March 1688 to open a new offensive against the Crimea suited Sophia's plans admirably, for, although the Russian government would have preferred more time for preparation, it was bound under the terms of the Russo-Polish treaty to act almost immediately. Things seemed to have taken a turn for the worse in Little Russia. Two Russian voivodes had been sent there with limited forces at the beginning of the year, but the Tatars had resumed their attacks and were now threatening Kiev itself. Mazeppa's Zaporozhye Cossacks lay low and the Poles declined to intervene, so the Regent sent her chief confidant to Little Russia to see what was happening.

'The Cossacks are trustworthy but the new hetman, Mazeppa, less so,' Shaklovity wrote in his report – thereby showing more discernment than Peter did later on.

Meanwhile, things had changed in Moscow. Egged on by his mentors, Peter suddenly demanded to be kept informed of affairs of state and started to attend sessions of the Duma, where he boldly asked questions and insisted on being given precise answers. When Shaklovity stirred up trouble among the musketeers, the young Tsar dispatched a message direct to Gordon asking him to send him the Butyrky Regiment. Gordon at once carried out the Tsar's order without consulting the Prime Minister, which greatly enraged Golitsyn despite his regard for the General. Before long, the Regent and her friends were forced to admit that the ranks of Peter's personal regiments were rapidly swelling. Four months later, the young Tsar's marriage furnished new and disquieting evidence of his approaching manhood. It was certainly not the ideal moment for Vasily Golitsyn to leave the capital, but it would have been a reflection on his courage if the army had left without him.

This time, elaborate precautions were taken to ensure that everything went without a hitch. Sophia attended councils of war in person and listened to the exchanges of views between her generals. Gordon submitted a new plan to Golitsyn. This demanded the construction, apart from the fort on the Samara, of several other minor fortresses along the route which the army was to take, each of which was to be situated at four days' march from the next. This would guarantee an uninterrupted supply of provisions and fodder, and field hospitals would be installed to deal with the sick and wounded. The plan also envisaged the construction of prefabricated bridges for transporting the army across rivers. Gordon's innovations injected an element of modernity into Russian military organization, but logistical precautions are valueless if unsupported by the human factor represented by the man who directs the battle. Although Sophia's long-standing affection for Golitsyn persuaded her to go on hoping for the miracle that would turn him into Alexander the Great, it is probable that Shaklovity, who had a healthy sense of reality, already regarded his team-mate with a disillusioned eye. No one knew better than he did that war, like rebellion, called for rapid decisions which the Grand Chancellor was incapable of making. However, it would hardly have been possible to appoint another commander-in-chief without damaging Golitsyn's prestige, and Golitsyn's prestige was closely linked with the Regent's.

While preparations for the coming campaign were in progress, Sophia's friends and associates became the target of sundry attacks by her enemies. Vasily Golitsyn received threatening letters, and a coffin was placed outside the door of his house together with a note warning him that a second defeat would mean his death. Then, without even waiting for the outcome of the campaign, a hired assassin hurled himself at the Prince one day as he was getting into his sleigh. Sophia made light of the unpleasant incident and tried to hush it up. The attempt was a failure, but the man involved was interrogated and executed in secret.

* * *

The campaign was supposed to start in February 1689, before the great thaw could set in and hamper the movement of troops. The Russians had mustered 100,000 men, not counting some 20,000 Cossacks commanded by Mazeppa. Many of the infantry and cavalry regiments were led by foreign officers such as Gordon, Lefort and von Werden. As for artillery, La Neuville estimates it at 700 pieces and Ustryalov, more conservatively, at 400.

The army got under way a month late, and Golitsyn, who had been detained in the capital by urgent business, did not join it until later, in the neighbourhood of Sumy. Gordon's advice proved its worth, but his evident respect for Tsar Peter was beginning to undermine the Prince's and the Regent's confidence in him. The spring was exceptionally cold and the thaw did not set in until April, transforming streams into boiling torrents and hindering the army's advance.

The Tatars, who were the first to attack, fell upon Sheremetev's regiment in the Nogayskaya Steppe on May 13th. Surprised and outnumbered, Sheremetev's men fled in disorder, exposing the supply train's line of advance. Golitsyn and his troops managed to retrieve the situation, but the Tatars, advancing in silence and attacking in force, invisible yet omnipresent and familiar with the smallest natural feature of their native district, were formidable foes. On May 16th, while the plain was being lashed by a violent storm, they reappeared on the right flank of the Russian army and attacked the rear formations. Six hours of confused fighting ensued, at the end of which the enemy broke off the engagement in good order, under pressure from the Russian artillery.

Golitsyn's objective was Perekop, a key town whose possession would enable him to control the Crimean isthmus. Despite the losses incurred and the size of the opposing forces, which had been swelled by Turkish troops and Circassian highlanders, Golitsyn's army reached Perekop on May 20th and took up its position outside the town.

What happened then is shrouded in mystery. Golitsyn's incomprehensible refusal to take advantage of his position gave birth to rumours which reflected on his honour, but the true explanation of the inexplicable lay in the Prince's mentality. Instead of exploiting the situation, which had great possibilities and could well have led to the capture of Perekop, he agreed to negotiate with the enemy only a few hours after coming in sight of the town. No one knows on whose initiative this step was taken, but the whole affair suggests that the commander-in-chief of the Russian army was afraid to order his men into action.

Thus, with victory in his grasp, Golitsyn defaulted, transforming triumph into disaster and dragging the Regent and her party down with him.

Lengthy negotiations were just what the Khan of Perekop needed to give him time to improve the defences of his town, and the Tatars, who always preferred surprise attacks to pitched battles, were equally delighted.

Golitsyn appears to have been completely demoralized, for his handling of the negotiations was – uncharacteristically – as maladroit as his military tactics had been. The conditions imposed by the Russians were far from severe. Golitsyn demanded an assurance from the Tatars that they would keep out of Polish and Ukrainian territory in future. He also demanded the cancellation of any indemnities due to the Khan from Russia under previous agreements and the release of Russian prisoners. The Tatars haggled with all the skill of merchants in a bazaar. While the Khan kept his head and tried to extract more money from Moscow in compensation for signing an armistice, the Tatars claimed that they had very few prisoners and that the majority had already regained their freedom by embracing Islam.

Golitsyn consulted his staff but declined to accept any of their suggestions unless they tallied with his wish to have done with the whole tiresome business as speedily as possible. In his eagerness to get back to Moscow, he ordered the siege to be raised and set off for Russia before a treaty had even been signed, so the arduous and inglorious journey home was attended by all the dangers which an armistice would have eliminated. Tatar and Turkish guerillas harassed the Russian army continually and the steppe blazed up in its path once more. C. Bickford O'Brien points out that if the Khan had decided to pursue the Russians in force their withdrawal might have been transformed into a rout.

Russian soldiers of the period used to impress the local girls by marching through the streets singing songs which boasted of their easy way of life.

> The soldier does not have to plough,
> He carries no scythe in his hands,
> He eats and drinks without working,
> He wears the bright attire of the Tsar's service.

But cheerful refrains like these gave way to sentiments of another kind when the Russians were far from their native land, as witness this plaintive song addressed by a Russian soldier to his faithful companion, the horse:

> O Country! O Country! O unknown land!
> It is not you, my good charger, that carries me hither,
> Nor the fleet wind, nor the racing rivers,
> But the compulsion of the soldier,
> The dread service of the Tsar.
> No father nor mother, no brothers nor sisters,
> No young wife nor little children
> In this strange and distant land.

Harassed and weary, hungry or thirsty, falling by the wayside and watching their horses die, the Russian forces took four days to withdraw from Perekop to the Dnieper, but miraculously preserved their discipline and good order.

It should be stressed that, even though it had been sacrificed to Golitsyn's military incompetence, the Russian army did further the interests of the Allies. Without gaining either glory or material advantage, Russia diverted enemy forces which might have been employed elsewhere – much as she did at the start of the 1914–18 war. The Poles were able to gain successes in the west because the Russians kept the Tatars on their eastern frontiers occupied. The Turks had to be more careful as a consequence of Russia's entry into the war, and this, as the Soviet historian Babushkina points out in *The International Importance of the Crimean Campaigns* (Moscow, 1950), helped the Allies to gain victories in Hungary, Dalmatia and Morea.

CHAPTER THIRTY-FOUR

WHILE Vasily Golitsyn was betraying the Regent's trust by his feeble behaviour outside Perekop, Sophia was facing troubles at home. Although she was too shrewd to minimize the danger, she continued to cheer her dejected lover with messages of unfailing tenderness, as she had done during the first campaign. Shaklovity, who shuttled between Moscow and the theatre of operations, bluntly reminded the Prince that another setback would put his life in jeopardy. He proposed drastic remedies, but Golitsyn refused to become involved in any political intrigues and Shaklovity returned to the capital convinced that the Regent's welfare now depended on him alone.

Sophia had resorted to her old policy of drumming up popular support. Refusing to settle matters by assassinating her half-brother, she tried to establish a durable version of the relationship known to modern diplomats as peaceful coexistence – a formula more easily defined than achieved.

Since Peter showed a blatant lack of interest in the Church, Sophia redoubled her processions and pilgrimages. On July 5th, 1689, she ordered a *Te Deum* to commemorate the victory of Orthodoxy over the Old Believers, a victory in which she had played a personal part. She went to the cathedral accompanied by Tsar Ivan, having previously arranged that the choir should sing the canon 'I am encompassed by dangers on every side' to remind the people that they were threatened by the Naryshkins.

July 8th was the Feast of Our Lady of Kazan, the day when a large procession traditionally wended its way from the Kremlin to the Cathedral of Kazan to commemorate the liberation of Moscow from the Poles in 1612. It was customary for the Tsar, carrying icons, to join the cortège as it moved from his private chapel to the two cathedrals in the Kremlin and thence into the city proper, where Mass was celebrated in the Cathedral of Our Lady of Kazan.

This being one ceremony which Tsar Peter could not decently avoid, he arrived from Kolomenskoye, fairly certain that since Sophia had never attended it in the past he would be spared her presence. But when the two

Tsars and their retinue left their apartments, icons in hand, the Regent emerged from hers also carrying an icon and fully resolved to join the procession. She found it a particularly propitious moment for such a gesture because she knew that Vasily Golitsyn was nearing the capital.

Entering the Cathedral of the Assumption, the Regent performed her devotions before the relics and, clad in regal splendour, prepared to accompany her brothers into the city. This proved too much for Peter, who flew into a rage and brusquely forbade her to follow them. A violent argument ensued, much to the embarrassment of those present, but Sophia refused to give way. In the face of her resistance, Peter did not go farther than the Cathedral of the Archangel, where he deserted the procession and immediately set off for Kolomenskoye without bothering to conceal his fury, leaving Tsar Ivan and the Regent to continue the pilgrimage on their own.

This first public clash was a preliminary to the open warfare that was to follow. Coolly, the Regent continued her outings. On July 14th she went alone to the Church of St Vladimir; on the 15th she paid a second visit; and on the 18th she set off on a pilgrimage to a monastery just outside Moscow, but hurried back when a messenger informed her that Prince Golitsyn and the Crimean expeditionary force were at the gates of the capital.

Once again, the Regent prepared to celebrate defeat as though it were a resounding victory. Although her own attitude was governed by propaganda requirements, the allied kings whom Golitsyn had prematurely informed of his would-be victory, even before concluding the campaign, did in fact send the commander-in-chief heartfelt messages of congratulation – John Sobieski's arrived on September 16th and the Emperor's on November 22nd – after the fall of the regime.

While waiting, Sophia ordered the joy-bells to be rung and assumed all the prerogatives of sovereignty. She ordered the voivodes commanding regiments to station the icons that had accompanied them to the Crimea at the head of the parade. At eight o'clock in the morning she went to a church in the Arbat and heard a *Te Deum*. Then she made her way to the city's outer gates, where she greeted the sacred icons with great reverence and gave her hand to Golitsyn, the voivodes and the boyars. Placing herself at the head of her 'victorious' troops, she led them to the Kremlin, where Tsar Ivan was waiting at the entrance to the palace. Ivan and Sophia then heard another *Te Deum* sung by the Patriarch in the Cathedral of the Assumption, after which the tsarevna had the icons taken to the Kremlin and placed in one of the royal chapels.

Their devotions completed, Tsar Ivan and the Regent received voivodes, officials and regimental commanders in the audience-chamber and thanked them graciously for their meritorious service.

Tsar Peter, who refused to play his sister's game, was conspicuous by his absence. He received his friends Lefort and Gordon in private and learnt from them the true state of affairs, but he declined to receive Vasily Golitsyn in spite of Sophia's threats and entreaties.

Tongues were wagging in earnest now. The boyars in Peter's clique went so far as to accuse the commander-in-chief of having taken bribes from the Tatars, and echoes of this calumny can be found in the memoirs of one Zheliabuzhsky: 'The boyar Prince Vasily Golitsyn accepted two barrels of gold pieces from the Tatars at Perekop, which pieces were later seen in circulation in Moscow, though in copper, for they were but thinly gilded.'

Peter stubbornly refused to appear at any of the receptions held in honour of the returning heroes, but the Regent affected not to notice this affront. She continued to distribute awards and drafted a decree investing the leaders of the expedition with the Order of the Nation. Peter refused to sign the document for seven days and only did so when Sophia increased her pressure, but when Golitsyn came to express his gratitude he flatly refused to see him. 'It was clear to all,' wrote Gordon in his journal, 'that the younger Tsar's consent had been wrung from him by force, which only incensed him against Golitsyn and the Tsarevna Sophia's advisers the more.'

Sophia persevered with her religious tours. On July 23rd there was a pilgrimage to the new Convent of the Virgins, where another *Te Deum* was sung in gratitude to the Lord of Hosts for the infidels' defeat. The Regent was still surrounded by her military leaders. On July 25th, her aunt Anna's name-day, Sophia entertained noblemen and officers to wine and vodka in the state apartments. On July 27th there was yet another pilgrimage to the Convent of the Virgins. This time, Sophia was so disturbed by the rumours that were circulating that she travelled with an escort of junior musketeer officers. Vespers ended at four o'clock in the morning. On emerging, the Regent harangued her bodyguards on the subject of Tsarina Natalia.

'There have been calamities before,' she said, 'but God has preserved us. Now we are threatened by a new peril. Are we acceptable to you? If so, defend us; if not, we shall leave the country.' The musketeers' response to her appeal was somewhat ambiguous:

'It shall be according to your will. We are ready to obey your orders. We shall perform whatsoever you command.'

'Well, then,' Sophia told them, 'await the call.'

* * *

Working in consultation with Sylvester Medviedev, Shaklovity laid plans for a coup d'état which would make Sophia joint occupant of the throne in her own right. Although he did not envisage the murder of the younger Tsar, he seemed indifferent as to whether his proposed course of action cost the latter's life. The Regent was still active but no longer seemed to know what she wanted. For the first time, her actions lacked coherence.

Vasily Golitsyn had become an encumbrance to the Regent's party, plainly demonstrating, if proof were still needed, that he could only work effectively under peaceful conditions.

On July 28th, Gordon noted: 'All saw clearly that the breach was complete.' On the 31st, he made another entry: 'Passions and vexations grow without cease.'

The last act of the drama was approaching. From now on, it was inconceivable that Peter would allow Sophia to usurp his place and continue to direct the affairs of a country whose anointed tsar he was. The outcome was not, however, a foregone conclusion. Though the ranks of his supporters were steadily growing, partly because of Golitsyn's unpopularity and partly because of the Russians' contempt for women in general, the fact remained that Sophia had run the country efficiently and with a firm hand for seven years. The people had grown used to regarding her as the source of rewards and punishments, whereas the young Tsar was still a relatively unfamiliar figure. His only known attributes were a violent temperament and a fondness for the German Quarter.

Again, while Patriarch Joachim might suspect Sophia and her friends of Latinism, the people could only compare the pious regularity with which the Regent and Tsar Ivan attended religious services with the younger Tsar's patent lack of interest in the Church. Nevertheless, between popular sympathy for the Regent and the popular revolt which would have been needed to keep her in power lay a gulf which the masses were not prepared to cross, the more so because they knew that victory would go to those who had arms, and they had none.

Shaklovity had taken the precaution of arming his musketeers, but Peter already had a complete private army at his disposal and was a force to be reckoned with.

Two significant incidents occurred on August 4th, 1689, when Peter was celebrating his wife Eudoxia's name-day at Izmailovo. The young couple had thrown open their doors to visitors, and among the many people who came to pay their respects to the Tsarina was Theodore Shaklovity, who had never lacked courage and probably wanted to gauge the atmosphere in the enemy camp. Peter took advantage of his presence to summon him to hand over the musketeer Streshnev, who was a sworn enemy of his. Shaklovity refused to obey, and Peter had him arrested on the spot. Then, probably feeling that he had bitten off more than he could chew for the moment, he released him. It was the first overt act of war, and Sophia's party took it as such.

During the night of August 4th, the Regent entertained some musketeer officers in the Terem.

'How much longer must we suffer thus?' she demanded. 'We are persecuted by Boris Golitsyn and by the Naryshkins. They have fuddled Tsar Peter's wits with drink and they treat my brother Ivan without respect. Nay, they call me a whore and even say that I am not Tsar Alexis's daughter. They wish to behead Prince Vasily, who has done much good and has made peace with Poland. I have endeavoured to set all to rights, but they are wresting power from my grasp. May we count on you? If you have no need of us, we shall go with my brother to seek refuge elsewhere.'

* * *

There was mounting anxiety in both camps. Although neither seemed prepared to make a definite move for the time being, the interested parties grew steadily more apprehensive. Sophia was convinced that Peter's supporters intended to get rid of her by foul play, while Peter's clique was certain that Sophia was getting ready to kill the Tsar and his advisers. From now on, their actions were dictated by fear.

On August 7th an anonymous letter arrived, informing the Regent that Peter's *poteshny* were proposing to march from Preobrazhenskoye to Moscow by night, seize the Kremlin and kill Ivan and his sisters. The gates of the Kremlin were shut at once. Shaklovity reinforced the garrison with a hundred musketeers of proven loyalty and posted another three hundred fully armed men at the Lubianka.

No one knew how much truth there was in Sophia's information, but speculation was rife. There was even some anxiety about her intentions among the musketeers of the 'Stirrup' or Guards Regiments, who leapt to the conclusion that she was planning an attack on Preobrazhenskoye.

During this alert, Peter Plestcheyev, one of Peter's Gentlemen of the Bedchamber, arrived at the Kremlin accompanied by three men. They were allowed to enter and then arrested. Theodore Shaklovity interrogated Plestcheyev in person and tried to find out what was going on in the enemy camp. Several musketeers hostile to Sophia found this comparatively trivial incident so alarming that they slipped out of the Kremlin and galloped all the way to Preobrazhenskoye to warn the younger Tsar that he was in mortal danger.

Roused abruptly in the middle of the night, Peter panicked. Feet bare and nightshirt flapping, the future conqueror of King Charles XII rushed out into the courtyard without bothering to dress and, vaulting on to a horse, galloped off into a neighbouring wood, where servants later brought him his clothes. Dressed at last but still shaking with terror, the younger Tsar galloped hell for leather to the monastery of the Holy Trinity and St Sergius, where his entire family had taken refuge when their lives were threatened by Khovansky. Exhausted, racked with convulsions, mad with impotent rage and trembling with fear, Peter rushed into Abbot Vincenti's cell and threw himself sobbing on to the couch. His sense of humiliation was so acute that he never entirely recovered from it.

The following day, Tsarina Natalia, the *poteshny* and the men of Peter's Preobrazhensky regiment arrived at the monastery to join him.

* * *

Meanwhile, calm had returned to the Kremlin. Since the night had passed without incident and there was as yet no news of Peter's flight, Sophia and Shaklovity went to the Cathedral of Kazan before dawn to give thanks, escorted by a single detachment of musketeer guardsmen. On returning to the palace, the Regent, whose spirits had completely revived, gave orders for the musketeers to be sent home. It was only then that news reached the Kremlin of Peter's flight and his departure for the monastery of the Holy Trinity.

The Regent's entourage pretended to attach little importance to this development. 'If it please the madman to flee, let him flee,' was Shaklovity's terse comment. Sophia, however, took her half-brother's flight very seriously. By advertising the fact that he feared for his own safety the young Tsar would assume the role of victim in popular eyes, and Sophia knew from personal experience that pity could breed active support.

On August 9th, Peter asked Sophia and Ivan for an explanation of the musketeers' stand-to-arms in the Kremlin two nights before, and for the first time in her life Sophia found herself compelled to justify her actions to her younger brother.

At this juncture, a traitor in the classical tradition appeared on the scene, namely Ivan Tsikler, the musketeer officer whom Platonov later called 'the very incarnation of treachery'. A man of boundless ambition, Tsikler made his living by fishing in troubled waters and had played a part in the disturbances of May 15th, 1682. Officially, it was Peter who summoned him to the monastery of the Holy Trinity, but Gordon's journal and several other sources state that Tsikler himself requested an audience of the younger Tsar. Resentful because he had never managed to win Sophia's entire confidence and because his only reward from her had been a sum of money and the rank of colonel, Tsikler had decided to seek his fortune elsewhere.

On August 14th, possibly thanks to the renegade colonel's 'revelations', Peter called eighteen other musketeer colonels together and ordered them to join him with all their men. He also sent for two regular regiments. Gordon received a summons, too, but despite his cordial relationship with the young Tsar he observed etiquette by asking Vasily Golitsyn's permission, which was refused. The Grand Chancellor and his son Alexis, who had just got married, were likewise summoned to the monastery of the Holy Trinity, as was Theodore Shaklovity in his capacity as head of the Office of Musketeers. Peter was evidently trying to prove to Sophia that he was now master.

But Sophia was not beaten yet. When Peter requested her to hand over some men she told his emissaries: 'I shall not surrender the nine men whom you seek, for if I do so they will bear false witness against nine hundred more.'

The worst of the crisis might have been avoided and its disastrous consequences reduced to a minimum if Sophia had only conceded defeat, but surrender would have meant the forfeiture not only of her power but of her freedom, and freedom had become her *raison d'être*. Sophia was in her prime. She knew that she could still be of service to the country and that her personal interests coincided with those of the State, which was more than could be said of Peter at this stage. By obeying his orders she would be losing her friends and denuding herself of military protection. Without a moment's hesitation, she summoned the musketeer colonels to the Kremlin and forbade them, on pain of death, to interfere in the dispute between herself and her brother.

Peter's course of action during these momentous days was largely dictated by the Grand Chancellor's cousin, Prince Boris Golitsyn, whose agile brain and forceful character were destined to restore the Naryshkins' fortunes. He was the only man on their side, apart from Tsar Peter, who possessed any real measure of intelligence.

Having taken steps to assure her personal protection, the Regent tried to effect a reconciliation with her brother on equal terms. She dispatched Peter's confessor and Ivan's beloved tutor, the elderly Prince Prozorovsky, to the monastery of the Holy Trinity to plead for the re-establishment of family unity, but the mediators returned to the Kremlin empty-handed.

Between the 19th and 22nd of August, Patriarch Joachim made his way to the monastery entrusted with the same mission. But the Patriarch, who detested Boris Golitsyn as much as he loathed Sylvester Medviedev, yet cherished the naïve conviction that the Naryshkins belonged to the traditionalist camp, made no effort to settle matters and calmly remained at Peter's side, already savouring his triumph over the Latinists. His defection was significant, for it indicated to the people that the head of the Church had made his choice. Some sources state that this was when the Patriarch excommunicated the Regent for disobedience.

On August 27th, Tsar Peter repeated his order to the musketeers and soldiers of the Moscow garrison to join him on pain of death. The result was a stampede. A tide of humanity flowed along the road leading from the capital to the monastery of the Holy Trinity. Among the first to join Peter were the foreigners of the German Quarter – merchants and craftsmen as well as soldiers. We are told that Gordon asked some of them to present his excuses to the Tsar, not knowing if his arrival would be considered opportune.

Peter welcomed his supporters in the company of Tsarina Natalia and the Patriarch. He openly accused Shaklovity of plotting against his life.

* * *

Sophia was now deserted save for a few devoted supporters – so few, in fact, that she was forced to acknowledge the full extent of the disaster that had overtaken her. Defeated at last but still dignified and unflustered, she prepared to take the road to Canossa. After fortifying herself by visiting the Cathedral of the Assumption to hear Mass, she made the traditional tour of the Kremlin's cathedrals and churches. Finally, going to the Church of Kazan, the woman who had ruled a great country took the icon of Our Lady of Kazan reverently in her hands and set off for the monastery of the Holy Trinity, escorted by a little band of loyalists which included Prince Vasily Golitsyn and his son, the Princes Odoyevsky, Dolgoruky and Tcherkassky, and Theodore Shaklovity.

Next day, the impressive cortège was met by a Prince Gagarin, who informed Sophia that she must return to Moscow on the Tsar's orders. Sophia turned a deaf ear and continued on her way. Buturlin, Peter's second courier, proved equally ineffectual, and the party eventually reached a point some six or seven miles from the monastery. However, knowing the tsarevna's powers of persuasion, the Naryshkin faction was determined to prevent a meeting between brother and sister at all costs. Peter's third emissary informed the ex-Regent in forceful terms that if she did not return to the Kremlin immediately she would run the risk of 'an affront'.

This time Sophia complied, and the game was irretrievably lost.

By August 31st Sophia was back in Moscow, complaining in her customary fashion to the few musketeers who still remained loyal to her that she had only escaped death by a hair's breadth. Prince Vasily Golitsyn had once again retired to his country estate, but Shaklovity, who refused to abandon hope, stationed his musketeers on the monastery road. Then a Colonel Metchayev arrived with an escort of musketeers in Peter's service, bringing a letter from the Tsar ordering his sister to hand over Shaklovity.

Sophia was furious and at once ordered the messenger to be beheaded, but no executioner happened to be available – 'fortunately', as Gordon remarked. The tsarevna proceeded to harangue her musketeers, forbidding them to obey any orders which Peter might send them.

On September 1st, New Year's Day, sizeable crowds collected inside the Kremlin to offer Sophia their best wishes. She received them very graciously and made a brief speech. 'Mischief-makers are setting me and my brother Ivan at odds with Tsar Peter,' she told them. She pointed out that she had governed Russia for seven years to the satisfaction of all, that she had weakened the enemies of Christendom and signed advantageous treaties of peace with Russia's neighbours. She concluded her address by promising rewards to all those who remained loyal to her and threatening all traitors with death.

Gordon commented, 'The Princess spoke superbly,' but fine words have seldom changed the course of history.

* * *

On September 2nd, Peter lost patience and sent two musketeer colonels to Moscow to secure Shaklovity's surrender. His letter was addressed not to Sophia, whom he now discounted, but to his brother Ivan, and contained ostensible proof of the favourite's guilt.

Ivan's gentle and prayerful soul found the enmity between his brother and sister highly distressing because he was equally attached to both. He also missed his old tutor and confidant, Prozorovsky, who was still at the monastery of the Holy Trinity. His reply to Peter was that he would hand over Shaklovity on condition that Prozorovsky came to collect him.

On September 4th a fresh calamity occurred. All the foreign regiments, which had hitherto remained neutral in what they regarded as a domestic dispute, rallied to Peter. They were led by Gordon, whose reluctance to meddle in politics had given way to a realization that Russia had lost a regent but gained a tsar.

On September 6th, musketeers belonging to the various regiments still in Moscow requested Sophia to hand over Shaklovity 'to restore peace'. Sophia ranted and raved, but the threatening murmur of the armed mob showed her that she was powerless.

When Prozorovsky arrived, Sophia did not try to prevent him from seeing Ivan. It is possible that the Tsar's old tutor passed on the rumours of Sophia's interference in his marital life. Whatever the truth, Ivan's attitude towards his sister changed, and he told her that he would not fall out with his beloved brother even for her, 'let alone that thief Shaklovity'.

That settled Shaklovity's fate. Having gambled for high stakes and lost, he unflinchingly took the road that led to certain death.

Sophia now had no reason for continuing the struggle, though she generously tried to protect the few friends who had remained at her side by ordering them to leave her and make their peace with Peter. It is said that Vasily Golitsyn advised the Regent to seek asylum in Poland, but that she refused with the words: 'By so doing, I should only concede that I was guilty of the charges levelled at me.' With his mistress's consent, and after being advised by his cousin Boris to throw himself on Peter's mercy without delay, Vasily Golitsyn set off with due pomp for the monastery of the Holy Trinity, accompanied by his son. His conscience was clear. He had never contemplated a coup d'état nor taken part in any conspiracy. The only points at issue were the two unfortunate Crimean campaigns, but he felt that they were outweighed by the excellent treaties and wise administrative measures for which he had been responsible.

* * *

As he descended from his carriage at the gates of the monastery, the Grand Chancellor was unceremoniously arrested and taken to an inn, where he was told to await the sovereign's pleasure. After an interval, the two princes, father and son, were conducted under armed guard into the monastery precincts and stationed at the foot of the steps leading into Tsar Peter's provisional palace. There, surrounded by a hostile crowd which openly relished their humiliation, they waited to learn their fate.

The boyar Streshnev emerged carrying a document which he handed

to a clerk. 'The Tsars Ivan and Peter,' read the latter, 'command th
Prince Vasily Golitsyn and his son Alexis be deprived of the dignity ar
rank of boyar, in that they did seek, without the Tsars' consent, to i
gratiate themselves with the Tsarevna Sophia by assisting her to proclai
herself sovereign; in that they did share in all her deliberations witho
consulting the two Tsars; in that they did officially honour the tsarevı
with the title of sovereign ... Moreover, on arriving before Pereko
Prince Vasily took no action, thereby causing great harm to the State .
Their Majesties command that they be sent into banishment. All the
estates, hereditary and acquired, and all that they possess shall be share
among others. Their serfs and domestic servants, with the exception
peasants, shall be freed.'

A search of the cellars in Golitsyn's town house produced 100,000 gol
ducats and forty puds[1] of silver plate confiscated from Samoilovitc
together with magnificent icons, manuscripts and books in vario
languages, rare wines, garments embroidered with gold thread an
adorned with precious stones, jewels, 'German' furniture and engraving
clocks and watches, Venetian mirrors and celebrated portraits of tsars an
kings, many of which had been presented to him by the sitters themselve

The Grand Chancellor's enemies later accused Boris Golitsyn of havin
censored the report of Shaklovity's interrogation so as to eliminat
evidence which might incriminate his cousin, but there is no proof th
Boris Golitsyn ever interceded on Vasily's behalf. The *deus ex machin*
of Peter's first victory did, however, escort his relatives into exile, a nob
gesture which did nothing to endear him to the Tsar's other supporter

Vasily and Alexis Golitsyn were banished to a place not far fror
Moscow where they would probably have ended their days in peace an
oblivion if an unfrocked monk named Ivashka, who wanted to curr
favour with the authorities, had not denounced them for sedition in 169
Even though Ivashka confessed later that his allegations had bee
unfounded, the unfortunate Golitsyns and their entire family, includin
young children, were sent off to the fortress of Pustozersk, wher
Artamon Matveyev had languished years before. Like Matveyev, Golitsy
wrote letters imploring royal forgiveness: 'Take pity on us, poor, unfortu
nate and helpless that we are. Have pity on our wives and on our childrer
who are only seven, three and two years old.' His efforts were in vair
for Peter never forgot a grudge. Later transferred to remote Pinega, th
great diplomat ended his days there in 1713 without ever being pardonec

* * *

[1] 1 pud = 35 lb.

Theodore Shaklovity was brutally tortured. When he had reached the end of his tether and could hardly wait for death to end his sufferings he asked his captors for pen and ink and wrote a confession. Even then, he remained loyal to Sophia and never implicated her in the case. While confessing that he had plotted against Tsar Peter's entourage and had planned to get rid of 'the Mother-Bear' (Tsarina Natalia), he swore before God that he had never contemplated an attempt on the Tsar's life.

The Case of Theodore Shaklovity, a large four-volumed work published in the nineteenth century, gives a detailed description not only of the enquiries themselves but also of life in contemporary Russia. We are told that Shaklovity went to consult Sylvester Medviedev, who supported his plans and added that Patriarch Joachim could be made to crown the Tsarevna under duress. When sounded on the subject, Vasily Golitsyn apparently wrote to Shaklovity that he found the suggestion so extraordinary that he had 'lost his memory'.

Naturally enough, the bill of indictment was an extremely long one. Shaklovity was charged with all manner of crimes. He had been seen to drink to the health of Ivan, Sophia and Golitsyn but had refused to drink to Peter ... He had been heard to say that Boris Golitsyn and the Naryshkins wanted to poison Sophia, and that it would be necessary to kill Boris, the Naryshkins and the three Apraxins, who were relatives of Tsar Theodore's widow ... He was also accused of planning to kill the Patriarch.

Shaklovity's final interrogation took place in the torture-chamber on September 12th, 1689. He continued to show great courage and declared that, by accusing Sophia of usurping the Tsars' powers and threatening her with armed might, Natalia had put the Regent in fear of her life. Neither Sophia nor Golitsyn had ever entertained 'evil thoughts' with regard to Tsar Peter. If the Terem had said that Tsar Peter would not live long, he, Shaklovity, had never heard them do so ... As to the scheme to crown Sophia, 'neither Prince Vasily, nor I, Theodore, ever contemplated it. These rumours come from abroad.'

Up to the last minute, Shaklovity refused to admit the existence of any criminal conspiracy, nor was any real evidence of one ever laid before his judges. The whole case rested on unverifiable denunciations – not that anyone bothered about such technicalities. Shaklovity was condemned to death by a special tribunal presided over by the boyar Streshnev and executed the same day, September 12th, 1689. His scaffold was erected on the road to Moscow, near the monastery of the Holy Trinity.

* * *

The Regent's third friend, Sylvester Medviedev, tried to reach th
Polish frontier but was arrested in the provinces and interrogated unde
torture like Shaklovity. His principal accuser was Patriarch Joachim, whos
character does not emerge from the affair unscathed. The Patriarc
attacked his Latinist foe with alacrity, presenting the judge with a repor
five pages long in which he added the crime of heresy to that of treason
Like Shaklovity, Medviedev stood firm and never recanted. His allege
confession of heresy is universally recognized as apocryphal. He, too, wa
condemned to death but was not executed until 1691, after a laboriou
inquiry which failed to elicit any real basis for the charges laid agains
him.

Medviedev was censured for his friendship with the Regent an
Shaklovity, his heretical doctrines, and the fact that he had referred t
Sophia as 'Autocrat' and Patriarch Joachim as 'ignorant'. When investiga-
tors discovered that his house contained a hundred of the engraving
described in a previous chapter, Peter ordered them and any other
depicting Sophia to be destroyed.

* * *

Back in the Kremlin, Sophia awaited Peter's decision in solitary state
She had already been deprived of all her titles and prerogatives by a roya
decree on September 7th, before Shaklovity's death and Golitsyn'
deportation.

The Terem was in a ferment. Sophia's sisters were greatly perturbe
because at least two of them, Martha and Catherine, had behave
indiscreetly and were afraid that inquiries would disclose the seamier sid
of their private life. Sophia had provided a protective barrier behind whic
they felt safe, but they did not know what Peter had in store for them
Catherine, the harder of the two, issued her serving-women with precis
instructions as to what to say if interrogated, and her good friend th
astrologer sent her a message saying: 'Never fear. The stars foretell that n
harm shall befall you.' The stars were right, for Catherine was left i
peace. Only Martha, who was closer to Sophia, experienced complet
disgrace.

At last, the Tsar's orders arrived. The ex-Regent was to retire to the nev
Convent of the Virgins and live there in solitude without being compelle
to take the veil. Martha was sent to another convent. Their aunt Tatian
showed her customary charity by interceding on their behalf and sendin
them the wherewithal to buy comforts.

From every point of view, it was the end of the Terem. Sophia ha

mancipated it. In his eagerness to sweep away tradition, Peter suppressed
t altogether.

At the age of thirty-seven, Sophia found herself a woman without a
uture. The convent gates had closed upon her dreams. Her friends were
cattered like dead leaves, her dear ones ignominiously dead or separated
rom her by the winds of Siberia, her dreams of glory transmuted into
egrets for what might have been. As a literate woman, the tsarevna may
vell have wished to confide her thoughts to a private journal and so
ustify herself in the eyes of posterity, but she lived under strict surveillance
nd nothing that could plead her cause had any chance of escaping
lestruction. She did, however, manage to keep in touch with a few
levoted supporters through the agency of the beggar-women and
tinerant nuns who were admitted to the convent.

While travelling into exile with his family, Vasily Golitsyn met Prince
Kropotkin, who handed him a letter of affectionate sympathy from
Sophia, together with some money to be spent on easing the hardships of
he journey. Despite her own misfortunes, Sophia remained loyal to those
who had served her in the past, but her messenger was soon arrested and
he was unable to correspond with her friend from then onwards. To all
ntents and purposes, Sophia was a dead woman.

Logically, our story should end here. If it does not, this is because the
Regent's prestige remained so high that her very name was enough to
unleash another storm in the early years of Peter's reign.

CHAPTER THIRTY-FIVE

THE following undated letter from Tsar Peter to his half-brother Tsar Ivan is generally supposed to have been written on or about September 12th, 1689, possibly even after the execution of Theodore Shaklovity.

> My little brother Sovereign Tsar Ivan Alexeyevitch and my sister-in-law, your spouse, and your children: may God have you in His holy keeping. I inform you and, by the same token, I request your consent to that which follows: by the grace of God, it is to our two persons that there has been entrusted the sceptre of the government of our patrimony, the Russian State, as witness the collective enactment of our Mothers, the Holy Churches of the East [i.e. the coronation ceremony of 1682], our brothers the foreign sovereigns being acquainted of our accession to the throne and the third person who has governed with us on equal terms being nowhere mentioned. And, since our sister, the Tsarevna Sophia Alexeyevna, has begun to govern our State of her own will, her government is a disgrace to our persons and a burden to the nation. You know, Sovereign, with what impatience we have had to endure it. Today, the miscreants Fedka Shaklovity and his companions, no longer content with our favour and heedless of their oaths, intended, with other traitors, to kill us and our mother. For this, they have been put to the torture and have acknowledged their guilt.
>
> It is now time, Sovereign brother, for our two persons to govern by ourselves the empire which God has entrusted to us, for we have come of age and we forbid the third, shameful person, our sister the Tsarevna Sophia Alexeyevna, to consider herself equal to our two male persons, whether in the matter of titles or the conduct of affairs. May your will, Sovereign brother, be identical, for, though she has begun by governing and has on her own authority and without our consent assumed the title of regent, she has it in mind to crown herself with the crown of the Tsars, to our future detriment.
>
> It would be wrong, Sovereign, if, after our coming of age, this

> shameful person were permitted to reign over the country despite us. I entreat and inform you, Sovereign brother, suffer me, Sovereign, by your fraternal leave, to act for our good and the tranquillity of the nation, according to the decision of just arbiters and without referring to you, that all those who are not agreeable to us may be dismissed and that our state may soon return to peace and joy. Later, when we are reunited, we shall deliberate together on all matters. As for me, Sovereign brother, I am ready to respect you as my father. For the rest, I have given orders to Prince Peter Prozorovsky to relate all that has occurred by word of mouth and to receive your response to this missive. Writing in affliction, your brother Peter wishes you good health and salutes you.

Now that Sophia was shut up in a nunnery, Ivan was hardly likely to place any obstacles in Peter's path, wherever it led. But with victory assured and 'the third, shameful person' banished from public life, the young Tsar simply returned to his war-games and his barbaric diversions in the German Quarter, leaving the conduct of affairs to a small group of henchmen who quickly set about destroying Sophia's achievements.

The members of Peter's clique were scarcely distinguished by their ability. 'Tsarina Natalia,' wrote Prince Kurakin, 'is incapable of governing, albeit she is a virtuous princess of worthy inclinations. She lacks application and has no gift for affairs; she is light-minded.' Her twenty-five-year-old brother, the boyar Lev Naryshkin, who replaced Vasily Golitsyn at the Ministry of Foreign Affairs but did not assume the title of Grand Chancellor or Keeper of the Privy Seal, was a sorry creature.

'His character can be very speedily described,' wrote Kurakin. 'He is an intemperate and conceited man of less than middling intelligence and uncongenial disposition, albeit he cannot properly be called a rogue. He does some good at times, but for no reason and only according to the state of his humour.' Prompted by jealousy, young Naryshkin hastened to rid the government of the only man in Peter's circle who was worth anything at all, Prince Boris Golitsyn, the guiding light of the political operation which had brought the young Tsar to power. Kurakin, an impartial observer, called him 'a man of great intelligence and subtlety of mind' and added: 'He was not industrious, for he was over-fond of amusements and, above all, he was addicted to drink.'

Boris Golitsyn, who liked foreigners as much as his cousin Vasily, was responsible for bringing Gordon and Lefort over to Peter's side. However, Lev Naryshkin succeeded in ousting him from his nephew's circle, and it was not long before the brilliant but indolent prince lost his influence over

Peter and vanished from the political scene. Lev Naryshkin was a man of unbounded avarice whose ruling passion in life was money. Not content with appropriating a large number of estates in the vicinity of Moscow, he persuaded Tsar Peter to make him a gift of the factories at Tula, which had been founded by Marcelis and accounted for the bulk of the country's output of arms and cast iron. But even that did not satisfy him. He proceeded to ruin his competitors by getting Peter to sign a decree stipulating that all government departments must purchase their supplies from him and forbidding them to buy anything from other foundries.

Peter's other ministers included the boyar Tikhon Streshnev, who had presided over the interrogation and torture of Shaklovity and his confederates. An elderly man, Streshnev had formerly acted as Peter's second tutor and was still on close terms with him. 'Concerning his character,' wrote Kurakin, 'we can only say that he was a treacherous man of evil disposition and very moderate intelligence, and well versed in intrigues.' Finally, there was Prince Romodanovsky, the chief of the secret police. 'He was a singular character,' Kurakin tells us, 'physically a monster and morally a tyrant.' Guided by their personal interests, these unprepossessing individuals quickly demolished the machinery of government which Sophia and her associates had built up, an administration which, according to Miliukov, 'united all the elements of reform in a moderate national spirit'.

The young Tsar himself shared Lefort's and Gordon's enthusiasm for what were known in contemporary parlance as 'the sports of Mars and Neptune' – i.e. took a keen interest in war and seamanship – but he did not forget to sacrifice to Venus and Bacchus as well. Drinking-bouts and orgies continued to lure him into the German Quarter. After one such party, Gordon, who was getting on in years, noted in his journal that the previous night's debauch had compelled him to keep to his bed.

Peter may seldom have appeared at religious ceremonies – and then only when he could not decently stay away – but he was always ready to organize manœuvres or firework displays. These entertainments were not without their dangers. In 1690, Gordon was wounded in the leg during a review and retired to bed for a week. One of the Tsar's friends, Prince Ivan Dolgoruky, was killed on manœuvres, and a nobleman on Peter's staff succumbed during a fireworks display when five pounds of unexploded rocket fell on his head.

Though married and the father of a family, Peter retained the mentality of an irresponsible teenager. In 1690, when his wife gave birth to a son and heir, Alexis, he doled out vodka and wine and then went off to enjoy himself at Fily, the Naryshkins' new estate.

Tsar Ivan lived far from this boisterous and rip-roaring world in the company of his daughters, his wife and his two old tutors, the Princes Prozorovsky and Troyekurov. A man of the highest integrity, Prozorovsky managed his former pupil's personal exchequer, which was largely devoted to the distribution of alms. At the age of twenty-seven, Ivan looked like an old man. Despite his rapidly failing health, the elder Tsar continued to fast and attend divine office. Unlike Peter, who refrained from making any pilgrimages to the Convent of the Virgins for fear of meeting Sophia, Ivan often went there and never failed to visit his sister.

As for Patriarch Joachim, his triumph was short-lived. Although he had at last got rid of Sylvester Medviedev, chased the Jesuits out of Russia and ousted Western scholars from the capital, what he now saw around him probably made him yearn for the good old days. The Patriarch sensed that religious life was threatened by a new danger. He was worried by the immorality rife in the German Quarter and by the steady growth of foreign influence. No one in the new government took any interest in spiritual life. Before he died in October 1689, the Patriarch had an opportunity to assess the reign which he had welcomed with such high hopes, and his last will and testament reflected his profound anxiety for the future. In it, he vehemently denounced the influence exerted on Peter by the foreigners of the German Quarter, adjured the Tsars to prohibit friendly intercourse between their subjects and Catholics, Lutherans, Calvinists or Mohammedans, and entreated them not to give heretics positions of authority in the Orthodox army.

Tsar Peter made no pretence of mourning the death of the old man who had supported him since his infancy. Adrian, Metropolitan of Kiev, who was elected in Joachim's place, was the last Russian patriarch to hold office until the 1917 Revolution. Peter took care to suppress not only men but also institutions which might one day become a source of opposition or criticism.

Tsarina Natalia's joy at seeing her son firmly established on the throne was alloyed with the anxiety which her beloved 'Petrushka's' riotous life caused her. On January 21st, 1694, Peter was enjoying himself at a friend's house. On the 25th, he was notified that his mother was unwell and hurried home to find her dying. Despite the young Tsar's affection for his devoted mother, he was a creature of instinct and illness exasperated him. He remained at Natalia's bedside for only two or three hours before returning to the pleasures of Preobrazhenskoye, leaving her to die alone.

Tsar Ivan, the 'Mother-Bear's' stepson, escorted her coffin to the cathedral alone, but Peter refused to budge from Preobrazhenskoye and his absence was inexorably recorded in the annals of the Court.

On January 6th, 1696, after attending a ceremonial benediction of the waters of the Moskva, Tsar Ivan took to his bed. Two weeks later, on the 29th, he died as quietly as he had lived, having nominally occupied the Russian throne for thirteen years. Three daughters survived him, of whom one was destined to rule Russia, surrounded by Germans, under the name of Anna Ivanovna. His widow, Tsarina Prascovia, and Tsar Theodore's widow, Tsarina Martha, were both treated extremely well by Peter for the rest of their lives.

But if Tsar Peter treated his sisters-in-law civilly he showed absolutely no consideration for his own unfortunate wife, Tsarina Eudoxia, whom he grew to detest more and more. He urged her to take the veil, but she refused, sorrowfully reflecting that her only crime had been to bear her husband an heir who would one day replace him on the throne. However, the Tsar felt no affection for his son either. The type of woman who appealed to him was Anna Mons, Lefort's former mistress, whom he kept in lavish style. Later, when he had got rid of the wife chosen for him by Natalia, he selected a tsarina who was more to his taste, namely Martha Skavronski,[1] a servant girl who had once been the mistress of his other favourite, Alexander Menshikov.

The Tsar spent more time in the German Quarter than in the venerable Kremlin palace. His democratic leanings prompted him to demand to be treated as an equal, but an ill-judged piece of familiarity or a chance remark could send him into a fury – and his contorted face, twitching limbs and rolling eyes were enough to send a chill through the gayest gathering.

From the moment when he seized power, Peter did his brutal best to shock public opinion and pour scorn on ancient traditions. In February 1700, while reorganizing the Kremlin, he came upon records of the enormous sums devoted to charity by the Terem. After Theodore's death, Tsarina Martha had fed three hundred paupers for five days at her own expense. During another period of mourning his aunt, the Tsarevna Tatiana, had fed two hundred people for nine days and her sister Eudoxia three hundred and fifty. On yet another occasion, the Terem celebrated a day of family rejoicing by distributing food to one thousand three hundred and seventy-one paupers and prisoners.

In Peter's practical and unsentimental view, this was money ill spent. His reaction on reading the report was to scribble on it: 'Distribute what remains to the poor in the streets and suffer them to enter the Terem no longer.'

[1] Later Empress Catherine I. Of Lithuanian origin, she adopted the name Catherine subsequently.

This marked the end of the traditional contact between the royal family and the least fortunate of their subjects. Paternalism was now a thing of the past.

No psychological portrait of Peter would be complete without a reference to his hatred for the old Russia, the boyars and everything that reminded him of his childhood terrors.

At the age of ten Peter had witnessed a massacre. He had seen Artamon Matveyev, whom he looked on as a grandfather, torn to pieces. He had seen his uncle tortured and the boyars who were loyal to him butchered before his eyes, and there is little doubt that he expected to be spitted on the musketeers' bloody pikes himself. Many years later, the Tsar confessed that he still trembled sometimes when thinking of the musketeers and found it hard to sleep. Three days of bloodshed and violence followed by months of apprehension as the royal family scuttled from one palace to the next, trying to keep one step ahead of Khovansky, had taken their toll.

Seven years later, as a youth of seventeen, Peter once more experienced the terror and anguish of imminent death when, demented with fear, he mistakenly imagined that Sophia was trying to assassinate him and galloped off in his nightshirt. It was these memories and his enduring sense of humiliation that had engendered his lasting hatred of the old Moscow. The German Quarter evoked no such tormenting memories. On the other hand, Peter's boon companions and his instructors in the arts of war were quite incapable of furnishing him with any spiritual ideals or moral principles.

Contemptuous of human dignity, humiliating the Church, breaking the pride of the nobility, deriding national traditions and totally impervious to spiritual values, Peter may well be regarded as a precursor of the modern materialistic tendencies.

In 1694 Peter 'married' his jester, Turgeniev. He ordered all the boyars and officials of the Duma to attend the grotesque ceremony and forced them to dress in garments made of sacking – embellished, just to complete the parody on ceremonial robes, with cats' paws and squirrels' tails. Shod with bales of straw and wearing mouse-skin gloves, the illustrious members of this squalid procession rode on pigs or in carriages drawn by goats and dogs. The jester and his 'bride' travelled in the Tsar's finest carriage. Their retinue consisted of men who had served Russia with distinction and bore the greatest names in the country: Trubetskoy, Sheremetev, Golitsyn, Gagarin and many others. The latter walked on foot dressed in gorgeous traditional robes. It was Peter's way of combating the survival of the rights of precedence, which Tsar Theodore had abolished with such dignity and which the Regent had taken further steps to suppress.

A little later, the Tsar devised another entertainment which was an exact forerunner of the anti-religious processions organized by Demian Biedny in the days of militant Communism. Peter derided the Church by setting up a sacrilegious 'Drunkards' Council' presided over by Prince Romodanovsky. Horror-stricken, the common people watched courtiers dressed as Orthodox and Catholic monks, priests and Templars filing by to the sound of Bacchanalian chants and ribald songs while the Tsar laughed gleefully at this fresh assault on human dignity. Still later, Peter's old tutor had occasion to regret the fact that he had flattered his pupil rather than educated him. At the opening of Lefort's new mansion in 1699, Peter forced Zotov to lead another parade of jesters. The old man walked along 'bearing the regalia of Bacchus, Cupid and Venus' and followed by a band of tipsy revellers, one of whom – alas – was a Schakovskoy. Some of the participants were dressed as cardinals, while others smoked 'the devil's herb' or carried goblets filled with wine. After the victory at Poltava, the Tsar invested Zotov with the title 'Count', which was unknown in Russia. However, this honour did not save the luckless man from fresh humiliation. Despite his own entreaties and those of his grown-up sons, he was compelled to marry an elderly widow of hideous aspect. The bridegroom was dressed as a cardinal and the guests as Catholic bishops, Cistercian monks, Indians and burgomasters. Having injured everyone else's dignity, Peter proceeded to injure his own by making one of his noblemen impersonate the 'King of Pressburg', i.e. himself, Pressburg being the name of the first fortress he ever built.

These few characteristics, selected at random from many other equally revealing traits, are enough to show that the Regent's successor was her exact antithesis. They also help to explain the wind of change that was destined to sweep through Russia.

Little by little, Peter began to exercise his sovereign authority, and it comes as no surprise to learn that his first venture was a military one.

In the spring of 1695, the Tsar emulated Sophia and Golitsyn by sending a large army against the Tatars of the Crimea. The failure of his preliminary expedition brought him a taste of the difficulties that had contributed to Golitsyn's downfall. A year later, by subjecting the country to crippling taxation, the Tsar had raised the money to build a powerful fleet of thirty vessels. He planned to attack his main objective, the town of Azov, by land and sea simultaneously, aided by experienced engineers and artillerymen borrowed for the occasion from the Emperor, the Netherlands and Brandenburg.

Azov was duly taken, and Peter returned to Moscow to savour his triumph. Like Sophia, he rewarded his companions in arms on a lavish scale. Lefort received the lion's share and became, as Vasily Golitsyn had done, the possessor of estates and gold pieces, priceless materials and rare furs. The bells pealed out in Moscow and elsewhere, and Peter marked the occasion by attending a *Te Deum*. This was preceded by a spectacular military parade which marched under triumphal arches to the roar of cannon-fire. Golovin, Peter's '*Generalkriegskommissar*', and Lefort were seated in carriages. General Gordon marched on foot preceded by his personal standard and surrounded by soldiers dressed in the Turkish style. One novel feature of the occasion was that the Tsar simply took his place at the head of his regiment, as if to demonstrate that he was just another soldier. It is only fair to point out that the capture of Azov was more spectacular than useful, since the Sea of Azov was land-locked and the victory afforded Russia no additional opportunities for commercial development.

* * *

This book being devoted to Peter's predecessors and Sophia in particular, we shall pass briefly over the first few years of the young Tsar's reign. Like Vasily Golitsyn, he recognized the need to send young Russians to be trained in Europe, but what interested him was the practical value of such a policy. His chief concern was not general education nor the arts nor contact with Western ideas, but technical competence.

The Tsar tried to make himself a master of all trades. He also prepared to realize a long-cherished project: to satisfy his passionate curiosity about the free and prosperous European nations of which he had heard so much from his friends in the German Quarter.

CHAPTER THIRTY-SIX

WHILE he was trying his hand at war for the first time, Peter left his boyars to govern the country under Streshnev's supervision. The new ministers did nothing to further the country's social and economic development, and the people, who were used to being the object of the Regent's unwearying attention, soon realized that no one was taking any more interest in them. They were exasperated to see foreigners carrying off 'plum' jobs and winning the lion's share of the Tsar's favour. Xenophobia was latent but widespread, especially among merchants and military men. The boyars had good reason to feel dissatisfied with their new sovereign. As for the musketeers, who had been severely punished for their past misdemeanours, their personal experience of Sophia's justice and Theodore Shaklovity's discipline, which had been backed up by efficient organization, encouraged them to compare the new regime unfavourably with the old.

During the preparations for Peter's journey abroad, a plot was hatched against his life by a group of men who were united only in their hatred of the young tyrant. The brains of the conspiracy was Ivan Tsikler, the musketeer colonel who had deserted Sophia during the critical days when Peter was still mustering support.

Since he still possessed some influence with the musketeers, Tsikler had little difficulty in persuading a few malcontents to join the conspiracy. He also got into touch with two senior dignitaries, Alexis Sokovnin and Alexis Pushkin, who detested the Tsar for less personal reasons and saw his reign as a threat to the country's future. A Don Cossack was also party to the plot. According to one author, Sophia bore full responsibility for stirring up popular unrest through the beggar-women who were allowed to visit her and priests who spread rumours of the Tsar's impious behaviour. However, the masses hardly needed anyone to bring Peter's impiety home to them. Korb, a foreigner, saw for himself the anger aroused in the capital by his sacrilegious masquerade.

Being familiar with the Tsar's habits and movements, the ringleaders of the conspiracy proposed to put their plans into effect on the evening of

January 22nd, 1697, when Peter was due to sup with Lefort. Since one of Peter's hobbies was fire-fighting, they knew that a blaze started in a street near the favourite's house would automatically bring him running to the scene, and that, they decided, would be an opportune moment to kill him.

Gordon tells us that Pushkin's wife warned the Tsar of the plot, but it is more probable that, as other authors suggest, the conspirators were denounced by two junior musketeer officers named Elizarov and Solin. John Perry, who arrived in Russia after the events of 1698, when rumours of the plot were still circulating, stated that it was an expression of the aristocracy's dissatisfaction with and opposition to the new order, while Player, who visited Moscow in 1699, attributed it to a fairly widespread desire to rid the country not only of Peter but of all foreign residents.

The Tsar took pleasure in arresting the culprits in person. Under trial and torture – synonymous procedures in Peter's day – Sokovnin and Pushkin admitted to having acted from personal hatred. In an attempt to ingratiate himself with Peter, Tsikler claimed that he had acted on Sophia's orders, and, although the other condemned men exonerated the ex-Regent, Peter eagerly seized on Tsikler's story. Mad with rage, he hurried to the new Convent of the Virgins and, despite his half-sister's protestations of innocence, hurled himself at her with every intention of killing her. Popular legend has it that a little serving-girl belonging to the Princess threw herself at the Tsar's feet crying: 'Sovereign, spare your sister! Do not shed your own blood! Do not commit the sin of Cain!'

Peter vented his spleen on the Miloslavskys in a macabre fashion. On the day when Tsikler, Sokovnin and Pushkin were due to be executed, Peter ordered the remains of Ivan Miloslavsky to be exhumed and laid at the foot of the scaffold so that his old enemy's bones would be sprayed with the condemned men's blood.

The executions, which took place in March 1697, were followed by a large number of deportations, notably that of Theodore Lopukhin, Tsarina Eudoxia's father.

No doubt satisfied that he had taught his potential enemies a salutary lesson, Peter resumed his preparations for a foreign tour, instructing Lev Naryshkin to persuade the Tsarina to enter a nunnery before he returned.

* * *

The 'embassy extraordinary' which left Moscow bound for Western Europe was officially led by Lefort and included Golovin, an excellent politician, and Voznitsyn, former Russian ambassador in Persia, Turkey, Poland and Austria. Peter, who wanted complete freedom of action, travelled under the pseudonym 'Peter Mihailov'.

For the first time, the Tsar crossed the Baltic, whose waters he dreamed of turning into a Russian sea. He visited the Hanseatic city-ports and travelled on to Königsberg. In Germany, where his incognito deceived no one, Princess Sophia of Hanover and her daughter Sophia Charlotte of Brandenburg were eager to meet him. Their verdict – 'an excellent man but a very wicked one' – was not far short of the mark. A sapper lieutenant-colonel named Sternfeld initiated 'Peter Mihailov' into the latest advances in gunnery technique. Leaving Germany, the truly 'extraordinary' embassy moved on to the Low Countries. Here Peter felt completely at home. He spent a considerable length of time in Amsterdam and in Saardam, where he gained practical experience of seamanship.

Finally, the Tsar went off to England to learn the theory of navigation. King William offered the royal seaman a yacht, which sent him into transports of delight, and he studied ship-handling under the supervision of Kneller. The Bishop of Salisbury described him as follows: 'He is a man who has extraordinary abilities and who knows a variety of things, bearing in mind his poor education, which leaps to the eye every minute. He is ardent, impulsive, passionate and extremely uncouth. Constant addiction to drink aggravates his condition. He seems born to be a shipwright rather than a tsar.'

The tour was a genuine success, even though Louis XIV, who was still as prejudiced as ever against Russia, 'courteously dissuaded' the Tsar from visiting France as he had planned. The King had ample grounds for dissatisfaction. Peter's government had inherited Russian membership of the Coalition from its predecessor. What was more, the Poles had just elected Peter's candidate, Frederick Augustus, Elector of Saxony, as their new king in preference to the Prince de Conti, who had Louis's support. The King's refusal to receive the Tsar was destined to have serious repercussions on Peter's foreign policy, though it did not affect his good humour at the time. He was just planning a trip to Venice when a courier brought him news of a new insurrection by the musketeers. The three men whom he had left to govern Russia in his absence under the leadership of Prince Romodanovsky were trustworthy, but Peter knew from experience how difficult it was to control popular uprisings. 'The Miloslavsky seed is sprouting afresh!' he exclaimed on being told the news, and ordered all sail to be set for home.

Had Peter only remained quietly abroad, the pages of history would not be darkened by the horrors that are inseparable from his name.

* * *

What had been happening in Moscow? We know that unrest had grown steadily and that the government had taken no steps to remedy its underlying causes. Only nine years had passed since Sophia's defeat, so comparisons could still be drawn between the period of the Regency and the years during which Peter's government had been in power. They did not operate in the new regime's favour.

The Tsar's departure had at once given rise to a wave of hope and speculation. People felt that, if his return could be prevented, Sophia might be persuaded to emerge from her monastery and reassume control.

All the ex-Regent's friends and associates were dead or deported. There was no one on whom she could rely to lead such a movement, still less take over the reins of government in the event of its success, yet her prestige was still so great that her name alone provided the rebels with a rallying-cry.

Describing these events, Lévesque echoes many other historians in commenting that the very fact that the revolt originated so far from the capital was evidence of Sophia's non-complicity. The French historian, who was a model of impartiality, wrote of the Regency: 'This party [Sophia's], while it may have been born of bribery, grew by reason of the Princess's wise administration. Those who did not know her, even those who expected nothing of her, liked her government.'

As usual, the musketeers were well to the fore. Compelled to serve long and unpleasant tours of duty on the Russian frontiers, they began to desert. In March 1698, a regiment in the Azov garrison which had been hoping to be relieved and posted back to Moscow was sent to Velikiye-Luki on the Polish border. One hundred and fifty-five men deserted and made their way back to the capital. This time, although it was not the first case of collective desertion and although the government had not even attempted to round the deserters up on previous occasions, Prince Troyekurov, head of the Office of Musketeers, gave orders for the men to be arrested. The musketeers of Moscow at once made common cause with their imprisoned comrades and succeeded in freeing them by force. The boyars sent regular troops to chase the rebels out of the capital, but the situation deteriorated rapidly and soon became critical. Prolonged contact with the Zaporozhye Cossacks had left its mark on the musketeers, who had acquired a number of their habits and a substantial dose of their independence of mind.

On June 16th, 1698, surrounded by a 'circle'[1] (yet another symptom of Cossack influence) on the banks of the Dvina, a musketeer named Mazlov read out a letter purporting to have been written by Sophia. It is hard to believe that the letter was not spurious, but the musketeers accepted it without further proof.

'You must go,' ran the letter, 'all four regiments of you, to the Convent of the Virgins and bivouac there. Then send me a petition entreating me to go to Moscow and govern you as in former times.'

Nothing could have inflamed the musketeers more or suited their inclinations better. Their programme was simple. They would go to Moscow, destroy the German Quarter and kill the foreigners 'who are the cause of the contempt in which the Tsar holds Orthodoxy'. Sophia could then govern in the name of Tsarevitch Alexis, Peter's son, and Golitsyn, of whom the musketeers retained agreeable memories, could be recalled from exile. As for Peter himself, he must simply be prevented from returning from the distant lands which meant more to him than his native Russian soil.

'Loyal to our Christian faith, we, our fathers and forefathers have served the Grand Sovereigns, and we have sworn to defend piety to the death,' wrote the musketeers in their first missive to the government. They went on to accuse 'the heretic Lefort' of having deliberately sacrificed their lives in the battles for Azov and of having tried to starve the survivors to death after the campaign by marching them back through desolate steppes where the only source of food was carrion.

News of the uprising soon reached Moscow, where memories of the past were still fresh. The population was seized with panic. Many Muscovites abandoned their houses and hurriedly sought refuge on their country estates, taking their treasured possessions with them.

On June 17th, the rebellious musketeers met the army sent against them by the boyars near the monastery of the Resurrection, not far from the capital. The government troops, who numbered about 3,700, were commanded by Sheyin, General Gordon and Prince Kolzo Massalsky.

Sheyin began by sending Gordon into the opposing camp to talk terms. Gordon called upon the musketeers in the government's name to return to their garrisons and hand over the first one hundred and fifty deserters to reach Moscow, who were officially regarded as the instigators of the mutiny.

'We shall die,' replied the musketeers, 'or we shall go to Moscow, though it be for three days only. That done, we shall be ready to be sent to such places as are designated by the Tsar.'

[1] The Cossack Assembly took the form of a circle.

'Do not count on it,' reported Gordon. 'You will never be allowed to enter Moscow.'

'Only death shall prevent us,' was the rebels' response. They proceeded to air their grievances, many of which were justified. They were paid in copper coinage whose purchasing power was sufficient to meet their expenses for only two weeks in every four. Separated from their families for months and sometimes years, never granted leave, always stationed in trouble-spots and deprived of military honours, they argued that only extreme measures could gain them a hearing.

'I give you fair warning,' Gordon told them, 'that if you refuse to submit you can expect no quarter.'

Neither side would yield, and both camps prepared for battle. Prayers for divine benediction were said in front of both the government and rebel lines. The government troops enjoyed an overwhelming superiority over the musketeers, for Gordon had trained twenty-five cannon on them and their encampment was completely surrounded by Sheyin's cavalry.

Gordon, who still hoped to avoid bloodshed, twice sent emissaries to the musketeers in an attempt to persuade them to surrender on the government's terms, but their response was always the same: 'We have no fear of you. We are ready to die.' At last, Gordon gave the order to open fire. Two, three, four salvoes crashed out, and the musketeers' resistance was broken. They fled in disorder, abandoning their dead and wounded where they lay. It only remained for Sheyin's troops to round up the fugitives and put them in chains.

Having crushed the revolt, the boyars ordered an inquiry into its causes. Under torture, the captured musketeers admitted their plan to seize Moscow, kill the foreigners and boyars and prevent Peter's return. Not one of them denounced Sophia or alleged that she was involved, even by implication. Sheyin ordered the ringleaders to be hanged on the spot and had the others sent off to prisons or monasteries. With order firmly restored, the boyars regarded the bloody interlude as closed.

* * *

Peter did not take the same view. The long return journey had done nothing to appease his fury and he was determined to eliminate every vestige of opposition once and for all.

The Tsar entered the capital a month after the revolt had been quelled, just when things were returning to normal. His response to the boyars who came to welcome him home was to cut off their beards with his own hands, an indignity which only two of the oldest were spared. Lev Naryshkin had failed to persuade the unfortunate Tsarina to part with her child and renounce secular life, so Peter banished her to a nunnery by force. When the almoner of the place refused to make her take the veil without her consent, the Tsar threw him into gaol and found a more accommodating priest. Moscow and Russia were lashed by a storm of terror and bathed in a river of blood. The events of 1682 paled into insignificance beside the reprisals instituted by Peter the Great.

Peter's own Preobrazhensky Regiment began the bloody purge on August 25th, the day after his return. One thousand seven hundred and forty of the musketeers whom Sheyin had spared were transferred to the palace at Preobrazhenskoye, where the dread Theodore Romodanovsky subjected them to more torture, this time under Peter's personal supervision. Fourteen torture-chambers were installed on the Tsar's estate, each one in charge of a trusted henchman. Contemporary reports are quite explicit about the reign of terror with which Peter signalled his final break with the past. Thirty furnaces were lit each day so that the wretched victims of the Tsar's wrath could be slowly roasted alive on grills placed beneath them. Peter watched the process with evident relish, ordering doctors to revive any men who fainted so that torture could begin anew. The musketeers admitted that they had meant to kill the Germans and ask Sophia to resume her regency. They even admitted having intended to oppose Peter's return. But they never, even in their death-throes, accused Sophia of inciting the revolt.

Determined to implicate his sister at all costs, Peter kept up the pressure until one man gasped that he had read a letter which Sophia had sent to the musketeers via a beggar-woman. Sophia's nurse, Rodimitsa, and four of her chambermaids, one of them pregnant, were also arrested and tortured without result.

After torture came the executions. Finding the headsman too slow at his job, Peter picked up the axe himself and sent his subjects' heads rolling in the dust, a royal giant with contorted features, foam-flecked lips and clothes stained with his victims' blood. He spared at least one man's life, or so tradition would have us believe. Mounting the scaffold one day to watch the executioner at work, Peter was hailed by a musketeer of imposing build[1] who called out: 'Turn to, Sovereign! The space is for me to lay me low!' Peter was so captivated by this display of sangfroid that he granted him his life.

Peter invited the foreigners in his service to help in the inquisition, but Lefort and von Blomberg declined this peculiar honour on the

[1] A man called Orlov, reputed to be an ancestor of Catherine II's two favourites.

grounds that it would be inconsistent with their national codes of behaviour.

* * *

Bodies dangled from gibbets erected at every gate into the capital, serving as an object lesson to the horrified crowds that gathered round them. Patriarch Adrian was equally horrified by the Tsar's brutality and came to beg him to be more merciful, carrying the icon of the Holy Virgin in his hands. Peter, who was drunk with blood by this time, gave him a hostile reception. 'Why do you come bearing an icon?' he ranted at the head of the Church. 'Away with you! Restore it to its place at once and cease meddling in matters that do not concern you. I revere God and the Holy Virgin more than you, but it behoves me to safeguard the country and rid it of all the scoundrels who mean it harm.'

The Patriarch withdrew in some trepidation, and Peter demonstrated his reverence for God and the Holy Virgin by lopping off five more heads.

A long line of tumbrils progressed along the Moscow road, each carrying two condemned men with lighted candles in their hands. Their wives and children ran alongside in the dust, lamenting loudly. Records inform us that two hundred and one men were hanged in a single day.

Musketeers' wives were likewise tortured and killed. Between the 15th and 21st of October, seven hundred and seventy-two men were beheaded or had their tongues cut out. On October 17th, no less than one hundred and nine musketeers were beheaded while Peter sat watching on horseback. Finally, a hundred and ninety-five musketeers were hanged under Sophia's windows, three of them holding in their lifeless hands pieces of paper meant to represent the petition calling on the ex-Regent to seize power. The last executions took place in February 1699, six months after the end of the revolt. A further hundred and seventy-seven people were subjected to various forms of torture and their bodies left unburied on the Tsar's orders until springtime, when they were thrown into common graves and buried beneath stones bearing inscriptions recording their crimes. The sight of fleshless skulls impaled on iron spikes was to remind the Muscovites of their sovereign's cruelty for a long time to come.

From then onwards, the traumatic fear which had bedevilled Peter's nervous system was accompanied by the moral and psychological perversion which afflicts anyone who consistently violates the laws of humanity. No one can inflict torture and death, devote himself to an orgy of blood-letting and revel in atrocities without becoming marked for life. Henceforward, Peter was destined to live with the madness which made his genius so dangerous.

* * *

Sophia's elder sister Martha, who was close to her despite their enforced separation, was personally interrogated by the Tsar. She admitted having heard from Yukova, her serving-woman, that the musketeers intended to mutiny in Sophia's name, but assured him that this was the extent of her knowledge. Peter had Yukova tortured, and Yukova denounced a colonel. The colonel was arrested, but while he was being tortured the servant revived and admitted that he had had no hand in the matter and that she had blurted out the first name that had come into her head. In brief, for all his efforts, Peter unearthed no evidence which directly incriminated Sophia. Since her rank exempted her from standing trial before a civil tribunal, he convened a national council of clergy. Sophia comported herself with great dignity, denying the charge of conspiracy and protesting that she had taken no part in the revolt. Her explanation of the fact that musketeers and other malcontents had called on her name was clear and concise. 'It was,' she said, 'because my government cared for the musketeers and the people that they preserved their esteem for and confidence in me.'

The churchmen apparently preserved their independence of mind and failed to condemn the tsarevna, for Peter carefully destroyed all record of their proceedings and final verdict, and Sophia was forced to take the veil at her brother's personal command.

On October 21st, 1698, the Tsarevna Sophia became the nun Suzanna and her sister Martha entered another convent under the name Margaret.

This marked the real end of the Regent's career. Kept under strict surveillance, guarded by soldiers and unable to correspond with the outside world except by sending her sisters and aunts messages which were censored by the frightful Romodanovsky, she survived for another six years, a nun without a vocation and a woman haunted by thoughts of past glory, memories of how her friends had died and ghastly visions of the dead musketeers who had stretched their lifeless hands towards her window.

Death finally released Sophia from her living tomb in 1704, at the age of forty-seven.

EPILOGUE

PETER'S hatred pursued Sophia beyond the grave. For many years, the Regent's reputation and achievements were enveloped in a conspiracy of silence or, worse still, calumny. Documents which could have helped to rehabilitate her disappeared from the archives and historians were commissioned by Peter to blacken her memory. Catherine II was the first to come to her defence, for obvious reasons, in a work published anonymously under the title *Antidote*. 'I believe,' she said, 'that Sophia has not been rendered the justice due to her. She conducted the affairs of the Empire for many years with all the sagacity that anyone could have desired. Her following was large.'

As time passed and people ventured to scrutinize her reforms more closely, Sophia became the object of more impartial study. In the nineteenth century, Karamzin wrote: 'She was one of the most remarkable women Russia has ever known.'

Sophia's gradual rehabilitation was accompanied by a more critical examination of the reign of Peter I. Without minimizing the scope of his reforms, some Russian historians suggested that his claims to greatness were not as overwhelming as had for so long been imagined. In one of his works Miliukov went so far as to stress that 'Peter never, in fact, directed the reforms of his reign.'

'He groped his way forward,' wrote the same historian, 'and a collection of people who were not ready to understand these reforms were obliged, by force of circumstance, to carry them out.' Miliukov added that the necessity for reform penetrated Peter's consciousness not as a result of systematic reflection (as in the case of Ordyn-Nastchokin and Vasily Golitsyn) but disjointedly and in an empirical manner, according to the frequency with which he was confronted with difficult problems – that he did, in fact, take decisions when compelled to take them by the needs of the moment.

Peter had no regard for the individual and his love of Russia never extended to the Russians themselves.[1] His victory over Sophia marked the disappearance from the Russian State of the idea of the *personne*

[1] Peter's celebrated political testament: 'Know this of Peter, that life matters little to him provided that Russia lives', is acknowledged to be apocryphal.

humaine, an idea which forms the nucleus of Western Civilization and which had hitherto existed in Russia, though in a special guise, by virtue of the Christian principles to which her rulers subscribed. Peter was less concerned with educating his subjects than with drilling them into obedience. In his determination to be the country's sole master, he broke the backbone of the Orthodox Church, the Russian patriarchate, thereby prompting a contemporary churchman to remark graphically: 'We were eagles, but we have become oxen beneath the yoke.' Ecclesiastical administration was placed in the hands of a 'Minister of Religion'.[1] Russia's first emperor confined all orders of society to barracks, as it were, and forcibly repressed any budding independence of mind, but he succeeded in realizing his predecessors' military ambitions at vast cost and his victories and conquests endeared him to Russian chauvinists for nearly three centuries to come.

At the close of the family drama which we have described Russia embarked on a course that was destined to warp her future in a disastrous way. Under Alexis, Theodore and Sophia, Russia tried to draw nearer the Mediterranean world, which could have supplied the cultural ingredients needed to refine her robust but unpolished national character. Gradually and without upheaval, Alexis, Theodore and Sophia tried to introduce Western ways while at the same time preserving the essential characteristics which make up the true genius and *raison d'être* of any nation. Peter swept everything aside, paving the way for the October Revolution.

With his practical mind, utter lack of mysticism and single-minded pursuit of technical efficiency, Peter turned to the Germanic West, though not to the Germany of philosophers, poets and musicians. Like Vasily Golitsyn, he sent troublesome young men to study abroad, but their centres of learning were shipyards, workshops and parade-grounds rather than universities.

Everything conspired to wrest Peter I away from Mediterranean influence. Saint-Simon, whom Rambaud aptly called 'the first French Russophile', was right when he deplored Louis XIV's refusal to establish friendly relations with Russia and referred to France's attitude as 'insane mistrust'.

Material civilization, the only kind which Peter was interested in introducing into his country, creates no profound or effective ties between donor and recipient. Sophia and Golitsyn cherished a disinterested love of

[1] It is, however, a crude fallacy to regard this civil servant as having played any form of spiritual role in the Russian Church, nor is it true, as some suggest, that the Tsar became its spiritual head.

the West. Peter expressed his own attitude towards it unequivocally by proclaiming: 'We have need of Europe for only a brief time: then we shall turn our backs on her.'

Though betrayed, the West continued to lavish superlatives on the man who spurned her. Voltaire's shameless flattery veiled the true features of the brilliant but barbarous reformer like a cloud of incense, and even now, centuries after his death, people still pay tribute to the man responsible for ensuring that part of Western Europe's legacy to Russia was the systematic violence and coercion whose fruits are being gathered in our own day.

BIBLIOGRAPHY

MANUSCRIPT SOURCES

Archives du Ministère des Affaires Étrangères, Paris
Baluze, 1686–1704.
Correspondance de la Picqueterie, 1660–83.
Russie, Mémoires et documents, vol. III.

Lenin Library, Moscow:

Anonymous: 'O zatchatii i rojdenii Petra Vélikogo' (The conception and birth of Peter the Great).
Krekchine, Petr: 'Zapiski Sobstvennii' (XVII s).
Matvéev, Andrei: 'Zapiski Russkogo Posla, 1709–1711' (Diary of a Russian Ambassador); 'Istoria Streletskogo bunta' (The story of the musketeers' revolt); 'O nevinnom zatochenii boyarina Matvéeva' (Of the imprisonment of the innocent boyard Matvéev).
'Perepiska Kniazia Vassilia Golitsma' (Correspondence of the Prince Vassily Golitzine): letters from his wife, his sister the Princess Trubezkoy, his son, his cousin Boris Golitzine, from Prince Fédor Kourankin, Ilya Chirikoff, Prince Andronnik Tcherkassky, Prince Dolgoruky, Doctor Gaden, etc.

PRINCIPAL PRINTED SOURCES

Adelung, F. von, *Kritisch-literarische Übersicht des Russlands bis 1700*, St Petersburg and Leipzig, 1846.
Aleppo, Archdeacon Paul of: *Putechestvie antiokhhiiskogo patriarkha Makaria v Rossiu v polovine XVII veka*, Chtenia, 1898.
Aristov, N.: *Moskovskii smuty vo vrermia pravlienia Sophii A*, Warsaw, 1871.
Artsibacheff, N.: *Povestvovanie o Rossii*, Moscow, 1843.
Avvakun, archpriest: *Jitie Protopopa Avakuma im samim napisanoie*, Moscow, 1934.
Bantych-Kamensky, N.: *Illustrations de la Russie*, Paris, 1829.
Belov: *Ob Istoricheskom znachenii russkogo boyarstva*, St Petersburg, 1886.
Bergh, V.: *Tsarstvovanié Tsaria Fedora Alexeevicha*, St Petersburg, 1834.
Brückner, A.: *Patrick Gordon i ego dnevnik*, St Petersburg, 1878; *Istoria Petra Velikogo*, St Petersburg, 1882.
Bogoslavski: *Petr I*, Leningrad, 1940.
Buxhoevden, Baroness Sophia: *A cavalier in Moscovy*, London, **1932.**

Collins, Samuel: *The Present State of Russia*, London, 1671.
Evréinov, N.: *Istoria Russkogo teatra*, New York, 1955.
Fédotof, G. P.: *The Russian Religious Mind*, Cambridge (Mass.), 1947.
Herberstein, Sigismund, and others: *Notes Upon Russia*, London, 1851–2.
Hilkov, Prince Andrei: *Yadro Rossiiskoi istorii*, Moscow, 1770.
Ikonikoff: *Tsaritzi tsari iz doma Romanovykh*, Kiev, 1914.
Illovaisky: *Istoria Rossii*, Moscow, 1905.
Jablochkov, M.: *Istoria Dvorianskogo Soslovia v Rossii*, St Petersburg, 1863.
Karamzin, N.: *Istoria Gosudarstva Rossiiskogo*, St Petersburg, 1818.
Kliuchevsky, Vassili: *Kurs Russkoi Istorii*, Moscow, 1908.
Koch, Christopher von: 'Pisma' (letters) in *Russkaya Starina*, 1878.
Korb, Johan: *Dnevnik* (*Diary*), Chtenia, 1867; *Récit de la sanglante révolte des Strelets*, Paris, 1859.
Kostomarov, N.: *Ocherk Domashnei jizni* . . , St Petersburg, 1887; *Russkaya istoria v jizneopisaniakh*, St Petersburg, 1892.
Kotoshikhin, Grigory: *O Rossii v tsarstvovanie Alexeia Mikailovitcha*, St Petersburg, 1840.
Kurakin, Prince F.: *Bumagi Kniazia Borisa Kurakina*, St Petersburg, 1890–1902.
Kovalevsky, Pierre: *Manuel d'histoire russe*, Paris, 1948.
Krijanich, Yuri: *Russkoie Gosudarstvo v poloviné XVII veka*, St Petersburg, 1859.
Lubimenko, Inna: *Les relations commerciales et politiques de l'Angleterre avec la Russie avant Pierre le Grand*, Paris, 1933.
Marais, Mathieu: *Journal et mémoires*, Paris, 1890.
Mayerberg, Baron Augustin von: *Putechestvié v Moskoviu*, Moscow, 1874.
Medvedev, Sylvestre, *Sozertsanie kratkoie*, Chtenia, 1894 and 1896.
Miege, Guy: *La relation de trois ambassades de Mgr le comte de Carlisle de la part du serenissime et très puissant prince Charles II, Roy de la Grande-Bretagne*, Rouen, 1700.
Milioukov, P.: *La régence de Sophie* (*Histoire de Russie*), Paris, 1932.
Mordovtsev: *Russkié istoricheskie jenshchini*, St Petersburg, 1874.
Neuville, de la (Adrien Baillet): *Zapisski* and *Relation curieuse et nouvelle de la Moscovie*, Paris, 1698.
O'Brien, Bickford C.: *Russia under two Tzars*, Univ. of California, 1952.
Oléarius, Adam: *Voyages très curieux et très renommés faits en Moscovie*, Amsterdam, 1727.
Palmer, William: *The Patriarch and the Tsar*, London, 1873–6.
Pascal, Pierre: *Avacum et les debuts du Rasskol*, Paris, 1938.
Platonov, S.: *Lektsii po russkoi istorii*, St Petersburg, 1907; *Moskva i Zapad*, Moscow, 1912.
Pogodin, N.: *Drevnyaya i Novaya Rossia*, 1875.
Rambaud, A.: *Receuil des Instructions données aux ambassadeurs en Russie*, Paris, 1890.
Rozysknoie delo o Fédore Shaklovitom i ego soobshchnikakh (The case of Fédor Shaklovity and his accomplices), St Petersburg, 1884–93.

Shebalski, Petr: *Pravlenie Tsarevny Sophii*, Moscow, 1856.
Shmourlo, E.: 'Padenié Tsarevni Sophii', *Journal Min. Inst. Publ.*, 1896; *Vostok i zapad v russkoi istorii*, Youriev, 1895; 'From Krizanic to the slavophils,' *The Slavonic Review*, 1927.
Soloviev, S.: *Istoria Rossii*, St Petersburg, 1894–5; *Publichnii chtenia o Petre*, Moscow, 1872.
Tatistchev: *Istoria Rossiiskaya*, Moscow, 1768–1848.
Tereshchenko, A.: *Opyt Obozrenia Jizni sanovnikov ...* , St Petersburg, 1837.
Ustrialov, N.: *Istoria tsarstvovania Petra velikogo*, St Petersburg, 1858–63.
Zabelin, I.: *Byt Russkih Tsarits*, Moscow, 1901.
Zaozerski, A.: *Tsar Alexi Mikhailovich v svoem khoziastvé*, Moscow, 1917.

OTHER SOURCES

Brockhaus and Eron Encyclopedias.
Bolshaia Sovetskaya Encyclopedias.
Ocherki Russkoi istorii XVII veka (various authors), Académie des sciences, Moscow, 1955.
Akty sobrannii v bibliotekahh, etc., édition de l'Académie des sciences de St Petersburg, 1838.

Drevnyaya russkaya vivliotheka, Novikov, Moscow, 1788–91.
Deiania Petra Velikogo, Novikov, Moscow (XVIII s).
Podmoskovié (various authors), Moscow, 1955.
Proshloie Moskvi, Sytine, Moscow, 1946.
Po Kremliu (guide to the Kremlin), Moscow, 1956.
Istoria Russkoi Arkhitekturi (various authors), Moscow, 1956.
Moskva, Lopatin, Moscow, 1960.
Istoria Russkoi Slovessnosti Parfizief, Kazan, 1886.
Istoria drevnei russkoi slovesnosti, N. Gudzi, Moscow, 1945.
Khhrestomatia po drevnei russkoi literature, Gudzi, Moscow, 1955.

REFERENCES ON ART

The works of Grabar, Lazarevsky, and Tiulin.

INDEX

MOSCVA
ad Archetypum Foedori Borissowitsi
A. Kremlena gorod, Aula Imperatoris
B. Kitay gorod Urbs media
D. Skorodom, Urbs exterior
C. Tzari gorod Urbs Caesarea
E. Streletska sloboda, vel Vicus militaris
a. Curia
b. Patriarchium
h. Forum equarium
i. Balneae publicae
k. Forum lignarium
m. Equile
Moscua fluvius
CAIANIA
CARELIA
SWEDEN
Finlandt
NOORDZEE
DANIA
MARE BALTICVM
LIEFLANT
PRVSSIA
LITTAW
POLONIA
WOLYNIA
PODOLIA
MOLDAVIA
VALACHIA
BVLGARIA
ROMANIA
SEVERA
MOSCOVIA
CARGAPOLIA
CRIMEA, SEV
PALVS MEOTIS
PONTVS EVXINVS qui ZORNO
NATOLIA
ARCHIPELAGO
Laloga Albus Lac.
Album
Kimi Lappmarck
TABVLA
RVSSIAE
ex autographo, quod delineandum curavit Foedor filius Tzaris Boris desum-ta; et ad fluvios Duinam, Zuchanam, aliaque loca, quantum ex tabulis et notitiis ad nos dela-tis fieri potuit, amplificata : et
Magno Domino, Tzari et Magno Duci Michaeli Foedrowits omnium Russorum, Autocratori Wolodimeriae, Mos-coviae et Novogardiae, Tzari Cazaniae, Tzari Astracaniae, Tzari Siberiae, Domino Plescoviae Magno Duci Smolenscoviae, Otweriae, Iugoriae, Per-miae, Wiatkiae, Bulgariae etc. Item Domino et Magno Duci Novogardiae Inferioris etc. Domino regionum Iveriae Kartaliniae et Grusiniae Tzari etc.
dedicata ab
Hesselo Gerardo
M.DC.XIIII
Amstelodami
Excusum Apud Guilie